God and the New Cosmology

D1546292

God and the New Cosmology

The Anthropic Design Argument

M. A. Corey

Rowman & Littlefield Publishers, Inc.

ROWMAN & LITTLEFIELD PUBLISHERS, INC.

Published in the United States of America
by Rowman & Littlefield Publishers, Inc.
4720 Boston Way, Lanham, Maryland 20706

Copyright © 1993 by M. A. Corey

British Cataloging in Publication Information Available

Library of Congress Cataloging-in-Publication Data

Corey, Michael Anthony.
God and the new cosmology : the anthropic design argument /
M.A. Corey.
p.   cm.
Includes bibliographical references and index.
1. God—Proof, Cosmological.   2. God—Proof, Teleological.
3. Anthropic principle.   4. Natural theology.   5. Religion and
science.   I. Title.
BT102.C672   1993
212'.1—dc20   92–33254 CIP

ISBN 0–8476–7801–6 (cloth : alk. paper)
ISBN 0–8476–7802–4 (paper : alk. paper)

Printed in the United States of America

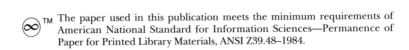
™ The paper used in this publication meets the minimum requirements of
American National Standard for Information Sciences—Permanence of
Paper for Printed Library Materials, ANSI Z39.48–1984.

For my father

Contents

Acknowledgments

I would like to extend my appreciation to the following people for making a significant contribution to this manuscript. Thanks to:

Mike Sr., Jeanette, Johnny and Danny, for helping to make this book possible.

David Ray Griffin, of the School of Theology at Claremont, for his extensive critique of the manuscript and help with the title.

John Hick and Stephen T. Davis, of The Claremont Graduate School, for their helpful suggestions regarding the content of this manuscript.

The entire staff of The Claremont Graduate School, for creating an outstanding academic environment where projects such as this one can thrive.

Nahia, for encouraging me throughout the long and arduous creative process.

Barbara Oden, of W.V. State College, for stimulating my interest in the theory of evolution. Also to Professors Brimhall, Kagen, Hutto, and Jackson, for making the physical sciences come alive.

Father Olof Scott, Olive Crummett, Thelma Woody, Bonnie Maddox, Charlotte Pritt, and Billie McNabb, for their wonderful inspiration over the years.

Elliot, Janice, and Tina, who made specific suggestions regarding the content of this manuscript.

Steve Levine, whose creative genius always manages to inspire me.

Gordon and Transallegheny Books, for their uncompromising commitment to good literature.

Beth, whose writing talent never ceases to amaze me.

The Desert Palms Motel, Tula's Place, Altan's Pickle Patch, Bagel Heaven, Les Deux Magots, Le Flore, and Café De La Paix, for providing a fertile breeding ground for many of the ideas contained herein.

CHAPTER 1

Introduction

"Any coincidence," said Miss Marple to herself, "is always worth noticing.
You can throw it away later if it *is* only a coincidence."

AGATHA CHRISTIE

1.1 Overview

It is no secret that science-based arguments for the existence of God have
become increasingly unpopular during the past few centuries. Although the
majority of scientists and philosophers during this period were sympathetic
to the cause of natural theology (especially in England), the advent of Darwinism in the latter part of the nineteenth century, with its extreme emphasis
on naturalistic explanations for the rise of life, had a devastating impact on
the credibility of the natural theologian's arguments. Since the existence
of the present universal order could now be conceived almost entirely in
naturalistic terms (or so it seemed), God was no longer needed as a vital
explanatory hypothesis.

The vast increase in our scientific understanding of the world during the
present century has only served to exacerbate the decline of the natural
theologian's claims. Now that we can understand where we came from and
what we are made of in unprecedented detail, it would appear as though
natural theology has all but been extinguished as a viable means of shedding
light on the possible existence of a Creator.

However, just as certain depressed economical markets have a strange
way of turning around to the upside at precisely the time when they appear
to have fizzled out completely, certain intellectual movements seem to behave in a similar manner. Such appears to be the case with natural theology.
At the very time when many moderns have been prepared to bury this
important historical movement once and for all, it has suddenly appeared
back on the intellectual scene, this time armed with an imposing array of
new scientific support.

Most of this support has inadvertently come from within the ranks of
modern theoretical physics, which itself has taken a very interesting turn in
recent years. For in the midst of their almost routine foraying into the underlying structure of the physical realm, physicists and cosmologists have stumbled upon a collection of physical "coincidences" that seem to pervay a

1

deep truth about the nature of the universe: In spite of the many complex requirements for the existence of carbon-based life forms, the physical universe nevertheless displays a remarkable fitness for the evolution of life.

At first this observation seems almost tautologous; *of course* the universe is fit for life, otherwise we wouldn't be here to observe it! On a deeper level, however, this fitness turns out to be utterly mysterious, because it involves the apparent fine-tuning of a wide range of seemingly unrelated physical parameters. It is this cooperative fine-tuning that demands a larger explanation, because the resultant life-supporting character of the universe has turned out to be exceedingly improbable.

In an effort to account for these remarkable life-facilitating "coincidences," physicist Brandon Carter in 1974 devised a multi-faceted explanation he called the "Anthropic Principle," which attempts to relate the structure of the physical universe to the specific requirements of *human* existence. Carter's initial aim was to "argue against (an) exaggerated subservience to the Copernican principle." For while Copernicus was justified in his assertion that we not "assume gratuitously that we occupy a central position in the cosmos," Carter argued that it does not necessarily follow that our position on this planet cannot be privileged in *any* way. To the contrary, our location in the universe "is necessarily privileged to the extent of being compatible with our existence as observers."[1]

In the years since Carter's initial anthropic limitation of the Copernican dogma, several versions of the so-called Anthropic Principle have subsequently been put forth by the scientific community. The "weak" form, known as the Weak Anthropic Principle (WAP), has been formulated by John D. Barrow and Frank J. Tipler in the following terms:

> WEAK ANTHROPIC PRINCIPLE: The observed values of all physical and cosmological quantities are not equally probable but they take on values restricted by the requirement that there exist sites where carbon-based life can evolve and by the requirement that the universe be old enough for it to have already done so.[2]

The WAP thus seeks no deeper level of explanation than to note that, given our current existence, we could never expect to observe a universe significantly different from our own. Obviously, though, the WAP does not seek to explain *why* or *how* the universe actually came to be structured in this life-supporting manner; it simply notes that, while the universe is the way it is for unknown reasons, given our current existence it could not have been otherwise.

At its most fundamental level, then, the WAP follows the widely accepted principle that whenever one measures anything, one must always take into account the particular properties of the measuring instrument.[3] In this case, the "measuring instrument" happens to be ourselves, so our conclusions must take into account the particular set of circumstances that give rise to our privileged position as observers.[4] Thus, the WAP asserts that, given our existence as observers, we must necessarily observe the kind of universe we presently inhabit.[5]

In an effort to provide a more satisfying explanation for the many apparent coincidences in nature, Carter also devised the Strong Anthropic Principle (SAP), which has been formulated by Barrow and Tipler in the following terms:

STRONG ANTHROPIC PRINCIPLE: The universe must have those properties which allow life to develop within it at some stage in its history.[6]

Although the SAP does not attempt to explain *why* the universe must be such as to eventually allow life to form, it nevertheless affirms that this must be so.[7]

As John Casti has pointed out, the gap separating the SAP from the traditional Design Argument for the existence of God[8] is no more than a "hairsbreadth, omitting only an explicit invocation of a Designer."[9] This leads us to the first corollary of the SAP, which can be stated as the following:

There exists one possible universe "designed" with the goal of generating and sustaining "observers."[10]

A second corollary of the SAP is derived from the findings of modern quantum mechanics. Dubbed the Participatory Anthropic Principle (PAP) by physicist John A. Wheeler, its principal originator, it asserts the following:

PARTICIPATORY ANTHROPIC PRINCIPLE: Observers are necessary to bring the universe into being.[11]

The PAP follows from the idea held by many quantum physicists that a living consciousness is necessary to collapse the various wave functions of physical reality, so as to impart a definite quantum determinancy to them.

The third and final corollary of the SAP has been dubbed the Final Anthropic Principle (FAP) by Barrow and Tipler. It can be stated as the following:

FINAL ANTHROPIC PRINCIPLE: Intelligent information-processing must come into existence in the universe, and, once it comes into existence, it will never die out.[12]

Casti's version of the FAP adds the following:

> Once life is created, it will endure forever, become infinitely knowledge-able, and ultimately mold the universe to its will.[13]

The FAP thus has an obvious religious quality to it, in that it affirms a positive universal purpose to human evolution which cannot be thwarted by any possible power.

The SAP in all its forms seeks to account for the utterly improbable nature of the many "coincidences" in nature by asserting that the universe *had* to have been such as to admit life at some point in its history. It correctly surmises that the odds for these "coincidences" to have independently happened by chance are so vanishingly small that they must have been in some sense deliberate. The FAP even goes so far as to generalize from this extreme improbability to the point of asserting that intelligent life will eventually grow to the point of becoming almost godlike.

Overall, the SAP implies a strong sense of necessity as far as the evolution of life is concerned, due to its claim that the universe *must* contain those properties that are conducive to life's evolution. We will now consider three possible ways of interpreting this strong sense of cosmic necessity. Only the final one, however, holds up under scrutiny:

1) *Life does in fact exist; therefore the universe "must" possess those properties that are capable of giving rise to it.* This assertion, however, reduces to the WAP, because of its possibly contingent status. For while the present existence of life compels us to conclude that the universe "must" be biocentric in nature, this is far from a necessary truth, because the universe might not have existed at all, or if it did happen to exist, it might not have been biocentric.

2) *There is only one logically possible universe; therefore, since life is known to exist, the universe "must" be biocentric in nature.* This too falls short of a necessary state of affairs, because it is always possible that this one logically consistent universe might not have ever existed.

Clearly, then, if the SAP is to be valid (i.e., if the universe is to be such that it had to have brought about life at some point in its history), a factor must be found that would have made the existence of the universe a *necessary* truth from the very beginning. Such a demand for absolute cosmic necessity is very difficult to imagine apart from the existence of some sort of necessary being or principle that would have made the evolution of life inevitable. This leads us to consider the final way of interpreting the SAP:

3) *The universe must be such as to admit life at some point in its history because of the action of a necessary being or principle that rendered this outcome inevitable.* This is the only explanation for the SAP that holds up under scrutiny, because there is no way to guarantee the inevitability of life's

evolution apart from the invoking of some sort of principle of absolute cosmic necessity. Traditionally, this vehicle of cosmic necessity has been called "God" (although it is possible to conceive of it in impersonal terms, as some Hindus and others have done).

In general, the anthropic family of principles reverses the pattern of logic typically employed in scientific reasoning.[14] Normally, scientists begin with an initial situation and the various laws of nature, and then come to predict a future state of affairs. "Anthropic" reasoning, on the other hand, proceeds in the opposite direction: One starts with the final observed state (the present) and then acts to constrain or limit the initial conditions in such a way that they are consistent with our existence as observers.[15]

Not all thinkers, however, are impressed by the various "anthropic" formulations. Martin Gardner, for instance, was so disgusted by Barrow and Tipler's grandiose claims regarding the Final Anthropic Principle that he renamed it "the completely ridiculous anthropic principle, or CRAP!"[16] Although one cannot help but sympathize with Gardner's exasperation regarding some of these formulations, the ultimate question at issue here is whether or not there is an element of truth in this kind of "anthropic" thinking. As we will see in the coming pages, the answer to this question is an unqualified "yes."

As Barrow and Tipler have pointed out, there have been surprisingly few attempts to work out a precise statement of the Anthropic Principle in the years since it was initially formulated.[17] Astrophysicists have apparently wanted to leave a little flexibility in its formulation so that its deeper significance might become more apparent in the future.[18]

One of the major goals of the present study is to work out a scientifically and philosophically accurate treatment of the Anthropic Principle in all of its various manifestations. I seek to do this for two reasons: 1) because of the intriguing nature of the subject matter, and 2) because such an analysis promises to help increase our understanding about the universe in which we live.

Many commentators on the Anthropic Principle have intuitively felt that it contains a deep element of truth about our overall position in the cosmos, but most have been at a loss to describe what this truth might actually be. In the following pages I will attempt to explore the many "hidden recesses" of the Anthropic Principle, so as to determine what it can possibly tell us, if anything, about our role in the cosmos.

1.2 The Humanoid Principle

Interestingly enough, none of the individual manifestations of the Anthropic Principle is specifically committed solely to the existence of human life *per se*. Each can be understood as referring to intelligent *humanoid* forms of life, and not necessarily to humans only. Thus, there could very well be intelligent humanoid observers on other planets who could easily contribute a significant amount to the overall validity of the "Anthropic" Principle.

In this sense, the "Anthropic" Principle is something of a misnomer, since there is nothing intrinsic to it that requires the existence of distinctly human observers. The WAP only requires *some* form of intelligent observership in the universe, while the SAP only requires that the evolution of *life* itself be inevitable, not the evolution of human or humanoid life *per se*. Even Wheeler's Participatory Anthropic Principle (PAP) can be undertstood in a non-anthropic sense, since other forms of life are also presumably capable of observing the universe into existence (granting the truth of this theory). Even the first corrollary to the SAP—which states that there is one possible universe that has been deliberately designed by a Higher Power so as to allow observers to come into being—can be understood in a non-anthropic sense, since other forms of intelligent life could just as easily fulfill its lofty requirements. The same can be said to apply to the Final Anthropic Principle (FAP): other forms of intelligent life could survive forever, and amass an infinite degree of knowledge in the process.

Properly speaking, then, the Anthropic Principle should be called the *Humanoid Principle*, since other human-like forms of intelligence are equally capable of rendering it valid. The fact that we have no direct proof of the existence of these humanoid extraterrestrials does not seriously affect this distinction, because: 1) there is always the chance that they *might* exist, and 2) there is nothing in any of the Anthropic Principles that requires the existence of human life in particular. At best, then, the Anthropic Principle as it currently stands only supports a *moderate* anthropocentric view of reality, which sees humans as only *one* source of importance in the universe.

In deference to this new terminology, we can devise humanoid versions to the Weak, Strong, Participatory, and Final Anthropic Principles, in which the word "humanoid" is simply substituted for the word "anthropic." This would result in the Weak Humanoid Principle (WHP), the Strong Humanoid Principle (SHP), the Participatory Humanoid Principle (PHP), and the Final Humanoid Principle (FHP).[19] The point is simply that human-like beings on other planets are just as capable of rendering the co-called Anthropic Principle valid as humans are.

With this in mind, there are two possible alternatives that could be taken as far as the terminology of the Anthropic Principle is concerned. On the one hand, the word "anthropic" could simply be dropped altogether in favor of the world "humanoid." This would result in the Weak, Strong, Participatory, and Final Humanoid Principles, as noted above. On the other hand, the meaning of the word "anthropic" could simply be extended beyond its traditional meaning of "human" to include possible human-like observers on other planets (or even other forms of intelligent life on *this* planet, such as whales or dolphins).

In order to remain consistent with existing convention (and thereby to simplify matters as much as possible), I have chosen to retain the word "anthropic" in its larger descriptive sense throughout the remainder of this manuscript. Its meaning will thus be extended to include all possible human-like observers, both on this planet and throughout the universe.

1.3   An Anthropic or Biocentric Universe?

Before we move on to consider the actual evidence for the Anthropic Principle, it will be instructive to distinguish between two possible interpretations of the physical evidence: an anthropic interpretation, which holds that human and human-like beings are the "reason" why the structure of the universe is so conducive to supporting biological life, and a more general biocentric interpretation, which holds that generic biological life (and thus not necessarily humanoid life) is the "reason" for this life-supporting structure.

Thus far, most authors who have written on this subject have simply assumed that any cosmic "intention" to evolve life must have had intelligent human life as its ultimate goal; hence the "Anthropic" Principle. However, it could be argued that the cosmological evidence that has been recruited in support of the Anthropic Principle can properly be said, in and of itself, to support only a *Biocentric Principle*, and *not* any type of Anthropic Principle *per se*.

Strictly speaking, this contention is correct: there is no way to derive any type of Anthropic or Humanoid Principle directly from the so-called anthropic evidence. The *most* that one can do, given the evidence at hand, is to argue for *Intelligent Contrivance* in the universe, which, at most, can only be said to support the existence of a *biocentric* universe, and not necessarily an anthropic one *per se*. Thus, the declaration of an anthropic universe amounts to an *additional* argument beyond the one for Intelligent Contrivance, because there is no way to infer from the physical evidence alone whether a deliberately contrived universe has been designed explicitly for humans, or whether it has been designed merely for biological life in general. The theoretical jump from a Biocentric to an Anthropic Principle thus involves an anthropocentric generalization from the scientific evidence that isn't grounded as much on the empirical evidence as it is on a variety of philosophical and theological intuitions about humanity's importance in the overall universal order.

While some may consider this distinction to be irrelevant, given the irreducible fact of our own existence, there is always the chance that we were never directly intended to exist by the creative powers that exist in the universe. It is possible that only life in general was originally intended, and that we only evolved as a kind of unforeseen "happy accident."[20] In this case, we would only be justified in arguing for a Biocentric Principle, and for the Intelligent Contrivance that necessarily accompanies it. As a consequence, it behooves us to draw a clear distinction between a general state of biocentric contrivance in the universe, on the one hand, and a more specific state in which human and human-like beings themselves are directly intended as the chief locus of value.

Because of the distinctness of these two arguments, they will be examined separately throughout the remainder of this book. To begin with, I will seek to show that the existing scientific evidence argues convincingly for a deliberately contrived (and therefore biocentric) universe. Once this assertion has been reasonably established, I will move on to consider the various interpretations of the cosmological evidence that have been proposed over the years. From there I will move on to consider whether or not the Biocentric Principle constitutes a legitimate "proof" of the existence of God. At this point I will move on to consider whether or not an anthropic generalization from the biocentric evidence is in fact justifiable. This will be followed by a detailed examination of the various theological implications surrounding the "anthropic" evidence. Finally, I will seek to defend the practice of natural theology in general, so that a suitable "bridge" can be built between the disciplines of science and religion. First, however, I will seek to place the current discussion of the cosmological evidence in context by providing a brief history of teleological thought. Having done this, I will move on to develop a new form of the Design Argument, which will be based upon the most recent scientific evidence to date surrounding the Anthropic Cosmological Principle.

Notes

1. Brandon Carter, "Large number coincidences and the anthropic principle in cosmology," *Confrontation of Cosmological Theories with Observation*, ed. M.S. Longair (Dordrecht: Reidel, 1974), p. 291.
2. John D. Barrow and Frank J. Tipler, *The Anthropic Cosmological Principle* (New York: Oxford University Press, 1986), p. 16.
3. John L. Casti, *Paradigms Lost* (New York: William Morrow and Co., 1989), p. 479.
4. Ibid., p. 480.
5. Although some have argued that the self-referential quality of the WAP renders it tautologous by its very nature, the true significance of the WAP can be found in its ability to cause us to question *how* and *why* the universe originally came to be such that it was capable of supporting intelligent life.
6. Barrow and Tipler, p. 21.
7. It is instructive at this point to note that the SAP as formulated here only refers

to a biocentric, or life-supporting, universe, and not necessarily one that supports *human* observers, as does the WAP. We will have more to say on this important distinction later.

8. Indeed, the strong version of the Anthropic Principle is so closely associated with the teleology of Intelligent Design that physicist Heinz Pagels once quipped that it is " . . . the closest that some atheists can get to God."

9. John L. Casti, *Paradigms Lost*, pp. 481–482.

10. Barrow and Tipler, p. 22.

11. Ibid.

12. Ibid., p. 23.

13. Casti, p. 482.

14. Ibid., pp. 480–481.

15. Ibid.

16. See Martin Gardner, "WAP, SAP, PAP, and FAP." *The New York Review of Books* 33(8 May, 1986):22–25.

17. Barrow and Tipler, p. 15.

18. Ibid.

19. My motivation here is simply to work out a series of accurate definitions of the various Anthropic Principles. However, this does not necessarily mean that I affirm any of them.

20. Interestingly enough, this is the only proper use of the word "accident" in cosmological theory. An "accident" is normally understood as being a malfunctioning, and therefore unintended, byproduct of a purposive system that has been initiated by some sort of intelligent creative force. That is to say, the very concept of an "accident" *presupposes* a pre-existing world of volition where some things happen expectedly, and others do not. It would thus be correct to say that an individual who had intended a certain consequence with his behavior *accidentally* produced another, unexpected event.

With the random origin of the universe, however, we aren't talking about the accidental production of an unintended effect by a volitional being; we are rather talking about the spontaneous origin of the entire cause-and-effect realm by pure happenstance. While we may be justified in calling such a hypothetical event a product of chance, we are *not* justified in calling it a bona fide *accident*. As a consequence, it is inappropriate to refer to the universe itself as being an "accident," even hypothetically, because this sort of use removes the notion of an "accident" from a purposive system to one of absolute, non-purposive chaos, and this is a concept that the word "accident" was never intended to cover.

CHAPTER 2

A Brief History of Teleological Thought

> . . . the very order, changes, and movements in the universe, the very
> beauty of form in all that is visible, proclaim, however silently, both that
> the world was created and also that its Creator could be none other than
> God whose greatness and beauty are both ineffable and invisible.
>
> St. Augustine, *The City of God*

The essence of both the Biocentric and the Anthropic Principles lies in
their affirmation of some sort of cosmic purpose in the universe. This renders "biocentric" and "anthropic" reasoning teleological, or goal-oriented,
by definition.

Although scientists routinely shun any mention of teleology in the universe, largely for fear of its theological implications, teleological thought has
had a long and distinguished history. In this chapter we will endeavor to
chart the development of teleological thinking in the West, beginning with
the ancient world and continuing on to the present, so as to get an idea of
the historical background out of which the Biocentric and Anthropic Principles have emerged.

2.1 Teleology, Eutaxiology, and the Concept of Design

From the outset an important distinction needs to be drawn between two
concepts that are often confused in the literature: teleology and *eutaxiology*.
Teleology is, of course, a reference to the purposeful, goal-directed nature
of any given process. Eutaxiology, on the other hand, isn't concerned with
the final goal or purpose of a given process *per se*; it is simply a reference
to the degree of order and complexity which is found in that process.

This distinction is important, because one can appreciate the design and
order in a given object without necessarily positing any higher purpose or
goal to that object. At the same time, though, most examples of design and
order in the world have some sort of larger goal or purpose associated
with them. One can appreciate the order contained in a watch in a purely
eutaxiological manner, but this order nevertheless exists for a purpose,
which is to tell time. Thus eutaxiology *implies* teleology; both are separate,
yet related, aspects of the phenomenon of mechanistic order.

Teleology in turn implies the existence of some sort of design, because goals can usually be attained only in a system that has been explicitly designed for a particular purpose. Although it is possible to imagine an undesigned "system" that is nevertheless capable of achieving certain ends, we usually tend to identify the existence of a given design with its particular goal-making capacity. By the same token, we tend to identify the absence of design by the absence of any such goal-making capacity. It is for this reason that teleological ideas have been closely associated with design arguments in the past. Today many thinkers continue to regard the two concepts as virtually synonymous. This is undoubtedly why most non-theistic scientists and philosophers tend to steer away from a teleological world view: because of the religious implications that are almost inevitably entailed with one.

2.2 Early Background of Teleological Thought

If it is possible to identify a single unifying theme in the history of man's thinking about the universe, it must have something to do with the intelligibility and goal-directed nature of the cosmos. Since the beginning of recorded history all major civilizations have maintained a belief in some sort of creation story, and with it a belief in the overall purposiveness of the universe. The ancient Egyptians and Persians, for example, took the existence of this Universal Mind for granted; they even developed impressive astronomical techniques for mapping out the heavens.

However, of all the ancient influences upon the modern concept of teleology, the ancient Hebrews have undoubtedly had the greatest impact. For not only did they take the existence of a Divine Universal Teleology for granted, they also established a fruitful foundation for the later pursuit of concrete scientific knowledge through their belief in a Transcendent Law-Giver. The fundamental idea here is that if there is an Intelligent Creator in existence who has established an orderly decree through the issuance of immutable physical laws, then the actual contents of the universe itself might be intelligible to human beings. This ancient idea provided the impetus for the scientific study of the universe many hundreds of centuries later. Concrete evidence for this relationship between the scientific pursuit of knowledge and belief in a Divine Law-Giver can be found in the fact that the majority of British scientists at the close of the nineteenth century were practicing Christians.[1]

2.3 Greek and Roman Philosophy

If the universe as a whole is actually teleological in nature, one would naturally expect a good many critical thinkers down through history to have noticed this characteristic. And indeed they have. Beginning with the pre-

Socratic philosophers in ancient Greece and running through to the present day, teleological reasoning has had a profound impact on the development of human intellectual thought.

Anaxagoras of Clazomenae (500–428 BC) was probably the first philosophical thinker in the West to attribute the obvious order in the universe to a larger plan or design. Working on the Greek island of Ionia during the fifth century BC (which was where Western science also had its origin), Anaxagoras attributed the existence of order in the universe to the influence of cosmic "Mind," an idea that was to be pursued in great detail in later centuries.[2] Once the universe became ordered, however, Anaxagoras felt that the influence of Mind came to an end. This was an important foreshadowing of the deistic movement that was to come much later, which also saw the universe as functioning entirely on its own power after having been initially created by a Supernatural Power. Curiously, though, Anaxagoras failed to take the concept of an ordering Mind to its natural conclusion: that of attributing a higher teleological purpose to the universe as a whole. He simply noted that the universe had originally been created by the influence of some sort of cosmic Mind.

Anaxagoras' ideas were later challenged by both Socrates (470–399 BC) and his student Plato (427–347 BC), both of whom believed that in addition to providing the initial order to the universe, Mind also acted to sustain it at all times. In his timeless genius, Plato came to the realization that matter cannot induce motion in and of itself. Consequently, since matter is currently in motion, he reasoned that there had to have been a Higher Cause that originally set it in motion. Moreover, both Socrates and Plato saw the obvious structural design in the human body as being direct evidence of a cosmic Mind.

The Cretan philosopher Diogenes (400–325 BC) was also deeply influenced by the degree of order in the natural world. He was impressed by the optimal arrangement of the various global cycles, such as the four seasons and night and day, and believed that such a fortunate arrangement could not have been possible without the Creative Intelligence of a Higher Power.

The greatest Greek teleologist to have ever lived, however, was undoubtedly Plato's student Aristotle (384–322 BC). For Aristotle, the ingenious structural and functional design contained in all life forms was itself *ipso facto* proof of an "intelligent natural world that functions according to some deliberate design." Not surprisingly, then, Aristotle regarded the notion of an accidental world created by the chance collision of atoms, introduced by Democritus and Leucippus, as ridiculous and in stark contradiction to the observed facts.

Aristotle postulated the existence of a larger "end" (*telos*) to which all events were magnetically attracted. He believed that it was this end or purpose which gave every object in the universe its ultimate meaning and significance.

As a consequence, Aristotle actively opposed the growing idea that a thing can be fully explained when one simply learns what it is made of. Rather, Aristotle believed that in order to understand the true meaning of any given object, three other causes besides this "material cause" had to be ascertained: the "efficient cause," which was the object or process that produced the object in question, the "formal cause," which was the intrinsic pattern or form of the object that distinguished it from all other objects, and the "final cause," which was simply the final purpose for which the object was created.

It was in this latter observation that Aristotle revealed his true genius. He saw the purposeful design of the universe as self-evident. Consequently, he came to the momentous conclusion that the best way to understand the ultimate meaning of a thing is by ascertaining its "final cause," or the purpose that the thing serves in the Universal Teleological Economy.

Entelechy was the term Aristotle used to describe the internal perfecting principle that brought things to serve their final teleological purpose. In modern humanistic psychology, Aristotle's principle of entelechy has become known as the "tendency for self-actualization," whereas in Jungian depth psychology it has become known as the "urge to individuation." In both instances, the teleological drive is towards full character development.

Moving on, we find that one of Aristotle's associates, Tyrtamus of Eresos (372–287 BC), challenged the master's emphasis on final causation, for he saw much in the world that seemed to have no discernable purpose at all: hurricanes, tornadoes, earthquakes, famine, disease, and the like. Indeed, many people continue to cite these natural catastrophes, not only as evidence against any larger teleological purpose to the world, but also as evidence against the existence of a good and all-powerful Creator. "How," it is wondered, "could a good and loving God allow such tragedies to happen in the world, especially when so many innocent men, women, and children are victims? If God can even remotely be described as being good He[3] will want to prevent such catastrophes, and if He is all-powerful He will be able to prevent them, yet they still occur on a regular basis. Consequently, either God is not totally good, not totally powerful, or else He doesn't exist at all."

As I plan to show in detail in a forthcoming work on the problem of evil, such a naïve view of natural evil is mistaken because it fails to consider the distinct possibility that these "acts of God" may be a logically necessary feature both of man's process of character development and of the nature of the physical world itself (insofar as they could all could emanate from an intrinsically necessary set of properties in the Human Essence). We should never be so arrogant as to assume that a given object or process in nature has no Higher Purpose, just because no purpose is immediately apparent, or because it produces a seemingly negative effect in the world.

The Stoic school of philosophy, begun by Zeno of Citium (334–262 BC), would have largely agreed with the above view, since the Stoics believed that everything that happened in the world was for the good of all concerned, even if it didn't superficially appear to be so at first glance. Being ardent supporters of the Teleological Design Argument, the Stoics adopted an anthropocentric view of man as the very pinnacle of creation, wherein they believed that everything else in the world was created for man's overall benefit.

Cicero (106–43 BC) went even further than this and asserted that not only the existence but also the various characteristics of the creating deities could be inferred from the highly ordered works of their hands. (The idea of a single all-encompassing Creator, known as monotheism, hadn't yet taken hold in the ancient world.) For Cicero, the ubiquitous presence of order and design in the world made the existence of the gods obvious:

> When we see some example of a mechanism, such as a globe or clock or some such device, do we doubt that it is the creation of a conscious intelligence? So when we see the movement of the heavenly bodies . . . how can we doubt that these too are not only the works of reason but of a reason which is perfect and divine?[4]

Later thinkers, such as Augustine, Aquinas, and most notably Paley, were to seize upon this same basic idea to argue convincingly for the existence of a transcendent Creator God. The rapid advance in scientific knowledge throughout the Renaissance, Enlightenment, and Modern periods functioned to greatly add to the persuasive power of this fundamental argument, largely because of the heightened understanding of natural order it engendered, which in turn served to strengthen the impression that our highly ordered physical world could not have been formed by chance alone.

The Greek physician Galen (131–201) expanded upon Cicero's views by arguing that the underlying Purpose of the Creator could be ascertained by an intimate inspection of all that He has created in the world. For Galen, the human hand alone was reason enough to conclude that a Supernatural Intelligence had to have been responsible for creating the world and all that is in it:

> Let us, then, scrutinize this member of our body, and inquire, not simply whether it be in itself useful for all the purposes of life and adapted to an animal endued with the highest intelligence, but whether its entire structure be not such that it could not be improved upon by any conceivable alteration.[5]

The notion of a goal-directed cosmos was introduced into the Roman Empire by the natural historian Pliny (23–79) and Boethius (470–525), who as Barrow and Tipler point out, mediated the transition from Roman to Scholastic thinking.[6] Both Pliny and Boethius were convinced that the order and design in nature were not the product of chance, but were instead the deliberate creation of a Supernatural Intelligence.

From this point onward, Greek ideas concerning teleology were disseminated into Arabic culture, as the Arabs were the principal translators of the early Greek texts. Thus it was only natural that the Muslim religion, which was to develop later amongst the Arabs, would contain deep teleological underpinnings. The Christian world was also to make extensive use of these anthropocentric ideas, beginning primarily with the efforts of St. Thomas Aquinas.

2.4 Medieval Philosophy

Moving on to the Medieval period, we find a variety of thinkers carrying on the teleological views of their goal-oriented forebearers. The most accomplished and influential of these Medieval thinkers was undoubtedly St. Thomas Aquinas (1225–1274), who incorporated the Aristotelian tradition into the overall framework of Christian theology. He used the argument from design to prove the existence of God in his famous "Fifth Way":

> The fifth way begins from the guidedness of things. For we observe that some things which lack knowledge, such as natural bodies, work towards an end. This is apparent from the fact they always or most usually work in the same way and move towards what is best. From which it is clear that they reach their end not by chance but by intention. For those things which do not have knowledge do not tend to an end, except under the direction of someone who knows and understands: the arrow, for example, is shot by the archer. There is, therefore, an intelligent personal being by whom everything in nature is ordered to its end.[7]

For many of these Medieval thinkers, the obvious link between man and the natural world was strongly suggestive of a Common Designer. For instance, Raymonde of Sebonde (c. 1400), the originator of the field of natural theology, wrote that:

> There could not be so great an agreement and likeness between man and the trees, plants, and animals, if there were two designers, rulers or artificers in nature; nor would the operation of plants and trees be carried on so regularly after the manner of human operations, nor would they all be so much in man's likeness, except that He which guided and directed the operations of these trees and plants were the same Being that gave man

understanding and that ordered the operations of trees which are after the manner of works done by understanding, since in trees and plants there is no reason or understanding. And of far more strength is the oneness of matter and sameness of life in man, animals, trees and plants an evidence of the oneness of their Maker.[8]

2.5 Renaissance and Early Modern Thought

With the advent of the Renaissance period we begin to find many of the individuals who did the important foundational work for the science we have today. Of these Renaissance thinkers, a surprising number were overtly teleological in their world view.

Nicholas Copernicus (1473–1543), for example, was a thoroughgoing teleologist, in spite of his bold assertion that the Sun, and not the Earth, was the center of the solar system (which actually has nothing at all to do with the existence of purposiveness in the universe). Indeed, Copernicus used many of Aristotle's goal-oriented ideas to help him construct a mechanical model of the solar system in which the Sun, and not the Earth, was the center. He even seems to have retained an anthropocentric view of the cosmos in spite of his ideas on the relative position of the Earth in the heavens, for he went to the trouble to show that in relation to the stars themselves, the distance of the Earth from the center of the solar system was negligible.

Copernicus' anthropocentrism is a bit surprising, as his work is typically associated with the scientific *removal* of man from the center of the universe. We aren't told in the scientific literature that Copernicus was a teleologically-oriented theist who used his goal-oriented ideas to place the Earth in its proper cosmic perspective in relation to God. We're simply led to believe that Copernicus removed mankind from *any* privileged position in the universe by virtue of his removal of the Earth from the center of the solar system.[9]

It was this perversion of Copernicus' major thesis that initially led Brandon Carter to propose the Anthropic Principle back in 1974. Carter correctly surmised that mankind's removal from the "center" of the universe at the hands of the Copernican dogma didn't necessarily mean that humanity wasn't privileged in *any* way. Indeed, Carter found that it was *necessarily* the case that mankind be "privileged" to the extent that the universe itself be compatible with human observers.

In contrast to Copernicus' anthropocentrism, Galileo Galilei (1564–1642) found a man-centered view of the heavens distasteful and presumptuous, as he supposed that God surely had more important things to do than deal primarily with us. Even so, Galileo's rejection of anthropocentrism seems to have had far more to do with his desire for an objective view of reality than it did with any explicit rejection of Divine Creatorship *per se*.

Johannes Kepler (1571–1630), the man who discovered the geometry of the planetary orbits in our solar system, was also an avowed teleologist who subscribed to the belief that all things were deliberately made for man by God. Indeed, he used his obsessive belief that God had created the universe according to some perfect numerical principle to help him search for—and find—the individual geometries of the planetary orbits in our solar system.

It is important to note, however, that not all Renaissance and early modern scientists were so enthusiastic about teleological thinking. Montaigne (1533–1592), for instance, believed that any degree of anthropocentrism is simply unwarranted, since we cannot know precisely what position we occupy in the ultimate scheme of things. Francis Bacon (1561–1626), one of the originators of the modern scientific method, was even more vehement in his criticism of teleological and anthropocentric thinking, especially in relation to scientific study. Although he didn't want to go so far as to deny that "final causation" actually exists, he believed that the pursuit of such issues belonged in the field of philosophy and not in science. As a consequence, he pushed strongly for a complete separation of empirical science from mere metaphysical speculation.

Even so, one of Bacon's scientific contemporaries, William Harvey (1578–1657), retained a firm belief in Aristotelian teleology and proceeded to discover the human circulatory system because of it. Harvey initially approached the question of how the blood moved within the body by asking himself how a Purposeful Designer would have constructed such a system. Following his observation that the various valves within the veins of the body allow blood to travel towards the heart, but not away from it, Harvey developed a sudden insight into the circulatory design which he believed the Creator had deliberately built into the body. This is but one instance among many of a teleological world view leading to a major scientific discovery; von Baer's discovery of the mammalian ova is another.

The seventeenth century saw a more mechanical view of the cosmos gradually take hold. This transition from an organic to a more mechanistic world view was in part due to the rise of more complex machinery in the growing industrial society of the time; it was also due to the many scientific discoveries which seemed to show the universe to be a type of Grand Mechanistic Clockwork.

Teleological thinking, however, flourished within this mechanistic period as well, due to the direct philosophical implications of a mechanistic world view: any proposed mechanism *by definition* seems to require both a designer and an ultimate purpose; therefore, if the universe is a machine, it must require a Grand Designer and an Ultimate Purpose.

Robert Boyle (1627–1691), discoverer of the famous gas law which continues to plague chemistry students to this day, was perhaps the most vocal supporter of the mechanistic design argument during this period. For Boyle, the many examples of intricate design in the natural world were proof enough of a Grand Designer. Indeed, because of his intense belief in the world as a giant mechanism, he was utterly convinced that the larger purpose of the world could be ascertained through an intimate analysis of its inner workings.

Boyle thus believed that a teleological world view was actually *supported* by scientific investigation, since such empirical inquiries almost invariably revealed an impressive underlying order to the cosmos. Indeed, he even went so far as to assert that a robust belief in a teleological universe could provide the impetus for further discoveries in the various fields of scientific research.

Nowhere do we find more support for this contention than in the work of Sir Isaac Newton (1642–1727), easily the greatest scientific genius of his age. Newton was a thoroughgoing teleologist who believed that cosmic order was "created by God at first and conserved by him to this Day in the same state and condition."[10] It was this undying belief in a Divinely-Inspired Universal Order that led Newton to make his many worldshaking discoveries regarding gravitation and motion.

Another intellectual heavyweight who was to give the study of teleology a new twist was the German philosopher and mathematician Gottfried Leibniz (1646–1716). For Leibniz, there was no question that the universe was created by a Supreme Being for a larger purpose; the very intelligence exemplified by the creation made this a self-evident proposition.

Leibniz wasn't content, however, to simply affirm the existence of a universal Creator. He chose to go one step further and assert that, while there are an infinite number of possible worlds that God could have created, His Goodness and Omniscience obliged Him to create the best of all possible worlds, which Leibniz believed to be our own.

Leibniz's Principle of Radical Optimism has been severely criticized over the years because of the tremendous amount of gratuitous evil that seems to routinely take place in our world. But even if one refuses to grant that this is the best possible world in terms of the amount of evil that takes place daily here, Leibniz's case becomes far more convincing when it is considered on a purely physical level. For as we shall see, the most recent scientific evidence indicates that this may very well be the *only* possible world (and therefore the best) in terms of its underlying physical structure, since it appears as though no other combination of fundamental constants is capable of producing a biocentric world like our own. If this turns out to be true, then Leibniz's Principle of Radical Optimism will be vindicated on the deepest level of all.

2.6 Eighteenth-Century Thought

William Paley (1743–1805) was yet another free thinker who strongly supported a teleological world view in his writings. His highly influential work *Natural Theology* has turned out to be one of the most important and widely read books on science and religion ever written. Even Charles Darwin[11] confessed that he had been deeply influenced by Paley's work while a student at Cambridge.

For Paley, the idea that the present world order could have been the result of blind chance was unthinkable. There were far too many extraordinary examples of design in the natural world to make this even a remote possibility. Any appearance of chance in the natural order was simply attributed to the inevitable "ignorance of the observer," rather than to any truly random aggregation of particles. It was this conviction that led Paley to argue for the existence of God in *Natural Theology* using the classic argument from design.

In one of the most memorable descriptions of the argument from design ever written, Paley shows how one cannot have a design without a designer:

> In crossing a heath, suppose I pitched my foot against a stone and were asked how the stone came to be there; I might possibly answer that, for anything I knew to the contrary, it had lain there for ever: nor would it perhaps be very easy to show the absurdity of this answer. But supposing I had found a watch upon the ground and it should be enquired how the watch happened to be in that place; I should hardly think of the answer which I had before given, that for anything I knew, the watch might always have been there. Yet why should not this answer serve for the watch as well as for the stone? For this reason, and for no other, viz. that when we come to inspect the watch, we perceive . . . that its several parts are framed and put together for a purpose.[12]

The remainder of Paley's book is concerned with showing how the many life-supporting features of our world constitute powerful evidence for the existence of Intelligent Design in the universe. This line of argument is strikingly similar to the "anthropic" arguments of today, which seek to show how the basic structure of physical reality itself is intimately related to the existence of all life on Earth.

For instance, Paley was aware of the fact that the gravitational inverse square law, upon which all life on Earth intimately depends, is only possible in a universe of precisely three dimensions. He therefore saw the present existence of a three-dimensional universe as evidence for the existence of a Divine Intelligence.

Voltaire (1694–1778), the famous French writer, agreed that "a watch proves a watch-maker, and . . . a universe proves a God."[13] He was further convinced that humans could not be the product of blind chance, since:

> We are intelligent beings, and intelligent beings could not have been formed by a blind, brute, insensible thing.[14]

Nevertheless, Voltaire was still radically opposed to the anthropocentric notion that humans are the center of God's creation, largely because of our ignorance of the true purpose of the various universal constituents.

The work of French mathematician Moreau de Maupertuis (1698–1759) further helped to establish the validity of teleological thinking in matters scientific. Maupertuis set out to accomplish the ambitious project of creating a mathematical quantification of Leibniz's proclamation that ours is the best of all possible worlds. What he came up with was his famous integral principle of variation known as the Least Action Principle.

In a paper presented to the French academy of sciences in 1744, Maupertuis showed that the behavior of impacting bodies could be predicted by assuming that the mathematical product of their mass, velocity, and distance (mvs) will always be a minimum; hence the notion of "least action." The significance of this assertion lay in the direct implication that Final Causes (i.e., a minimum mvs product) were in fact operative in nature. This Maupertuis took to be proof of a Divine Creator, who alone was thought to operate in nature via Final Causes.

The publication of David Hume's *Dialogues Concerning Natural Religion* in 1779, however, put a severe damper on the progress of teleological thought as the eighteenth century began to draw to a close. In this very persuasive work, Hume pointed out several glaring weaknesses in the traditional Design Argument which, for many readers, had the effect of completely nullifying any type of teleological argument for the existence of God. We will explore Hume's anti-theistic arguments in detail in Chapter 11.

Immanuel Kant (1724–1804) further helped to discredit the Design Argument—and with it the validity of teleological thought—through the promulgating of his unique theory of knowledge. For Kant, it was impossible to either prove or disprove statements about the real world using reason alone, because of the inherent uncertainty regarding the mind's intrinsic categories of perception. Since we can only know our own idiosyncratic perception of an object, and never the thing itself, it seems to follow that we can never know anything for sure about the inherent nature of reality. This being the case, Kant believed that we could never know for sure whether the universe was truly teleological in nature, or whether we just perceived it to be this way because of the intractable order-imposing capacity of the human mind. He therefore believed that the Teleological Argument could never be used to absolutely establish the existence of God (although he was sympathetic to the argument on other grounds).

The demise of teleological thinking in the Western world was secured by the gradual advance of the modern world view, in which the animated, organismic ideas of the ancients eventually came to be supplanted by a more inanimate, objective, and reductionistic perspective, which in turn seemed to make any sort of theological explanation of the scientific world almost obsolete. The realities of Darwinian evolutionism which were to come later only served to reinforce the perception that scientific truth was inherently non-theological, because it seemed to show that the present diversity of living organisms in the world could have come about by purely natural means.

2.7 Nineteenth- and Twentieth-Century Thought

Although Maupertuis was mistaken in his assumption of least action in all possible cases, he was largely correct in calling his Principle of Least Action a teleological interpretation of physics.[15] Indeed, several of this century's greatest physicists, such as Max Planck, John Wheeler, and Richard Feynmann, have independently come to the conclusion that Maupertuis' Least Action Principle may in fact be more fundamental than non-teleological mechanistic principles in explaining natural phenomena.[16]

Following Helmholtz's assertion that the Action Principle could predict new physical laws, the great quantum physicist Max Planck also took sides with the teleological Action Principle, not just because of his own religious convictions, but because he felt that the Action Principle was more in line with both the relativistic and quantum nature of modern physics. Indeed, Planck's famous mathematical constant is expressed in units of Action.

Moreover, in a verification of Helmholtz's predictions regarding the Action Principle, the German mathematician Hilbert was able to derive the final form of Einstein's field equations independently of Einstein using only the stipulation that they had to follow from Action precursors.[17]

However, the most impressive utilization of a teleological Action Principle in the realm of theoretical physics was performed by Richard Feynman and John Wheeler at Princeton University. Feynman and Wheeler together worked out a classical theory of electrodynamics which predicted that the behavior of a given particle in the present is not only determined by the behavior of other particles in the past, but also by the behavior of particles *in the future*! This is clearly a teleological way of conceptualizing the quantum behavior of subatomic particles, and it subsequently led Feynman to develop his "sum-over-histories" interpretation of quantuam mechanics, which is simply a way of conceiving quantum reality in terms of an Action Principle.[18]

In spite of these impressive achievements, Feynman pressed on, and later developed the Feynman Rules for the scattering of subatomic particles. Utilizing these rules, scientists were able to develop a workable version of guage symmetry theory, which is a complex series of formulas that physicists now use to attempt to understand the underlying nature of physical reality. This in turn led Weinberg and Salam to discover a gauge theory which had the surprising effect of unifying the weak nuclear force with the electromagnetic force. Indeed, this was such an important step in the quest for a unified physical theory that Weinberg and Salam were awarded a Nobel Prize in 1979 for their efforts.

For our purposes in this book, it is important to understand that virtually all of modern particle physics is now based on guage theories which were largely derived from Feynman's sum-over-histories method of interpreting Maupertuis' original Action Principle. It is for this reason that Barrow and Tipler have concluded that "teleological thinking has become essential to modern mathematical physics."[19]

Nevertheless, in spite of the overwhelming amount of evidence in favor of a scientific teleology, most scientists today openly reject the notion of a goal-directed cosmos. Even the word teleology itself is regarded with an almost superstitious suspicion by many scientists, largely because of its inevitable association with the idea of a Grand Designer. Atheistic scientists apparently want the idea of God to have no part in their scientific models, so they tend to reject any philosophical system that is even remotely teleological in nature. Biologists have even gone so far as to deliberately substitute the word "teleonomy" for teleology, so that they can refer to the obvious purposiveness displayed by living organisms without making any undue religious statements. Robert Brandon is thus correct in his surmisal that the word teleology tends to cause an "allergic reaction" in most non-theistic scientists.[20]

Even so, an objective assessment of the available evidence, especially in the fields of astrophysics and biology, leads almost inescapably to a teleological view of the universe. The reason is not far to seek: just about everything in the physical universe tends to a goal, whether it be the Earth's revolution about the Sun or the tiger's search for prey. Indeed, if this weren't the case, we probably wouldn't be here to wonder about it, since a non-teleological "universe"[21] would almost surely be incapable of supporting our existence (since it is the goal-directed nature of the universe's atoms and molecules that makes our biocentric universe possible in the first place). Perhaps this is why non-theistic scientists are so adamantly opposed to a scientific teleology: precisely because it *does* in fact seem to be true almost everywhere we look.

Indeed, one wouldn't think that an obviously untrue proposal would generate such passionate rejections on the part of otherwise rational scientists. It simply wouldn't be worth their time. Everything changes, however, if there is some element of truth to the teleological paradigm, because an acknowledgement of this truth would bring the non-theistic scientist that much closer to the conclusion he or she most wants to avoid: the prospect of Intelligent Design in the heavens.

In other words, it isn't goal-directedness *per se* that these learned individuals find so unpalatable; it is the direct implication of a Divine Creator, which seems to follow inescapably from a teleological world view, that they find offensive. Even so, few scientists have been able to mount a serious attack on the teleological paradigm over the years, in spite of a large number of heroic attempts.

Indeed, as Barrow and Tipler have pointed out, the only significant argument against a scientific teleology that has stood the test of time doesn't even attempt to deny the obvious purposiveness of physical reality. It simply cites the unfinished and changing nature of the entire universe itself as the chief piece of evidence counting against a goal-directed universe. This is said to be[22] the real way in which our world differs from a watch: an unfinished watch doesn't work, whereas our world persists in working in spite of the fact that it still appears to be unfinished. If the world were deliberately made by an All-Powerful Creator, one would perhaps expect it to be "finished" by the time it came to be inhabited by intelligent beings. Since it still appears to be unfinished, the notion of Intelligent Design seems to suffer.[23]

It is fallacious, however, to use the apparent unfinished nature of the physical universe as evidence against Intelligent Design, because there is always the possibility that this "unfinished" character was precisely what was intended by the Creator all along. Indeed, as John Hick[24] and others have pointed out, the "unfinished" nature of the world and universe serves the all-important function of promoting human character growth through a wide variety of psychospiritual mechanisms. From this point of view, the "unfinished" character of the universe is just an illusion, since it disappears just as soon as we view the world from the perspective of human development. On this view, the universe is really "finished" with respect to its presumed function in promoting human character growth.

If this is the case, however, the "unfinished" nature of the universe *cannot* be used as evidence against a cosmic teleology, since this perceived incompletion can be subsumed under a still larger developmental goal. To the extent that this hypothesis is valid, it leaves goal-directed thinking virtually unchallenged in the realm of science and religion.

2.8 The Influence of Darwinism on Teleological Thought

The progress of teleological thought took a violent nosedive in 1859 with the publication of Charles Darwin's (1809–1882) earthshaking book *The Origin of Species*. Up until this point, the various examples of design in the living world were generally taken to be direct evidence of a Grand Designer, as it was largely inconceivable that these complex designs could have originated entirely on their own, due only to natural causes. With his theory of natural selection, however, Darwin attempted to show that the struggle for survival in and of itself was capable of creating the extreme diversity of living creatures we now see in the world. His arguments were seen as being extremely persuasive, especially by the scientific community, since the theory of natural selection not only purported to explain the rise of new species, but also the extinction of those species that were unable to adapt quickly enough to a harsh and changing environment. Since scientists were now in apparent possession of an entirely naturalistic theory to explain the existence of life, many rejected any notion of a Divine Teleology as being not only unnecessary, but also unlikely as well, given Darwin's monumental achievement.

Not everyone, however, saw Darwin's findings as necessitating the abandonment of a Divine Teleology. Asa Gray (1810–1888), a Calvinist professor of botany at Harvard, saw much of value in Darwin's work, since it not only seemed to explain the findings of his own botanical studies, it also seemed to explain the extinction of species as well, which traditional creationism was hard-pressed to account for. Gray was thus able to retain his belief in a teleological universe in spite of Darwin's discovery of natural selection, which he simply believed to be the natural mechanism God ordained for controlling the rise and fall of species. Indeed, Gray was of the opinion that if a theistically-minded person "cannot recognize design in Nature because of evolution, he may be ranked with those of whom it was said 'Except ye see signs and wonders ye will not believe.'"[25]

Darwin was surprisingly sympathetic to Gray's interpretation of his work, for he realized that:

> . . . it is just as noble a conception of the Deity to believe that he created a few original forms capable of self-development into other and needful forms.[26]

Gray was certainly on the right track, for even if we assume that Darwin was correct in all of his judgments (which he most certainly was not), the possibility remains that natural selection is simply the naturalistic tool that God ordained to control the rise and fall of species in the world. If God exists at all, we know that He has delegated a great deal of creative power to the naturalistic forces that are constantly at work in our world. For instance, God's Hand didn't directly carve out the Grand Canyon long ago; the Colorado River did.

By the same token, God seems to have delegated much of the controlling power behind the rise and fall of species to natural selection and other naturalistic forces. Even so, this delegation of creative power doesn't make God any less responsible for the creation and proliferation of life, any more than the use of a paintbrush made van Gogh any less responsible for his art. It would thus be utterly ridiculous to reject the notion of a Divine Teleology just because we seem to have discovered some of the naturalistic tools that God used to create the world. If anything, the world is *more* of a teleological place *because* of Darwin's theory of natural selection, since it shows that naturalistic powers *are* in fact geared to producing a final end product.

Erasmus Darwin (1731–1802), the grandfather of Charles Darwin, was also of the opinion that God had chosen to create the world through the use of natural processes. Speaking in reference to the beliefs of philosopher David Hume, the elder Darwin once wrote that Hume:

> . . . concludes that the world itself might have been generated, rather than created; that is, it might have been gradually produced from very small beginnings increasing by the activity of its inherent principles, rather than by a sudden evolution of the whole by the Almighty fiat—What a magnificent idea of the infinite power to cause the causes of effects, rather than to cause the effects themselves.[27]

2.9 The Return to a Scientific Teleology

Despite the tremendous importance of teleological thinking throughout most of human intellectual history, the rise of scientific naturalism in the nineteenth and early twentieth centuries all but eliminated the notion of teleology from serious scientific consideration.

It wasn't until the publication of Henderson's *The Fitness of the Environment* in 1907 that teleological ideas began to be seriously considered again by many individuals. In this ground-breaking work, Henderson noted how the underlying structure of the physical and chemical realms are perfectly suited for the evolution of life. For many people, this perfect suitability was taken to be strongly indicative of Intelligent Design.

Indeed, the recent rise in popularity of the Anthropic Principle in both scientific and lay circles may be signaling the beginning of a conceptual return to a more teleologically based cosmology in the Western world. For many scientifically oriented individuals, the overwhelming evidence of contrivance in the structural details of the natural world necessitates some degree of affirmation in the overall purposiveness displayed by the cosmos. To the extent that this return to a scientific teleology actually takes place, the Anthropic Principle can be understood as providing the essential conceptual link between the modern scientific period and the more traditional teleology of times past.

2.10 Teleology and Holism

One of the guises through which the concept of teleology has reasserted itself in recent years is the resurgence of holism, which has found support in many different areas of physics.

The concept of nonlocality—in which causal influences are thought to be capable of traveling faster than light—has been instrumental in the rebirth of the holo-movement. Bell's Theorem, for instance, shows that causal influences between two physically separated particles can happen *instantaneously*, even though in the traditional Newtonian conception of the world this is impossible. The significance of this remarkable phenomenon lies in its suggestion that the entire universe exists in a state of undivided wholeness, in which causal influences in one area can have an instantaneous impact elsewhere. Physicist David Bohm's concept of the implicate order, in which the information of the entire universe is enfolded into each of its constituent parts, is based on this idea of a universal holism.

According to philosopher of science Errol E. Harris of Northwestern University, the true meaning of teleological phenomena can only be understood when it is considered in terms of the implicit assumptions of holism:

> It is the immanence of the principle of order in the parts of a structured whole that constitutes its teleology . . . The nature, disposition, and behaviour of the part can be accounted for only by reference to this immanent principle, where the discovery of efficient causes leaves unexplained the structure and dynamic regulation of movements within the whole. Such explanation of the part in terms of the whole is what is properly termed teleological. In the case of a dynamic movement or a genetic process, subjection of the phases to the governance of the principle of wholeness will determine the end, which is typically the completion of some whole; thus a teleological process is one of genesis of a whole, and if the process is consciously directed it is purposive.
>
> The objections to teleological explanation so frequently voiced since the 16th-century reaction against Aristotle now fall away. The complaint that it reverses the order of causation, making a future event the cause of the present no longer applies, because the teleological effect is now seen to result from the principle of systematic wholeness immanent in the part and in the process of generation of the total structure.[28]

To their great credit, the ancient Greeks anticipated the science of holism with their concept of teleological *organism,* in which they conceived of the entire universe as a single, interconnected entity, on the analogy of a living organism. The more we learn about the underlying order of the universe, the more we are discovering that the ancient Greeks had it right all along.

2.11 Conclusion

The teleological world view discussed in this chapter has enjoyed a particularly distinguished following over the years, beginning with Plato and Aristotle in ancient Greece and moving on through Augustine, Aquinas,

Copernicus, Boyle, Newton, Planck, and a whole host of other important thinkers. While the modern agnostic period may have put a temporary damper on this time-honored teleological tradition, the Anthropic Principle seems well on its way towards bringing us back to the historically dominant position once again.

Notes

1. John D. Barrow, *The World Within the World* (New York: Oxford University Press, 1990), p. 32.
2. John D. Barrow and Frank J. Tipler, *The Anthropic Cosmological Principle* (Oxford University Press, 1986), pp. 32–33.
3. I use the male personal pronoun to refer to the Deity for the sake of literary simplicity and existing convention. I do *not* mean to imply that God is a male, or to show any disrespect for feminist theology.
4. Cicero, *The Nature of the Gods*, translated by H.C.P. McGregor (London: Penguin, 1972), p. 89.
5. Galen, *On the Usefulness of the Parts of the Body*, translated by M. T. May (New York: Cornell University Press, 1968).
6. Barrow and Tipler, p. 45.
7. Thomas Aquinas, *Summa Theologica*, Q.2, Art. 3.
8. Raymonde, *Studies in the History of Natural Theology*, (Cambridge: Cambridge University Press, 1915).
9. This type of slanting of the facts in the scientific literature suggests a deep anti-theistic bias on the part of most scientists, who show a pervasive tendency to interpret the existing facts in a non-theistic manner.
10. Taken from Barrow and Tipler, *The Anthropic Cosmological Principle*, p. 60.
11. Although Darwin's ideas have been widely used by atheists to support a non-theistic world view, it is important to note that Darwin himself was not an atheist. To the contrary, Darwin believed that the world itself had been originally created by a Supreme Being; he even believed that the variations which provide the raw material for biological evolution were somehow inspired by the Creator. However, the one thing he did not believe was that the plant and animal kingdoms had been created ready-made at some point in the distant past. In this sense Darwin was a classic deist, insofar as he believed that God created the universe at the very beginning of time and then left it alone to develop according to its own laws.
12. William Paley, *Natural Theology* (London: Baldwyn and Company, 1819).
13. Taken from Barrow and Tipler, p. 64.
14. Voltaire, 'Atheist atheism,' *Philosophical Dictionary* (1769), transl. and ed. P. Gay, 2 Vols (New York: Basic Books, 1955).
15. Barrow and Tipler, p. 149.
16. Ibid., pp. 151–152.
17. Ibid.
18. Ibid., p. 152.
19. Ibid.
20. Robert N. Brandon, "Adaptation Explanations: Are Adaptations for the Good of Replicators or Interactors?" *Evolution at a Crossroads*, David J. Depew and Bruce H. Weber eds. (Cambridge: The MIT Press, 1985), p. 81.
21. The notion of a non-teleological universe is almost surely a contradiction in

terms, since a genuine uni-verse is by definition a unified whole, and unified wholes are always goal-directed by their very nature. (At the very least, the minimum goal that would be accomplished by any such unified whole would be the maintenance of a singular identity through the cohesion of all its constituent parts.) For a "universe" to be truly non-teleological, then, it would have to be anarchic to its innermost core, but such an anarchic entity could not possibly qualify as being a unified whole, since true anarchy is by definition the opposite of holism. Therefore, the concept of a universe contains within itself the specification of a unified whole, and unified wholes are always goal-directed by their very nature. It follows, then, that to the extent that the universe is truly a universe, it *must* be teleological by its very nature.

22. Barrow and Tipler, pp. 28–30.
23. This argument betrays the extremely close association between teleology and Intelligent Design that has persisted over the years. Most thinkers have deemed it to be next to impossible for the universe to be explicitly goal-directed without simultaneously being Intelligently Designed as well.
24. John Hick, *Evil and the God of Love* (New York: Harper and Row, 1977).
25. Asa Gray, *Darwiniana* (New York: Appleton, 1876).
26. Taken form Barrow and Tipler, p. 85.
27. Erasmus Darwin, *Zoonomia*, 2 vol. (London, 1974).
28. Errol E. Harris, *Cosmos and Anthropos* (Atlantic Highlands, New Jersey: Humanities Press International, Inc., 1991), p. 168.

CHAPTER 3

The Immediate Background of the
Biocentric and Anthropic Principles

In the beginning God created the heavens and the earth.

GENESIS 1:1

I want to know how God created the world. I am not interested in this or that phenomenon, in the spectrum of this or that element. I want to know His thoughts, the rest are details.

ALBERT EINSTEIN

3.1 Science Acknowledges a Beginning to the Universe

One of the greatest pieces of evidence supporting a theistic world view is undoubtedly the scientific confirmation of a definite universal beginning, which is said to have occurred approximately 15 billion years ago. Prior to this discovery, many scientists believed in the so-called Steady-State theory of the universe, which simply asserted that there was no beginning to the universe because it is eternal. With the advent of the widely accepted Big Bang theory of universal origins, however, scientists have been forced to concede that the universe as we know it did in fact have a violent beginning sometime in the distant past.[1]

Science's discovery of the beginning of the universe began in 1913, when American astronomer Vesto Melvin Slipher inadvertently discovered that the spectra of several distant galaxies were strongly displaced towards the red, or lower frequency, end of the electromagnetic spectrum. This famous "red shift" is the result of the Doppler Effect, in which objects that are moving away from us have—by virtue of their own receding motion—their light spectra shifted toward the red end of the visible spectrum. Today we know that this galactic redshift is an indication that our neighboring galaxies are moving away from us and each other at tremendous velocities, up to two million miles per hour.

In 1913, however, the implications of this Doppler-induced red shift were still poorly understood, because no one had yet developed a reliable way to measure the immense distances to our neighboring galaxies. As a consequence, Slipher and his colleagues were unable to come to any definite

29

conclusions regarding their findings; all they knew was that their photographs of the galaxies surrounding the Milky Way were persistently redshifted.

Interestingly enough, though, when Slipher reported his findings to the American Astronomical Society in 1914, his audience spontaneously stood up and cheered, even though they weren't exactly sure what they were cheering about! Evidently they were able to sense the profound importance of Slipher's discovery for the up-and-coming science of cosmology.

Then, in 1915, Albert Einstein completed his general theory of relativity. Much to Einstein's initial dismay, however, the simplest solution to his equations revealed an expanding universe, which was something he did not believe in and had not anticipated (largely because an expanding universe implies a beginning, and a beginning implies a Creator). To the contrary, Einstein believed in a static and unchanging universe, which is what the majority of astronomical observations up to that point had indicated. As a consequence, Einstein devised an addition to his equations, the so-called cosmological constant, which enabled them to reflect a non-expanding universe. He later called this the greatest mistake of his career.

The purpose of the cosmological constant was to counteract the pull of gravity, so that the entire universe could be maintained in a static state. Einstein should have realized, however, that such a precarious state of cosmic balance would have been *extremely* unstable (not unlike a gigantic house of cards), such that even the smallest amount of disturbance in the balance would tend to become magnified until the entire universe would begin collapsing in on itself. This of course would even preclude the planetary orbits, since even the slightest movement by a major celestial body would be capable of upsetting the delicate universal balance. No wonder Einstein called the cosmological constant the greatest mistake he ever made.[2]

In the same year that Einstein went public with his static model of the universe (1917), the Dutch astronomer Willem de Sitter solved Einstein's equations and also came to the conclusion that the universe is expanding. Five years later in 1922 the Russian mathematician Alexander Friedmann discovered a simple algebraic error in Einstein's equations which, when corrected, clearly showed the universe to be expanding.

At first Einstein protested. He simply couldn't believe that the universe was really expanding in this way, again because of the broader theological implications that were inherent in such a finding. Although he claimed to have believed in "Spinoza's God," who revealed Himself in the orderly workings of nature, Einstein found it much more difficult to believe in a personal Deity who had actually created the universe at a specific point in the past.[3]

Then, in 1929, Milton Humason and Edwin Hubble showed once and for all that the various galaxies in our region of the universe are all moving away from each other at a rate that is directly proportional to their distance from the Milky Way. According to their calculations, some galaxies were found to be moving at the dizzying velocity of over 100 million miles per hour! In one fell swoop, Hubble and Humason were able to provide concrete experimental support for de Sitter's mathematical portrait of an expanding universe. With this finding, the static model of the universe originally envisioned by Einstein became obsolete almost overnight.

Still more evidence supporting the notion of a concrete beginning to the universe was found in the Second Law of Thermodynamics, which basically says that the total amount of disorder in the universe can never decrease. In other words, the universe is running down like a clock. If it is running down, it must have been "wound up" sometime in the past. It is this initial "winding up" period that corresponds to the thermodynamic beginning of the cosmos.

Yet, despite all the evidence indicating an actual beginning to the universe, there were still those who were not convinced. Finally, in 1965, two Bell Laboratory employees named Arno Penzias and Robert Wilson accidentally discovered a faint (3° Kelvin) background radiation that was apparently bathing the entire universe. Scientists soon identified this faint microwave background as a cosmic relic of the Big Bang itself. The Russian-American physicist George Gamow had predicted the existence of this background radiation back in 1948 on the basis of his "hot" model of the universe, but few took his prediction seriously until it was actually confirmed by direct observation.

Based on his calculations regarding the Big Bang, Gamow also predicted that approximately 25% of all the matter in the universe should be helium, with the other 75% or so being made up of hydrogen. Gamow was again vindicated when it was later discovered that hydrogen and helium do indeed comprise approximately 75% and 25% of the universe respectively.

It remained for an English mathematician named Roger Penrose and premier physicist Stephen Hawking to demonstrate once and for all that the Big Bang was not only theoretically plausible, it was physically *necessary* (provided that certain basic assumptions about the universe were to hold true). Interestingly enough, they found the proof they needed in the peculiar qualities surrounding massive collapsed stars, otherwise known as black holes.

Stars are normally comprised of a delicate balance between a gravitational pull inward, which is exerted by the matter contained within the star, and an explosive push outward, which is produced by the nuclear fusion reactions that are constantly going on inside the star's fiery core. When a star begins to run out of nuclear fuel, however, the gravitational forces within it begin to take precedence over the decreasing amount of explosive force being generated by the star's nuclear furnace. Once this critical balance point is surpassed in a dying star, the matter within it spontaneously begins to collapse in upon itself at a steadily increasing rate of speed. If the star's total mass happens to be less than a certain critical amount—known as the Chandrasekhar limit—the collapsed star will reach a point where its inward pull of gravity is just offset by the outward push generated by the Pauli Exclusion Principle, which forces atomic particles away from one another. There is, however, a limit to the amount of outward force that can be generated by the Pauli Exclusion Principle—it is the amount of force that would be capable of accelerating particles within the star to the speed of light (which is the cosmic speed limit according to Einstein's theory of relativity). Thus, in a sufficiently dense star that exceeds the Chandrasekhar limit, the inward pull of gravity would be able to overwhelm the outward push exerted by the Pauli Exclusion Principle, and the star would begin a calamitous period of runaway contraction. This period of contraction would continue until a point of zero size and infinite density—known as a singularity—is eventually reached. A singularity of this type is termed a black hole, because its gravitational pull is so great that not even light itself can escape from it.[4]

Interestingly enough, Einstein's theory of general relativity states that the entire universe itself also began as a singularity, a point of zero size and infinite density in which all the matter and energy in the universe is said to have been concentrated. For some unknown reason this "cosmic egg" is thought to have exploded with just the right vigor to ensure the development of a life-supporting universe several billion years later.

The Belgian priest and mathematician Georges Lemaître had anticipated the discovery of the Big Bang singularity back in 1927 with his publication of the first conceptual link between Slipher's redshifts and the expanding universe of general relativity. But Lemaître went even further. While other scientists, such as England's Sir Arthur Eddington, were forcing themselves to reject the notion of a concrete universal beginning (again because of its profound religious implications), Lemaître went straight to the heart of the matter and made the first scientific prediction of a Big Bang singularity. He reasoned that if the entire universe was presently expanding, there must have been a time when it was much closer together. Going back to the very beginning, he concluded that the primordial universe must have been very dense indeed, perhaps even infinitely dense, and therefore infinitely small. Lemaître called his prophetic conceptualization of the cosmic egg "the primordial atom," and called its explosion "the big noise." Several years later the British astrophysicist Fred Hoyle, who was openly antagonistic to the whole idea of a singular creation event, sarcastically called it "the big bang," and the name stuck.

The inference of a concrete universal beginning based on the present-day rate of cosmic expansion is much more precarious than it may initially seem, because our theoretical models could very well turn out to be mistaken. As John Barrow explains:

The cosmological solutions of Einstein's equations which model the present state of the expanding universe most successfully are those in which the expansion proceeds at exactly the same rate in every direction. This is only an approximation of reality, but none the less currently a very good one indeed. But in the past things might not have been so symmetrical. Could it not be that the retrodiction of a past 'Bang' in which the entire universe was squeezed to a point arises entirely as a consequence of following the expansion backwards in a perfectly symmetrical fashion? If one disturbed the symmetry slightly, then the disparities would grow as one went backwards, and the Bang might be de-focused and have never really occurred. Or could not some unknown force of Nature emerge to change the result of our naïve extrapolation back to a beginning? Or more subtly, maybe we have simply chosen a defective way of mapping the expansion of the universe, and it is only this *description*, rather than the universe itself, that becomes degenerate at the apparent Big Bang? Something like this occurs on a geographer's globe as we approach the North and South Poles. The meridians intersect and pile up to create a 'co-ordinate singularity' at the Poles, but nothing odd happens on the Earth's real surface. Another set of map coordinates could be introduced near the Poles to overcome this pathology of our mapping description.[5]

In the face of these legitimate considerations, Hawking and Penrose devised a theorem[6] which showed that, if the following conditions were in effect, the universe *had* to have had a singular beginning somewhere in the distant past, regardless of any modeling ambiguities on our part: 1) gravity must be attractive and act upon everything, 2) the universe must be expanding today and contain a sufficient quantity of matter to produce at least one black hole, 3) time travel must be impossible, and 4) Einstein's general theory of relativity must accurately describe the universe. If these four conditions hold, then general relativity requires there to be a singular boundary to space, time, and matter somewhere in the distant past.[7] Since none of these four conditions are in serious dispute today, it follows that the universe probably *did* have a singular beginning long ago.[8]

One of the most remarkable features of Hawking and Penrose's Singularity Theorem is that it posits a concrete universal beginning to space and time as well as to matter.[9] This is an extremely radical proposal which makes the modern scientific view almost identical with the Biblical account of the creation described in the book of Genesis.

It is important to note, however, that a theistic interpretation of the Big Bang is *not* absolutely dependent on the existence of a Big Bang singularity at the beginning of space-time. It is only unreservedly committed to the general idea of the universe as a Divine Creation, which of course leaves open any and all physical mechanisms that God might have employed in the service of cosmic evolution. Strictly speaking, theism isn't even dependent on the notion of temporal beginning to the universe, since it is possible that an eternal God could have been maintaining an infinite universe for all of eternity.

Nevertheless, the modern scientific belief in a concrete universal beginning is still strongly supportive of the Biblical doctrine of creation. For as long as the universe did in fact experience a definite beginning at some point in the distant past, there had to have been a sufficient reason for the universe to begin as it did. Moreover, as we shall see in more detail in the next chapter, these cosmic initial conditions are now known to have been *incredibly* fine-tuned with respect to their eventual capacity to produce a life-supporting universe. It follows, then, that there *had* to have been a sufficient reason for this initial fine-tuning at the Big Bang, upon which our own lives now so intimately depend.

Significantly, though, science itself will apparently never be able to probe back to the very beginning of space-time because the very laws of science themselves break down as one nears the moment of creation. It appears, then, that the cause of the Big Bang must remain forever beyond the reach of science, as astrophysicist Robert Jastrow has so eloquently described in his popular little book *God and the Astronomers*:

> At this moment it seems as though science will never be able to raise the curtain on the mystery of creation. For the scientist who has lived by his faith in the power of reason, the story ends like a bad dream. He has scaled the mountains of ignorance; he is about to conquer the highest peak; as he pulls himself over the final rock, he is greeted by a band of theologians who have been sitting there for centuries.[10]

It would seem, then, that the moment of creation—and with it the possible role of a Divine Creator—will forever be protected from the probing minds of modern-day scientists. All that can be said with relative certainty is that the universe did indeed experience a concrete beginning at some point in the distant past. But this in turn raises the question of who or what could have served as a sufficient reason for the birth of the universe. This question becomes all the more perplexing when we take into consideration the apparent creation of the universe out of "nothing," along with the simultaneous fine-tuning of its many life-supporting parameters. On this score, the age-old notion of a Divine Creator may very well turn out to be the most credible explanation of all. Whittaker agrees:

> When the development of the system of the world is traced backwards by the light of laws of nature, we arrive finally at a moment when that development begins. This is the ultimate point of physical science, the farthest glimpse that we can obtain of the material universe by our natural faculties. There is no ground for supposing that matter . . . existed before this in an inert condition, and was in some way galvanized into activity at

a certain instant: for what could have determined this instant rather than all the other instants of past eternity? It is simpler to postulate a creation *ex nihilo*, an operation of Divine Will to constitute Nature from nothingness.[11]

It is for this reason that theism is strongly supported by the notion of a concrete beginning to space-time (even though it isn't *absolutely* dependent upon it). Hence, anything that points away from a universe of infinite age and infinite spatial extent and towards a concrete universal beginning at a finite point in the past will tend to support the theist's overall case.

Fortunately for the theist, several intriguing scientific observations have effectively ruled out a universe of infinite age and spatial extent. For one thing, the night sky is essentially dark, but this isn't what we would expect if there were an infinite number of stars in the heavens. As Thomas Digges[12] first pointed out in 1576, a universe with an infinite number of stars should produce a bright night sky. Edmund Halley reiterated this same paradox in 1715.[13] For a time it was thought that Heinrich Olbers had solved the paradox in 1823, through his suggestion that a significant proportion of light in an infinite universe would be absorbed by interstellar dust clouds.[14]

In 1879, however, Josef Stefan showed that radiant energy isn't just absorbed by a body; it is also radiated outward at a definite proportional rate. According to this momentous finding, Olber's proposed interstellar medium would eventually reach a temperature where it would radiate out as much energy as it was receiving.[15] This would especially be true in an infinitely old universe, since the interstellar dust clouds would have an infinite amount of time to absorb and re-radiate this energy back out into space. In an infinite universe with an infinite number of stars, then, the night sky would have to be much brighter than the one we currently have. Therefore, the universe probably does *not* contain an infinite number of stars.

More evidence against a universe of infinite spatial extent comes from Einstein's theory of general relativity, which states that the curvature of light in response to gravity creates a finite spatial limit beyond which earth bound observations cannot be made.[16] Even so, the red shifts of galaxies at this finite spatial limit should, according to general relativity, equal infinity.[17] This is clearly not the case, so it does not appear as though we live in a universe of infinite spatial extent. (That is, as long as Einstein's theory of general relativity is correct, which it very much seems to be. Several extremely sophisticated experiments have recently verified general relativity to within 5 decimal places.)

In addition, one would expect that an infinitely old universe would contain many stars that are at or near their natural age limit. However, no stars have ever been discovered that are older than 17 billion years or so, this in spite of the fact that recent calculations have shown[18] that some stars are capable of reaching an upper age-limit of around 80 billion years! This seems to be clear evidence against an infinitely old universe.

Indeed, according to astronomer Hugh Ross, *all* galaxies are middle-aged.[19] No newly formed or extinct galaxies have ever been discovered; hence, all galaxies were probably formed at a definite time in the finite past. This hypothesis is supported by the most recent models of galaxy formation in an expanding universe, which predict a very narrow window following the Big Bang in which galaxy formation could possibly take place. Beyond this point, matter would be too dispersed because of the ceaseless universal expansion to be able to condense into coherent galaxies.

Moreover, galaxies look progressively younger as one looks further and further out into the heavens.[20] In an infinite universe, though, one would not expect such an age-distance gradient to occur.

One of the most common ways of getting around the Big Bang's implication of a definite universal beginning has been the notion of an oscillating universe, in which the universe is said to oscillate back and forth between successive cycles of expansion and contraction. Each time this oscillating universe collapses back in on itself, it spontaneously re-expands in a tremendous burst of energy until gravity eventually halts the expansion and gives way to another phase of contraction. With this superficially clever theoretical maneuver, one can affirm the reality of the Big Bang and yet still not be held to a concrete universal beginning.

Indeed, some theoreticians believe that this oscillating universe model is able to account for the many improbable physical coincidences that have led to the evolution of life. On this view, if there have indeed been an infinite number of oscillations in the cosmic past, then *one* of these oscillations could have *accidentally* produced all those fundamental parameters that are necessary for the evolution of life, and of course we would then inevitably find ourselves living within one of these lucky oscillations.

Three pieces of evidence, however, strongly discredit any notion of an oscillating universe. To begin with, cosmologists are by no means certain that our present universe will *ever* collapse back on itself. Indeed, according to applied physicist and theologian, Gerald L. Schroeder, author of the book *Genesis and the Big Bang*, the latest evidence indicates that we actually live in an "open" universe, which means that the present universal expansion will probably continue indefinitely.[21] Schroeder argues that there simply isn't enough matter in the universe to ever cause it to collapse back in on itself, since current measurements indicate that our universe contains only 10 to 20% of the amount of matter needed to eventually halt the present expansion.[22] This critical amount of matter is known to cosmologists, appropriately enough, as the *critical density* of the universe. While it is possible that non-luminous "dark matter" could be the missing element that would give the universe this critical density, many consider this possibility to be unlikely, given the tremendous amount that would be required for the task.

In addition, sophisticated computer analyses of Doppler shift data indicate that the present expansion of the universe will probably continue forever.[23] That is, the rate of slowing of the various galaxies around us does not appear to be sufficient to ever cause them to halt their present expansion. But if our universe is destined to go on expanding forever, it obviously could not be involved in a never-ending pattern of expansion and contraction.

However, the most convincing evidence that the universe has not been oscillating forever is thermodynamic in nature. Each cycle of expansion and contraction in such an oscillating universe must produce an *overall* increase in entropy, or disorder.[24] This increase in entropy would reveal itself as an increase in the number of photons, or light particles, relative to those particles with a rest mass (which comprise matter as we know it).

Accordingly, with each successive oscillation, there should be an *increase* in the ratio between photons and nuclear particles. It follows, then, that an *infinite* number of oscillations

would, according to thermodynamics, have raised the ratio of photons to nuclear particles to infinity. Because the number of photons is finite, for the ratio to equal infinity, the number of particles must equal zero. Zero particles means that there would be no material universe. But our very existence attests that this is not the case. There is a material universe and we are part of it.[25]

This evidence from thermodynamics is so persuasive that even atheistic physicist Steven Weinberg was compelled to admit that "it is hard to see how the universe could have previously experienced an infinite number of cycles."[26]

The work of Russian physicists Igor Novikov and Yakob Zel'dovich strongly supports this non-cyclic contention. In 1973 they showed that the maximum radius of a cyclic universe would necessarily increase from cycle to cycle.[27] While this means that an oscillating universe may experience an infinite future, it necessarily constrains such a universe to a finite past, since the steadily increasing radius would be able to be traced back to a first cycle. Therefore, the present universe could not have been oscillating for an infinite amount of time in the past.

But even if we assume that there is enough matter in the universe to eventually halt its present expansion, it does *not* necessarily follow that the ensuing contraction will result in another Big Bang type of explosion or "bounce." For one thing, there is no known physical mechanism[28] that is capable of reversing a cosmic contraction. The work of Novikov and Zel'dovich has substantiated this conclusion, insofar as they have shown that a uniform isotropic compression becomes wildly unstable near the end of the contraction, leading to an inevitable fragmenting of the collapsing medium.[29]

Ross builds on this conclusion by noting that the universe is by far the most entropic (i.e., disorder-producing) phenomenon known.[30] As a consequence, even if the universe were to eventually collapse back in on itself, it " . . . would *not* produce a bounce. Far too much of the energy of the universe is dissipated in unreclaimable form to fuel a bounce. Like a clump of wet clay falling on a carpet, the universe, if it did collapse, would go "splat."[31]

But if we do not live in an eternal, oscillating universe, we are left with the conclusion that the Big Bang *was* in all likelihood a unique event, which of course is to say that there *was* an actual beginning to the universe some 15 billion years ago. Such a conclusion is significant for a number of different reasons, not the least of which is the fact that we are now compelled to come up with a realistic explanation for the sudden, perfect appearance of this primordial explosion.

Unfortunately for the cosmologist, however, the familiar chain of cause and effect (which of course is the whole basis of science) abruptly terminates as we approach the beginning of the Big Bang. This mystical endpoint is known as "Planck's Wall," and it dates all the way back to when the universe was but a mere 10^{-43} seconds old.[32] But even though our scientific capacity to ascertain causality abruptly terminates at this point, a larger causality intrinsic to the universe itself *had* to have been operative from the very beginning, otherwise the universe would have had no reason to come into being. By the same token, the Big Bang *had* to have been caused by some larger force, otherwise it never would have occurred in the precise fashion it did. It is this transcendent Original Cause that a growing number of thinkers now understand to be God.[33]

Robert Jastrow agrees:

> Now we see how the astronomical evidence leads to a Biblical view of the origin of the world. The details differ, but the essential elements in the astonomical and Biblical accounts of Genesis are the same: the chain of events leading to man commenced suddenly and sharply at a definite moment in time, in a flash of light and energy.[34]

This statement is all the more remarkable when we consider the fact that Jastrow himself is a self-avowed agnostic.

In order to learn more about the initial conditions surrounding the birth of the universe, physicists take their cosmological equations that describe the universe's present-day expansion and run them backwards until the beginning of time is reached. In the process, an impressive amount of information regarding the early stages of the universe is produced.[35]

So much information, in fact, has been produced in this fashion that it is sometimes tempting to believe that we will one day be able to come up with an all-encompassing "theory of everything," which will be able to single-handedly unify the four fundamental forces of physics *and* predict the values of nature's physical constants. We shouldn't get too excited about our chances for discovering such a theory, however, because the fact is that we have *not* been given all of the keys that would lead to a total understanding of the cosmos. The limitations posed by our human intellect, our measuring apparatus, and the intrinsic uncertainty of quantum reality itself—all conspire together to make this virtually impossible. Worse still, all our equations break down at Planck's Wall, and for good reason: the temperature of the primordial universe beyond this point was so high that the four fundamental forces of physics were all dissolved, presumably in the form of a single all-encompassing force. This in turn made it impossible for any direct information about the birth of the universe to survive intact. Planck's Wall thus seems to represent:

. . . the universe's ultimatum: There will be no further hedging of equations, no more jumping over points too complex or obscure to understand. This is where all your calculations and all your thinking must be brought together in the clearest statement in the history of mankind about the cosmos before you will know how it began. And still you may never know—exactly.[36]

Notes

1. "Because it is impossible to probe back beyond "Planck's Wall," when the universe was a mere 10^{-43} seconds old (due to a breakdown in the cosmological equations), it is impossible to determine whether some form of matter preceded the Big Bang, or whether matter itself was created *ex nihilo* (out of nothing) during the Big Bang itself. As a consequence, we will stick to the dominant scientific position, which says that matter in its current form did indeed have a concrete beginning around 15 billion years ago.
2. Ironically, though, the cosmological constant has made startling comeback in recent years, in the form of the energy density of the quantum vacuum. We will have much more to say about the cosmological constant in Chapter 5.
3. Most of Einstein's reluctance to accept a personal Creator was caused by the horrendous fact of evil in the world. In Einstein's mind, a personal, omnipotent Creator would have to be responsible for generating all the world's ills, and this was completely unacceptable to him.
4. Hawking has subsequently shown that due to quantum considerations, a black hole can still emit radiation at the edge of its "event horizon," which is the boundary point of its sphere of gravitational attraction. This radiation has appropriately been termed "Hawking radiation."

5. John D. Barrow, *The World Within the World* (New York: Oxford University Press, 1990), pp. 227–228.
6. A theorem is substantially more than a theory, insofar as if its premises hold true, its conclusion follows by logic alone. It is even possible for the conclusion to be true if one or more of its premises turn out to be mistaken.
7. Ibid., p. 228.
8. Of course, there will always be scientists who will take issue with even the most basic of physical assumptions, including the four basic conditions which underlie Hawking and Penrose's Singularity Theorem. At present, however, these four conditions comprise the foundational bedrock upon which virtually the whole of modern astrophysics is based.
9. Hawking has recently revised his original conception of the Big Bang to be more consistent with a quantum view of gravity. On this view, while the universe still begins with a Big Bang, it doesn't necessarily begin with a Big Bang singularity.
10. Robert Jastrow, *God and the Astronomers* (New York: Warner Books, 1978), p. 125.
11. Taken from John D. Barrow's *The World Within the World*, p. 227.
12. E.R. Harrison, "The dark night sky riddle: a 'paradox' that resisted solution," *Science*, 226. (1984), pp. 941–945.
13. Stanley L. Jaki, *The Paradox of Olbers' Paradox* (New York: Herder and Herder, 1969), p. 72–143.
14. Ibid.
15. Herman Bondi, *Cosmology* (Cambridge: Cambridge University Press, 1960), p. 21.
16. Hugh Ross, *The Fingerprint of God* (Orange, CA: Promise Publishing, 1990), p. 81.
17. Ibid.
18. Ibid., p. 91.
19. Ibid.
20. Ibid.
21. Gerald L. Schroeder, *Genesis and the Big Bang* (New York: Bantam Books, 1990, pp. 78–79.
22. Ibid., p. 78.
23. Ibid.
24. Ibid., p. 80.
25. Ibid., p. 81.
26. Ibid., p. 80.
27. Igor D. Novikov and Yakob Zel'dovich. "Physical Processes Near Cosmological Singularities," in *Annual Review of Astronomy and Astrophysics*, 11. (1973), pp. 387–412.
28. Hugh Ross, *The Fingerprint of God*, pp. 104–105.
29. Novikov and Zel'dovich, p. 401.
30. Ross, *The Fingerprint of God*, p. 105.
31. Ibid.
32. The Planck time of 10^{-43} seconds corresponds to the fundamental limit with which time can be accurately measured in quantum physics.
33. This is an example of the Cosmological Argument for the Existence of God, which attempts to trace the chain of cause-and-effect in the universe back to an original Uncaused Cause.
34. Robert Jastrow, *God and the Astronomers*, pp. 13–14.
35. It is truly remarkable that Einstein's equations are able to describe both the

current expansion of the universe as well as its very beginning, using only mathematics and the insight of an incomparable genius. Such a prodigious accomplishment seems to indicate rather conclusively that the science of mathematics represents much more than the various idiosyncrasies surrounding human thought; it actually describes the inner workings of the physical universe itself. This is a miracle in and of itself, and explains why so many mathematicians tend to be mystically inclined.

36. John Boslough, *Stephen Hawking's Universe* (New York: William Morrow, 1985), p. 104.

CHAPTER 4

Evidence for the Biocentric Principle

Although we talk so much about coincidence we do not really believe in it. In our heart of hearts we think better of the universe, we are secretly convinced that it is not such a slipshod, haphazard affair, that everything in it has meaning.

J.B. PRIESTLEY

4.1 Where Did the Original Evolving Matter Come From?

Non-theistic evolutionists claim that matter haphazardly evolved into the phenomenon of biological life with no Outside Help. In doing so, they generally ignore the question of where the original matter came from in the first place, i.e., they take the previous existence of some sort of matter-energy for granted. While scientists generally agree that our present universe began at the Big Bang some 15 billion years ago, the question of where the original matter-energy actually came from has not been resolved, largely because of our inability to probe back in time beyond Planck's Wall, when the universe was a mere 10^{-43} seconds old. As we saw in the preceding chapter, it is at this critical point that the cosmological equations totally break down, so it is impossible for scientists to state for a certainty what happened at the very beginning of space-time. This inability to get behind the cosmic drama is extremely disheartening for most scientists, who want nothing less than a total understanding of the origin and meaning of the universe.

At the same time, though, we can rest assured that the universe did in fact have a sufficient reason for its spontaneous appearance, otherwise it never would have come into existence in the first place. Given a sufficient reason for this spontaneous appearance, we must now ask ourselves *where* this matter originally came from. Some thinkers believe that it arose out of a pre-existing chaos of finite actualities that has been around forever. They therefore believe (to one extent or another) that the Big Bang was simply a reorganization of this pre-existing realm. Others believe that the postulated Big Bang was the origin of (finite) existence as such. This latter position is analogous to the theological idea of creation *ex nihilo* (out of nothing).

There isn't a shred of evidence indicating that matter has been around forever. On the other hand, there *is* a great deal of evidence indicating a

42

finite age to the universe, as we saw in the previous chapter. It is then but a small step to conclude that the matter within the universe is equally finite in age.[1]

Significantly, one of the most important predictions of the grand unifying theories (GUTs) in physics—a finite age for the proton—supports this idea that matter in its present form has not been around forever. Although the predicted age for the proton is immense, with an average decay time of some 10^{31} years, it is nonetheless finite. Therefore, if this particular prediction of the GUTs is correct, and if protons are no longer being created in present-day cosmic processes in sufficient numbers to replace those that have decayed away, matter in its present form *cannot* be infinite in age.

Moreover, since there is no way to verify the existence of an eternally existing material realm, and since all the available evidence points in the direction of a finite age to matter, we will confine ourselves in this book to the dominant scientific position, which states that matter had a definite beginning around 15 billion years ago in the original Big Bang explosion.

The first piece of evidence, then, that can be recruited in support of the Biocentric Principle is the fact that the "right" kind of matter (i.e., the kind that is capable of evolving into biological life) happened to spontaneously come into existence some 15 thousand million years ago.[2] The significance of this one event, of course, cannot be overstated, because it is what made the subsequent evolution of life possible.

4.1.1 Creation Out of Nothing?

According to several recent cosmological models, the primordial stuff of the universe may have come into existence in a sudden quantum appearance out of "nothing." In this way of thinking, matter could very well have sprung into existence *ex nihilo*,[3] much as the ancient Church Fathers believed.

However, a few scientists have interpreted this idea of quantum creation out of nothing as support for a non-theistic view of cosmogenesis. The basic idea here is that if the universe could have spontaneously leaped into existence as a single quantum fluctuation, then a traditional Creator is no longer needed to make it happen.

This view is fallacious, however, because sudden quantum appearances don't really take place out of "nothing." A larger quantum field is first required before this can happen, but a quantum field can hardly be described as being "nothing." Rather, it is a thing of unsearchable order and complexity, whose origin we can't even begin to explain. Thus, trying to account for the appearance of the universe as a sudden quantum fluctuation doesn't do away with the need for a Creator at all; it simply moves the whole problem backwards one step to the unknown origin of the quantum field itself. However, the best explanation for the origin of the primordial quantum field appears to be none other than God Himself! Therefore, all the recent scientific talk about a possible creation of the universe *ex nihilo* is actually in line with a *theistic* view of cosmogenesis that has been around for centuries. Indeed, this remarkable convergence of ancient theology with modern science undoubtedly qualifies as one of the most important intellectual developments of the twentieth century.

4.2   The Cosmic Prevalence of Matter Over Antimatter

Experiments in high-energy particle accelerators have revealed further difficulties with the proposed quantum appearance of matter "out of nothing." The most troublesome of these difficulties is the regular appearance of matter in matter/antimatter pairs during high-energy particle experiments.

Building on their extensive experience with these particle accelerators, scientists now believe that when matter first appeared at the Big Bang, it did so in matter/antimatter pairs. Three reasons have been cited in support of this conclusion:

1. Except for their overall charge, particles and their corresponding antiparticles are identical.
2. Because the cumulative charge of matter/antimatter pairs equals zero, their simultaneous appearance doesn't violate the Law of the Conservation of Energy.
3. When modern-day physicists create particles in the laboratory, they always appear in pairs.

This type of pair creation in the laboratory has tremendous repercussions for our understanding of the ultimate origin of matter, because it is a well-known fact that whenever particles and their corresponding antiparticles come into close proximity with one another, they quickly annihilate each other in a sudden burst of energy. Accordingly, if matter made its original appearance in matter/antimatter pairs, it is difficult to see how any matter at all could have survived the initial period of annihilation.[4]

If we assume, as most physicists do, that matter did indeed make its initial appearance in the form of matter/antimatter pairs, there obviously had to have been an initial imbalance between the quantities of matter and antimatter that were initially produced, with a miniscule, but nevertheless significant, preponderance of matter; otherwise, our present universe, which appears to be made solely out of matter, could never have evolved. Amazingly, several unified theories of the strong, weak, and electromagnetic interactions have predicted a tiny asymmetry in the decay rates of particles and antiparticles.[5] Although this predicted asymmetry is slight—adding up to a final balance of a billion and one protons to a billion antiprotons—it is nevertheless enough to have resulted in a gloriously detailed universe comprised solely of matter.[6]

Science has no explanation whatever for why such a fundamental asymmetry between matter and antimatter should happen to exist. It seems almost too good to be true, because it is this "tiny" asymmetry to which we owe our very lives.

A conventional reading of the Biocentric Principle states that this fundamental asymmetry exists "because" we and other life forms are here.[7] That is to say, because this asymmetry is a necessary condition for our own existence, we can't help but observe it to be true. While this is a self-evident statement, it doesn't explain *why* this asymmetry between matter and antimatter exists in the first place. It only recognizes that this asymmetry is an essential prerequisite for the existence of life.

It is here that we must depart from a conventional reading of the Biocentric Principle so we can postulate a sufficient reason for this fundamental asymmetry. The apparent significance of life's existence, along with the fact that this asymmetry *had* to exist before *we* and other life forms could possibly exist, seems to lead us to the conclusion that there might be a causal connection between this asymmetry and the existence of life. From here, of course, it is but a small step to the traditional Argument from Design, which states that God created the primordial universe in such a way as to ensure the eventual appearance of life.

4.3 The Amount of Matter in the Universe and the Rate of Cosmic Expansion

Another cosmic "coincidence" that is intimately tied to the biocentricity of the universe concerns the overall amount of matter in existence. As cosmologists have known for a number of years now, there had to have been a precisely determined amount of matter produced by the Big Bang explosion or else our present biocentric universe could never have formed. Too much matter and the gravitational pull would have been enough to counteract the explosive force of the Big Bang, thereby causing the entire universe to collapse back in on itself like a gigantic black hole. Too little matter and there would not have been enough attractive gravitational force to cause the matter to bunch together into galaxies and solar systems; instead, the matter in the universe would have remained diffuse and disorganized forever.[8]

It is extremely unlikely that a random explosion of the "cosmic egg" would have just happened to produce the precise amount of material density to make our present biocentric universe possible.[9] Indeed, given the near infinite range of possible densities that could have been produced by the Big Bang, it seems far more likely that there was a larger principle at work from the very beginning that would have ensured the production of the "right" amount of matter for our own eventual appearance.

The Big Bang also had to have exploded with just the right degree of vigor or else our present biocentric universe could never have formed. Too little velocity and the universe would have collapsed back in on itself shortly after the Big Bang because of gravitational forces; too much velocity, and the matter would have streaked away so fast that it would have been impossible for galaxies and solar systems to subsequently form. Indeed, as Stephen Hawking[10] has pointed out, this balance between universal collapse and eternal expansion is so precise that scientists have not yet been able to decide on which side of the dividing line our universe actually lies. As a consequence, we still do not know whether the universe will continue to expand forever, or whether it will begin to contract someday in the future, leading eventually to what has been called the "Big Crunch."

The large-scale properties of the universe also depend on a uniform expansion rate. Specifically, the coherence of light depends on the universe doubling in size at a uniform rate (i.e., in the same interval of time). As the universe expands, the space between the galaxies is continually stretching, which in turn "stretches" light rays traveling in the interstellar medium, producing light of longer wavelengths. This is the origin of the famous "red shift" which Slipher first detected in 1913, and which Hubble used in 1929 to deduce that the galaxies were receding from one another at tremendous velocities.

Now, as space continues to expand and light rays continue to stretch, the possibility arises that they might stretch to an *infinite* wavelength, thereby making it impossible for the light rays to convey any useful information. It turns out that the only way light can avoid getting stretched to an infinite wavelength in an expanding universe is if the universe expands at a precisely uniform rate. Given the infinite number of possible expansion rates, it is nothing short of remarkable that our present universe is expanding at *precisely* a uniform rate. Even more remarkable, though, is the fact that our own existence as observers is intimately tied to this large-scale uniformity. However, the only possible way that the universe could be capable of such a uniform expansion rate is if the amount of matter produced by the Big Bang was perfectly balanced with the subsequent rate of cosmic expansion.

Another way of looking at this seemingly lucky "accident" involves the energy density of matter p, which determines the gravitating power of the entire universe. A higher density causes a greater gravitational force, and vice versa. Now, there is a critical value, know as p_{crit}, above which gravity would beat the force of the cosmic expansion and cause the entire universe to collapse back in on itself. Thus, in order for there to be a minimum degree of stability to the universe, the rate of cosmic expansion has to just beat the inward force of gravity, which means that the value of p has to be exceedingly close to p_{crit}. Fortunately for us, nature has caused the difference between p and p_{crit} to vary by less than 1 part in 10^{60} at the Planck time, when the universe was a mere 10^{-43} seconds old. Like a bullet that is fired into the sky with just enough velocity for it to avoid being pulled back to Earth by gravity, the entire universe itself is also expanding with just enough velocity for it to avoid collapsing back in on itself.

Another fortunate consequence of the universe expanding at close to the critical rate has to do with the general geometry of space-time. An expansion rate that is close to critical produces a "flat" universe that approximates the "normal" geometry of Euclid, in which the sum of a triangle's three angles equals precisely 180 degrees. ("Flatness" in this sense corresponds to a rate of cosmic expansion that just equals the inward pull of gravity.) Had the universe expanded at a significantly different rate, the geometry of space-time would have been curved, with the strange result that the sum of a triangle's three angles would have either been more or less than 180 degrees.

Given the incredible amount of fine-tuning that was necessary to allow the universe to expand at precisely this critical rate (accurate to within 1 part in 10^{60}), many scientists are understandably overwhelmed. Physicist Paul Davies has put it this way:

> We know of no reason why p is not a purely arbitrary number. Nature could apparently have chosen any value at all. To choose p so close to p_{crit}, fine-tuned to such stunning accuracy, is surely one of the great mysteries of cosmology. Had this exceedingly delicate tuning of values been even slightly upset, the subsequent structure of the universe would have been totally different. If the crucial ratio had been 10^{-57} rather than 10^{60}, the universe would not even exist, having collapsed to oblivion after just a few million years.[11]

Davies goes on to describe how the "natural" value that describes the curvature of the universe, which is represented by a natural relation between the gravitational constant, Planck's constant, and the speed of light, is 10^{60} times *greater* than the actual curvature value "chosen" at the beginning of the Hubble expansion. Incredibly, had nature chosen this "natural" curvature value, the universe would have only been able to survive a mere 10^{-43} seconds, after which it would have either recollapsed into nothingness or exploded into oblivion. As Davies concludes:

> To achieve a universe with a longevity some 60 orders of magnitude longer than the natural fundamental unit of cosmic time t_p requires a balancing act between p and p_{crit} of staggering precision.[12]

The implications of the above-stated observation are truly astounding. We are being asked to believe that, at the beginning of the Hubble expansion, nature "chose" a universal expansion rate—itself comprised of a critical interaction between three separate physical constants—which was over 60 orders of magnitude smaller than the "natural" value that these constants would have ordinarily produced on their own. The result of this "unnatural" choice is that our universe has expanded at *precisely* the proper rate to ensure the evolution of intelligent observers. *Is this not glaring evidence of some form of Intelligent Contrivance in the universe, whose purpose was evidently to ensure the eventual development of biological life?*

Cosmologist John Gribbin and astrophysicist Martin Rees are equally impressed by the incredible precision of the Hubble expansion rate, since it makes the flatness parameter:

> . . . the most accurately measured number in all of physics, and suggests a fine-tuning of the universe, to set up conditions suitable for the emergence of stars, galaxies, and life, of exquisite precision.
>
> If this were indeed a coincidence, then it would be a fluke so extraordinary as to make all other cosmic coincidences pale into insignificance. It seems much more reasonable to suppose that there is something in the laws of physics [God?] that requires the universe to be *precisely* flat. After all, the critical density for flatness is the *only* special density; no other value has any cosmic significance at all. It makes more sense to accept that the universe had to be born with *exactly* the critical expansion rate than to believe that by blind luck it happened to start out within 1 part in 10^{60} of the critical value.[13]

It is nothing short of amazing to realize that a "mere" change of 1 part in 10^{60} in the density parameter, in either direction, would have made the universe completely uninhabitable for life as we know it. It strains credulity too much to believe that such a perfect degree of balance could have ever happened by chance, especially when we realize that our lives were made possible by this unbelievable act of cosmic precision.

According to physicist George Greenstein, though, the further back one goes in the history of the universe, the closer the difference between p and p_{crit} had to have been in order to keep the universe from collapsing back in on itself instantaneously.[14] For instance, when the universe was a year old, it was only 0.00003% denser than critical, while when it was just an hour old, it was only 0.00000008% denser than critical. At this profoundly sensitive stage, the slightest perturbation would have caused the universe to recollapse, yet the cosmic expansion continued on without a hitch.

Remarkably, the further back in time one probes, the more perfect the adjustment between p and p_{crit} automatically becomes, so that when one reaches the unsearchable moment of creation itself, the adjustment between

p and p_{crit} was not one part in a billion; it was one part in *infinity*. As Greenstein declares, creation was perfect.[15]

This level of perfection completely defies the laws of chance, because the odds for a particular value to be chosen out of an infinity of possible choices turns out to be zero.[16] Accordingly, it seems infinitely unlikely that the "choice" of the universe's actual density could have ever been made by blind chance alone. As John Gribbin has put it:

In principle, the Universe could have had *any* density. A billionth, or a billion times, the critical density, or anything in between, or even anything outside that range. Why should it lie so close to the *only* special density that comes into the cosmological equations of relativity? Surely this cannot be a coincidence—and surely, some cosmologists have speculated, if this is *not* a coincidence then the density of the Universe must be precisely the critical density?[17]

But what cosmic power could have possibly ensured that the density of the universe be *precisely* the critical density? Since blind chance alone could not possibly have performed such a stupendous feat, there seems to be only one other Alternative left to choose from. It is for this reason that more and more scientists are becoming sympathetic to the religious point of view.

George Greenstein, for instance, admits[18] that the "theistic hypothesis" seems to be the most sensible explanation for the existing facts, but he nevertheless ends up rejecting it on the prevailing scientific premise that "God is not an explanation."[19] This highly dubious rationale is based on a fallacious assumption regarding God's relationship to His creation, but for space's sake we cannot discuss this issue further until Chapter 5.

Other scientists are also openly mentioning the idea of God in their books. For instance, the back cover of John Gribbin and Martin Rees' book *Cosmic Coincidences* openly asks two of the most important questions ever framed by scientists: "Was the Universe made for man?" and "What was in the mind of God fifteen billion years ago?" The word God also fills the pages of Stephen Hawking's bestselling book *A Brief History of Time*. Hawking even goes so far as to claim that his ultimate scientific purpose is nothing less than to know the mind of God Himself. (Talk about blind ambition!) With all this talk about God by some of the greatest minds in all of history, along with all the compelling evidence for Design from physics and cosmology, it is very difficult to see how the word "God" could merely be a referent to nothing at all.

4.4 The Role of Dark Matter in Cosmogenesis

Precise measurements of the present density of the universe reveal a curious fact: there is approximately ten times less visible matter in existence than is necessary to make the universe "flat." Yet, it is also known that the universe is very nearly flat on the largest possible scale of measurement. These observations have led cosmologists to postulate the existence of non-luminous "dark matter" throughout the universe, which would supply the missing mass needed to make the universe flat. All sorts of possible candidates for this missing mass have been suggested in recent years, but as yet nothing definite has been discovered.

While we are still uncertain about the identity of this missing mass, we are pretty clear about how much of it has to exist in the universe: it is precisely the amount that is necessary to give the universe its all-important critical density. Since life can only exist in a universe whose energy density is close to critical, the quantity of dark matter in the universe works out to be yet another cosmic "coincidence" upon which we owe our very lives.

Dark matter is also necessary for the evolution of life in yet another way: without it the galaxies and solar systems of the universe would probably never have been able to form. It is now thought that clouds of dark matter originally functioned as cosmic "potholes," around which the galaxies themselves eventually came to be condensed.[20] The problem with this conceptualization is that it is hard to see how these non-luminous irregularities could have possibly formed in a universe as smooth and homogeneous as our own. Evidently other processes were also involved in galaxy formation, the cumulative effect of which was to allow galaxies to form in spite of the incredibly smooth distribution of matter in the early universe.

4.4.1 Evidence for the Existence of Dark Matter

One of the primary reasons why astronomers believe in the existence of dark matter has to do with their observations of spiral galaxy rotation patterns. Normally in such a pattern of spiral rotation, the outer edges would be expected to move much more slowly than the inner regions of the spiral, as is true of the planetary orbits in our solar system. With spiral galaxies, however, the outer regions move at precisely the same velocity as the inner regions. This would be impossible without the existence of a "halo" of dark matter outside the boundary of the galaxy to equilibrate the overall rotational velocity. Because all spiral galaxies seem to rotate in this manner, we are led to postulate that the amount and distribution of dark matter in the universe must be incomprehensibly precise, not just for each galaxy individually, but for the entire visible universe as a whole.

In order for the rotational velocity of any given spiral galaxy to be absolutely uniform across the entire range of its diameter, the halo of dark matter that surrounds it must be very precisely positioned with respect to the stars inside the galaxy in order to be able to counterbalance the pull of gravity from within the spiral.[21] Given the number of stars in each spiral galaxy, along with the number of spiral galaxies in existence, this is a cosmic balancing act of outrageous, unprecedented precision.

Scientists, of course, are at a complete loss to explain why the amount and distribution of this halo of dark matter should exactly counterbalance the expected fall-off in rotation velocity from the center of each galaxy. This is known as the "Halo Conspiracy," and it seems to be completely insoluble in the absence of Intelligent Design.

When scientists extrapolate backwards from the orbits of the stars in each spiral galaxy, they are able to get a pretty good estimate of the amount of dark matter that probably exists in the universe. According to the most recent estimates, there is at least 10 times as much dark matter in the universe as visible matter. This renders over 90% of the universe non-luminous.[22]

Further evidence for the existence of dark matter in the universe has recently been obtained by Tony Tyson, a physicist working at AT&T Bell Laboratories.[23] Using the sophisticated technique of gravitational lensing—in which the light from a background curtain of visible galaxies is distorted into an arc by the gravitational pull of invisible matter—Tyson found that the light from many of these distant galaxies is indeed distorted by the presence of dark matter.

Significantly, Tyson's calculations have shown that this dark matter is some 9 to 10 times more prevalent (or 9 to 10 times more massive) than the "normal" luminous matter we can see. Remarkably, this is the same quantity of dark matter that is needed to initiate galaxy formation, explain spiral galaxy rotation patterns *and* make the universe flat. Numerical convergences like these are what help to make cosmologists so confident about the overall validity of their theories.

4.5   The Time Frame for Galaxy Formation

As physicist James Trefil explains in *The Dark Side of the Universe*, there are several intriguing reasons why galaxies should never have formed in the early universe (even though we obviously know that they did.)[24]

For one thing, galaxies could never have formed before the atoms themselves formed, since atoms are the primary consituents of normal "baryonic" matter. However, atoms were unable to form in significant numbers until the universe was approximately 500,000 years old, due to the powerful interaction between radiation and the plasma which preceded the formation of coherent atoms. Beginning at the 100,000-year mark, though, radiation began to *decouple* (separate from) this embryonic plasma, with the result that solid atoms were finally able to form in appreciable numbers. Atom formation continued on until approximately the 1,000,000-year mark, at which point essentially all of the initial plasma had condensed into atoms.

The problem with the above time frame regarding atom formation is that it does not leave much time for galaxy formation to occur. In order for galaxies to form, matter must be close enough together to condense around a gravitational focal point. However, given the perpetual Hubble expansion, by the time there are enough atoms in existence to condense into galaxies, they will have already become far enough apart to make any type of gravitational condensation extremely unlikely.

As a result, there is a very narrow window between the time atoms arrive on the scene and the critical point where matter becomes too sparse to be able to condense into galaxies. It is apparently in this small cosmological window that the various galaxies in the universe actually formed.

4.5.1   Big Bang Ripples: The "Holy Grail" of Cosmology

The single most pressing problem facing galaxy formation theorists has to do with the remarkable uniformity of the microwave background. If galaxy formation began with clumps of matter, and if radiation also clumps with matter (as it is known to do), we naturally would expect the original condensations of matter that led to galaxies to leave behind a clumping of radiation as well, the remnants of which should be visible today as clumps or anisotropies in the microwave background. Yet, prior to April 23, 1992, these anisotropies were nowhere to be found, since the microwave background had repeatedly been measured to be uniform in all directions to within 1 part in 10,000.

Indeed, this incredible uniformity had been widely recognized as being the single most damaging piece of evidence against the Big Bang. For if the Big Bang happened the way theorists imagined it did, there *had* to be anisotropies in the microwave background; otherwise, matter would have been unable to begin the clumping process that eventually led to galaxy formation.

In order to determine whether or not these anisotropies actually exist—and therefore whether or not the standard Big Bang model is really true—a way had to be found to measure the temperature of the microwave background to unprecedented levels of accuracy. The Cosmic Background Explorer (COBE) satellite was ingeniously designed to perform this very function.

On April 23, 1992, after compiling data from the orbiting COBE satellite for over two years, project leader George Smoot and his team at UC Berkeley finally had enough evidence to go public with their remarkable findings. On that date they announced to the world that they had finally discovered empirical proof for the birth of the universe: tiny anisotropies or fluctuations in the microwave background as small as 1 part in 100,000, which in all likelihood served as the gravitational focal points around which the various galaxies originally formed. Though these fluctuations are *exceedingly* tiny, amounting to only 30 millions of a kelvin, they are nonetheless big enough to represent the earliest stages of matter-clumping in the universe.[25]

Taken together, these fluctuations comprise the largest and most ancient structures ever observed: extremely thin clouds or ripples that stretch across two thirds of the known universe. These ripples date back to when the universe was only 300,000 years old, and they contain the earliest known precursors to the present universal configuration.[26] In this sense they are like cosmic fossils, which together make up the primordial blueprint for the structure of the entire universe.

Physicists and cosmologists reacted to the COBE satellite's findings with uncharacteristic elation and euphoria. Stephen Hawking, who holds the same chair of physics at Cambridge that Isaac Newton once held, was quoted as saying that it is "the discovery of the century, if not all time." University of Chicago physicist Michael Turner even went so far as to proclaim that "We have found the Holy Grail of cosmology." However, it was COBE project leader George Smoot who delivered the most astounding quote. He said, "What we have found is evidence for the birth of the universe. If you're religious, it's like looking at God."

These are very big words to come from the mouths of ordinarily conservative scientists, but they are very much deserved. For as scientific historian Frederic B. Burnham pointed out in the Los Angeles Times, these findings regarding the Big Bang make the theistic explanation for the birth of the universe "a more respectable hypothesis" today than at any time in the last century.

Further confirmation for the Big Bang was obtained from the COBE satellite's measurement of the spectrum of the microwave background. The simplest model of the Big Bang predicts that the radiation produced by this primordial explosion should have the characteristics of a perfect blackbody, which is to say that it should trace out a perfectly smooth spectral curve. Astonishingly, this is precisely the spectrum that the COBE satellite actually detected in the microwave background!

In order for this particular Big Bang model to work, however, there must be roughly nine times as much exotic matter in the universe as ordinary "baryonic" matter. Interestingly enough, this is also the amount of exotic matter that is needed to make the universe "flat." This would appear to be a highly significant theoretical congruence, because a flat space-time is thought to be an important prerequisite for the existence of life.

Prior to the COBE satellite's findings, it was thought that primordial field defects known as *textures* might have been responsible for building the large-scale structure of the universe. However, texture theory predicts the existence of a few very large temperature fluctuations, which were not found by the COBE satellite. As a result, texture-based cosmologies have now been effectively ruled out.

String theorists have proposed yet another possible mechanism for galaxy formation. Instead of using ordinary matter as the gravitational condensation point for the building of galaxies, they believe that incredibly massive cosmic strings could have done the trick. (A cosmic string is an exceedingly tiny [about 10^{-33} cm across], one-dimensional crack in the fabric of space-time that is capable of producing all of the particles and forces of physical reality in the form of different vibrations or "tones.") Remarkably, the actual pattern of galaxies in the night sky bears a striking resemblance to the way cosmic strings ought to behave if they actually exist.[27]

Unfortunately, there doesn't seem to be any way of proving just yet whether or not cosmic strings really exist, or whether they were actually involved in the condensation of galaxies. Therefore, we can only guess about the role that cosmic strings may have played in galaxy formation. All we can say for sure is that galaxies and superclusters did indeed form sometime in the distant past, and that we owe our lives to this critical stage of cosmic history.

4.6   The Roughness Parameter

From the foregoing discussion it is clear that the initial distribution of matter in our biocentric universe could not have been *perfectly* smooth; otherwise, matter would not have been capable of congealing together into galaxies, and life would have had no place in which to evolve. At the same time, though, too much cosmic "roughness" would have caused the universe to either collapse back on itself early on, or to have developed into a vast sea of black holes, which would have been separated by mostly barren space. In either case life as we know it would never have been able to evolve.

In order for the universe to be capable of supporting life, then, the degree of roughness within it must be *very* precipitously balanced between near infinite extremes on either side. Interestingly enough, the value[28] of this "roughness parameter" can be expressed in terms of a pure number: 10^{-5}. Had the value of this parameter been even slightly different, life could never have evolved here because galaxies would have been incapable of forming.[29]

This fact is all the more remarkable when we consider the infinite range of possible values that this parameter *could* have occupied. Yet, against all the odds, the one value that was essential for the evolution of life is the one that was actually "picked." Surely this cannot be just a coincidence. But if it wasn't a coincidence, then the specific value of this roughness parameter had to have been deliberately chosen, and there is only one possible Being in the entire universe who would have been in a position to do the choosing at that point in time. Thus, a commonsense interpretation of the facts tells us that the value of the roughness parameter was probably selected on purpose by a Higher Power so that a suitable environnment could be created for the evolution of life.

4.7 The Size of the Universe

Another intriguing characteristic of the present cosmic order is the overall sparseness of matter in the universe, a property originally thought to represent evidence *against* deliberate design.[30] On this view, perpetrated by Bertrand Russell, the vast reaches of uninhabitable emptiness in the universe could serve no conceivable function to a Supreme Designer; therefore the odds for the existence of such a Designer were deemed to be exceedingly remote.[31]

At first glance this argument appears to be valid. If life is so important to the Grand Designer, why would He put it on such a small "speck of dust" in such an unfathomably large and ancient universe, with some 10^{22} other stars as a "supporting cast"? Moreover, as Russell has asked:

Why should the best things in the history of the world [such as life and mind] come late rather than early? Would not the reverse order have done just as well? . . . Before the Copernican revolution, it was natural to suppose that God's purposes were specially concerned with the Earth, but now this has become an unplausible hypothesis. If the purpose of the Cosmos is to evolve mind, we must regard it as rather incompetent in having produced so little in such a long time.[32]

Recent cosmological research, however, has yielded a fascinating explanation for this nagging problem: *the universe is as big and old as it is because were it any younger or smaller, it would have been incapable of evolving intelligent life.* There is a minimum cosmological time that it takes to produce a world where intelligent (and non-intelligent) life forms can develop through normal evolutionary pathways. These evolutionary pathways are themselves divided into three separate cosmic epochs: 1) an initial stellar synthesis epoch, wherein the heavier organic elements upon which life depends, such as carbon, oxygen, and iron, are synthesized deep within stellar interiors over approximately 10 billion years of time, 2) an intermediate epoch, wherein these heavier elements are spewed into space by huge supernova explosions, and are then allowed to crystallize into concrete solar systems, and 3) a final biosynthesis epoch, wherein life gradually evolves into progressively more complex forms over billions of years of organic evolution.

When the minimum times for these major cosmic epochs are calculated, we find that the *minimum* age for the development of intelligent life is approximately 15 billion years, which is also the estimated age of our present universe. Ironically, then, when we take into account the rate of the Hubble expansion during this entire time period, we find that our incomprehensibly large universe is nevertheless the *smallest one possible* that would allow for the evolution of life in this manner. Consequently, it follows that the vast reaches of empty space which characterize our present universe are *absolutely necessary* for the evolution and continued existence of all carbon-based life forms.

The upshot of this astonishing realization is that the immense size and age of the universe can no longer be used as evidence against the existence of a Grand Designer, for as we have just seen, ours is the smallest and youngest universe that could possibly evolve life through natural evolutionary pathways. If anything, then, the size and age of the universe can be used as evidence *for*, and not against, the existence of a Grand Designer, for the following reason: if the evolution of life were merely a random event, one would never expect it to happen just as soon as it possibly could. The random shuffling of atoms requires a great deal of time to produce anything interesting, so the random evolution of life would naturally be expected to take many billions of years longer than the minimum possible time frame for such a complex occurrence. Yet, life evolved just as soon as it possibly could (both in terms of the physical environment on Earth and in the cosmos at large), in spite of all the overwhelming odds against it. In this one fact alone we can almost see the Hand of God directly at work, organizing the structure of the universe in an optimal fashion so that life could be produced as quickly as possible.

4.7.1   The Advantage of a Sparse Universe

There is a second life-facilitating function to the vast reaches of empty space in the universe. It has to do with preserving the orbital integrity of planets like our own Earth against the disturbing gravitational influences of other celestial bodies. Had the universe been any more compact, the immense gravitational power of wandering stars and other large gravitating objects would have jerked the Earth out of its delicate orbit about the Sun long before life ever got chance to evolve here. This of course would have destroyed the life-supporting capacity of the Earth forevermore.[33] Alternatively, had life been lucky enough to evolve here before the appearance of such a disturbing gravitational influence, it would have only been a matter of time until one would have come close enough to the Earth to knock it out of its orbit about the Sun.

Even worse, a wandering star could have come close enough to our own Sun in a significantly smaller universe to become trapped by the Sun's immense gravitational field. This of course would have quickly rendered the

Earth uninhabitable, either through a direct collision of the Earth with the vagabond star, or through the severe climatic disruptions that would have inevitably resulted from the star's additional heat input. But even if the star's presence in our solar system didn't immediately exterminate all life here, it would have only been a matter of time until a collision between the wandering star and our own Sun would have incinerated the entire solar system.

However, a collision between the two stars would not have to actually happen in order for the Earth to be rendered totally uninhabitable, nor would the Earth have to be completely jerked out of its orbit by a wandering star in order for its entire ecosystem to be wiped out. These same ominous events would have also transpired if a distantly passing star succeeded in pulling the Earth out of its nearly concentric orbit about the Sun. We mustn't forget that the stability of the Earth's climate is absolutely dependent on the reception of a near constant amount of heat energy from the Sun. In order for this to occur, the Earth must remain more or less the same distance from the Sun at all times. This is "why" the Earth's orbit is anomalously circular, when the orbits of most of the other planets in our solar system are elliptical: a circular orbit ensures that the Earth will be bathed in a more or less constant amount of heat energy from the Sun at all times.

The extreme sensitivity of the Earth's ecosystem to the strength of the Sun's incoming radiation is well-illustrated by the seasonal variations in temperature that are caused by the Earth's 23.27-degree tilt on its axis of rotation. This relatively small amount of tilt varies the angle, and subsequently the strength, of the Sun's incoming rays sufficiently to alter the Earth's surface temperature by as much as 175 degrees Farenheit in different regions (from approximately 50 degrees below zero to approximately 125 degrees above zero), *and this is while the Earth's overall distance from the Sun remains more or less constant.* Given this extremely delicate balance of the Earth's climate to its distance from the Sun, it clearly would not take much of a change in this distance to render the Earth either too hot or too cold to support the rigid needs of biological life.

Thus, even if a wandering star were to pass within only a few million miles of our solar system, it would nevertheless be close enough to induce a significant change in the Earth's orbital radius, and hence in its climatic stability, and this would be enough to render the Earth uninhabitable forevermore. Fortunately for us, though, due to the vast reaches of empty space in the universe, along with the fact that all stars are rapidly moving away from one another, it is exceedingly unlikely that any star will ever pass close enough to our planet to affect its orbital integrity. Indeed, the nearest star to our solar system, Proxima Centauri, is over four and a half light years away from us; that is, it takes light traveling at 186,282 miles per second over four and half *years* to reach us. This tremendous degree of sparseness in the universe virtually guarantees that the Earth's orbit will remain undisturbed by any passing stars for the rest of our Sun's lifetime, at which point *it* will be the sole cause for the Earth's eventual demise. Fortunately for us, this point lies billions of years in the future.

We are also protected from the gravitational influences of distant stars by the fact that the gravitational force happens to vary by the inverse square of the distance between any two gravitating bodies. This means that the force of gravity declines sharply as the distance between gravitating objects is increased. Had this Inverse Square Law occupied another value, it is conceivable that we would have been much more susceptible to the gravitating influences of distant stars, with the result that our planet's orbital integrity would have been greatly jeapordized.

The fact that our universe exists in precisely three spatial dimensions further protects the orbital integrity of the Earth in two separate ways: 1) the Inverse Square Law is only possible in a universe of three spatial dimensions, and 2) a three-dimensional universe provides the maximal degree of stability for all planetary orbits. (More on this important subject will be said later.)

Now, how is it that the universe happens to exist in precisely the right number of spatial dimensions to guarantee the maximal degree of stability for all planetary orbits? How is it that the gravitational force between two bodies happens to vary at precisely the right rate to protect the orbital integrity of the Earth from the disruptive gravitational effects of distant stars and galaxies? And how is it that our universe has precisely the right degree of sparseness to guarantee the Earth's orbital integrity over the billions of years of life's gradual evolution? Of course, one could argue that these are just colossal cosmic coincidences, whose haphazard occurrence accidentally allowed life to evolve. As we are about to see, however, such a conclusion is untenable in the light of all the remaining cosmic "coincidences" which work together, against all the odds, to produce a life-supporting universe.

4.8   The Temperature of Nuclear Stability

The temperature of nuclear stability in the universe—which marks the point at which radiation began to decouple from embryonic matter—is highly significant from a biocentric point of view. Had this temperature (just under 10^9 kelvins) been much different than its present value, our biocentric universe could never have formed. As physicist Gerald Schroeder explains:

> If $10^{10°}$K. was the temperature of stability, then stability would have been reached at approximately one second after the Big Bang. The composition of the universe at that time was approximately 25 percent neutrons and 75 percent protons and the particle plus energy density of the universe was

some 400,000 times that of water. This high density would have caused rapid fusion among particles and therefore rapid building of heavier nuclei.

How would this affect us? First of all, we probably would not be here. Immediately, the composition of the universe would have shifted from its present 75 percent hydrogen and 25 percent helium to a 50–50 ratio as the abundant free neutrons joined with protons to form helium. The high particle density would have changed more, perhaps all, of the hydrogen into nuclei of heavier elements. Little or no hydrogen would have remained. No hydrogen means no significant solar radiation. The stellar furnaces would not have burned as they do today, because the energy of stars is fueled almost entirely by the fusion of hydrogen into helium. Those elements heavier than helium, which life now gleans from the residues of supernovas, would have been abundant. But the hot spots of the universe, which we call stars, would not be there to provide life-giving energy.

Had nuclear stability been delayed until the universal temperature cooled to $10^{8\circ}$K., then instead of having an abundance of heavier elements and a dearth of hydrogen, as we saw in the previous scenario, there would be hydrogen and not much else in the universe. Approximately 300 minutes had elapsed before the expansion of the universe had lowered the temperature to $10^{8\circ}$K. Although neutrons bound in a nucleus are stable and do not decay radioactively, free neutrons are radioactive. They decay with a 15-minute half-period. The 300 minutes that elapsed before reaching $10^{8\circ}$K. would have allowed almost complete decay of all free neutrons. Nuclear synthesis requires neutrons. A universe with no neutrons means a universe composed of hydrogen and no other elements. There is no place for life in such a universe.[34]

Remarkably, then, we find that the biocentric nature of our universe extends to the very origin of the physical realm itself. Prior to this discovery, who would have ever thought that the temperature of nuclear stability in the primeval cosmos could have had such a profound effect on the later evolution of life?

Indeed, this extension of the universe's biocentricity to the most foundational levels of physical reality is *in and of itself* strongly indicative of Intelligent Design. Had the evolution of life in the universe been dependent on local, recent factors only, such as the particular arrangement of atoms on a planet, we might have been able to argue more persuasively for a possible random origin of life. However, now that we know that the biocentric nature of the cosmos dates back to the very origins of the universe itself, and extends to each and every one of the foundational parameters that comprise physical reality, it is hard to see how it could have been produced by anything *but* Intelligent Design.

4.9 The Role of Deuterium

Deuterium, otherwise known as heavy hydrogen (because it consists of one proton and one neutron), also formed in the Big Bang as an isotope of regular hydrogen (which consists of only a single nuclear proton). While only 0.002% of all hydrogen nuclei in the universe are in the isotopic form of deuterium, this rare cosmic impurity turns out to be a vital ingredient in the birth of main-sequence stars like our Sun.[35]

When these proto-stars are just beginning to form, they are not yet hot enough to fuse hydrogen into helium, as all main-sequence stars do, since a temperature of 10 million kelvins is required to do the trick. Therefore, a second form of energy is required to heat the proto-star up to this enormous temperature. Gravitational friction alone at the center of the proto-star is incapable of producing such a tremendous amount of heat energy, since at most it can only produce a temperature of around 1 million kelvins. Fortunately for us, deuterium *can* burn at this relatively low temperature, and since deuterium comprises approximately 0.002% of all the hydrogen in existence, there is just enough deuterium inside the proto-star to get the fusion sequence going.

It is this process of deuterium-burning that prepares the proto-star to enter the main-sequence, through complex convection patterns that gradually enlarge the proto-star's size and increase its temperature. Once the proto-star's fiery interior reaches a temperature of around 10 million kelvins, its vast stores of normal isotopic hydrogen can then begin fusing into helium. It is at this point that the proto-star enters the main-sequence and becomes an adult star. From here on out it will be a steady producer of radiant energy for thousands of millions of years to come.

Biological life, of course, is completely dependent on precisely this type of stable energy source. If such main-sequence stars were unable to form, or if they were unable to maintain a relatively constant temperature, biological life as we know it would be incapable of existing at all. Thus, the existence of biological life hinges on the prior existence of deuterium, which happens to exist in just the right concentration to encourage this "jump-starting" of the proto-star's nuclear furnace. The existence of deuterium, in turn, depends on a wide variety of fundamental cosmological parameters, including the strength of the strong force and the particular explosion dynamics that were displayed by the Big Bang.

The profound importance of deuterium in the evolution of life is all the more remarkable when the extreme rarity of the deuteron in the universe is duly taken into account. An isotope that exists in such small quantities might not have existed at all, or it might have existed in such minute quantities as to have been totally incapable of participating in stellar nuclear reactions. In either case, we clearly wouldn't have been around to discuss the fact, so we very much owe our lives to this rare isotope of hydrogen, and to the various cosmic parameters that enabled it to form in precisely the "right" amount to allow main-sequence stars like our Sun to come into being.

4.10 Design at the Sub-Atomic Level

Another instance of perfect calibration in the universe involves the mass of neutrinos, the smallest (5×10^{-35} kg) and most abundant particles in the known universe. Although they are far smaller than electrons, the huge numbers of neutrinos in existence could easily work together to exert a significant gravitational effect on the rest of the universe. Indeed, as physicist Paul Davies points out in his book *The Accidental Universe*, had the neutrino been just a tiny fraction bigger, the entire universe would have collapsed in on itself shortly after the Big Bang because of the neutrinos' cumulative gravitational effect:

Although a mass of 5×10^{-35} kg is extremely small compared to all other known particles, the high density of neutrinos in the universe (about 10^9 m^{-3}) implies that the accumulated neutrino mass could outweigh all the stars. Indeed, had the neutrino mass turned out to be, say, 5×10^{-34} kg instead, then the gravitating power of the primeval background would have caused a drastic alteration in the expansion of the universe, possibly even halting it completely before now. It is then a remarkable thought that an apparently insignificant change in such a tiny mass would result in our living in a *contracting* rather than an expanding universe.[36]

Another area in which the size of the neutrino figures prominently concerns the rate and quality of galactic motion. By virtue of their tremendous numbers, neutrinos are able to exert a significant viscous drag on galactic motion, such that had the mass of the neutrino been any larger or smaller, present galactic structures would be impossible.[37]

It also turns out that there had to have been a precise balance between the two fundamental constituents of atomic nuclei, protons and neutrons, or else the universe as we know it could never have formed. This balance, in turn, is determined by the complex interaction of a number of fundamental physical constants, each of which happens to possess the right value to ensure the "proper" proton/neutron ratio.

This ratio is all the more incredible when one considers the fact that protons and neutrons themselves are evidently made out of even smaller particles known as quarks, which themselves have to be exactly the right size to ensure a mass difference between protons and neutrons of 10^{-3} of the proton mass. If this mass difference were only one third of its present value, then neutrons could not have decayed to produce protons, because they would not have had enough mass to form an electron. Similarly, if the neutron mass were only 0.998 of its actual value, free protons would probably decay into neutrons by a process known as positron emission. If this were the case, there would probably be no atoms at all in the universe.[38]

As Davies points out, the above relation between the relative sizes of protons and neutrons is itself derived from a seemingly "accidental" relation between the strength of gravity, the strength of the weak force, and the mass difference between protons and neutrons.[39] Had this not been the case, virtually all of the nuclei in existence would have been either protons or neutrons. Either way, the complex chemistry upon which life depends would have been impossible.

Yet another example of near perfect balance in the subatomic realm can be found in the ratio of protons to electrons, which establishes the role of gravity in relation to the electromagnetic force.[40] As we noted earlier, a certain number of protons and electrons were able to survive the primordial annihilation between matter and antimatter at the Big Bang. Amazingly, the number of protons and electrons that were left unscathed were equivalent to within 1 part in 10^{37}. As Ross has pointed out, had this primordial balance between protons and electrons been any different, the electromagnetic force would have so completely dominated the gravitational force that stars, galaxies, and people could never have evolved.[41]

Still another source of wonder in the subatomic realm can be found in the respective electrical charges of protons and electrons. Although the proton is many orders of magnitude larger than an electron, it possesses exactly the opposite quantity of electrical charge. As a consequence, equal numbers of protons and electrons cancel one another out, producing a net charge of zero. This is vitally important for the evolution of biological life forms, because this perfect degree of electrical balance in the atom is a vital prerequisite for the complex biochemistry upon which life depends.

Indeed, had the electrical charge of an electron not been perfectly offset by the charge of a proton, our world would have never had the chance to form at all, since atoms and molecules would have been so unstable that they never would have been able to endure the test of time. Indeed, calculations indicate that if this perfect degree of electrical balance were to be altered by as little as as 1 part in 100 billion, our bodies would instantaneously explode.[42]

With this in mind, how are we to explain the perfect degree of electrical balance between the proton and the electron? It obviously cannot be a function of mere size, as we might expect *a priori*, because the proton is so much larger than the electron. One could conceivably posit a type of natural selection of subatomic particles, in which an entire range of charged protons and electrons would originally exist, but in which only those particles whose charges were perfectly balanced would be allowed to continue to exist. The problem with such a conjecture is twofold: 1) there is no evidence that this could have ever been the case, as we have no good reason to believe that protons or electrons ever existed with even a slightly varying amount of electrical charge, and 2) even if there originally had been such a wide range of charged protons and electrons, we would still have to explain where the correctly charged particles themselves originally came from, and how they could have come to be the only particles in existence.

A far simpler and more satisfying way to explain this perfect electrical balance between protons and electrons is to assert that they were deliberately designed to be this way by a Larger Creative Power. This hypothesis has the added value of being consistent with all the other explanations being offered in this chapter for the other cosmic coincidences that happen to exist in our universe.

The strength of the electromagnetic coupling constant, which determines how strongly electrons are bound to protons in atoms, is also intimately related to the evolution of biological life forms.[43] As you will recall, complex molecules are formed by the spontaneous interaction between the electrons of different atoms. The behavior of these electrons, in turn, is directly determined by the strength of the electromagnetic coupling constant. Had this constant been slightly smaller, relatively few electrons would have been able to remain in "orbit" about nuclei. Had it been slightly stronger, covalent bonding—in which atoms share electrons with one another—would have not been possible. In either case, the complex chemistry upon which life depends would have been strictly impossible.

Digging deeper, we find two other principles at work at the subatomic level which function to stabilize atomic interactions, thereby guaranteeing the stability of all matter and, as a consequence, enabling complex chemistries to result. The first stabilizing force, known as the *Pauli Exclusion Principle*, acts to guarantee that no more than one particular kind of particle and spin can occupy a single quantum state at the same time. If this Exclusion Principle did not apply, all electrons would occupy the lowest quantum state, since it is the orbital with the lowest energy. This would have two disastrous effects: 1) The various positively and negatively charged particles in an atom would spontaneously rearrange themselves so that interactions between their nearest neighbors would predominate. This would result in the spontaneous collapse of the entire atomic structure into a single particle of enormous density, thereby destroying any further possibility for complex chemical interactions. 2) By destroying the multiple shell structure of the heavier atoms, upon which most of the known chemical properties of the elements absolutely depend, the vast majority of these properties would disappear. This would make any type of complex biochemistry strictly impossible, with the result that no carbon-based life forms at all would have been able to evolve on this planet.

As Barrow and Tipler point out, it is possible to imagine a world where the Pauli Exclusion Principle did not apply, but it would be a very different world containing superdense objects that would possess no capacity at all for complex organization.[44] Our very lives thus depend on the existence of the Pauli Exclusion Principle, yet we have no idea where it came from or why it works the way it does. All we know is that it does indeed work, and that it is this very functionality that has enabled life to form.

The second stabilizing force at the subatomic level is the quantization of electronic energy levels. As Bohr originally showed in 1913, electrons can only exist at discrete levels about the nucleus, which amount to multiples of Planck's universal quantum of energy. The great benefit of this quantum nature of the atom is that it allows for all atoms of a particular atomic number and weight to be both identical and stable in the face of a continual bombardment of energy from without. In a non-quantum atom, electrons could possess all possible energy states, and therefore all possible orbital distances from the nucleus. This of course would render all atoms different from one another, and would allow electrons to continually change their energy levels in response to the slightest amount of incoming energy, be it in the form of photons, cosmic rays, or whatever. This in turn would make a given atom's chemical properties subject to change at a moment's notice, thereby making any stable form of chemical interaction absolutely impossible. Fortunately, the existence of discrete quantum states greatly stabilizes each individual atom, because an entire quantum of energy is needed to alter a given electron's particular energy level.

As Barrow and Tipler point out, the atomic stability which is engendered by quantization ironically flies in the face of the popular perception of quantum theory, which sees it as being the very essence of randomness and indeterminism. In reality, however, quantization forms the physical basis for much of the stability and fidelity that is regularly observed in the natural world.[45]

Another important source of atomic stability is the stability of the proton itself, which is one of the primary constituents of atoms. Indeed, this stability of the proton turns out to be absolutely essential for the evolution of life, for had the proton been significantly less stable, life-destroying doses of radiation would have been a much more common occurrence in matter. Similarly, had protons been significantly more stable (i.e., less easily formed and less susceptible to decay), less matter would have been produced in the Big Bang, and life would have therefore been impossible.[46]

4.11 Cosmic "Coincidences" Involving Nature's Fundamental Constants

Of all the cosmic "coincidences" in the natural realm, the most remarkable undoubtedly have to do with the specific values of the physical constants themselves, since they ultimately determine the gross properties of the entire macro world.

Take the gravitational constant (*G*) for example. Although it is by far the weakest of the four physical forces, it is nevertheless sufficiently powerful to have determined the specific large-scale structure of the entire visible universe. Indeed, had the gravitational constant differed from its present value by even one part in 10^{50}, the structure of the entire universe would have been radically different.[47]

The precise value of the gravitational constant is also intimately related to the types of stars that can form in the cosmos, which in turn is one of the most important factors in the evolution of life, as we have seen. Had the gravitational constant been an order of magnitude larger than it is, most stars would have been "blue giants," whose life cycles are so brief that they would have exhausted their nuclear fuel long before life would have ever had a chance to evolve. Similarly, had the gravitational constant been an order of magnitude smaller than it is, far fewer stars would have formed, and the majority of these would have been "red dwarfs," which do not produce enough heat to support life. As it turns out, life can only evolve around stable "main sequence" stars like our own Sun, which alone are able to burn bright enough and long enough to allow for the gradual evolution of life. Incredibly enough, though, in order for these main sequence stars to form in any appreciable numbers, the gravitational constant could only have occupied one possible value, which of course turns out to be precisely its presently observed value.

However, the gravitational constant doesn't work alone in determining the types of stars that can form through normal evolutionary pathways. It works in concert with the electromagnetic fine structure constant and the ratio between the mass of the electron and proton to ensure that the majority of stars which are formed will be "main sequence" stars like our own Sun. As Paul Davies has pointed out in *The Accidental Universe*, this seemingly fortuitous relation between three independent physical constants is all the more remarkable because in order for typical stars like our Sun to be able to form in any appreciable numbers, both sides of the inequality which relates these fundamental values must come very close to the huge number 10^{-39}.[48] This is because the danger of convective instability within a star puts a stringent limitation on the values these constants can possess if stars like our Sun are to be able to routinely form. Given this very narrow convective window in which stars like our Sun can form, along with the requirement that the strength of gravity, on the one hand, and the product of the electromagnetic fine structure constant and the electron/proton mass ratio, on the other, must both add up to approximately 10^{-39}, one might initially suppose such a feat to be next to impossible, especially in a genuinely accidental universe. Fortunately, the strength of the gravitational force in the above-stated inequality works out to be 5.9×10^{-39}, while the product of the electromagnetic fine structure constant and the electron/proton mass ratio works out to be 2.0×10^{39}; this inequality is sufficiently close to unity to allow the majority of stars which form to be "main sequence" stars like our own Sun. As Davies comments:

> Nature has evidently picked the values of the fundamental constants in such a way that typical stars lie very close indeed to the boundary of convective instability. The fact that the two sides of the inequality . . . are such enormous numbers, and yet lie so close to one another, is truly astonishing. If gravity were *very* slightly weaker, or electromagnetism *very* slightly stronger, or the electron slightly less massive relative to the proton, all stars would be red dwarfs. A corresponding tiny change the other way, and they would all be blue giants. Carter has argued that a star's surface convection plays an important role in planetary formation, so that a world where gravity was very slightly less weak might have no planets. In either case, weaker or stronger, the nature of the universe would be radically different.[49]

The value of the strong nuclear force, which binds atomic nuclei together, also helps to determine both the micro and macro properties of the entire universe. Had it been slightly stronger, protons and neutrons would have tended to bind together more frequently and more firmly.[50] This would have had the disastrous effect of making hydrogen, which is the only element in existence that contains a single nuclear proton, a rare element in the universe. Not only would this have spelled catastrophe for stars like our Sun, which depend on an abundance of hydrogen for their primary nuclear fuel, it would have also vastly reduced the cosmic supply of elements heavier than iron, upon which life so intimately depends.[51] (These elements result from the fission, or splitting, of very heavy elements.) In either case, life would have been impossible.

Moreover, had the strong nuclear force been slightly stronger in relation to the electromagnetic force, reality would have largely been comprised of a strange entity known as the di-proton, which consists of two protons bound together (and which fortunately does not exist in reality). This would have been catastrophic to the nuclear reactions that fuel our Sun, since they would have quickly become so powerful that the Sun itself would have exploded.[52]

Similarly, had the strong nuclear force been slightly weaker, multi-proton nuclei would not have been able to hold together, so hydrogen would have been the only element in existence.[53] This would have made the evolution of life—which depends upon the existence of many elements heavier than hydrogen—strictly impossible.

A second consequence of a slightly less energetic strong force would be that the nucleus consisting of one proton and neutron, known as the deuteron, would have been unable to form in stellar interiors.[54] This would have been catastrophic to the chain of nuclear reactions that power the stars, as we have seen, since the deuteron is an essential intermediate in the eventual fusion of hydrogen into helium, and it is this fusion that produces the characteristic nuclear energy of all stars. Thus, the long-term stability of stellar fusion is dependent on the specific value of the strong nuclear force.

In view of these stunning realizations, we owe our very lives to the specific values of these fundamental constants, yet we have no idea where they came from or how they came to occupy their present life-facilitating values. All we know is that were they any different at all, we would not be here to discuss the fact.

4.11.1 Discussion

Perhaps the most remarkable thing about these fundamental physical forces is that they do not work in isolation from one another. To the contrary, there is a deep level of cooperation in nature between the different physical forces, such that, in the absence of this cooperation, our present world could not exist. For instance, if the gravitational constant were only a wee bit stronger in relation to the strong nuclear force, the universe would have been a great deal smaller and faster than it presently is, with the result that stars like our own Sun would have been much smaller and would have lasted only around a year. On the other hand, if gravity were any weaker in relation to the strong force, then the various galaxies and solar systems in the cosmos would never have been able to form in the first place. Either way, life would have been impossible.

Similarly, had the electromagnetic force been slightly stronger in relation to the strong force, the heavier elements which are so important to life would have been nonexistent. If the strong force is held constant, we learn that the fine structure constant must be less than approximately 0.1 in order for heavier elements such as carbon to be able to exist.[55]

A delicate "coincidence" also seems to have been at work between the gravitational interaction and the weak nuclear force at the very beginning of the universal expansion, for it was this "coincidence" that produced the hydrogen and helium which in turn made the evolution of life possible. As it turns out, the primordial nuclear reactions which produced these initial elements are only possible within an exceedingly narrow range of universal temperatures (around 5×10^9 kelvins) and universal ages (anywhere between 0.04 seconds and 500 seconds). Had these reactions taken place at any time prior to 0.04 seconds, all incipient nuclei would have been instantly photodisintegrated; had they taken place at any time after approximately

500 seconds, the reacting nuclei would have possessed too little energy to overcome electrical barriers so as to come within range of the nuclear force.

Fortunately, by virtue of the intimate cooperation between the gravitational and weak interactions, sufficient matter to produce a biocentric universe was indeed formed in the initial nucleosynthesis "window" of the cosmic expansion—75% in the form of hydrogen and 25% in the form of helium. Had this cooperation not occurred, the universe would have been comprised either of 100% hydrogen or 100% helium, if indeed any atoms at all would have been capable of forming. While there does not seem to be any "anthropic" problems associated with a primordial universe consisting of 100% hydrogen, life would have been impossible in a universe consisting of 100% helium. This is because hydrogen would not have been available to form compounds essential to life, such as water; in addition, exclusively helium-burning stars would have been far too short-lived to allow any significant evolution of life to occur.

Remarkably, the gross properties of all atomic and molecular structures can ultimately be traced to the specific values of only two dimensionless physical parameters: the fine structure constant [which is approximately equal to $(137)^{-1}$], and the electron-to-proton mass ratio [which is approximately equal to $(1836)^{-1}$].[56] We clearly owe our lives to the specific values of these fundamental parameters, for had either of their values been even slightly different, we never would have evolved to discuss the fact.

A commonsense interpretation of the facts suggests that a Larger Creative Principle was probably at work in the early universe coordinating events so as to make the later evolution of life possible. Davies agrees:

. . . the nature of the physical world depends delicately on seemingly fortuitous cooperation between distinct branches of physics. In particular, accidental numerical relations between quantities as unconnected as the fine structure constants for gravity and electromagnetism, or between the strengths of nuclear forces and the thermodynamic condition of the primeval universe, suggest that many of the familiar systems that populate the universe are the result of exceedingly improbable coincidences.

Turning to the subject of cosmology—the study of the overall structure and evolution of the universe—we encounter further cosmic cooperation of such a wildly improbable nature, it becomes hard to resist the impression that some basic principle is at work.[57]

4.12   Evidence for Design in the Invariant and Cooperative Aspects of Nature's Physical Constants

As Barrow and Tipler have pointed out, one of the most widespread misconceptions in learned academic circles is the belief that the smallest details of physical reality could have been determined by the Darwinian process of natural selection working in local environments. To the contrary, modern physicists have learned that:

> . . . there exist invariant properties of the natural world and its elementary components which render inevitable the gross size and structure of almost all of its composite objects. The size of bodies like stars, planets, and even people are neither random nor the result of any progressive selection process, but simply manifestations of the different strengths of the various forces of nature.[58]

The upshot of this fundamental insight is that each of these invariant physical constants had to have been perfectly calibrated, both individually and with respect to one another, for our present world to have been able to come into existence. As Davies points out, the slightest variation in any of them would have thus ensured that our delicately balanced world would have never been able to evolve:

> What is specially interesting is that, in many cases, only a modest alteration of values would result in a drastic restructuring of the system concerned. Evidently the particular world organization that we perceive is possible only because of some delicate 'fine-tuning' of these values.[59]

This fine-tuning is all the more remarkable when we realize that these fundamental constants work together at the macro level to allow our concrete world to come into existence. There is thus an incomprehensible *cooperation* in the specific values of these constants, without which we would not be here to think about it.

Davies has this to say about the reality of cooperation in the cosmic drama:

> It is clear that for nature to produce a cosmos even remotely resembling our own, many apparently unconnected branches of physics have to cooperate to a remarkable degree.

All this prompts the question of why, from the infinite range of possible values that nature could have selected for the fundamental constants, and from the infinite variety of initial conditions that could have characterized the primeval universe, the actual values and conditions conspire to produce the particular range of very special features that we observe. For clearly the universe is a very special place: exceedingly uniform on a large scale, yet not so precisely uniform that galaxies could not form; extremely low entropy per proton and hence cool enough for chemistry to happen; almost zero cosmic repulsion and an expansion rate tuned to the energy content to unbelievable accuracy; values for the strengths of its forces that permit nuclei to exist, yet do not burn up all the cosmic hydrogen, and many more apparent accidents of fortune.[60]

In response to this "anthropic" brand of argument it is often claimed that life would have probably evolved to fit virtually *any* kind of physical situation. Or alternatively, it is often claimed that a change in one of the constants would not spell disaster for biological evolution, since the other constants could presumably compensate for this alteration with changes of their own. Accordingly, the present values of the fundamental constants are said to *not* be sacrosanct, since life could presumably have developed in almost any kind of universe.

This is an incredibly naïve argument, because it shows a profound lack of understanding about the many complexities that are involved in the evolution of a biocentric universe. For instance, had the explosive vigor of the Big Bang, the density of matter in the universe, or the value of G differed even slightly from their actual values, *no coherent universe at all would have been able to form*; either the universe would have collapsed back on itself in the first few seconds after the initial explosion, or else it would have exploded with such force that galaxies and stars (and indirectly, people) would have never been able to form.

Similarly, the profound level of cooperation between each and every one of the fundamental constants makes it exceedingly unlikely that *even one* of these parameters could have occupied a different value. Since there are so many inter-level connections between all of the fundamental constants, even a minor change in one would destroy the functional cohesion of the entire unit. Moreover, the values of all the other constants could *not* adequately compensate for such a minor change, because any such large-scale alteration would remove the entire physical realm from the very narrow window of opportunity in which a coherent life-supporting universe can form. As Gribbin and Rees put it:

> If we modify the value of one of the fundamental constants, something invariably goes wrong, leading to a universe that is inhospitable to life as we know it. When we adjust a second constant in an attempt to fix the problem(s), the result, generally, is to create three new problems for every one that we "solve." The conditions in our universe really do seem to be uniquely suitable for life forms like ourselves, and perhaps even for any form of organic complexity.[61]

John Barrow concurs:

> The fact that so many of Nature's most important creations owe their gross size and structure to the mysterious values of the constants of Nature places our own existence in a new and illuminating perspective. We can

see how the conditions necessary for our own existence are contingent upon the values taken by the constants. At first one might imagine that a change in the value of a constant would simply shift the size of everything a little, but that there would still exist stars and atoms. However, this turns out to be too naïve a view. It transpires that there exist a number of very unusual coincidences regarding the values of particular combinations of the constants of Nature which are necessary conditions for our own existence. Were the fine-structure constant to differ by roughly one per cent from it actual value, then the structure of stars would be dramatically different. Indeed, there is every reason to suspect that we would not be here to discuss the matter.[62]

This being the case, how are we to explain the fact that all of the fundamental constants have spontaneously taken on the precise values needed to produce a coherent, life-supporting universe, in spite of truly overwhelming odds to the contrary? How are we to explain the profound level of functional cooperation between the various fundamental constants, such that *in complex unison* they are able to produce a universe that is hospitable to life?

It seems apparent that these "coincidences" point to some kind of intelligent selection, *not just in a retroactive, self-selective sense, but in proactive, deliberate sense.* As many physicists have said, our existence actually *constrains* the type of universe we could ever expect to inhabit, and even "selects" it; hence the doctrine of the Anthropic (i.e. human-centered) Principle.[63]

What it all comes down to is *how* our present universe was selected. There are only two possibilities: either it evolved entirely by chance, in which case it was self-selected by our own existence as observers (retroactive selection), or else it was deliberately selected *in advance* by an Intelligent Power (which qualifies as proactive selection). Given: 1) the incredible degree of fine-tuning that is displayed by each of these fundamental physical parameters, 2) the remarkable degree of cooperation that had to occur between all of these parameters before our biocentric universe could have come into being, and 3) the tremendous improbability that any one of these "coincidences" could have occurred by chance alone, it seems almost self-evident that some form of Intelligent Power probably selected in a proactive (i.e., deliberate, *a priori*) fashion the type of universe we presently inhabit.

Put another way, there *has* to be some degree of Intelligent Design behind the specific values of the invariant physical constants, since their very cooperation towards such a sophisticated end product suggests that they were deliberately calibrated with all the other values "in Mind"; otherwise, how could they possibly interact with one another in so complex and delicate a fashion as to produce the marvel of biological life? Had the present values of these physical constants been free to vary with respect to one another through some cosmic form of natural selection, it might have been possible to suppose that they originally had had some degree of dynamic interaction with one another during the evolution of the universe, with the result that their presently observed values could have developed in an entirely natural and undesigned fashion. As Barrow and Tipler point out, however, such a notion is untenable in light of the most recent cosmological findings, since we now know that the specific values of these physical constants have remained invariant from essentially the very beginning of the Hubble expansion (hence the term "constant of nature").

But if the specific values of these fundamental constants have been invariant from (more or less) the very beginning, then it directly follows that our present physical world, which is a direct function of the coordinated interaction of these specific physical values, was implicit in the birth of the constants themselves shortly following the Big Bang. This of course means that our present world has existed in the form of a direct future *potentiality* from the very beginning, which in turn seems to imply the existence of Intelligent Design, for there seems to be no other reasonable way to explain how the physical constants themselves could have taken on their present life-facilitating values "all at once" shortly following the birth of the universe itself.

One possible way to account for the sudden appearance of these cooperative, life-facilitating parameters is to simply assume that they all took on their present values by chance, so that it was only by the most unlikely of events that life was able to evolve here. But surely there must come a point where the degree of cooperation between an increasing number of independent values becomes so profound that the only reasonable way to account for it is in terms of Intelligent Design. This appears to be precisely the case with the evolution of the universe: there is such a high degree of functional cooperation between so many seemingly independent constants that the only rational way to account for it seems to be in terms of Intelligent Design.

The fact that an alternative explanation for the values of the constants is "possible" (by simply calling them accidents of nature) does *not* automatically render the whole situation ambiguous, nor does it significantly detract from the persuasive power of this theistic interpretation.[64] For one thing, it is far from obvious that our biocentric universe could have ever evolved in a purely accidental manner. But even if it could, the outrageous unlikelihood of this ever happening in the real world makes the theistic interpretation *far* more probable, and hence *far* more satisfying.

4.13   Cosmic Repulsion

When Einstein first formulated his general theory of relativity in 1915, he sought to construct a static model of the universe (i.e., one that was neither expanding nor contracting), because this was the dominant view in cosmology at the time. In order to do so, Einstein had to interject a repulsive value into his equations, which he called the cosmological constant, in order to counteract the force of gravity. Although Einstein quickly eliminated the cosmological constant from his equations when he learned that the universe was expanding, modern developments have indicated that such a repulsive force may indeed be acting across empty space.[65]

In addition, quantum field theory posits the existence of a "vacuum energy" which is a direct function of all the possible particles in existence. This vacuum energy must be considered alongside any type of repulsive force that may be acting across "empty" space. When these comparative calculations are made, it appears as though the cosmological repulsive force is almost exactly counterbalanced by the quantum repulsive force that happens to be acting in the opposite direction. The accuracy of this unbelievable balancing act has been calculated to be better than 1 part in 10^{50}. The effect of this counterbalancing is to render the cosmological repulsive force inactive in cosmic gravitational dynamics.

As Davies points out, had the gravitational or weak force constants varied by more than 1 part in 10^{50}, the precise counterbalance against this cosmic repulsive force would have been upset, with the effect that the gross structure of the entire universe would have been radically altered.[66] When the Grand Unified Theories of particle physics are used to make the calculation, the precision of the matching must be increased to greater than 1 part in 10^{100}.[67]

We are the beneficiaries of this exceedingly precise balancing act, because a non-zero value for the vacuum energy density of the universe (i.e., the cosmological constant) would cause profound distortions in space-time geometry, so much so, in fact, that we probably would not be around to be aware of it. Fortunately for us, no concrete evidence for a non-zero cosmological constant has ever been found, even though a number of galactic surveys extending billions of light years into space have been conducted over the years, and have shown absolutely no evidence for any measurable form of space-time distortion.[68] (We will have more to say about the non-vanishing value of the cosmological constant in the next chapter.)

This amazing counterbalancing precision is not the only aspect of the cosmic repulsive force that is conducive to life. The specific value of this repulsive force also turns out to be extremely important in this capacity, as the gross features of the entire universe itself are known to be remarkably sensitive to the strength of this force. Thus, had the strength of this repulsive force been any greater, it would have made a significant contribution to the overall rate of universal expansion, since it by definition grows in strength with distance (partly because ordinary gravitational effects lessen with distance). Had it been greater by several orders of magnitude, the universal expansion would have been explosive, with the effect that galaxy formation could have never occurred.

Interestingly, some cosmologists have suggested that this cosmic repulsive force may have been the original cause of the Big Bang explosion (through an "inflationary" type scenario).[69] If this were indeed the case, the subsequent development of a quantum vacuum energy could very well have cancelled out the later effect of this cosmic repulsive force on the overall rate of cosmic expansion. The result of this cancellation would have been the uniform rate of cosmic expansion that we observe today throughout the visible universe.

4.14 Life and the Degree of Entropy in the Universe

As Ross has pointed out, the entropy level of the universe—which determines the degree to which disorder is spontaneously produced—is intimately related to the degree to which massive systems such as stars and galaxies are able to condense.[70] The entropy level of the universe can be calculated by determining the ratio between photons and baryons (i.e., protons and neutrons) in the universe. This ratio works out to be approximately a billion to one. Hence, the universe itself turns out to be the most entropic entity in existence.

Significantly, had the universe's entropy level been slightly larger, no galaxies at all would have been able to form. Conversely, had the universe's entropy level been slightly smaller, the resulting galaxies would have trapped so much radiation that any fragmentation into stars would have been effectively thwarted.[71] In either case, life would have never been able to form.

Once again we find that an important physical parameter happens to occupy the precise value that is required for the evolution of life. Given the utter ubiquity and importance of the universe's entropy level, along with the exceedingly rigid and narrow degree of universal entropy that is demanded by all carbon-based life forms, the best explanation for this particular physical parameter again seems to be Intelligent Design.

4.15 The Importance of the Velocity of Light in the Evolution of Life

As Hugh Ross explains in *The Fingerprint of God,* the velocity of light can be expressed as a function of any of the fundamental forces of physics. It can also be expressed as a function of one of the fine structure constants.[72]

This means that the velocity of light is intimately related to all of these constants, such that any alteration in light's velocity would necessitate a corresponding alteration in the values of each of these constants. But life as we know it is absolutely dependent on the presently observed values for each of these constants. Therefore, life could not exist in a universe in which the velocity of light deviated even minutely from its present value of 299,792,458 meters per second.[73]

The significance of this fact cannot be overemphasized, because there seems to be no other discernible "reason" why the velocity of light should occupy its present value. In a universe dominated solely by chance, the velocity of light could conceivably have occupied any of a wide range of possible values (if indeed light could have existed at all in such a "universe"). So, to think that velocity of light just happened to occupy its present value purely by chance, and that this value just happened to be the only one that would be conducive to the evolution of life, *vis-à-vis* the values of all the other constants, is a bit too coincidental to be plausible.

It won't do to simply attribute the velocity of light to the laws of physics, because one must then ask why the laws of physics *themselves* are such as to make the velocity of light so perfectly attuned to the many interdependent requirements for the existence of life. There thus doesn't seem to be any non-theistic response to this enigma that doesn't itself beg the fundamental question at issue here.

4.16 Photosynthesis and the Surface Temperature of the Sun

Another stunning cosmic "coincidence" involves the surface temperature of the Sun and its relationship to the particular needs of life on Earth. In order for the life-generating process of photosynthesis to take place, the spectral temperature of the Sun's incident light must closely approximate the molecular binding energy of around 1 rydberg.[74] If it exceeded this value, all life on Earth would either be sterilized or completely annihilated. If it was significantly below this value, the crucial photosynthetic reactions which maintain the viability of our ecosystem would proceed much too slowly to be of any benefit to the rigid demands of a living world.

In other words, sunlight simply must be of the right color in order for photosynthetic reactions to occur in an optimal fashion. However, it would be wrong to assume that, had incident sunlight been of a different overall color, another type of molecule besides chlorophyll would have evolved to take advantage of it. The fact is, due to the specific quantum states that are common to all the elements, *all* molecules absorb light of approximately the same color. Thus, given this necessary requirement of all molecular structures, the Sun's spectral temperature had to have been just right, or else photosynthetic reactions would have never occurred on this planet. Fortunately, due to a separate series of nuclear "coincidences" at work in the stars themselves, our Sun not only possesses the right spectral temperature to fuel Earth-based photosynthetic reactions, it is also sufficiently long-lived to give carbon-based life forms enough time to evolve and prosper on this planet.

4.17   The Historical Increase in Solar Luminosity

In the non-teleological perspective currently espoused by the modern scientific community, we would normally expect solar events that don't causally impinge on the Earth to be totally independent of those events occurring on the Earth itself. Such an expectation follows directly from the very assumptions of the non-teleological perspective, for if there is no larger cosmic meaning and no coordinating Designer to tie such causally distinct events together, we would never expect *a priori* to see any significant degree of cooperation between them, especially if it had the fortunate effect of enabling life to evolve on this planet.[75]

Incredibly, though, in one of the most startling instances of cooperative change ever to occur during the evolution of life, it turns out that the Sun experienced a significant change in its luminosity at *precisely* the same time that certain life forms were appearing on the Earth, who were themselves capable of compensating for these extreme solar changes in such a way as to keep the Earth's overall temperature relatively constant.

Astronomer Owen Gingerich explains the details behind this intriguing transformation in the book *Is God a Creationist?*

From what astronomers have deduced about solar evolution, we believe that the Sun was perhaps 25 percent less luminous several billion years ago. Today, if the solar luminosity dropped by 25 percent, the oceans would freeze solid to the bottom, and it would take a substantial increase to thaw them out again. Life could not have originated on such a frozen globe, so it seems that the Earth's surface never suffered such frigid conditions. As it turns out, there is a very good reason for this. The original atmosphere would surely have consisted of hydrogen, by far the most abundant element in the universe, but this light element would have rapidly escaped, and a secondary atmosphere of carbon dioxide and water vapor would have formed from the outgassing of volcanoes. This secondary atmosphere would have produced a strong greenhouse effect, an effect that might be more readily explained with a locked car parked in the Sun on a hot summer day than with a greenhouse. When you open the car, it's like an oven inside. The glass lets in the photons of visible light from the Sun. Hot as the interior of the car may seem, it's quite cool compared to the Sun's surface, so the reradiation from inside the car is in the infrared. The glass is quite opaque for those longer wavelengths, and because the radiation can't get out, the car heats up inside. Similarly, the carbon dioxide and water vapor partially blocked the reradiation from the early Earth, raising its surface temperature above the mean freezing point of water.

Over the ages, as the Sun's luminosity rose, so did the surface temperature of the Earth, and had the atmosphere stayed constant, our planet would now have a runaway greenhouse effect, something like that found on the planet Venus; the Earth's oceans would have boiled away, leaving a hot, lifeless globe.

How did our atmosphere change over to oxygen just in the nick of time? Apparently, the earliest widely successful life form on Earth was a single-celled prokaryote, the so-called blue-greens, which survive to this day as stromatolites. Evidence for them appears in the preCambrian fossil record of a billion years ago. In the absence of predators, the algaelike organisms covered the oceans, extracting hydrogen from the water and releasing oxygen to the air. Nothing much seems to have happened for over a billion years, which is an interesting counterargument to those who claim intelligent life is the inevitable result whenever life forms. However, about 600 million years ago the oxygen content of the atmosphere rose rapidly, and then a series of events, quite possibly interrelated, took place: 1) eukariotic cells, that is, cells with their genetic information contained within a nucleus, originated, which allowed the invention of sex and the more efficient sharing of genetic material, and hence a more rapid adaptation of life forms to new environments; 2) more complicated organisms breathing oxygen, with its much higher energy yield, developed; and 3) the excess carbon dioxide was converted to limestone in the structure of these creatures, thus making the atmosphere more transparent in the infrared and thereby preventing the oceans from boiling away in a runaway greenhouse effect as the Sun brightened. The perfect timing of this complex configuration of circumstances is enough to amaze and bewilder many of my friends who look at all this in purely mechanistic terms—the survival of life on Earth seems such a close shave as to border on the miraculous. Can we not see here the designer's hand at work?[76]

4.18   The Transition to a Non-Toxic, Oxidizing Atmosphere

In order for green plants to be capable of producing oxygen via photosynthesis, light must be capable of reaching the surface of the Earth in sufficient quantities. However, the primeval atmosphere of the Earth was much too opaque to allow for the unrestricted passage of light through it.[77] Much of this opaqueness is thought to have been due to the presence of large quantities of methane and ammonia—which are bio-toxic poisons in their own right—in the atmosphere. Hence, before life could have ever been capable of evolving on the surface of the Earth in any appreciable quantities, a way had to be found to transform the Earth's toxic, opaque atmosphere into a non-toxic, translucent one.

This transformation was also needed so that the Earth's atmosphere could be transformed from a reducing one—in which elements tend to combine with hydrogen—to an oxidizing one, in which elements tend to combine with oxygen. An oxidizing atmosphere, of course, is absolutely essential for the development of life for 2 reasons: 1) routine metabolic processes require a certain minimum amount of oxygen in the atmosphere, and 2) life cannot evolve without an ozone shield to block out the Sun's harmful ultraviolet radiation, and ozone is comprised of three oxygen atoms.

In order for life to evolve, then, the Earth's toxic, reducing atmosphere had to have somehow purged itself of its high ammonia and methane content, so that the way could be paved for the transformation to a translucent, oxidizing atmosphere. At the same time, though, it had to retain almost all of its water vapor, because water is an absolutely essential ingredient for all Earth-based life forms.

It is generally thought that this selective loss of methane and ammonia occurred through a process of atmospheric evaporation; the methane and ammonia evaporated into outer space, while the water vapor was selectively retained within the Earth's atmosphere. However, as Hugh Ross[78] points out in *Genesis One: A Scientific Perspective*, this process of atmospheric evaporation had to have been very finely balanced indeed, because the molecular weights of these three substances are so close to one another. Methane, for instance, has a molecular weight of 16, ammonia has a molecular weight of 17, and water vapor has a molecular weight of 18. Hence, the climatological forces which facilitated this process had to have been just strong enough to allow for the evaporation of methane and ammonia, but not quite strong enough to allow for the evaporation of water vapor. This undoubtedly qualifies as one of the most remarkable events in the Earth's entire history, because water vapor is heavier than ammonia by a mere factor of 1 atomic unit.

In order for any molecule to be capable of evaporating from the Earth's atmosphere, its escape time must add up to a certain minimum amount. Now, the escape time of a molecule is known to be determined by a number[79] of discrete cosmic factors, including: 1) the mass of a planet, 2) the square of the planet's radius, 3) the square root of both the molecule's mass and the atmospheric temperature of the planet, and 4) the individual temperature gradient for each of the different layers in the planet's atmosphere. As far as the primeval Earth itself was concerned, this latter factor was greatly influenced by a series of other factors, including: 1) the gradual increase in the Sun's luminosity, which we discussed earlier, 2) the gravitational "mopping up" of interplanetary debris by the Sun and other gravitational bodies, and 3) the steady decrease in the Earth's volcanic activity.

It is astonishing to realize that all of these causally distinct factors had to have worked together to a very high degree of accuracy to have allowed for the selective evaporation of methane and ammonia, while simultaneously allowing for the selective retainment of water vapor.[80] Considering the very close proximity between the molecular weights of methane, ammonia, and water vapor, this almost certainly had to have been an Intelligently Contrived event.

Of course, there will always be those who insist on seeing such remarkable events as being purely accidental. However, in light of all the other cosmic "coincidences" we've discussed in this chapter, it just doesn't seem credible to believe that they *all* could have happened by chance alone, and that the only reason we're alive is because of the luckiest of accidents.

Many scientists like to attribute our existence to a mere selection effect, in which we can't help but find ourselves living in that part of the universe which just happens to be capable of supporting biological life. While it is necessarily the case that we can't help but observe ourselves in such a life-supporting world, this tautological observation can never be used as a *sufficient* explanation for our existence, because it doesn't explain how the universe originally came to occupy its present biocentric nature.

4.18.1 Atmospheric Oxygen Maintenance

Following the terrestrial compensation for the previously discussed change in solar luminosity, it was essential for the amount of oxygen in the atmosphere to be strictly regulated. For while a relatively high amount of oxygen in the atmosphere is important for virtually all forms of earthly life, too much oxygen is exceedingly destructive. Indeed, if the amount of oxygen in the atmosphere were to be increased even slightly beyond its present 21% concentration, forest fires would become far more prevalent. This is due to the fact that the probability of lightning starting a forest fire is known to increase by a whopping 70% for each 1% rise in the atmospheric oxygen content.[81] Once again we find yet another amazing balance in nature, without which most life forms would be unable to exist.

A possible naturalistic explanation for this degree of balance is to say that the atmospheric oxygen content has been fixed by a natural feedback-type mechanism on the Earth which is automatically connected to the amount of vegetation that has been burned by lightning-induced forest fires. In this mode of reasoning, once too much oxygen appears in the atmosphere, the increased number of forest fires automatically reduces the number of oxygen-producing plants to the point that a delicate balance between fire risk and atmospheric oxygen content can be achieved and maintained.

Such a natural feedback mechanism is no doubt operative in our world. But why does such a naturalistic process have to count against the Creative Design of a Higher Power? Why can't it simply be another natural process which God has ordained to control an important aspect of the Earth's environment?

4.19   The Requirements for a Stable Water Cycle

In order for life to evolve, a relatively stable water cycle first had to have been established to transfer water from the world's great bodies of water to the atmosphere, and then back to the surface of the Earth again in the form of rain or snow. This required an extremely delicate balancing act between evaporation and condensation forces in the Earth's atmosphere, which are themselves dependent on a number of different climatological factors, including air pressure, air temperature, surface gravity, a gradual decrease in volcanic activity, a gradual increase in the Sun's luminosity, continued development of an oxidizing atmosphere, and a stablization of the upper layers of the Earth's atmosphere.[82]

Again we find that a number of causally distinct environmental and cosmic forces had to have worked together in very precise fashion to allow for the development of an essential feature of the Earth's biocentricity.

4.20   The Timing of the Sun's T-Tauri Wind

As Gerald Schroeder explains in *Genesis and the Big Bang*, most stars in the early stages of their evolution are observed to lose tremendous amounts of matter in a single convulsive outburst.[83] This explosive period is known as the *T-Tauri Phase* of stellar evolution. In all likelihood, our own Sun experienced just such a violent outburst early in its history (during which time it probably expelled the equivalent of two or three solar masses).

Indeed, according to Schroeder, the Sun produced such a powerful solar wind during its T-Tauri Phase that it probably blew all residual interplanetary gases straight out of the solar system.[84] The devastation, however, affected far more than just these interplanetary gases; it also blew away the atmospheres of the planets as well. This of course presented a potentially catastrophic threat as far as the life-supporting capacity of the Earth was concerned, for had the Sun's T-Tauri wind occurred *after* the basic atmosphere of the Earth had already formed, it would have blown away these precious gases once and for all, with the result that life would have never been able to evolve here.

It is thus the timing of the Sun's T-Tauri wind, *vis-à-vis* the appearance of the Earth's atmosphere, that becomes the all-important issue with respect to the life-supporting capacity of our planet.[85] Had this T-Tauri wind occurred *before* the aggregation of matter into planets, all the potential water for our world—which originally clung to the surfaces of interstellar dust particles as frost—would have instantly been vaporized by the massive radiation.[86] This would have produced an Earth without water, and this of course would have been catastrophic to the later development of life. It is also possible that an "early" T-Tauri wind would have blown many of the uncongealed precursors of the Earth straight out of the solar system as well, which of course would have made it impossible for our planet to form in the first place.

On the other hand, had the Sun's T-Tauri wind taken place *after* the production of the Earth's atmosphere (which is thought to have taken place through the outgassing of volcanoes), it would have swept away these precious life-giving gases in short order.[87] Hence, in order for life to have eventually been capable of forming here, the Sun's T-Tauri wind had to have occurred *after* the congealing of matter into planets, but *before* the outgassing of the Earth's volcanoes. Fortunately for us, this appears to have been precisely what happened.

4.21   The Importance of the Ratio Between Photons and Protons

The ratio between photons (light particles) and protons, which is denoted by the symbol S, is also critical for the evolution of life, since it plays an important role in determining many of the gross features of our universe. Had this ratio been just 10^7 times bigger, the temperature of space would have been above the boiling point of water.[88] No water could then have existed, so our globe would have remained lifeless forever.[89]

Even a relatively small increase in the value of S would have altered the universe beyond recognition, since it would have severely threatened the development of galaxies.[90] As we have seen, galaxy formation could only have happened when the gravitational dynamics of the early universe became dominated by matter instead of radiation. The photon/proton ratio played a direct role in determining when this actually occurred; had this ratio been even slightly different, matter would have decoupled from radiation at a different time. This would have been catastrophic for the development of galaxies because, given the relentless Hubble expansion, a very narrow window existed in which galaxy formation could have possibly occurred. Beyond this critical point, the atoms and molecules in existence would have been too far apart to congeal into galaxies. It follows, then, that matter had to have decoupled from radiation while these particles were still close enough together to condense into galaxies. In order for this to have been possible, though, the value of S had to have been more or less the same as it is today.

4.22   The Smoothness of the Microwave Background

Another critical balance in nature concerns the temperature and intensity of the microwave background, which works out to be slightly less than 3°K, no matter which direction in space one happens to look. This degree of isotropy, or directional fidelity, is utterly remarkable, because those parts of the universe that have never been in causal contact with one another are nevertheless found to possess the same background temperature to better than 1 part in 10 thousand. This in turn requires that the rate of cosmic expansion at the Planck time of 10^{-43} seconds had to have been fine-tuned in all directions to within 1 part in 10^{40}.[91] The result of this incredible degree of fine-tuning is that from the largest possible perspective (about 6000 Mpc), the expansion dynamics of the universe are meticulously coordinated with one another, in spite of the fact that so many areas have evidently never been in causal contact for any appreciable length of time.

One way to explain this incredible degree of sameness is to postulate the existence of natural frictional processes in the early universe that would have acted over time to smooth out any irregularities. This is known as *chaotic cosmology*, and it seeks to make superfluous any knowledge of the initial conditions that gave rise to the present universe, since the proposed viscous processes would themselves over time have supposedly smoothed out any irregularities.[92]

The problem with this chaotic cosmological approach is that these proposed viscous processes can only smooth out irregularities that were not originally too large in magnitude and spatial extent. [93] Otherwise, the overall rate of cosmic expansion would have proceeded too rapidly to allow interparticle viscous reactions to occur. Significantly, calculations show that these initial irregularities could *not* have kept pace with the rate of cosmic expansion.

Another problem with chaotic cosmology is that the amount of dissipation that would have been necessary to induce a state of homogeneity and isotropy in the universe would have probably been far in excess of that which is currently observed in the microwave background.

According to Collins[94] and Hawking, this chaotic cosmological explanation of the universe's current degree of isotropy is false because the only physically realistic solutions to Einstein's equations have indicated that most irregularities would have reliably appeared only at *late* cosmic epochs; that is, unless the overall expansion rate of the universe turns out to be close to critical. This is because a "flat" universe seems to contain within itself the preconditions for cosmic isotropy. As we have seen, though, the rate of cosmic expansion is indeed so close to critical that it is impossible to tell at the present time whether the universe will go on expanding forever, or whether it will recollapse someday into what has been called the "Big Crunch."

But if the best way to explain the universe's current degree of isotropy is by tying it to the overall rate of cosmic expansion, we are again compelled to conclude that the original Big Bang explosion had to have been exceedingly fine-tuned in all directions and in all capacities. Indeed, calculations show that in order for space to have the temperature it now has (which in turn is critical for the development of a life-supporting world), the rate of cosmic expansion when the universe was a mere 10^{-43} seconds old had to have been globally fine-tuned to better than 1 part in 10^{40}. Otherwise, the universe would have turned out much differently, with the result that life as we know it would have never been possible.

The challenge is to discover the global force that would have been capable of fine-tuning the universe's initial expansion rate in this manner. For Collins and Hawking, who have worked extensively on this problem, "the isotropy of the universe and our existence are both results of the fact that the universe is expanding at just about the critical rate. Since we could not observe the universe to be different if we were not here, one can say, in a sense, that the isotropy of the universe is a consequence of our existence."[95]

This is a hard statement to pin down in terms of its exact meaning. On the one hand, Collins and Hawking are saying that both our existence and the isotropy of the universe are the natural consequences of the fact that the universe happens to be expanding at close to the critical rate. Such a statement seems to imply that an accidental relationship exists between human existence and the overall rate of cosmic expansion. On the other hand, it also seems to suggest that this expansion rate is so close to critical *because we exist*. This radical statement could be interpreted in two ways: 1) as a self-evident tautology which says nothing at all about *why* the universe itself is expanding at the critical rate, and 2) as an indication that the rate of cosmic expansion has been deliberately fine-tuned by a Higher Power, so as to facilitate the subsequent evolution of human observers.

4.23 The Homogeneity of the Universe

The homogeneity, or relative sameness, of the physical universe that we have been discussing is one of the most baffling problems in modern cosmology. Why such a gigantic and complex system should emerge out of the Big Bang in such an incredibly uniform manner is inexplicable in the absence of a Divine Coercive Agent, because it is very difficult to see how parts of the universe that are beyond the reach of light impulses could have had time to causally interact with one another after the initial explosion.

The reason for this has to do with what physicists call the *particle horizon*. Briefly, the particle horizon results from the fact that "the finite velocity of light partitions the universe into causally coherent volumes which have not had time to send light signals to each other since the beginning of the universe."[96] Assuming that nothing in the universe can travel faster than light, it follows that galaxies beyond this particle horizon cannot be causally connected with one another.

Nevertheless, the astonishing fact of the matter is that the temperature and distribution of matter in the universe is the same over the largest possible scale of measurement to within 1 part in 10,000! This is a level of cooperation that seems impossible without some form of high-level communication. As Davies explains:

> . . . the galaxies that lie in these causally disconnected regions of the universe—regions that have never been in any sort of physical contact—look remarkably similar. Moreover, the galaxies populate those disconnected regions at the same density and recede from their neighbors at the same rate. How is one to explain such an extraordinary degree of cooperation without communication?
>
> It is hard to resist the impression of something—some influence capable of transcending spacetime and the confinements of relativistic causality—possessing an overview of the entire cosmos at the instant of its creation, and manipulating all the causally disconnected parts to go bang with almost exactly the same vigour at the same time, and yet not so exactly coordinated as to preclude the small scale, slight irregularities that eventually formed the galaxies, and us.[97]

Now, what sort of "influence" could possibly exist that would transcend spacetime and possess an overview of the entire cosmos? The traditional notion of a Divine Creator seems to be pretty much the only conceivable power that would be capable of performing such a grandiose creative function.[98]

4.24 Guth's Inflationary Hypothesis

In one of the most recent attempts to explain the overall isotropy and homogeneity of the universe, physicist Alan Guth of MIT has suggested that a period of extremely rapid inflation immediately following the Big Bang could have itself been responsible for smoothing out the overall distribution of matter and energy in the cosmos.

In order to explain how this could have been possible, a distinction must first be drawn between the entire universe, which comprises every physical thing in existence, and the visible universe, which is demarcated by the distance light could have traveled since the Big Bang. By definition, of course, all we will ever be able to see is the visible universe. It follows, then, that we will never be able to establish with absolute certainty whether any part of physical reality happens to extend beyond this fundamental barrier.[99]

The inflationary hypothesis "solves" the horizon problem by vastly reducing the area of the primordial universe that could have expanded to produce our present-day visible universe. The advantage of this wholesale reduction in size is that it enables the region that did in fact expand into the visible universe to be in complete causal contact with itself.

In the non-inflationary Big Bang model of cosmogenesis, the size of the primordial universe that could have been causally connected is calculated by extrapolating backwards in time from the present-day rate of cosmic expansion. This produces an unacceptably large size for the universe of 1 centimeter when the universe was but a mere 10^{-35} of a second old. It is unacceptably large because there is no way even such a tiny region could have been causally connected, since the furthest light could have traveled in such a brief amount of time is 10^{-25} centimeters. This is where the process of inflation comes in. Because of the greatly accelerated rate of cosmic expansion that is purported to have taken place in an unimaginably brief 9.9×10^{-34} seconds, the region that could have given rise to our visible universe can be reduced to an area measuring 10^{-25} centimeters. This tiny region would have been within the range of light signals at that time, so it is assumed to have been in complete causal contact with itself at this early stage of cosmic history.[100] So, by assuming that this tiny homogenized region spontaneously inflated to produce the entire visible universe, we have a *de facto* explanation for the large-scale homogeneity of the cosmos.

In order for this inflationary scenario to work, however, the initial rate of inflation had to have been enormous, much greater than the rate of cosmic expansion we observe today. To make this possible, a new form of energy that would have been sufficient to the task had to be found. Guth found it in the energy of *grand unification*, that primordial moment when the original symmetry binding the strong, weak, and electromagnetic forces was first broken. The cataclysmic breaking of this original symmetry is thought by Guth to have liberated such an enormous amount of energy that the postulated rate of universal expansion could have indeed taken place.

The inflationary hypothesis provides a second mechanism by which the homogeneity and isotropy of the universe could have had their origin. Just as blowing up a lumpy balloon has the effect of smoothing out the lumps that originally existed on it, the rapid inflation of the universe itself is thought to have been capable of smoothing out whatever inhomogeneities that may have initially existed in it.

The inflationary paradigm has gone through a number of revisions since its original conception by Guth. Guth's original inflationary model, which was based on a period of fast symmetry breaking with the formation of bubbles, has since turned out to be inadequate because the high rate of cosmic expansion would have prevented the bubbles from joining together to bring the entire visible universe into the same overall phase.[101] In 1981, a young Russian by the name of Andrei Linde suggested that this problem could be overcome if the entire visible universe was originally contained inside a single bubble. This suggestion, which necessitated a process of slow symmetry breaking inside the bubble, was dubbed the "new inflationary model." It too was found to be inadequate on two separate counts: 1) it predicts a much greater variation in the microwave background than is actually observed, and 2) further research has cast doubt on whether or not there could have been a colossal phase transition the way the model requires. As a consequence, Hawking personally believes that "the new inflationary model is now dead as a scientific theory."[102]

The new inflationary model was superceded in 1983 by a chaotic inflationary model, also proposed by Linde. The chaotic model seems to possess all the advantages of the earlier inflationary models without being plagued by their shortcomings.[103]

The biocentric significance of this period of cosmic inflation (assuming it occurred at all) can be found in the fact that it had to have occurred in the very precise fashion that it did in order for the universe to have been capable of supporting biological life. Had it occurred any earlier or later, or taken place with a slightly different degree of vigor, or not stopped at precisely the right instant, the universe would have been a very different place, perhaps unrecognizably so. This is because the process of galaxy formation is intimately related to the overall cosmic expansion rate, as we have seen. Had this expansion rate occupied another value because of an unchecked inflationary process, the newly formed matter of the universe would have never been capable of congealing into galaxies, due to the severe limitations of the gravitational force.

It is hard to see how such a precisely orchestrated process of inflation could have occurred in just the right manner to ensure the development of a biocentric universe, especially considering the near infinite variety of problems that *could* have taken place with it. Once again, it seems as though the best way to account for this incredible degree of precision is in terms of a Larger Creative Influence, who would have been capable of overseeing the whole affair.

4.25 The Marvel of Intrastellar Carbon Formation

One of the most important prerequisites for the development of organic life is, of course, the element carbon. Unbeknownst to most people, all the carbon in our world—including the carbon in our bodies—was manufactured billions of years ago in the fiery interiors of dying red giant stars. We are quite literally, then, made of recycled star stuff.

Remarkably, though, if it weren't for a series of wildly improbable "coincidences" involving the ambient heat energy of a star and a peculiar nuclear property known as *resonance*, there would be virtually no carbon at all in the universe. This is a truly astonishing realization, and one which figures prominently in the cosmic conspiracy to evolve life that we have been discussing throughout this chapter. For this reason we shall devote a particular amount of attention to this all-important cosmic phenomenon.

There are two possible ways in which carbon can be manufactured inside of stars. The first mechanism involves the simultaneous fusion of three helium nuclei into a single carbon nucleus. The reaction rate, however, for this simultaneous triple collision is much too slow to enable a significant quantity of carbon to be formed in this manner. Something else needs to occur to enable this reaction to proceed at a more favorable rate, otherwise virtually no carbon at all would exist in the universe.

As it turns out, two helium nuclei are able to fuse together to produce a beryllium intermediate at a much faster rate than the triple collision of helium is able to produce a carbon nucleus. Once this beryllium intermediate is formed, an additional collision with a single helium nucleus is then able to produce the desired carbon product in appreciable numbers.

However, before this two-step reaction can take place, two nuclear factors need to exist to help the process along. First, the beryllium intermediate needs to be relatively long-lived, in comparison with the helium + helium reaction that gave rise to it. This is so as to allow the beryllium intermediate a sufficient amount of time to react with a helium nucleus before it decays.

However, this mechanism is complicated by the fact that the beryllium intermediate, which is necessary in the first stage of this process, is not the normal form of beryllium found in nature (which possesses one more neutron). To the contrary, it is the most wildly unstable isotope of beryllium known, which is only stable for a mere 0.000000000000001 of a second, after which point it flies apart.[104] Therefore, some other factor has to exist to compensate for this exceedingly short lifetime; otherwise, there wouldn't be enough of the beryllium substrate produced inside of these dying red giant stars to allow for the generation of sufficient quantities of carbon.

The discovery of this crucial additional factor came in 1953, when Cornell University astrophysicist Edwin Salpeter found that the beryllium intermediate inside these stars possesses just the right nuclear *resonance* level to help facilitate the production of sufficient quantities of carbon.

The term "nuclear resonance" refers to the natural vibration frequencies of atomic nuclei. Just as electrons are known to occupy different energy levels in an atom, so too are the nuclei themselves capable of occupying different energy levels, which are known as resonance energies. Resonance becomes a factor when two nuclei collide, for if the nuclear resonance of the composite structure (the potential product) matches the combined mass-energy of the two reactants, the two nuclei "resonate" when they collide, with the effect that there is a much greater chance that they will stick together and form a new product.

In other words, just as all physical objects naturally possess a sympathetic vibrational frequency, so too do all atomic nuclei. This sympathetic vibrational frequency of an atomic nucleus is known as its nuclear resonance level, and all nuclei possess a coordinated mixture of them. Nuclear reactions are either facilitated or hindered by the specific resonances of reacting nuclei in the following manner: if the sympathetic vibrational frequency of one of the reactants happen to "resonate" with the energy of an incoming nucleus, the two nuclei are more likely to fuse together; if no resonance at all occurs, they are more likely to "bounce off" one another and remain separate.

It is the phenomenon of nuclear resonance that enables the essential beryllium intermediate to be produced in appreciable quantities inside dying red giant stars, in spite of its extremely short lifetime. Fortunately for us, the reacting helium nucleus resonates with the beryllium intermediate in such a fashion that the latter substance is able to be produced in *much* greater quantities than otherwise would have obtained. This additional factor compensates for the unusually brief lifetime of the beryllium intermediate, and allows for its production in sufficient quantities to facilitate the eventual synthesis of carbon.

Before we move on, it is instructive to note that there is a deeper "reason" for the radical instability of the beryllium intermediate: it is crucial for the development of the *other* heavy elements upon which life so intimately depends. As Hugh Ross has pointed out, if this beryllium intermediate were even a tad bit more stable, the production of heavier elements would proceed so rapidly that violent stellar explosions would inevitably result, and this would effectively short-circuit the stepwise fusion of the heavier elements that are so crucial to life.[105]

In order for carbon-based life forms to be capable of existing, then, it was necessary for the lifetime of the beryllium intermediate to be balanced on a knife-edge between two extremes, both of which, had they obtained, would have made the evolution of life impossible. On the one hand, the lifetime of the beryllium intermediate had to have been short enough to slow the fusion process down in stars sufficiently, so as to prevent catastrophic intrastellar explosions from occurring. On the other hand, it had to have been long enough to allow enough time for a third helium nucleus to hit home so that a precious carbon-12 nucleus could be produced. Needless to say, the actual lifetime of the beryllium intermediate is precisely what it needs to be in order to allow for the production of carbon-based life forms such as ourselves.

Even so, the lifetime of the beryllium intermediate *still* isn't long enough by itself to allow for the production of significant quantities of carbon. Yet other nuclear factor has to intervene before this can take place.

It was here that British astrophysicist Sir Fred Hoyle made an incredible biocentrically motivated discovery. Reasoning backwards from the existence of life, Hoyle knew that carbon *had* to have been formed in sufficient quantities in dying red giant stars, so he doggedly set about looking for a suitable mechanism that would have been responsible for producing it. Hoyle expanded upon Salpeter's original discovery and proposed that a *second* nuclear resonance must be at work between helium, the reacting beryllium, and the final carbon product.

At first Hoyle was unsuccessful in locating this second resonance level. In an impressive display of biocentrically motivated faith, however, Hoyle persisted, because he knew that nuclei typically possess not one but *many* resonances. Working at Caltech with physicist Willy Fowler, he eventually found the resonance frequency he was looking for, which turned out to be precisely the 7.6 MeV energy level that he had originally predicted. As a direct consequence of this second resonance level, helium and the already facilitated beryllium intermediate are able to come together to form significant quantities of carbon when they wouldn't have otherwise been able to do so.

Going one step further, we find that the thermal energy of the nuclei in a typical star is almost exactly equivalent to the nuclear resonance level of the carbon nucleus. This further facilitates the production of carbon, as it ensures that the thermal energy of the reacting helium nucleus is almost exactly the same as the nuclear resonance level of the desired carbon product. The result of this happy "coincidence" is that the helium and beryllium nuclei are encouraged to stick together to form carbon, and this in turn ensures that relatively large quantities of carbon are regularly formed inside dying red giant stars.

As if that were not enough, there is a *third* resonance at work inside dying red giant stars that prevents the newly synthesized carbon from reacting with another helium nucleus to form oxygen. As it turns out, the oxygen nucleus possesses a resonance level that actually *discourages* its production from the fusion of carbon and helium nuclei. We owe our lives to this lucky "coincidence," for had a more favorable resonance level existed between carbon, helium, and oxygen, most of the carbon that is essential to life would have become transformed into oxygen, and we would not be here to wonder about it.

Overall, it is safe to say that, given the utter precision displayed by these nuclear resonances with respect to the synthesis of carbon, not even *one* of them could have been even slightly different without destroying the precious carbon yield. Had this change in the cosmic *status quo* occurred, carbon would have been an exceedingly rare element in the universe, and we in all likelihood would not be here.

In an intriguing essay entitled "Let There Be Light: Modern Cosmogony and Biblical Creation," astronomer Owen Gingerich explains how these unique nuclear properties have conspired together to facilitate the intrastellar production of carbon:

Carbon is the fourth most common atom in our galaxy, after hydrogen, helium, and oxygen, but it isn't very abundant; there are 250 helium atoms for every carbon atom. A carbon atom can be made by merging three helium nuclei, but a triple collision is tolerably rare. It would be easier if two helium nuclei would stick together to form beryllium, but beryllium is not very stable. Nevertheless, sometimes before the two helium nuclei can come unstuck, a third helium atom strikes home, and a carbon nucleus results. And here the details of the internal energy levels of the carbon nucleus become interesting: it turns out that there is precisely the right resonance within the carbon that helps this process along. Without it, there would be relatively few carbon atoms. Similarly, the internal details of the oxygen nucleus play a critical role. Oxygen can be formed by combining helium and carbon nuclei, but the corresponding resonance level in the oxygen nucleus is *half a percent too low* for the combination to stay together easily. Had the resonance level in the carbon been 4 percent higher, there would be essentially no carbon. Had that level in the oxygen been only half a percent higher, virtually all of the carbon would have been converted to oxygen. Without that carbon abundance, neither you nor I would be here tonight.[106]

As a direct consequence of this harmonious, teleological interplay between four distinct nuclear structures and three distinct resonances, carbon was able to be produced in stellar interiors in sufficient quantities to allow carbon-based life forms to subsequently evolve. In order for this to have happened, though, the nuclear resonance levels of beryllium, carbon, and oxygen nuclei had to have been meticulously fine-tuned to better than accuracy. This in turn required additional fine-tuning between the relative strengths of the nuclear and electromagnetic interactions, as well as between the relative masses of nucleons and electrons. The cumulative effect of this fine-tuning is that, against all the odds, carbon was able to form in sufficient quantities to make the evolution of carbon-based life forms possible.

It is hard to escape the notion that all of these previously mentioned structures and resonances were deliberately calibrated with all the others "in Mind," otherwise they probably would have never been able to cooperate with one another in such a precise and meticulous fashion to ensure the production of sufficient quantities of carbon. In addition, we mustn't forget that a high degree of cooperation between several distinct structures for a common end product is *itself* indicative of intelligent design.[107]

The elucidation of this relationship between organic life and nuclear resonance levels has to qualify as one of the greatest discoveries in the history of modern science, for it provides yet another powerful reason to believe that our physical universe has indeed been contrived by some sort of Divine "Superintellect" with the explicit goal of creating carbon-based life forms. There are simply too many "coincidences" at work here to allow for any other reasonable conclusion.[108]

Indeed, Fred Hoyle, the astrophysicist who discovered these nuclear resonances, was so persuaded by his findings that he has since come to the radical conclusion that they were probably the work of a Supernatural Contriver. For Hoyle, the meticulous fine-tuning of nuclear resonance levels that has made organic life possible is direct evidence of a kind of "put-up job" in the universe. In reference to the precise positioning of these nuclear resonances, Hoyle has written that:

> If you wanted to produce carbon and oxygen in roughly equal quantities by stellar nucleosynthesis, these are the two levels you would have to fix, and your fixing would have to be just about where these levels are actually found to be. Would you not say to yourself, "Some supercalculating intellect must have designed the properties of the carbon atom, otherwise the chances of my finding such an atom through the blind forces of nature would be utterly miniscule?" Of course you would . . . *A common sense interpretation of the facts suggests that a superintellect has monkeyed with physics, as well as with chemistry and biology, and that there are no blind forces worth speaking about in nature. The numbers one calculates from the facts seem to me so overwhelming as to put this conclusion almost beyond question* (emphasis mine).[109]

The significance of this statement from Hoyle cannot be overemphasized, not only because of its obvious theological implications, but also because of Hoyle's blatant atheistic background. At one time, Hoyle was a strong proponent of the infinite Steady State hypothesis (which he helped to formulate), not because of the persuasiveness of the scientific evidence *per se*, but because of its freedom from any need for a Divine Creator. Indeed, throughout his early writings Hoyle displayed himself to be a firmly entrenched atheist, and openly admitted that his cosmological theories were explicitly designed to support his non-theistic world view.

It is against this atheistic background that Sir Fred's admission of a "supercalculating intellect" at work in the universe is nothing short of remarkable. It also says something about the intrinsic persuasiveness of the cosmological data, for as Hoyle correctly points out, the numbers one calculates from the facts are indeed so overwhelming as to put the theistic hypothesis virtually beyond question.

4.26   The Role of Neutrinos and the Weak Nuclear Force in the Explosion of Supernovae

In order for carbon and the other heavy elements that are essential for life to become available for the formation of planets and, ultimately, people, they must find a way to become dispersed throughout the interstellar medium. This function is served by the magnificent explosions of supernovae, which release so much radiant energy into the heavens that for a time they are brighter than anything else in the night sky.[110]

However, had the weak nuclear force—which mediates radioactive decay—been any weaker, the neutrinos that cause supernova explosions would not have had sufficient power to do so.[111] Similarly, had the weak force been much stronger, the same neutrinos would have been hopelessly trapped within the cores of these dying stars.[112] Either way, the heavier organic elements which are so essential to life on Earth would never have been made available to the rest of the universe.

As we saw earlier, the strength of the weak force is also what determines how much hydrogen is converted into helium at the Big Bang. This dual role of the weak force strictly limits the possible values it can possess and still be conducive to life. As Gribbin and Rees point out:

> The weak force seems to be just about as weak as it can be in order to avoid all the original hydrogen being converted into helium. Supernovae might still work (exploding by a different mechanism) if the force were a little stronger, but if the force were weaker the neutrinos could not drive any kind of explosion; the Universe would be even more comfortably dominated (baryonically speaking) by hydrogen if the force were a little stronger. But the window of opportunity for a universe in which there is *some* helium, *and* exploding supernovae, is very narrow.[113]

4.27   Large Number Coincidences

Another intriguing phenomenon in the study of cosmology involves the many large number coincidences surrounding the number 10^{40}. Why such a huge number should keep cropping up in completely different areas of physics is a complete mystery, but it seems to reflect a deeper level of Design in the universe than many scientists are willing to admit.

For instance, the number 10^{40} is mathematically related to the gravitational fine structure constant, the number of charged particles in the universe, the ratio between the Hubble time and the Planck time, the ratio between the proton's Compton wavelength and the Planck time, the ratio between the strengths of electrical and gravitational forces in a hydrogen atom, and the ratio between the present epoch and the time it takes light to travel across the proton's Compton wavelength.[114] It is also mathematically related to the weak fine structure constant, the cosmic photon/proton ratio, and both the number of stars in a galaxy and the number of galaxies in the universe.[115] Given the extremely large magnitude of this number, there is no *a priori* reason why it should keep cropping up in so many different and seemingly unrelated branches of physics; that is, unless there is a deeper level of Intelligent Design to the universe than is superficially apparent.

The most famous of the large number coincidences was studied intently by British physicist Paul Dirac, who noted how the age of the universe in nuclear units is very close to the square root of the number of particles in the universe and to the square of the ratio between the electrical and gravitational forces, all three of which are represented by that magic number 10^{40}. Of this mysterious relationship, Dirac wrote that, "Such a coincidence we may presume is due to some deep connexion in Nature between cosmology and atomic theory."[116]

The "anthropic" significance of this coincidence lies in the fact that the age of the universe is always changing. Therefore, our choice of the "present" epoch is clearly related to our own existence as observers.

In other words, the fundamental question at issue here centers around why the age of the universe in nuclear units should be related numerically to both the number of particles in the universe and to the relative strengths of gravity and electromagnetism. Dirac attempted to explain this remarkable coincidence by suggesting that perhaps the gravitational constant G may not really be a constant at all, but may always be changing, so that the strength of the gravitational constant will *always* be related to the overall age of the universe and to the overall number of particles in existence. There is, however, no evidence whatsoever that the value of G has ever varied from its present value throughout the entire history of the cosmos.

In 1961, the American physicist Robert Dicke proposed a novel solution for this cosmological curiosity which has the further distinction of being one of the first attempts to employ anthropic-type thinking to explain an otherwise inexplicable problem. Dicke reasoned that the present cosmic epoch is itself intimately related to those larger cosmic processes that are themselves necessary for the existence of life. We know, for instance, that carbon-based life forms can only exist in a universe that is at least as old as one stellar generation, because carbon and the other heavy elements upon which life depends are actually *formed* within dying stars. Hence, we *can't help* but observe the present universal age, because it is the only one (within a few orders of magnitude) that is consistent with our own existence as observers. The present universal age, in turn, determines the number of particles that we can detect in the observable universe, due to the ongoing expansion of the universe and the subsequent widening of the particle horizon.[117] Hence, the number of particles in the observable universe is in fact related to the age of the universe, which itself is determined by the necessity that it be consistent with our own existence as observers.

Furthermore, the ratio of the electrical force to the gravitational force inside the hydrogen atom has a direct influence on the lifetime of stars.[118] This in turn is related to the present age of the universe, which is approximately equal to the lifetime of a typical star (due to the need for carbon, which is dispersed into space when dying red giant stars explode as supernovae). Hence, all three aspects of Dirac's large number coincidence—the present age of the universe, the relative strengths of gravity and electromagnetism, and the number of particles in the visible universe—can be "explained" by the requirement that they be consistent with our own existence as observers.

The significance of Dicke's explanation lies in the fact that "a *biological* explanation of a fundamental feature of our world has succeeded where theoretical *physics* has failed."[119] Although Dicke was unable to explain all the large number coincidences, he nevertheless succeeded in showing that the existence of life on Earth cannot be considered to be unrelated to the structure of the universe as a whole.

4.28 The Importance of Three Spatial Dimensions for the Evolution of Life

Another anthropically oriented area of inquiry involves the relationship of life to the existence of three spatial dimensions. As it turns out, life as we know it could not have evolved if space possessed a greater or lesser number of spatial dimensions.[120]

To begin with, three dimensions appear to be necessary for a sufficiently complex neural network, which in turn is a vital prerequisite for the evolution of intelligent life. The human brain, for instance, consists of trillions of neurons which are themselves interconnected in thousands of different ways. The end result of this complex network is a nervous system that is sufficiently complex to support the existence of intelligent life. However, had space possessed only two spatial dimensions, these complex neural interconnections would have been impossible, because any two non-parallel connections would have automatically crossed one another, thereby ruining the connection. This is what happens to a limited extent in multiple sclerosis; the loss of the important nerve-insulating substance known as myelin causes a tremendous confusion of nerve signals in the brain, with the result that decisive physical motion becomes next to impossible.

Three dimensions are also required for proper blood flow, for had space possessed only two dimensions, venous blood would have invariably become intermingled with arterial blood, with catastrophic results for the body. It is clear, then, that the existence of three spatial dimensions is absolutely mandatory for the proper functioning of both our minds and our bodies.

But what about four spatial dimensions? Although it is impossible to visualize the existence of four spatial dimensions (neglecting time, of course, which is often said to represent the fourth dimension), we can analyze the characteristics of a four-dimensional world using mathematics. While such a world might very well enable the neurons in our brains to be interconnected more effectively, we nevertheless would never be able to survive long enough to benefit from it, since the stability of our planet's orbit about the Sun is absolutely dependent on the existence of precisely three spatial dimensions.

Stability in this case can be defined as the resistance of the Earth to any increase in the Sun's gravitational attraction whenever the Earth's orbit, which is not perfectly circular, brings it closer to the Sun. This kind of orbital stability is also important when we consider the tremendous number of wandering objects in space that could possibly smash into the Earth with sufficient force to disturb its orbital integrity. A number of such objects (usually meteors) are known to have struck our world in the distant past. Each released cataclysmic amounts of energy that easily could have jolted the Earth out of its orbit about the Sun if the Earth's orbit were significantly less stable.

Indeed, had this actually been the case, even a relatively small perturbation from without would have pushed the Earth either closer to, or further away from, the Sun (depending on where the object would have struck our planet relative to the Earth's orbital trajectory). Had this occurred, the Earth would have been unable to compensate for the Sun's rapidly changing gravitational effects, with tragic consequences. The result would have been a highly volatile orbital period that would have become increasingly susceptible to further change. This in turn would have resulted in wildly fluctuating surface temperatures and weather patterns on the Earth, since our stable ecosystem is absolutely dependent on our being a relatively fixed distance from the Sun at all times, as we have seen. At best, life would have been exceedingly difficult and tenous in such a world; at worst, the possibility for life would have altogether been lost.

Significantly, it is possible to show that each increase in the spatial dimensionality of the universe above a single dimension reduces the overall stability of the Earth in its orbit about the Sun.[121] In a universe of only one dimension, for instance, orbits would have been extremely stable, due to the fact that the Sun's gravitational lines of force would have all been oriented in a straight line; this lack of spatial concentration would have kept the Sun's gravitational field constant no matter how close our planet came to it. This in turn would have greatly contributed to the stability of the Earth's orbit, since any movement of the Earth toward or away from the Sun wouldn't have altered the strength of the Sun's gravitational attraction. Similarly, in a two-dimensional universe, while the Sun's gravitational lines of force would have been more concentrated than in a one-dimensional universe, they still wouldn't have increased sufficiently to endanger the stability of the Earth's orbit. In our three-dimensional universe, however, the Sun's gravitational lines of force emanate out from it in all three spatial dimensions, producing a much more concentrated gravitational force the closer one draws to the

Sun. While this has the inevitable effect of reducing the stability of the Earth's orbit even further, it is still stable enough to have survived intact for billions of years.

At the same time, though, it is apparent from the above progression that each increase in spatial dimensionality necessarily brings with it a corresponding reduction in the Earth's capacity for a stable orbit. This being the case, three is the maximum number of spatial dimensions that would allow for the existence of stable orbits. As a consequence, any proposed increase to four spatial dimensions would render the Earth completely unstable in its yearly orbital trek about the Sun. This in turn would make the evolution of life impossible, because it would destroy the capacity of the Earth to remain in a stable orbit about the Sun. As Barrow and Tipler conclude:

> If hundreds of millions of years in stable orbit around the Sun are necessary for planetary life to develop then such life could only develop in a three-dimensional world.[122]

Interestingly, Newton's Inverse Square Law, which measures the rate at which the attraction between two gravitating bodies decreases as the distance between them increases, is itself dependent on the existence of precisely three spatial dimensions.[123] This observation becomes all the more remarkable when one realizes that the numerical relation exemplified by the Inverse Square Law is not free to vary in any way if the purpose of the universe is to evolve life. As William Paley demonstrated in 1802, had the force of gravity varied by some other relation besides the Inverse Square Law, stable gravitational patterns themselves would have been impossible, both on an intergalactic as well as a solar level. Barrow and Tipler have confirmed Paley's original observation by pointing out that the inverse Square Law:

> is unique in that it allows the local gravitational field within . . . [any given] . . . spherical region to be evaluated independently of the structure of the entire universe beyond its outer boundary. Without this remarkable safeguard our local world would be at the mercy of changes in the gravitational field far away across our galaxy and beyond.[124]

Paley's original conclusions about the Inverse Square Law seem to have been vindicated after all. It does indeed seem to signify a Higher Source of Intelligent Contrivance in the universe, the result of which has been the long-term stability of the Earth's orbit about the Sun. But even if one refuses to make such a large "leap of fact," one thing cannot be denied: had the Inverse Square Law occupied any other value, the structure of our world and universe would have been so different that life as we know it would have never been able to evolve.

Another area in which the tri-dimensionality of the universe directly impacts upon the possibility for biological life is in the existence of a stable chemistry. As Barrow and Tipler point out, matter can only be stable if the ground state energy of an atom is finite.[125] Quantum theorists have traditionally assumed that this stability was provided by the Heisenberg Uncertainty Principle, insofar as it seems to ensure, by virtue of its inherent indeterminancy, a finite energy to the ground state of an atom.[126] Interestingly enough, however, this assumption turns out to be false, for "it is, in principle, possible for the electron to be distributed in a number of widely separated wave packets. The packet close to the nucleus could then have an arbitrarily sharp momentum and position specification at the expense of huge uncertainty in the other packets. In this manner the ground-state energy might be made arbitrarily negative."[127]

In order to supply the required bound on this ground-state energy, a "much stronger, *non-linear* constraint is required in addition to the Heisenberg Uncertainty Principle."[128] As it turns out, the non-linear Sobolev inequality is capable of supplying this required bound; however—and this is the important point—this inequality is only possible in less than four spatial dimensions.[129] These results have been confirmed by a number of technical analyses, most notably those performed by Ehrenfest,[130] Buchel,[131] Tangherlini,[132] and Gurevich and Mostapenenko.[133]

The upshot of these technical analyses is that stable electron orbits are only possible in three spatial dimensions.[134] From this crucial observation Barrow and Tipler conclude that "the [present] dimensionality of the universe is a reason for the existence of chemistry and therefore, most probably, for chemists also."[135]

Still another area in which the dimensionality of the universe impacts upon the possibility for biological life concerns the unique physical requirements for the transmission of electromagnetic wave phenomena, upon which life so intimately depends. It has repeatedly been shown that the properties of electromagnetic wave equations are strongly related to the number of spatial dimensions.[136] In fact, stable information-processing and signal propagation are only possible in a universe of precisely three spatial dimensions, because of the unique physical properties that a tri-dimensional universe happens to possess.[137]

More specifically, calculations have shown that signal reverberation inevitably occurs in two-dimensional spaces, which means that signals emitted at different times can nevertheless be received simultaneously.[138] Furthermore, it has been shown that transmission of wave impulses in a distortion-free manner is impossible in regions with an even number of spatial dimensions.[139] Accordingly, many authors have come to the conclusion that life:

[can] only exist in an odd-dimensional world because living organisms

require high-fidelity information transmission at a neurological or mechanical level . . . Only three-dimensional worlds appear to possess the "nice" properties necessary for the transmission of high-fidelity signals because of the simultaneous realization of sharp and distortionless propagation.[140]

The upshot of these momentous observations is that if living organisms require high-fidelity wave transmissions for their existence, we couldn't possibly observe anything *but* a tri-dimensional universe.[141]

On a more remote level, Barrow and Tipler have also demonstrated that axial vector representations of such things as magnetic vectors and electromagnetic fields are intimately related to the tri-dimensionality of space as well.[142] The reason for this has to do with the geometrical observation that only those universes with three spatial dimensions possess a unique correspondence between rotational and translational degrees of freedom.[143] While this bit of scientific understanding may be largely inaccessible to the average reader, the final conclusion is the same: life as we know it is only possible in a world of precisely three spatial dimensions.

In summary, the tri-dimensionality of our universe is a mandatory precondition for the existence of biological life for the following reasons:

1. Planetary orbits are only stable in less than four spatial dimensions.
2. Electron orbits about the nucleus are only stable in less than four spatial dimensions.
3. Complex neural and vascular routings are only possible in greater than two spatial dimensions.
4. The Inverse Square Law is a direct consequence of tri-dimensionality.
5. Sharp, distortion-free electromagnetic wave propagation is only possible in three spatial dimensions.
6. Three spatial dimensions are necessary in order to provide an important geometrical correspondence between rotational and translational degrees of freedom, which in turn is necessary for the vector representations of magnetic vectors and electromagnetic fields.

Given these six crucial ties between tri-dimensionality and the existence of life, we now need to ask ourselves the following question: is it credible to believe that our present universe occupies precisely three spatial dimensions by chance alone?[144] The existence of so many other evidences of Intelligent Design in the universe would seem to make this a vanishingly small possibility.

Again, it is the complex, life-facilitating coordination between such a large number of independent "coincidences" that is the dead giveaway here. It simply does not appear to be credible to suppose that each of these "coincidences" could have just happened to possess precisely the right character and structure in relation to all the others to accidentally facilitate the production of biological life. Just as one would never expect to find 1000 separate mechanical structures of unrelated origin that just happened to work together to produce a jet airplane, one would also never expect to find a multitude of life-facilitating cosmic "coincidences" without there being a common origin to them as well.

Moreover, since we are talking here about the complete foundation of physical reality itself, which apparently has remained constant from the very beginning, we cannot appeal to the vacuous concept of natural selection to explain the genesis of this miraculous interlocking design. All the evidence accumulated thus far indicates that this physical foundation has possessed an optimal, life-supporting character from the very beginning. With this in mind, the challenge is now to come up with a suitable explanation for how this could have been the case. Since it is inconceivable that chance processes alone could have accomplished this instantaneous feat (due to the unavailability of natural selection at the Big Bang), we are compelled to resort to a coercive universal power that would have been capable of creating things correctly from the very start. Only one Possibility seems to suggest itself in this capacity.

Indeed, it doesn't simply strain credulity to believe otherwise; it is positively irrational to do so. While it may be possible to devise elaborate theoretical schemes to "explain" how these life-facilitating "coincidences" could have occurred solely by chance, such a view is profoundly counter-intuitive.

To borrow the useful idea of a "hard-core commonsense notion" from David Griffin—which is simply any idea that all people presuppose in practice, even if they verbally deny it—we all tend to unconsciously assume a common origin behind the independent parts of any functional mechanism in the world. This assumption is so deep that it can legitimately be called a hard-core commonsense notion, which all rational people presuppose in practice, even if they choose to verbally deny it.[145] It is this hard-core commonsense belief in the principles of holism that explains why no one in his right mind would question the common origin to the complete misfiring of 100 rifles during an execution. In the same way, it is very difficult to question the proposition that the many life-facilitating "coincidences" discussed in this chapter must have had some form of common origin. Their complex interaction towards a single functional goal would seem to make this a self-evident proposition.

The only possible retort to this argument is that the universe is not a thing in the same way that a fish or a river is a thing; it is a collection of things. It is therefore possible for certain principles to apply to self-contained things within the universe, but not to the entire universe itself. For instance, all members of a football team may have fathers, but this doesn't mean that the football team itself has a father.

At the same time, though, it would be a mistake to conclude that no analogies at all can be drawn from self-contained objects within the universe to the entire universe itself. Some analogies of this type are probably legitimate, while others are probably not. We simply must be judicious in our choice of analogies. Indeed, the very practice of cosmology itself is based on the universality of certain physical principles which *necessarily* must be studied piecemeal. One of these universal principles seems to be the supposition of a common origin behind the component parts of all complex functional mechanisms.

4.29 The Existence of Order *vis-à-vis* the Second Law of Thermodynamics

The Second Law of Thermodynamics—which basically says that the overall entropy or disorder of any closed system always increases—is one of the most firmly established laws in all of science. As Sir Arthur Eddington has pointed out:

> The law that entropy always increases—the Second Law of Thermodynamics—holds, I think, the supreme position among the laws of Nature. If someone points out to you that your pet theory of the universe is in disagreement with Maxwell's equations—then so much the worse for Maxwell's equations. If it is found to be contradicted by observation—well, these experimentalists do bungle things sometimes. But if your theory is found to be against the Second Law of thermodynamics I can give you no hope; there is nothing for it but to collapse in deepest humiliation.[146]

Given the universal validity of the Second Law of Thermodynamics, it is nothing short of remarkable that the universe began in a state of minimum entropy (i.e., disorder). Since the number of disordered states vastly exceeds the number of ordered states, we would expect on the basis of all the known laws of probability for the universe to have begun in a state of relative disorder. Yet, we know that this was most definitely *not* the case, because a state of minimum entropy at the beginning of time is a necessary condition for our own existence, since order can only arise in a relatively non-entropic system.

Once again, though, we cannot use the WAP to fully account for why the universe began in a relatively ordered state, because the fact that such a state is a necessary condition of our own existence does not *in itself* explain why it actually obtained in the first place. Something larger is needed to explain this apparent contrivance.

One of the major implications of the Second Law is that the universe is steadily winding down towards a future "Heat Death," in which the randomness and disorder of the universe will be at a maximum. This in turn will leave the entire universe dead and cold, possibly forevermore.[147]

Given these bleak considerations for the future, it isn't surprising that many individuals question the overall prudence of the Second Law. After all, wouldn't a world in which one's house automatically cleaned itself be preferable to one in which dirtiness continually increased of its own accord? Moreover, who wants to look forward to the future thermodynamic suicide of the universe? In light of these considerations, it is hard to see much positive value to the Second Law.

As always, though, nature turns out to be wiser than her severest critics. For even here, the Second Law paradoxically turns out to be indispensible to our present world order. To his great credit, the French physicist Poincaré succeeded in showing that the existence of a universe where entropy tends to go up is actually a *prerequisite* for any type of meaningful action. For in a world where entropy regularly went down, it would be impossible to make any intelligent predictions regarding the future status of a given situation. Friction, for example, would be a destabilizing force rather than a dampening force, while the temperatures of initially uniform bodies would spontaneously change without rhyme or reason. In such a world it would be difficult or impossible to anticipate the immediate future with any degree of accuracy; hence intelligent behavior would be impossible. Paradoxically, then, the constant rise in disorder experienced in one mode of physical reality leads to a more ordered (predictable) state of affairs in another mode of reality (the realm of intelligent creaturely action).

This hidden functionality of the Law of Entropy shouldn't surprise us, since every physical parameter we have examined in this chapter has facilitated the existence of life in one way or another. It should only be surprising in a world where Intelligent Design is deemed to be nonexistent.

4.30 The Three Arrows of Time

The laws of science themselves do not distinguish between the past and future.[148] Yet, our perception of time is very real. We remember the past, experience the present, and anticipate the future. This in a nutshell is the psychological arrow of time.

Interestingly enough, two broad features of the present universal character happen to coincide with our subjective experience of time: the ongoing expansion of the universe and the thermodynamic trend towards greater disorder in the cosmos. These constitute the cosmological and thermodynamic arrows of time, respectively.

A major problem in cosmology centers around why these three arrows of time should all point in the same direction. In other words, why should it be the case that disorder happens to increase, and the universe happens to expand, in the same direction that we subjectively experience time to flow? The answer seems simple enough: if the three arrows of time were not pointing in the same direction, the existence of observers on this planet would be impossible.[149] Hence, we can't help but observe a universe in which the three arrows of time point in the same direction, because this is a necessary condition for our own existence. This is the Weak Anthropic Principle at its finest.

However, asserting that the present situation couldn't have been otherwise does nothing to explain how the three arrows of time could have come to point in the same direction in the first place. The WAP simply helps us to appreciate the existence of those physical parameters that turn out to be essential for our own existence as observers; it doesn't tell us where these optimal parameters themselves originally came from.

This brings us to the primary thesis of this book, which can be stated as the following: *God deliberately designed the various physical parameters of the universe in such a way as to ensure the evolution of life on this planet. In this context, the WAP simply amounts to a retroactive acknowledgement of the optimal nature of these physical parameters in terms of their overall facilitation of biological processes. As such, the WAP is actually a scientific "compliment" to the outstanding ingenuity of the Creator Himself, for His perfect choice of those physical parameters that have enabled us and all terrestrial life forms to exist.*

Seen in this context, God deliberately designed the three arrows of time to point in the same direction because this is an essential precondition for the existence of human observers. While it is possible to imagine that the three arrows of time might not all point in the same direction elsewhere in the universe (a possibility that is strongly disconfirmed by scientific observation), and that we were only able to evolve in a region where they do happen to coincide, this still begs the question of how these three arrows originally came to coincide in our region of the cosmos in the first place. Since chance processes alone do not seem capable of performing such a grandiose task (especially in light of all the other "coincidences" in nature), we find ourselves back at the concept of Intelligent Design once again.

Further support for this theistic explanation comes from the universal character of both the Hubble expansion and the Law of Entropy, which are two of the most well-supported principles in all of modern science. There isn't a shred of evidence indicating that either of these principles might have been different at other times and places in the universe. But if this is indeed the case, then both the Law of Entropy and the Hubble expansion have been true from the Big Bang onward, which means that *the entire universe* has possessed the "right" orientation for the three arrows of time from the very beginning. This in turn means that we can't appeal to a plurality of basic conditions in the universe to "explain" how our local life-supporting environment could have originally come about.

4.31 The Miracle of Carbon

Carbon is uniquely qualified to be the structural backbone upon which the biochemistry of life can be based. Being situated in the first row of the Periodic Table, carbon is able to form multiple bonds extensively with its four available outer level electrons. This gives it the structural flexibility that is so important in the building of complex biochemical structures which are essential for life.

Carbon is required in a wide range of biological processes. For instance, carbon is a major ingredient of carbon dioxide, which is one of the most important organic[150] compounds in the biosphere. Since carbon dioxide is both an essential nutrient for plant photosynthesis *and* one of the most important products of cellular respiration, it provides a continuously renewable form of energy that is completely recyclable. The importance of this one feature alone should not be underestimated, for it is what has enabled our world to remain viable for billions of years, in spite of the constant production of vast quantities of organic waste.[151]

Carbon dioxide is able to serve a variety of important biological roles because of its ingenious structural configuration, which enables it to experience very little attraction to other carbon dioxide molecules. This allows carbon dioxide to be a gas within the range of temperatures that can support biological life. This is important, because it allows carbon dioxide—which is the final waste product of animal metabolism—to be removed from the body quite easily.

Moreover, carbon dioxide is unique among all known compounds in the fact that its concentration in air is essentially the same as its concentration in water. This allows carbon dioxide to freely move from air to water and from water to air, another property that makes the removal of carbon dioxide from the body (via the blood) relatively easy.

Carbon dioxide also has the marvelous ability to be hydrated in the body to form carbonic acid, which can then break down to form carbonate and bicarbonate. This allows carbon dioxide to act as a powerful pH regulator within the body, since both bicarbonate and carbonate can neutralize excess acidity in the blood quite effectively.

Carbon dioxide's life-supporting role even extends beyond its many activities in supporting animal metabolism. As Barrow and Tipler point out, carbon dioxide also plays a critical role in maintaining the Earth's temperature within a range that is favorable for life. It is able to do this because it acts as a barrier to prevent heat from escaping from the Earth's surface. This "greenhouse effect" raises the Earth's surface temperature tens of degrees higher than it would have otherwise been.[152]

Some have argued that silicon, being positioned just below carbon on the

Periodic Table, could possibly have taken carbon's place as the backbone of organic chemistry. Recent work by Sidgwick and others[153] has shown, however, that this is unlikely. For one thing, silicon is unable to form double bonds like carbon can, and double bonds are absolutely essential to any form of complex biochemistry. Silicon compounds are also not nearly as stable over time as carbon compounds are. This unusual stability of carbon encourages the formation of long molecular chains, which play an important role in the maintenance of life.

Moreover, the heat of formation in carbon's various compounds is usually relatively small, which means that the amount of energy needed to promote a reaction between carbon and other elements is also typically quite small. This enables many carbon compounds to form spontaneously, a feature that is crucial to the spontaneous evolution of life as well as to the support and maintenance of normal body metabolism.

Carbon is also blessed with the ability to store a maximal amount of information in its various compounds, due to its capacity to form a wider variety of compounds than almost any other element. As Barrow and Tipler point out, it is the information-carrying capacity of living systems, which is made possible by this unique property of carbon, that qualifies them as "living"; as a consequence, carbon compounds are now recognized to be "uniquely fitted to serve as the basis of life."[154]

One more point about carbon deserves mention before we move on. Even if carbon is not absolutely necessary to produce life, as some theorists like to believe, a universe very much like our own *still* has to exist before this alternative kind of life could possibly come into being. This is because some type of heavy element seems to be absolutely required before *any* kind of physical life[155] can evolve; life forms comprised solely of hydrogen and/or helium seem to be intrinsically impossible. But if this is so, then a universe containing these non-carbon-based life forms would *still* have to be about the same size, age, and overall configuration as our present universe, since the same stellar-cooking process is required to produce *all* of the heavier elements.[156] Therefore, since a universe very much like our own seems to be required before *any* kind of physical life can exist, and since carbon seems to be uniquely capable of producing both the complexity and spontaneity that all life forms undoubtedly require, we can feel reasonably safe in concluding that if other physical life forms exist in the universe, they are probably carbon-based as well.

4.32   The Importance of Nitrogen, Sulfur, and Phosphorus in Biochemistry

Although carbon is vitally important in making a complex biochemistry possible, it is by no means unique in this capacity. Nitrogen also plays an extremely important role in the formation and sustenance of life, as it is a vital component both in the amino acids of which proteins are made, as well as in the nitrogenous bases which provide the genetic information that is contained in the DNA molecule. It is the unique structure of the nitrogen molecule that enables it to be utilized so effectively by both proteins and nucleic acids. No other element could possibly take its place, and indeed, if the molecular properties of nitrogen were only slightly different, proteins and nucleic acids could never have formed.

The same thing can be said of sulfur and phosphorous compounds, which are utilized extensively by the cellular machinery of the body to produce energy through the breaking of high energy bonds. Adenosine triphosphate, or ATP, is the central energy producer of the cell. It releases energy when its high-energy phosphate bonds are broken; this energy then goes into the driving of other important life-supporting reactions.

Interestingly enough, the cell is unable to directly utilize the energy that is produced when sugars are oxidized, because too much energy is typically produced to be directly utilized by the cell. However, by harnessing this energy in the form of high energy phosphate bonds (at a 66% rate of efficiency), it becomes much more available over the long term for the cell's constant energy needs.

Sulfur also forms high-energy bonds that the cell can make efficient use of. These high-energy sulfur bonds can be found in thiol esters, mixed anhydrides of phosphoric and sulfuric acids, and sulphonium compounds. Indeed, sulfur and phosphorus are the only elements on the Periodic Table that are able to form high-energy bonds in this manner, which again reveals a precise molecular economy in the structure and function of living tissue.

4.33 The Miraculousness of Water

Although the existence of ordinary water is indispensible for the sustenance of life, we all tend to take water for granted. After all, it is one of the most common and seemingly least mysterious substances known. We drink it, swim in it, bathe in it, and squirt it at each other without the slightest thought about its inner molecular qualities and how they enable life to exist.

From a molecular and biochemical standpoint, however, the various properties of water are nothing short of miraculous, as no other compound even comes close to duplicating its many life-supporting properties. Indeed, if it weren't for these unique and anomalous properties of water, life as we know it would be absolutely impossible.

The unique properties of water immediately set it apart from all other similar hydride compounds. For instance, if the boiling points of all compounds similar to water are graphed as a function of their atomic weight, a simple extrapolation to the expected boiling point of water would produce a temperature of -100 degrees Celsius.[157] This, of course, is 200 degrees *less* than the observed value of $+100$ degrees Celsius for water.

The significance of this observation lies in the fact that if water did not have such a high boiling point, life as we know it would be impossible. However, when we analyze the various water-like hydride compounds, we instantly see that water is an isolated and special substance that does *not* reflect the properties of other similar compounds, as we would expect if the realm of organic chemistry were not specifically designed by an Intelligent Creator. Thus, the anomalous character of water is seen to be related to its capacity to support life, and it is this relationship that seems to point in the direction of an Intelligent Designer.

Of course, there is a structural explanation for water's anomalously high boiling point: because of the asymmetrical way the water molecule is constructed between one oxygen atom and two hydrogen atoms, it is an electro-chemically unbalanced structure. This "polar" nature renders one side of the water molecule more electronegative while rendering the other side more electropositive. This electrochemical polarity enables the positive end of one water molecule to be attracted to the negative end of an adjacent molecule. It is this process of "hydrogen bonding" that produces such an anomalously high boiling point for water, since the additional attractive force between water molecules that is produced by hydrogen bonding must be overcome before the boiling point can be reached.

Again, though, just because we know the molecular explanation for water's high boiling point doesn't mean that we know *where* such an ingenious molecular structure could have originally come from. While we can always perform the ultimate philosophical cop-out and claim that the remarkable structure of water is merely the result of a spectacular cosmic accident, the additional life-supporting properties of water that we are about to discuss make this conclusion completely untenable.

For instance, water is the only known substance whose solid phase (ice) is less dense than its liquid phase. This is why ice floats in water. The reason for this strange anomaly again lies in the unique and peculiar nature of water's molecular structure. But as Barrow and Tipler[158] point out, we are indeed fortunate that this is the case, for if it weren't, our oceans and lakes would have eventually frozen over, since ice would have accumulated on the bottom of these bodies of water instead of the top, and hence would have failed to entirely melt away during the summer. Fortunately, however, ice is less dense than water, so it forms on the surface of lakes and oceans first, and this in turn protects the marine life below from additional cooling.

Now why should water stand alone in its possession of this most unusual feature? This is an intriguing question that seems to lead to the following conclusion: since this one anomalous feature is crucial to the well-being of the Earth's life-supporting environment, it seems to follow that it was somehow engineered with this important effect "in Mind." Although there is no way to prove this assertion, a commonsense interpretation of the facts would indeed seem to lead to this conclusion.

Water also has an unusually high specific heat, higher in fact than almost all other organic compounds. The specific heat of a substance is the amount of heat that is required to raise its temperature one degree Celsius. Having such a high specific heat enables water to retain heat longer, which in turn helps to stabilize the temperature of the global environment. The fact that water also has a higher thermal conductivity than the majority of other liquids also makes it an optimal temperature stabilizer for the environment as well.

As we have seen, water has the highest heat of vaporization (boiling point) of any known substance. This enables water to act as the most effective coolant by evaporation known to man. It is undoubtedly this unique feature of water that has enabled sweating to be used as the premier cooling mechanism in much of the animal kingdom. The marathon runner is indebted to this unique quality of water for enabling him to run for hours at a time without succumbing to heat stroke.

Water also has an unusually high surface tension, which causes compounds that can act to reduce this tension to congregate near the surface. This in turn enables biochemical reactions to proceed at a much faster rate than they otherwise would. Indeed, were it not for this one property of water, existing rates of metabolism in living creatures would be impossible to maintain for very long.

Another anomalous feature of water is its unusually high dielectric constant, which is a measure of a substance's ability to dissociate (i.e., dissolve) ionic compounds into their respective ions. It is water's anomalously high dielectric constant that enables it to dissolve salt and other ionic substances so easily.

Water's high dielectric constant also allows it to spontaneously ionize itself into its constituent hydrogen and hydroxide ions; indeed, at any one time, 10^{-7} water molecules are dissociated because of this constant. This effect is exceedingly important in biochemical reactions since it furnishes a ready supply of the hydrogen and hydroxide ions upon which so many reactions depend. This in turn has the effect of greatly speeding up reaction rates in living organisms.

Water molecules also exhibit an important characteristic known as the *hydrophobic* (i.e., water-repelling) effect, again because of water's unique molecular structure. It is this hydrophobic effect that gives water the unique ability to shape proteins and nucleic acids into their biologically active configurations. Without this shaping effect, the enzymes upon which biochemical life is built could not function properly, because their biochemical activity is directly elicited by their three-dimensional configurations in space.

Another important result of this hydrophobic effect is that it seems to have played an important role in the formation of cell walls and cell membranes. Water has the ability to cause the non-polar ends of molecules to aggregate together, which happens to be the first step in the formation of cell walls and membranes. Indeed, the very origin of life itself seems to have been dependent on this hydrophobic characteristic of water, since the initial primordial cell could not have formed without first having a cell wall to protect it and to differentiate it from the rest of the world.

Given the absolute dependence of life on the water molecule's many anomalous properties, where did the structure of the water molecule itself ultimately come from? Science itself is unable to provide an adequate answer to this question. However, since life is absolutely dependent on the many anomalous properties of water just discussed, and since water stands alone in this life-supporting capacity, it seems to follow that the water molecule was probably designed on purpose to be the medium through which life could evolve and sustain itself. The standard scientific texts of course don't come right out and say this because it would be considered "unscientific." An unbiased view of the facts, however, leads almost inescapably to this conclusion.

4.33.1 Discussion

If the world were merely the result of a mindless accident, one would never expect every known instance in the molecular realm to be supportive of biological life in some fashion, but this is precisely what we find to be the case in our present world. Every subatomic particle appears to be ingeniously designed to support the existence of life, not only on its own, but also in concert with the many other subatomic particles that go into the making of life.

Lawrence J. Henderson, who was a professor of biological chemistry at Harvard during the early 1900s, also came to the conclusion that the specific properties of physical matter seem to be a kind of teleological "preparation" for the existence of life. For Henderson, the traditional notion of chance as an explanatory mechanism for the existence of life was incompatible with the seemingly tailor-made properties of physical matter:

> The chance that this unique ensemble of properties should occur by "accident" is almost infinitely small. The chance that each of the unit properties of the ensemble, by itself and in cooperation with the others, should "accidentally" contribute a maximum increment is also almost infinitely small. Therefore there is a relevant causal connection between the properties of the elements and the "freedom" of evolution.[159]

Henderson went even further. He argued that the absolute dependence of biological life forms on the physical properties of matter is strongly indicative of the existence of a biocentric universe:

> The properties of matter and the course of cosmic evolution are now seen to be intimately related to the structure of the living being and to its activities; they become, therefore, far more important in biology than has previously been suspected. For the whole evolutionary process, both cosmic and organic, is one, and the biologist may now rightly regard the universe in its very essence as biocentric.[160]

These views, of course, are just a small step away from crediting God Himself for the creation of such an enormously complicated "biocentric" universe. This is all the more remarkable when we remind ourselves that Henderson was writing primarily from the perspective of a physical scientist, not that of a theologian or minister.

Indeed, given the many complex physical properties that are required by living systems, it is hard to escape the notion that atoms and molecules have the chemical properties they do because of the unique requirements of biological life. Atheistic scientists, however, simply believe that our particular type of matter just happened to exist in the universe purely by accident. On this view, biological life really had no choice but to utilize this type of matter in its evolution, since it was the only type that was thought to be in existence at the time. But what are the odds that undesigned atoms and molecules could have accidentally fulfilled all of the many complex requirements for life? If there were truly an accidental relationship at work here, we would perhaps expect that *some* of the properties of matter would have been sufficient for the development of life, but certainly not *all* of them. Since there nevertheless exists a more or less perfect correlation between the properties of physical matter and the needs of biological life, the only other possible non-theistic explanation is that life would have developed no matter what the properties of physical matter would have been. Although at first this may seem like a genuine possibility, even a cursory examination of the absolute specificity of life's biochemical needs shows that this is most definitely *not* the case; indeed, it is a well-known assumption in the scientific community that had the properties of matter been any different, life almost certainly would never have arisen. This would again appear to leave us with only one other Explanation to choose from.

4.34 A Tailor-Made World

In *Other Worlds* Paul Davies[161] examines the exceedingly delicate balance of our existence on the scales of chance and seems to come to the same sort of theistic conclusion (though he is much more subtle about it). Specifi-

cally, Davies cites seven essential prerequisites that must be satisfied if life
is to be able to exist on this planet:

1. There must be an adequate supply of the elements which comprise our
   bodies, such as carbon, oxygen, hydrogen, phosphorus, and calcium.
2. There must be little or no risk of contamination by other poisonous
   chemicals, such as would be found in an atmosphere containing methane or ammonia.
3. The climatic temperature must remain within the narrow range of 5 to
   40 degrees Celsius, which is a mere 2% of the temperature range found
   within the solar system as a whole.
4. A stable supply of free energy must exist, which in our case is provided
   by the Sun.
5. Gravity must be strong enough to keep the atmosphere from escaping
   into space, but it must also be weak enough to enable us to move
   freely about on the Earth's surface.
6. A protective screen must exist to filter out the Sun's harmful ultraviolet
   rays, which in our case is provided by a layer of ozone in the upper
   atmosphere.
7. A magnetic field must exist in order to prevent cosmic subatomic particles from raining on the Earth.

As we have seen, it is the propitious nature of the Earth's orbit about the
Sun that makes it an ideal place for the existence of biological life. However,
it isn't simply the Earth's average distance from the Sun that gives it such
a hospitable temperature range; the *shape* of the Earth's orbit about the Sun
also figures prominently in this determination as well.

As it stands now, the Earth's orbit about the Sun is nearly circular, varying by only a relatively small 3%.[162] In this respect the geometry of the
Earth's orbital trajectory is quite anomalous, since the orbits of most of the
other planets in our solar system are much more elliptical. Mars, for instance, varies in its distance from the Sun by a whopping 50 million kilometers, as compared to a variance of only 4.5 million kilometers for the
Earth.[163] If the Earth's orbital trajectory were to experience this degree of
variance, everything on the surface of the Earth would be incinerated once
a year (during January, when the Earth is closest to the Sun). Indeed, as
Schroeder points out, if our distance from the Sun were only 7% less, the
atmosphere would be so hot that water vapor would be incapable of condens-
ing.[164] Oceans, lakes, and rivers would be nonexistent in such a world, as
would life itself.

In order to be capable of supporting biological life, then, the Earth must
be close enough to the Sun to be bathed in sufficient warmth, yet it can't be
too close, otherwise it will be bombarded with an excessive amount of life-

destroying ultraviolent (uv) radiation from the Sun.[165] Indeed, even at its current distance from the Sun, too much uv radiation exists to allow for the flourishing of life without an additional means of protection. Fortunately for Earth-based life, this extra protection exists in the form of an ozone layer high in the atmosphere.

Other forms of deadly cosmic radiation are deflected from the surface of the Earth by the Earth's powerful magnetic field, which is generated by the motion of molten iron deep in our planet's seething radioactive interior. A precise balance of this radioactivity is absolutely essential if life is to be capable of surviving here.[166] On the one hand, it is the heat generated by this radioactivity which is ultimately reponsible for producing the Earth's magnetic field (by causing the Earth's iron core to remain fluid enough to flow). On the other hand, an excessive amount of radioactiviy would render the surface of the Earth uninhabitable, as it was some 4 billion years ago.

The degree of volcanic activity on the Earth is also vitally important for the evolution of life.[167] Too little volcanic activity, and there wouldn't have been enough water liberated by volcanic explosions to fill the world's oceans, lakes, and rivers. (Liquid water is thought to have originated when water dissolved in molten rock escaped into the atmosphere in the form of steam during volcanic eruptions.)

Volcanoes are also known to be an important factor in the maintenance of suitable climactic temperatures for life, through the much-talked-about greenhouse effect. Volcanoes are now recognized[168] to be a significant source of atmospheric carbon dioxide, which is an important greenhouse gas (since it enables the Earth's atmosphere to trap sufficient quantities of solar radiation to significantly increase surface temperatures). Without this additional input of carbon dioxide from volcanoes, there probably wouldn't have been enough carbon dioxide in the Earth's atmosphere to maintain a life-supporting range of environnmental temperatures.

Too much volcanic activity, on the other hand, and the Earth's surface would have been too violent and unstable to support the gradual evolution of life; it would also have caused the Earth's atmosphere to be so dark and sooty that a nuclear-type winter would have ensued.

A similar degree of balance exists in the amount of seismic activity found on Earth. A certain amount must exist so that nutrients that have been channeled to ocean floors through river runoff can be recycled to the continents through a phenomenon known as tectonic uplift.[169] Yet, too much seismic activity would spell catastrophe for many forms of life, so it appears as though the Earth possesses just the right degree of seismic activity to make it a viable place for biological habitation.

Hugh Ross documents the existence of several other finely-tuned parameters which strictly limit the capacity of our planet to support life. For instance, if our solar system contained more than one star (which many systems do), tidal effects would severely disrupt the Earth's orbit, rendering it either too hot or too cold to support life.[170]

The Sun's date of birth and overall age are also intimately related to the Earth's capacity to support life. If the Sun were significantly younger, it wouldn't have had time to reach a stable burning phase, which means that its luminosity would have been subject to a life-devastating change in the future. On the other hand, if the Sun were significantly older, its luminosity would have either been subject to changing too quickly, or else it would have been in danger of running out of fuel and completely burning out.[171] Indeed, Brandon Carter has shown that the lifetime of G-type stars like our Sun provides a clearly defined upper bound on the length of time life can evolve on a planet.

The strength of the Earth's surface gravity, which is in turn directly related to the Earth's size and mass, is also very finely balanced between two competing extremes. On the one hand, the Earth must be sufficiently large to ensure that a life-supporting atmosphere of oxygen, nitrogen, carbon dioxide, and water vapor is gravitationally bound to the surface of the planet.[172] On the other hand, the Earth mustn't be too large, because the resulting increase in the pull of gravity would have caused the atmosphere to retain too much poisonous ammonia and methane to have been conducive to life.[173] It also would have generated destructive tidal effects in living bodies.[174] Moreover, a significantly larger Earth would have generated too much internal heat to have been compatible with the fragile needs of life.[175]

The Earth's degree of axial tilt is also an important part of the biocentric equation, for if it were greater or less, the Earth's surface temperature differences would have been too extreme to support the existence of life.[176]

Similarly, the Earth's period of rotation is also subject to a strict upper and lower bound if it is to be hospitable to life. A longer rotational period would have generated diurnal temperature differences that would have been too great for life, whereas a shorter rotational period would have caused atmospheric wind velocities to be too extreme.[177]

The Earth's gravitational interaction with the Moon is also very delicately balanced as far as life is concerned. If it were any greater, the resulting tidal effects on the Earth's atmosphere, oceans, and rotational period would have been too great for the fragile needs of life. Yet, if it were less, orbital obliquity changes would have caused severe climatic instabilities throughout the Earth's various ecosystems.[178]

Even the thickness of the Earth's crust is related to its capacity for supporting life. A thicker crust would have caused too much oxygen to be transferred from the atmosphere to the crust, whereas a thinner crust would have caused volcanic and tectonic activity to be too frequent and too violent for the fragile needs of living organisms.[179]

The albedo parameter—which compares the amount of light reflected off the Earth to the amount falling on the Earth's surface—is also vitally important for the needs of life. If it were much greater, a runaway ice age would have developed in the past, but if it were much less, a runaway greenhouse effect would have occurred.[180] Either way, life would have probably never evolved here.

The oxygen to nitrogen ratio in the atmosphere is also important for life, for had it been much greater, advanced life functions would have transpired too quickly. On the other hand, had it been much less, these same biochemical functions would have transpired too slowly.[181]

A similar degree of balance exists in the combined amount of carbon dioxide and water vapor in the atmosphere. If it were much greater, a runaway greenhouse effect would have developed sometime in the past, but if it were much less, there wouldn't have been *enough* of a greenhouse effect to keep our planet sufficiently warm for the evolution of life.[182]

The amount of oxygen in the atmosphere also appears to be optimal for the existence of life. Had it been much greater, plants and other combustible materials would have burned too easily, but had it been less, animals wouldn't have had enough oxygen to breathe.[183]

The same thing can be said of the amount of ozone in the atmosphere. Had it been much greater, the Earth's surface temperature would have been too low. On the other hand, had it been significantly less, the Earth's surface temperature would have been too high, and there would have been too much harmful ultraviolet radiation at the surface.[184]

Even the atmospheric discharge rate appears to have been fine-tuned for the benefit of life. Had it been any greater, terrestrial fires would have started much too easily. Yet, had it been significantly less, an insufficient quantity of nitrogen would have been fixed in the atmosphere to have been conducive to life.[185]

And then there are the extraordinarily complex recycling mechanisms that the Earth uses to convert waste products into usable forms of matter and energy. Thousands of exceedingly complex structures and mechanisms are known to cooperate with one another so that no unrecyclable forms of waste are ever produced anywhere in the world (except by man). This has enabled the Earth to be maintained in its precious life-supporting mode for thousands of millions of years.

4.34.1 The WAP and Natural Complexity

The one thing we should strive to keep in mind when pondering these life-supporting parameters is that they are all composite entities comprised of many smaller functional constituents, which cooperate *together* to form a given parameter. Hence, each of these life-supporting parameters is actually comprised of the cooperative influence of a great many independent factors, which conspire together to make life possible.

The point is simply that the level of design that is actually operating to make our world a habitable place is so staggering that it almost completely transcends our capacity to understand it. Yet many informed minds continue to believe that it is nothing more than a grand cosmic accident.

Of course, given the fact of life's existence, it is *necessarily the case* that these essential prerequisites for life *must* exist. It is important to remember, though, that we aren't referring here to an *a posteriori* commentary on the life-supporting capacity of our planet *per se*, which from this point of view isn't so remarkable; rather, we are referring to the original *generation* of these life-supporting prerequisites themselves, which by all accounts *is* astonishing.

One of the most popular ways to account for the genesis of these life-supporting parameters has been to use the WAP to argue for the existence of a multiplicity of worlds throughout the cosmos, in which the surface conditions vary on a smooth continuum. In such a widely varying universe life would only arise on those worlds that happened to possess the proper conditions.

The problem with this conception is twofold: 1) There is no good evidence indicating that such a smooth variance in surface conditions actually exists from world to world, and 2) It fails to consider the deeper questions of *how* and *why* the surface conditions on *any* planet ever originally came to occupy the proper life-facilitating conditions against all the odds.

The truth of the matter is that a certain small percentage of worlds out there *could* in fact be capable of supporting[186] biological life, but this wouldn't necessarily mean that these worlds had evolved by chance. A Cosmic Designer could have deliberately created such a cosmopolitan universe for His own purposes, and indeed several Biblical verses seem to hint at this tantalizing possibility.

In traditional theism it was assumed that God deliberately designed the Earth's environment in such a way as to make life possible. Today science has found such a deep balance and coordination in nature that many are once again turning to the God of traditional theism as the most probable explanation for it, not in response to blind religious devotion, but in response to a *rational compulsion* induced by the scientific facts themselves. As Davies points out:

> Considering that the universe is full of violence and cataclysms, our own little corner of the cosmos enjoys a benign tranquility. To those who believe that God made the world for mankind, it must seem that all these conditions are in no way a random or haphazard arrangement of circumstances,

but reflect a carefully prepared environment in which humans can live comfortably, a pre-ordained ecosystem into which life slots naturally and inevitably—a tailor-made world.[187]

4.35 The Rapidity of Life's Evolution

According to the non-theistic evolutionist, life was only able to evolve on this planet after a long series of chance molecular combinations happened to eventually produce the right organization for life. This assumption is based on the belief that the trial-and-error interworkings of a vast number of molecules will eventually produce a living cell. Like a thief who tries to open a lock by going through all possible numerical combinations, the non-theistic evolutionist believes that life was only able to evolve when its molecular constituents happened to stumble upon the right combination after a vast number of trial-and-error interactions.

Such a vast number of trial-and-error interactions of course requires an enormous amount of time in which to occur. The incredible complexity of even the "simplest" living cell means that many billions of years had to have been necessary to enable such a complex combination to come about by chance (if indeed life could have *ever* formed in this random manner).

The historical fact of life's evolution, however, strongly disconfirms this non-theistic prediction: instead of taking billions of years to evolve, the first living cell came into being just as soon as the cooling Earth could possibly support it.[188] This is perhaps the most significant "coincidence" of them all, and it is very much at odds with the predictions of non-theistic evolutionary theory. For if life evolved just as soon as it possibly could, then chance processes, which inherently take vast amounts of time, could never have produced it.[189] If, on the other hand, the universe was Intelligently Designed, we would naturally expect life to have evolved just as soon as it possibly could have. Since this is precisely what happened, the theistic explanation for the origin of life is to be preferred over the non-theistic explanation, since it is the one that is most consistent with the available evidence.

The non-theistic evolutionist, of course, is at a complete loss to explain how life could have evolved so quickly. Since random concatenations of order inherently take vast amounts of time, he cannot fall back on the incoherent "cosmic accident hypothesis" to explain the origin of life, so he really has little choice but to "abandon ship" and look for a better solution. The only other plausible solution, however, is the theistic one, which states that a Supernatural Intelligence designed the universe on purpose so that it could support biological life. On this theistic view, it was the great efficacy of God's Design that enabled life to evolve just as soon as it possibly could.

4.36   The Relative Size of the Human Body in the Universal Hierarchy of Objects

The final cosmic "coincidence" we are going to discuss in this chapter has to with the relative size of the human body (and to a greater or lesser extent, the relative sizes of all other mammalian life forms as well) in the cosmic hierarchy of objects. In order to make this determination, we are going to make use of a physical relation called called the *geometric mean*, which is used to compare objects of widely varying size. It is obtained by first multiplying the lengths or diameters of the objects being compared and then taking the square root of the product.

As it turns out, the size of a human being is the geometric mean between the size of a planet and the size of an atom, while the size of a planet is the geometric mean between the size of an atom and the size of the entire universe.[190] This seems to place humanity squarely in the middle of the cosmic hierarchy of objects. And, as if this weren't enough, astrophysicists also tell us that human life appeared on the Earth at approximately the halfway point in our Sun's life cycle.

Of course, there is no way to tell for sure whether this is a genuine coincidence (and therefore the product of mere chance) or whether it reveals the actual creative purpose of God Himself. Even so, one can't help but feel a nagging sense of suspicion about this intriguing relation, especially when it is considered alongside the other things we know about humanity.

In other words, could it be a mere coincidence that the most sophisticated and complex objects we know of in the entire universe (namely ourselves) happen to be poised midway between the smallest known compound objects (i.e., atoms) and the single largest known macroscopic object (i.e., the entire universe)? Could it also be a coincidence that we just happened to make our appearance at approximately the halfway point in our Sun's life cycle? Common sense dictates that there is probably more going on here than just a happy accident.

Notes

1. Since we can never prove for an absolute certainty that matter was created *ex nihilo* at the Big Bang, there is always the possibility that matter in some form could have existed prior to the formation of the present universe.
2. One of the greatest mysteries in all of science has to do with how matter originally came to possess the miraculous property of self-organization. This capacity for self-organization is itself a function of the internal structural characteristics of the atomic and subatomic particles themselves, so the question reduces to the following: how did matter originally come to acquire those precise structural characteristics that have enabled it to organize itself into the phenomenon of biological life? As we shall see a bit later, it is exceedingly difficult to account for these fundamental characteristics in the absence of a larger Designer.

3. See Barrow and Tipler's discussion of this important topic in *The Anthropic Cosmological Principle*, pp. 440–444.

4. Although it is conceivable that our present-day scientific laws and equations didn't apply during the initial period of cosmic evolution, there is no evidence whatsoever that this was ever actually the case following the Planck time of 10^{-43} seconds. Indeed, the entire science of cosmology is based on the well-founded assumption that our present-day laws and equations *do* in fact apply everywhere and everywhen in the universe following Planck's impenetrable Wall.

5. John D. Barrow, *Theories of Everything* (Oxford: Oxford University Press, 1991), pp. 133–134.

6. George Greenstein, *The Symbiotic Universe* (New York: William Morrow, 1988), pp. 143–148.

7. I am jumping the gun a bit by mentioning the relationship of the cosmos to our own existence, because the evidence presented in this chapter at best only supports a general doctrine of contrivance in the universe; an entirely different set of arguments is needed to establish that humans were the central goal of the creation. Even so, it is still a good deal easier to show that the universe was contrived using humanity as our central reference point instead of life in general.

8. Barrow and Tipler, pp. 376–379.

9. Although there is a sense in which *any* possible value for the amount of matter in the universe is highly unlikely, I am using the stipulation that life should be able to evolve as my primary reference point in making this evaluation.

10. Stephen Hawking, *A Brief History of Time*, pp. 121–122.

11. P.C.W. Davies, *The Accidental Universe*, p. 90.

12. Ibid.

13. John Gribbin and Martin Rees, *Cosmic Coincidences* (New York: Bantam Books, 1989), p. 26.

14. Greenstein, *The Symbiotic Universe*, pp. 134–135.

15. Ibid., p. 135.

16. Ibid.

17. John Gribbin, *The Omega Point*, (New York: Bantam Books, 1988), p. 43.

18. George Greenstein, *The Symbiotic Universe*, p. 27.

19. Ibid., p. 28.

20. John Gribbin and Martin Rees, *Cosmic Coincidences*, p. 53.

21. John Gribbin, *The Omega Point,* pp. 139–140.

22. James Trefil, *The Dark Side of the Universe* (New York: Doubleday, 1988), pp. 90–91.

23. Sam Flamsteed, "Probing the Edge of the Universe," *Discover*, Vol. 12, No. 7, July, 1991, pp. 43–47.

24. James Trefil, *The Dark Side of the Universe,* pp. 60–62.

25. Corey S. Powell, "The Golden Age of Cosmology," *Scientific American,* Vol. 267, No. 1, July, 1992, pp. 17–22.

26. Ibid.

27. Gribbin and Rees, *Cosmic Coincidences,* pp. 175–201.

28. Ibid., pp. 92–93.

29. Ibid.

30. Bertrand Russell, *Religion and Science* (New York: Oxford University Press, 1968), p. 216.

31. Barrow and Tipler, p. 384.

32. Quoted in Barrow and Tipler, p. 169.
33. George Greenstein, *The Symbiotic Universe*, pp. 18–21.
34. Gerald L. Schroeder, *Genesis and the Big Bang*, pp. 119–120.
35. Steven W. Stahler, "The Early Life of Stars," *Scientific American*, Vol. 265, No. 1, 1991, p. 51.
36. Paul Davies, *The Accidental Universe* (New York: Cambridge University Press, 1982), p. 61.
37. Ibid., pp. 61–62.
38. Ibid., pp. 62–64.
39. Ibid., pp. 63–64.
40. Hugh Ross, *The Fingerprint of God*, p. 123.
41. Ibid.
42. Greenstein, *The Symbiotic Universe*, pp. 64–65.
43. Ross, *The Fingerprint of God*, p. 123.
44. Barrow and Tipler, *The Anthropic Cosmological Principle*, p. 303.
45. Ibid., p. 305.
46. Hugh Ross, *The Fingerprint of God*, p. 125.
47. Davies, *The Accidental Universe*, p. 107.
48. Ibid., p. 73.
49. Ibid.
50. Ross, *The Fingerprint of God*, p. 122.
51. Ibid.
52. Greenstein, *The Symbiotic Universe*, p. 101.
53. Ross, *The Fingerprint of God*, p. 121.
54. Greenstein, *The Symbiotic Universe*, pp. 99–100.
55. Barrow and Tipler, *The Anthropic Cosmological Principle* pp. 289–305.
56. Ibid., pp. 295–296.
57. Davies, *The Accidental Universe*, p. 77.
58. Barrow and Tipler, *The Anthropic Cosmological Principle* p. 288.
59. Davies, *The Accidental Universe*, p. 60.
60. Ibid., p. 111.
61. Gribbin and Rees, *Cosmic Coincidences*, p. 269.
62. John D. Barrow, *Theories of Everything*, (Oxford: Oxford University Press, 1991), pp. 94–95.
63. Ibid., p. 112.
64. See Chapter 8 for a more thorough treatment of this important issue.
65. It should be pointed out that this postulated repulsive force has never actually been measured; it simply follows from the assumptions of quantum field theory. For more information on this intriguing subject, see P.C.W. Davies' *The Accidental Universe*, p. 106.
66. Ibid., p. 107.
67. Ibid.
68. Larry Abbott, "The Mystery of the Cosmological Constant," *Scientific American*, Vol. 3, No. 1, 1991, pp. 77–78.
69. Davies, *The Accidental Universe*, p. 109.
70. Hugh Ross, *The Fingerprint of God*, p. 124.
71. Ibid.
72. Ibid., p. 126.
73. Ibid.
74. Greenstein, *The Symbiotic Universe*, pp. 95–97.
75. Of course, the argument can always be made that such an immensely unlikely

instance of cooperation nevertheless occurred solely by chance, and it is only because it did in fact happen that life was able to evolve. Such an "explanation" might even be remotely believable if this were the only life-facilitating coincidence we were being asked to consider. However, given the simultaneous existence of so many *other* exceedingly unlikely coincidences in the evolution of life, the competing explanation—that of Deliberate Design—becomes far more likely and therefore far more believable.

76. Owen Gingerich, "Modern Cosmogony and Biblical Creation," in Roland Mushat Frye ed., *Is God a Creationist?* (New York: Charles Scribner's Sons, 1983), pp. 132–133.
77. Hugh Ross, *Genesis One: A Scientific Perspective* (Sierra Madre, CA: Wisemen Productions, 1983), pp. 6–7.
78. Ibid.
79. Ibid., p. 6.
80. Hugh Ross has estimated the odds for such a coordinated series of events to be far less than one in a billion (Ibid., p. 7.)
81. Barrow and Tipler, p. 544.
82. Hugh Ross, *Genesis One: A Scientific Perspective*, p. 7.
83. Gerald L. Schroeder, *Genesis and the Big Bang*, pp. 122–123.
84. Ibid., p. 122.
85. Ibid.
86. Ibid.
87. Ibid., p. 123.
88. Although the number 10^7 may seem like a large number, in comparison to the countless trillions of protons and photons in existence, it is very small indeed. In fact, it is nothing short of amazing that the numbers of photons and protons should be so closely matched, especially considering how important this matching is to the existence of life on this planet.
89. Davies, *The Accidental Universe*, p. 99.
90. Ibid.
91. Ibid., p. 97.
92. Barrow and Tipler, p. 178.
93. Ibid., p. 422.
94. Ibid., pp. 421–426.
95. C.B Collins and S.W. Hawking, *Astrophys. J.* 180, 317 (1973).
96. Barrow and Tipler, *The Anthropic Cosmological Principle*, pp. 419–420.
97. Davies, *The Accidental Universe*, p. 95.
98. Even if one were to argue that this transcendent coordinating influence may only be an impersonal creative force, it would still serve the same creator-type function as the traditional God of the Bible. In view of this observation, the ancient Hebrew prophets accurately anticipated the need for a Coordinating Transcendent Influence to explain the existence of our present world.
99. John D. Barrow, *Theories of Everything*, pp. 50–51.
100. The use of the speed of light to determine which areas of the primordial universe could have been in causal contact with one another may in fact be mistaken, as it is based on two rather implausible assumptions. This important issue will be discussed in more detail in the next chapter.
101. Stephen Hawking, *A Brief History of Time*, p. 130.
102. Ibid., p. 132.
103. Ibid.
104. George Greenstein, *The Symbiotic Universe*, p. 40.

105. Hugh Ross, *The Fingerprint of God*, p. 126.
106. Owen Gingerich, p. 134.
107. Please refer to Errol E. Harris' *Cosmos and Anthropos* (Atlantic Highlands, New Jersey: Humanities Press International, Inc., 1991) for an excellent philosophical analysis of functional holism and its relationship to the concept of design.
108. It is interesting to note that many of the physicists who write about these cosmic coincidences enclose the word "coincidence" in quotation marks, as I do. This would appear to signify a hidden realization that these events are probably not really coincidental at all.
109. Fred Hoyle, "The Universe: Past and Present Reflections," *Engineering and Science* (November 1981), pp. 8–12.
110. Many theistic researchers believe that the famous Star of Bethlehem was actually a supernova explosion.
111. Davies, *The Accidental Universe* (New York: Cambridge University Press, 1982), p. 68.
112. Ibid., p. 68.
113. Gribbin and Rees, *Cosmic Coincidences*, p. 254.
114. Davies, *The Accidental Universe*, p. 82.
115. Ibid.
116. Taken from Davies' *The Accidental Universe*, p. 81.
117. John Barrow, *The World Within the World*, p. 358.
118. Davies, *The Accidental Universe*, p. 55.
119. Ibid., p. 114.
120. In modern string theory anywhere between 10 and 26 universal dimensions are postulated to exist. However, all but 3 (plus 1 of time) are believed to have shrunk down to microscopic size. It is these 3 macroscopic dimensions that interest us here.
121. Greenstein, *The Symbiotic Universe*, pp. 111–116.
122. Barrow and Tipler, p. 262.
123. Ibid.
124. Barrow and Tipler, p. 264.
125. Ibid.
126. Ibid.
127. Ibid.
128. Ibid.
129. Ibid., p. 265.
130. P. Ehrenfest, *Proc. Amst. Acad. 20*, 200 (1917); *Ann. Physik 61*, 440, 1920.
131. Barrow and Tipler, p. 264.
132. F.R. Tangherlini, *Nuovo Cim. 27*, 636 (1963).
133. L. Gurevich and V. Mostepanenko, *Phys. Lett. A 35*, 201.
134. Barrow and Tipler, p. 265.
135. Ibid.
136. Ibid., p. 266.
137. Ibid.
138. Ibid., p. 268.
139. J. Hadarard, "Lectures on Cauchy's Problem in Linear Partial Differential Equations" (New Haven: Yale University Press, 1923).
140. Barrow and Tipler, p. 268.
141. Ibid., p. 269.
142. Ibid., p. 273.

143. Ibid., p. 272.
144. Although it is possible that our universe could possess 3 spatial dimensions *necessarily*, we have to then ask where this cosmic necessity *itself* came from. In the absence of an Intelligent Designer, we have no choice but to fall back on the precarious notion of "chance" to explain this necessity.
145. Although David Griffin's belief of what constitutes a hard-core commonsense notion tends to be reserved for the more general aspects of human experience, such as the notion of free will (see his discussion in *Primordial Truth and Postmodern Theology* [Albany: SUNY Press, 1989], co-authored with Huston Smith), the assumption of a common origin to the separate parts of a single functional whole nevertheless seems to be a hard-core common-sense notion for most people.
146. Taken from Barrow and Tipler, *The Anthropic Cosmological Principle*, p. 658.
147. Fortunately, this future Heat Death, if it occurs at all, won't happen for billions of years to come.
148. Stephen Hawking, *A Brief History of Time*, p. 144.
149. Ibid., p. 152.
150. Carbon is so intimately involved in the processes of life that the word "organic" simply refers to the fact that a given compound contains carbon.
151. We humans haven't even come close to designing such a non-polluting system of energy production. This fact alone should be able to convince even the most hardened skeptic that our world has been Intelligently Designed. For how could it be possible that chance processes alone could have devised such a wonderful non-polluting system, when our best engineers can't even *approach* such an idealistic goal?
152. Barrow and Tipler, p. 548.
153. Ibid., pp. 545–546.
154. Ibid., p. 547.
155. I am distinguishing here between physical beings and purely spiritual beings, the latter of which can presumably exist entirely in the absence of physical matter.
156. John Barrow, *The World Within the World*, p. 373.
157. Barrow and Tipler, p. 526.
158. Ibid., pp. 533–534.
159. L.J. Henderson, *The Order of Nature* (Cambridge: Harvard University Press, 1917), p. 191.
160. L.J. Henderson, *The Fitness of the Environment* (Glouster: Peter Smith, 1970), p. 312.
161. P.C.W. Davies, *Other Worlds* (New York: Simon and Schuster, 1980), p. 143.
162. Gerald L. Schroeder, *Genesis and the Big Bang*, p. 123.
163. Ibid.
164. Ibid.
165. Ibid., p. 124.
166. Ibid., p. 125.
167. Ibid., p. 126.
168. Corey S. Powell, "Greenhouse Gusher," in *Scientific American*, Vol. 265, No. 4, p. 20, October, 1991.
169. Hugh Ross, *The Fingerprint of God*, p. 131.
170. Ibid., p. 129.
171. Ibid.
172. Ibid., p. 130.

173. Ibid.
174. Errol E. Harris, *Cosmos and Anthropos* (Atlantic Highlands, New Jersey: Humanities Press International, Inc., 1991), p. 52.
175. Ibid.
176. Ross, *The Fingerprint of God*, p. 130.
177. Ibid.
178. Ibid.
179. Ibid., p. 131.
180. Ibid.
181. Ibid.
182. Ibid.
183. Ibid.
184. Ibid.
185. Ibid.
186. Given the trillions of planets in existence, this would amount to thousands or even millions of such life-supporting worlds.
187. Davies, *Other Worlds* (New York: Simon and Schuster, 1980), p. 143.
188. Gerald Schroeder *Genesis and the Big Bang*, pp. 157–158.
189. Ibid., p. 158.
190. Gribbin and Rees, *Cosmic Coincidences*, p. 67.

CHAPTER 5

Interpreting the Evidence

We find ourselves in a bewildering world. We want to make sense of what we see around us and to ask: What is the nature of the Universe? What is our place in it and where did it and we come from? Why is it the way it is?

STEPHEN HAWKING[1]

Why not consider the possibility that life is what it so evidently seems to be, the product of creative intelligence? Science would not come to an end, because the task would remain of deciphering the languages in which the genetic information is communicated, and in general finding out how the whole system *works*. What scientists would lose is not an inspiring research program, but the illusion of total mastery of nature. They would have to face the possibility that beyond the natural world there is a further reality which transcends science.

PHILIP E. JOHNSON[2]

5.1 God and the Nature of the Quantum Vacuum

As we saw in the previous chapter, one of the most startling findings of the new physics is that the vacuum of "empty" space isn't really empty. Rather, it is a dynamic, energy-filled mileu that arises partly from the negative pressure exerted by the naked vacuum itself (the so-called bare cosmological constant) and partly from quantum fluctuations within the vacuum, in which pairs of so-called virtual particles can spontaneously arise out of "nowhere," briefly interact, and then disappear. This vacuum energy density—which is assigned a value proportional to it known as the cosmological constant—is extremely intriguing, because it seems to imply that real world objects can arise "out of nothing."

Although this idea of something from "nothing" is new to the scientific establishment, it has been around for centuries as part of traditional theological dogma. Theologians have long maintained that God created the world out of nothing, and now it appears as though modern science has corroborated this belief.

One possible means of interpreting the vacuum of "empty" space is in terms of a metaphysical interface between the physical universe, on the one hand, and the hypothetical existence of a Divine Creator, on the other. It

123

would seem to be a logical deduction that if God does in fact exist and is in fact responsible for creating our world, then His Creative Activity would probably interface with the physical realm at the level of the vacuum quantum field itself. If so, then God Himself would in some sense be responsible for producing the observed energy density of the vacuum.

The fact that empty space can indeed give rise to "virtual particles" strongly supports this theistic interpretation, insofar as it implies that there is Someone or something on the other side of this metaphysical interface which is imparting a certain amount of energy to it. On this view, the "spontaneous" appearance and disappearance of virtual particles from this quantum field would be due to the activity of God in some fashion.

The science of modern physics, however, is not free to openly attribute this kind of phenomenon to the activity of a hypothetical Creator. As a consequence, it simply accepts the idea of a dynamic cosmic vacuum as a raw given, without taking the "unnecessary" extra step of invoking an unseen supernatural Agency to "explain" it.

5.2   Value of the Cosmological Constant

As we have seen, the value of the cosmological constant (which is expressed in units of 1 over distance squared) is intimately related to the gross structure of the entire physical universe (via its powerful ability to control the geometry of space-time). Significantly, though, the cosmological constant is not a simple quantity, nor is its contribution to the rest of the physical realm straightforward and uncomplicated. To the contrary, the cosmological constant represents the sum total of all the highly complex "free" parameters in the so-called Standard Model[3] of particle physics, along with contributions made by the naked vacuum and unknown physics. The cosmological constant, then, is a composite value that contains a very large number of contributing factors, many of which are presently unknown.

Given this fact, along with the scientific establishment's firm belief in a random origin to the physical universe, it was only natural for physicists to assume that the "free" parameters that gave rise to the cosmological constant were all causally and functionally independent of one another. On the basis of this one assumption alone, they predicted a value for the cosmological constant that turned out to be wrong by an incredible factor of at least 10^{46}. As physicist Larry Abbott of Brandeis University has aptly pointed out,

> Few theoretical estimates in the history of physics made on the basis of what seemed to be reasonable assumptions have ever been so inaccurate.[4]

In other words, the actual value of the cosmological constant is some 10^{46}

times *smaller* than our best calculations indicate it "should" be. This is an astonishing fact in and of itself, but even more astonishing is the fact that our present universe could never have existed if the cosmological constant occupied anything *other* than its present value. As Abbott has pointed out:

> The geometric structure of the universe is extremely sensitive to the value of the vacuum energy density. So important is this value that a constant proportional to the vacuum energy density has been defined. It is called the cosmological constant. If the vacuum energy density, or equivalently the cosmological constant, were as large as theories of elementary particles suggest, the universe in which we live would be dramatically different, with properties we would find both bizarre and unsettling.[5]

This is an extraordinary observation that suggests a hidden level of cooperation between the many different structural parameters that comprise the subatomic realm. This cooperation appears to be directed towards making the cosmological constant sufficiently small as to be compatible with the existence of a life-supporting universe.

Indeed, this appears to be why particle theorists were so off base in their prediction of the value of the cosmological constant to begin with: due to their private assumptions regarding the random origin of the universe, they were naturally expecting the "free" parameters of the Standard Model to be totally independent of one another with respect to their contribution to the overall value of the cosmological constant. As it turns out, however, this just doesn't appear to be the case at all. To the contrary, there appears to be an extremely intimate degree of hidden cooperation (and, therefore, of relative causal interdependence) between these physical parameters that functions to make the value of the cosmological constant some 10^{46} orders of magnitude smaller than would have otherwise been expected without this cooperation.

This kind of multi-level cooperation between so many seemingly "independent" factors is directly suggestive of Intelligent Design. Three factors lead to this conclusion; 1) the number of distinct parameters involved, 2) the many complex interconnections between these parameters, and 3) the overall purpose that this grand cooperative venture aims towards (that of making space-time flat so it can be conducive to life).

It follows, then, that had the particle theorists assumed in an *a priori* fashion some degree of cooperative interdependence between the physical parameters that comprise the Standard Model (i.e., had they assumed that the various terms in the overall sum of the vacuum energy density would end up cancelling each other out), their prediction of the value of the cosmological constant would have been *much* more accurate. As Abbot explains:

> The stupendous failure we have experienced in trying to predict the value

of the cosmological constant is far more than a mere embarrassment. Recall that the basic assumption we used to obtain our estimate [of the value of the cosmological constant] was that there are no unexpected cancellations among the various terms in the sum determining the total energy density of the vacuum. This expectation was based on the assumed independence of the free parameters of the Standard Model. Clearly, this assumption is spectacularly wrong. There must in fact be a miraculous conspiracy occurring among both the known and the unknown parameters governing particle physics, with the result that the many terms making up the cosmological constant add up to a quantity more than 46 orders of magnitude smaller than the individual terms in the sum. In other words, the small value of the cosmological constant is telling us that a remarkably precise and totally unexpected relation exists among all the parameters of the Standard Model [of particle physics], the bare cosmological constant and unknown physics.[6]

Another way of saying this is that in order for our life-supporting universe to exist, the cosmological constant must occupy a value that is some 10^{46} times smaller than our best calculations indicate it "should" be. This implies a hidden, cooperative arrangement between all of the individual parameters that make up our physical world, which *together* create a vacuum energy density that is at least 10^{46} times smaller than would have been expected without this cooperation. This is a truly *incredible* amount of intimate cooperation that is directly suggestive of Intelligent Design.

The very fact that this cooperation is on a level that is not superficially apparent is a lasting testimony to the profound intricacy and depth of Intelligence that is at work here. Evidently each of the many "free" parameters that make up the physical universe possesses a hidden variable which, when combined with the hidden variables of all the other physical parameters, produces a net cosmological constant that is some 10^{46} times *less* powerful than would have otherwise been expected apart from this profound degree of hidden cooperation.

The outrageous failure of modern particle theorists to accurately predict the value of the cosmological constant provides an excellent example of how an extreme non-theistic bias can adversely affect the accuracy of our physical predictions. Conversely, it suggests that a correct theological orientation to the universe will help us to greatly increase the accuracy of our physical theories in the future.[7]

Abbott, of course, fails to openly attribute the vanishingly small value of the cosmological constant to a Divinely-Inspired conspiracy between the fundamental parameters of the physical realm. He simply points out that this surprisingly tiny value has profound implications for our understanding of physics:

If we discount the possibility that the vanishingly small value of the cosmological constant is accidental, we must accept that it has profound implications for physics. Before we launch in constructing new unified models, however, we must face the dilemma that the relation implied by the vanishing of the cosmological constant is unnatural. The miraculous cancellations required to produce an acceptably small cosmological constant depend on all the parameters relevant to particle physics, known and unknown. To predict a zero (or small) value for the cosmological constant, a unified theory would face the imposing task of accounting for every parameter affecting particle physics. Even worse, achieving a sufficiently small cosmological constant requires that extremely precise (one part in 10^{46} or more) cancellations take place; the parameters would have to be predicted by the theory with extraordinary accuracy before any improvement in the situation regarding the cosmological constant would even be noticeable. Constructing such a theory, even if it does exist, seems to be an awesome if not impossible task.[8]

Needless to say, it would be ludicrous to the greatest possible extent to even *suggest* at this point that the physical parameters which gave rise to the cosmological constant were random in origin. There are simply far too many of them—and far too much cooperation between them aiming for a single unified end (our biocentric universe)—to *ever* be the result of chance processes alone.

To his credit, Abbott doesn't even *attempt* to attribute this interdependence to chance; rather, he openly *assumes* a non-accidental origin to the cosmological constant, because this is the only conclusion that is consistent with the existing evidence. After all, if we humans, in spite of our intelligence, will probably never be able to construct a viable unified theory that will accurately represent all of the physical parameters in the Standard Model that contribute to the cosmological constant, then how can we possibly believe that a random and accidental cosmic process could have *ever* given rise to it in the first place?

5.3 God and the Primordial Process of Spontaneous Symmetry Breaking

As we noted above, physicists believe that immediately following the occurrence of the Big Bang the universe was still so hot that the four fundamental forces of nature were symmetrically intertwined in a single superforce. As the universe cooled, however, a process called spontaneous symmetry breaking is believed to have taken place that caused these four fundamental forces to crystallize out of their primordial state of grand unification. Physicists believe that the exact nature of this crystallization process is not foreseeable in principle, but depends on the precise nature of small triggering fluctuations (otherwise known as chaos) that regularly occur in dynamical physical systems.

This process of spontaneous symmetry breaking is analogous to the initiation of chemical crystallization in a supersaturated solution, which is a solution containing a dissolved solute that has been cooled beyond the crystallization point, but in which crystallization has not yet occurred. A tiny addition of a crystalline "seed" is then all it takes to initiate a spontaneous process of crystallization. How this crystallization actually proceeds, however, is dependent on the tiny chaotic fluctuations in the solution that happen to exist at the time the seed is placed in it.

Similarly, in the microseconds immediately following the Big Bang, the universe was like a supersaturated symmetrical solution, awaiting the first tiny fluctuation to elicit a process of spontaneous symmetry breaking. Cosmologists believe that the specific nature of this primordial crystallization process depended in large part on the specific nature of the initial triggering fluctuation. On this view, different triggering fluctuations would have produced radically different universes.

We know for a fact, though, that the specific fluctuations which *did* actually occur in the newly born universe eventually produced a world that was capable of evolving intelligent life. It therefore appears as though these initial triggering fluctuations were of such an utterly precise character that the very pinnacle of order—intelligent life forms—were able to eventually evolve from them.

Assuming this to be true, we now have to ask ourselves the following question: what cosmic force was of such a precise and intelligent character that it was able to instigate the present level of universal order by initiating precisely the "right" type of cosmic fluctuation? It seems evident that one cannot attribute this initial triggering fluctuation to blind chance, because the odds of such a random fluctuation leading to our present highly ordered world are so sufficiently remote as to place them beyond the realm of statistical non-possibility. Thus, only one other sensible alternative seems to present itself; namely, that an Intelligent Designer somehow determined the exact nature of these initial triggering fluctuations, with the eventual goal of producing biological life forms in mind.

5.4 Inflation and Contrivance

As we have seen, the goal of Guth's "inflationary" paradigm is to eliminate any undue cosmological subservience to initial conditions by showing that "however the universe began—whether in chaos or in order—the inevitable effect of the laws of gravitation is to deliver it to us in the form we find today."[9]

Some writers have used the inflationary model's apparent freedom from initial conditions to argue against the notion of Intelligent Design, for the following reason: if the present universal character would have resulted no matter how the universe actually began, then there no longer seems to be any need for a larger Creator to unilaterally determine the initial conditions surrounding the Big Bang. Although this line of reasoning seems superficially appealing, it is undermined by one of its most basic underlying assumptions: namely, the constancy and specific character of the laws of Nature, which are themselves the most important of all initial conditions.

Most cosmologists would agree that the process of inflation is utterly dependent on the precise character of the laws of Nature, for if these laws were any different, the universe's inflationary epoch would have never occurred the way it apparently did. A different value for the gravitational constant, for example, would have so altered the behavior of the primordial universe that we probably would not be around to discuss the matter. It is thus fallacious to argue that the inflationary hypothesis eliminates the need for a precisely-defined set of initial conditions at the Big Bang, because the process of inflation is absolutely dependent on the most important initial condition of them all: the constancy and specific character of the laws of Nature.

In other words, as long as the goal of the inflationary paradigm is to show that the present universal character would have evolved regardless of the initial conditions at the Big Bang, then one cannot *simultaneously* refer to the laws of Nature as making inflation possible, because the laws of Nature themselves are known to comprise an integral part of these initial conditions. But the laws of Nature *did* make inflation possible. Therefore, the inflationary process cannot be said to be free from an absolute dependence on initial conditions.

When cosmologists refer to the initial conditions surrounding the Big Bang, they are actually referring to two very different things: 1) the internal composition and spatial configuration of those primordial actualities which were in existence (or came into existence) at that time, and 2) the specific laws of Nature, which had either been in existence eternally, or had come into existence at about the same time as the primordial actualities themselves. Although there may be some overlap between these two items (insofar as the laws of Nature would have partially determined the initial composition and configuration of these primordial actualities), a definite distinction can nevertheless be drawn between them. This distinction is based upon the fundamental ontological difference between concrete physical entities, on the one hand, and those natural laws that somehow govern how these entities actually behave, on the other.[10]

If we utilize this fundamental ontological distinction as our primary point of reference, it would seem as though some (perhaps all) of the laws of Nature had to have been in existence *prior to* the initial unfolding of the Big Bang, since they had to have somehow mediated the initial appearance (and initial spatial configuration) of the primordial actualities themselves. It would therefore seem that the laws of Nature must have in some sense *preceded* the actual Big Bang itself, otherwise the "cosmic egg" would have never existed in the first place, nor would it have been able to explode in such a precise and coherent manner as to produce our miraculous life-supporting universe.

But if this is the case, then the laws of Nature themselves are by far the most important of the initial conditions that were operative in the very beginning; at the very least, they are equivalent in importance to the initial composition and configuration of the primoridial entities that comprised the Big Bang. In either case, the inflationary scenario *cannot* account for the present structure of the universe without causal reference to these initial conditions, because inflation can never be construed to have happened *apart* from the laws of Nature. It is in this sense that we can say that the inflationary paradigm is just as dependent on initial conditions as non-inflationary scenarios are; it simply utilizes the laws of Nature to compensate for any irregularities that might have occurred during the initial stages of cosmic history.

As a result, even if we were to assume the validity of Guth's inflationary model, we *still* wouldn't free of the need for a larger Designer, because we would still have to explain where the laws of Nature *themselves* came from, and there doesn't seem to be any coherent way of doing this apart from the creative activity of a Grand Designer.

Interestingly enough, the Bible seems to contain a reference to a one-time inflationary force that God may have used to set the heavens in motion. As Gerald Schroeder[11] points out in *Genesis and the Big Bang*, a literal translation of Genesis 1:2 reveals a unique creative force, known as the "wind of God," which acted upon the primeval universe to set in it motion:

> And darkness was on the face of the deep [the infinite expanse that the universe was created in], and a wind of God moved on the face of the waters [the common substance from which the entire universe was created].

Another translation states that "God's wind stirred on the face of the waters."[12] Significantly, the Hebrew phrase that is translated as "God's wind" in this verse—a *ruach elokim*, or spiritual enactment of God's Will—is used only once in the entire book of Genesis. According to Schroeder, this is a clear reference to God's use of a one-time "stirring" or "moving" force in the very beginning that may have been identical to the inflationary scenario conceived by Guth. Scientists also believe that this inflationary force was a one-time phenomenon because of the unprecedented amount of energy that was unleashed at the Big Bang.

As Schroeder points out, scientists don't like to resort to one-time forces in their theories because it is too much like using a fudge factor.[13] For the inflationary epoch following the Big Bang, however, cosmologists make a clear exception, because such a one-time homogenizing force seems to have been necessary to produce the biocentric universe we presently observe. It thus may not be a coincidence that a *ruach elokim*, or wind of God, is also mentioned only once in the entire book of Genesis, for if it actually refers to some type of inflationary scenario, a single moment of inflationary expansion in the universe is all that was ever needed.

5.5 Can Inflation Solve the Horizon Problem?

As we saw in the last chapter, the horizon problem has to do with the fact that light has not had enough time since the Big Bang to travel between causally coherent parts of the visible universe. As a consequence, we would naturally expect these causally disconnected regions to be very different from one another. Remarkably, however, this is not at all the case, since the present-day universe is isotropic (similar in all directions) to within 1 part in 10,000. Because this isotropy has lessened considerably with the expansion of the universe, the Big Bang itself has been calculated to have been isotropic to within 1 part in 10^{40}, even though normal physical processes that are limited to the speed of light could not have had time to effect this incredible degree of smoothness.

The non-theistic inflationary paradigm discussed in the last chapter has been used to explain how this extraordinary degree of isotropy could have come about. On this view, the initial "cosmic egg" is assumed to have been non-homogeneous on the whole, because all its constituent parts couldn't have had enough time to causally interact with one another (not counting, of course, the coercive power of a Divine Creator). Then, because of natural forces that were resident in the egg itself, a single causally connected region spontaneously inflated to produce the entire visible universe. The homogeneity and isotropy of the visible universe is thus "explained" by the fact that its primordial constituents were all causally connected with one another.

Of course, just because these primordial constituents could have been in physical contact with one another for an unimaginably brief instant doesn't necessarily mean that they could have become homogenized by purely natural means. The process of homogenization through normal physical pathways typically requires a reasonable stretch of time in order to occur. However, because of the tremendous speed of light, which is used to determine the area of this initial region that could have been causally connected, only a vaporous microsecond would have been available for this homogenization to occur. It is very hard to see how such an incredibly precise degree of homogenization could have possibly resulted in such an imperceptibly small amount of time. It is also very hard to see how normal light rays could have ever caused such a remarkable degree of isotropy all by themselves, even if they were given a much longer period of time in which to act.

It would seem, then, that the use of the speed of light to determine which areas of the cosmic egg could have realistically been in causal contact with one another may in fact be mistaken. This, of course, compounds the horizon problem immensely, because it indicates that normal physical processes were probably incapable of producing the observed degree of cosmic isotropy in the early universe.

The theistic answer to the horizon problem therefore seems to be by far the better explanation, because it uses a known creative process—the coercive power of an intelligent designer—to produce the original homogenization of the universe. On this view, the primordial contents of the visible universe were homogenized just as soon as they came into existence.

Another weakness in the non-theistic inflationary view concerns its assumption that the remainder of the actual universe, which supposedly begins where our portion of the visible universe ends, is probably a very disordered, non-homogeneous place, since these other regions couldn't possibly have had enough time to causally interact with one another after the Big Bang. This does not seem to be a plausible hypothesis in light of all we know about the cosmos, since everything we have ever detected, from the smallest reaches of the subatomic world to the furthest reaches of the visible universe itself, definitely displays a tremendous amount of order and complexity. While this omnipresent degree of order is "explained" by the inflationary paradigm as being the result of a small, causally connected region that happened to inflate by a fantastic amount, it seems counterintuitive to suppose that this order is actually limited only to our visible portion of the universe. Given the utter pervasiveness of this cosmic order over truly immense distances, ranging from the very large to the very small, we have every reason to believe that it extends to the furthest reaches of physical reality itself, and not just to the furthest reaches of the visible universe.

Most scientists (apart from those who are committed to the traditional inflationary picture) would probably agree with this assertion, since it is in line with *all* scientific discoveries to date in *all* scientific disciplines. If it is indeed true, though, it automatically invalidates the inflationary solution to the horizon problem, because it means that *all* parts of the cosmic egg had to have been in causal contact with one another when the process of inflation began. Since there clearly wasn't enough time for such a global causal connection to occur after the Big Bang, it seems apparent that some type of Larger Cosmic Force probably acted to homogenize all parts of the cosmic egg from the very beginning. This Larger Force we can understand to be God.

Of course, this Primordial Creative Power could have used inflation to further homogenize things during the initial cosmic expansion, but this would eliminate inflation as the sole cause of the homogeneity of the universe.

Further evidence that the inflationary hypothesis cannot fully account for the incredible smoothness of the early universe can be found in the current cosmological supposition that there wasn't enough time in the very early universe for any two proto-galaxies to have communicated with one another.[14] If this was indeed the case, then our galaxy in its earliest stages couldn't possibly have communicated with any other galaxies in the visible universe, so there wouldn't have been enough time for *any* homogenization to occur between them through natural physical pathways. Yet, *all* areas of the visible universe, including the incidence and composition of the different galaxies, are still very much synchronized with one another. It would seem, then, that we have to postulate the existence of a Universal Homogenizing Force that transcends the limitations of conventional theory.

This need for a Universal Homogenizing Force is further supported by the non-scientific nature of the conventional inflationary "explanation," which has cleverly been constructed in such a way that it seems to be forever immune to falsification. It cannot be falsified because we will never be able to detect the existence of any disordered regions of the universe *by definition*, since they are defined as lying beyond the boundary of the visible universe. Since the theory cannot be falsified, it cannot claim to be truly scientific, because all scientific theories must in principle be falsifiable before they can be described as being "scientific." The conventional inflationary explanation also has a certain *ad hoc* quality to it, which is due to the fact that: 1) it seems to have been contrived just to make the non-theistic theory work, and 2) it is contrary to all our observations.

The conventional inflationary explanation for the homogeneity of the universe also violates the Principle of Theoretical Economy on a truly grand scale, since it necessitates the existence of a wide variety of inhomogeneous and permanently invisible regions of the universe just to make the theory work. It would be easier to simply employ Occam's Razor to cut them out of the theory altogether, and to postulate the activity of a Grand Designer, who would have deliberately acted to make the entire cosmic egg smooth from the very beginning.

5.6 Singularities in View of the Divine

As we have seen, the equations of general relativity point to the existence of an infinitely dense singularity at the beginning of the present cosmic epoch, from which all the space, time, and matter in the universe would have spontaneously come into existence. Although Stephen Hawking originally helped to establish this Singularity Theorem (along with Roger Penrose), he has since tried to show that the universe could indeed have begun without a Big Bang singularity.[15] This being the case, one might suspect that Hawking is somehow opposed to the existence of singularities in general, but this isn't so at all. To the contrary, Hawking possesses a very robust belief in the existence of black holes, which are singularities that are produced when sufficiently massive stars collapse in upon themselves until a final "point" of infinite density is eventually reached. Most cosmologists share Hawking's belief in black holes. Singularities, then, are a common feature of the modern cosmologist's world view, at least as far as the existence of black holes is concerned.

This concept of an infinitely dense point of matter, whose gravitational pull is so strong that not even light can escape (hence the term "black hole"), is an extremely interesting one, insofar as it is immensely difficult to see how so much matter could possibly be "squeezed" down to a point of infinite density.[16] Yet, physicists assure us that black holes are relatively common-place throughout the universe. Indeed, many cosmologists continue to believe that the entire universe itself probably arose from a similar "point" of infinite density, as we have seen.

This notion of a Big Bang singularity, which would have given birth to the entire universe, is so profoundly radical that it must be quietly meditated upon at some length before it can be fully appreciated. It is easy enough to *say* that the entire universe originally arose from a point of infinite density, but it is another thing altogether to fully realize *what* one is actually saying.

A simple analogy may help us to better understand what is implied by this notion of a Big Bang singularity. We humans tend to be rather impressed whenever we see a magician pull a rabbit out of a hat, but now we are being told by some of the most brilliant minds on the planet that our *entire universe* may have been "drawn" out of an infinitely dense point of matter-energy! This is an *incredibly* miraculous notion that seems to speak directly of some form of Divine Power. John Barrow agrees, insofar as he admits that "[i]n modern cosmology the role of the Creator is essentially assumed by the naked Big Bang singularity."[17]

How could it possibly be otherwise? That is to say, how could the notion of an entire universe arising from an infinitely dense point of matter-energy even *begin* to make sense apart from the action of an infinitely powerful Creator? While the skeptic might be able to dismiss the pulling of a rabbit out of a hat (or even the "pulling" of an entire zoo out of a hat) as feats that an ordinary mortal could conceivably accomplish, it would be next to impossible for him to make the same claim about the entire universe as a whole, as it seems to be strictly impossible for an entire universe to be "pulled" out of a hat (or even worse, for an entire universe to be pulled out of an infinitely small point of matter-energy) without the enabling Power of a Supreme Being. It would seem, then, that the Miraculous Power of the

Creator is implicit within the very notion of the Big Bang, regardless of the size of the "cosmic egg" that initially gave rise to it.

The implications of this realization are truly monumental, as Hugh Ross has pointed out:

> Atheism, Darwinism, and virtually all the "isms" emanating from the eighteenth to twentieth century philosophies are built upon the assumption, the incorrect assumption, that the universe is infinite. The [Big Bang] singularity has brought us face to face with the cause—or causer—beyond/behind/before the universe and all that it contains, including life itself.[18]

Far from pointing away from the God of traditional theism, then, the evidence of the Big Bang instead makes the existence of such a God virtually inescapable.

5.7 What Happened Before the Big Bang?

As we have seen, science cannot probe back beyond Planck's Wall, when the universe was but a mere 10^{-43} seconds old, because the very equations that are used to study the universe break down at this precipitous point. The reason for this is now pretty well understood: the enormous temperatures that existed so close to the beginning (about $10^{32°}C$) caused a state of fluid interchange between matter and energy, according to Einstein's famous formula $E = MC^2$. Any matter that came into being instantly became transformed into energy, and vice versa. As a consequence of this tremendous high energy state, the very early universe was incapable of maintaining a sufficient degree of order within itself to transmit usable information about what had happened previously.[19]

Interestingly enough, the creation account in Genesis seems to convey this very point, as Biblical tradition also teaches that what happened at or before the beginning of time is unknowable by man.[20] This conclusion was reached, not through a routine analysis of the words contained in the Bible, but through a careful examination of the *shapes* of the letters that comprise the original Hebrew text. Biblical scholars believe that all aspects of the ancient Hebrew scriptures can convey important meaning, including the shapes of the individual letters themselves.[21] As it turns out, the first word of the first line of Genesis ("In the beginning . . . ") begins with the Hebrew letter beth, which is closed on three sides and open in the forward direction only.[22] This has been taken to mean that humans have access only to those events that transpired *after* the original creation, not during it or before it.

The Biblical scholar Nahmanides was aware of this interpretation of the creation over seven centuries ago, long before anything concrete was known about the origin of the universe. Amazingly enough, modern science seems to have vindicated this ancient teaching.

5.7.1   The Creation of Space and Time at the Beginning

As we have seen, cosmologists now believe that space and time did not exist prior to the Big Bang. Rather, space and time are thought to have come into existence "out of nothing" when the universe itself exploded into being. This belief also strongly supports the Biblical contention of an absolute beginning to the universe.

Incredibly, though, Nahmanides in the thirteenth century concluded the very same thing, using only the text of Genesis 1:5 as a guide: " . . . and there was evening and morning, day one."[23] The original text does not state that it was the "first day." Had this been so, it would have implied a preexisting series of days, which in turn would have implied the prior existence of time. The use of the phrase "day one," however, implies that time itself began with the creation of the universe.[24] The use of the ordinal words "second," "third," and so on during the remaining "days" of the creation "week" further supports this interpretation, since by the time the "second day" rolled around a definite series of temporal events ("days") had been established.

Both Maimonides and Nahmanides reached a similar conclusion about the creation of space at the very beginning. Instead of believing that space somehow existed prior to the creation (and that the universe was created in this preexisting space), they held that space itself was also created at the beginning. Amazingly enough, this radical teaching has been confirmed by modern science almost a thousand years later.[25]

Even more remarkable is the fact that cabalist theorists working 500 years ago were able to conclude, entirely through their own mental effort, that the whole universe was in a dynamic state of expansion. They reasoned that God, being infinite, would have originally contracted when He created the universe. This, in turn, is thought to have caused the newly-created universe itself to expand.[26] Hubble's discovery of our expanding universe in 1929 confirmed this esoteric cabalist teaching.

Cabalist theorists were also able to deduce the existence of a ten-dimensional universe from the ten repetitions of the phrase "And God said . . ." in the first chapter of Genesis. Only four of these dimensions, however, were believed to be physically measurable. The other six were believed to have contracted into the submicroscopic realm shortly after the creation.[27]

Incredibly, modern string theory also predicts the existence of a ten-dimensional universe, six of which have allegedly contracted into the submicroscopic realm shortly after the initial creation event. (The four remaining dimensions—length, width, height, and time—are now known to comprise the entire macroscopic realm.) To their great credit, the cabalists were able to anticipate this modern scientific theory over 500 years ago.

5.8 Additional Biblical Parallels With Modern Cosmology

The Bible also indicates that an initial darkness followed the immediate creation of the universe (i.e., the Big Bang):

And darkness was on the face of the deep . . . (Gen. 1:2.).

This ancient statement reveals an astonishing amount of scientific insight, as it is now known that the primeval universe had to have been dark because of two independent factors: 1) because light could not escape from the "cosmic egg" that initially gave rise to the universe because of the enormous gravitational field[28] exerted by it, and 2) because any photons of light that may have existed after the Big Bang were initially trapped within a hot plasma of free electrons, and so could not travel as uninterrupted light waves. The universe had to cool for a while before light could "decouple" from matter and become visible. The Bible heralds this epic event with God's command in Gen. 1:3:

"Let there be light," and there was light.

Indeed, the entire creation account in Genesis is described in a sequential, evolutionary-type fashion. For while Gen. 1:1 tells us that "In the beginning God created the heavens and the earth," the Baylonian Talmud tells us that this was *not* an instantaneous event, because of the redundancy of the Hebrew word *et* (meaning "the") which precedes the words "heavens" and "earth." Consequently, the Talmud[29] teaches that "In the initial act of creation, the potential existed for all that ever will be contained in the universe."[30]
In contrast, Exodus 20:11 tells us that "For six days God made the heavens and the earth." Thus, God created the *potential* for everything that was ever to exist at the beginning of time, but it took Him six subsequent "days" in His own space-time reference frame to form the universe through natural evolutionary pathways.[31] In our own space-time reference frame, however, this same "six day" creation took some 15 billion years!
This immense difference in subjective time frames is the legacy of time dilation that Einstein's theory of relativity has left us with. There is simply no such thing as an absolute measure of time in the entire universe because each object has its own unique frame of reference, which is determined by its own velocity and proximity to a gravitational field. Thus, as Einstein's Twin Paradox[32] clearly shows, what can take 6 days for one observer can actually take 15 billion years for another! It is this notion of the relativity of

time that leads Schroeder to conclude that God's creation of the universe took both six days *and* 15 billion years *simultaneously*.[33] With this stunning realization, the apparent discrepancy between Genesis' 6 days of creation and the modern scientific account is resolved once and for all.

5.9   The Miracle of Perfect Universal Balance

As we learned in the previous chapter, the universe is comprised of a vast number of competing structures and forces that are aligned in such a way as to render inevitable many of the macroscopic aspects of our world (such as the sizes of things). In order for this cooperation to occur, a remarkable degree of balance must be achieved and maintained by all of these opposing forces, against stupendous odds to the contrary.

An analogy may help us to better understand the delicacy of this universal balance. It is as if the entire physical universe were poised on a huge see-saw, with trillions of counterbalanced weights arrayed on either side of the fulcrum, and an infinite distance to the ground on either side. In order for life to be possible on our planet, the see-saw must be perfectly balanced so that it is utterly flat. The addition of even an imperceptible micron of weight on either side of the fulcrum is therefore intolerable, since it would disturb the balance sufficiently to produce a universe that is inhospitable to life.

Now, it is apparent that in order for the see-saw to be perfectly balanced, the various weights on either side of the fulcrum must be perfectly matched. This of course requires a precise mass and location for each weight. However, it is precisely here that something remarkable begins to show itself: the odds against a perfect balance being obtained purely by accident seem to be *infinite*, since there are an infinite number of different masses and locations that could possibly be chosen.

The upshot of this reality is that an accidental universe, like the one proposed by nontheistic scientists, probably could not have formed under any conceivable set of circumstances, since the odds against such a "possibility" actually happening appear to be infinitely remote.[34]

Barrow and Tipler seem to agree, for they point out with understated astonishment that according to the work of Collins[35] and Hawking, in which the initial boundary conditions of Einstein's equations were systematically varied in order to determine the types of universes that could possibly result:

. . . the presently observed universe may have evolved from very special initial conditions. The present universe possesses features which are of infinitesimal probability amongst the entire range of possibilities. However, if one restricts this range by the stipulation that observers should be able to exist then the probability of the present dynamical configuration may become finite.[36]

That is to say, since there is an infinite range of possibilities for the various features of our universe, there is accordingly an infinitesimal probability for their actual occurrence, which is simply a way of saying that it is infinitely improbable for our present universe to have come into being by chance alone. Yet the universe has in fact come into being. Therefore, some way must be found to restrict this infinite range of possibility. Barrow and Tipler suggest that if the stipulation that observers should be able to exist is used to restrict this range (presumably any type of living consciousness will do), the probability of our present universe coming into existence may become finite, or within the range of possibility.[37]

In other words, a way must be found to single out a certain constellation of finite life-supporting features out of an infinite series of universal possibilities. Since these physical parameters have conspired together to make life possible, it makes sense to propose that it may very well have been the stipulation that life should be able to exist which made the probability of our present universal configuration finite or possible. This of course creates the problem of how such a stipulation could have actually taken place in the real world. *The most sensible way to account for this biocentric stipulation is to suppose that some form of Larger Intelligence deliberately placed it on the evolving universe.*

5.10   The Mind of God and Bohm's Concept of the Implicate Order

One other interesting observation seems to follow from the invariant properties of nature's physical constants. As noted previously, it directly follows from this invariance that our present world was an implicit feature of the universe when the constants themselves were born. Barring the occurrence of an incalcuably improbable cosmic accident, the only reasonable way to account for the coordinated calibration of these constants "all at once" is in terms of the calculating Mind of the Designer Himself, as it is only God's Intelligent Foresight[38] that could have anticipated the physical requirements for life from the very beginning.

The implicit nature of life at the Big Bang gives us an important theoretical tool for understanding physicist David Bohm's concept of the "implicate order," in which all the information in the entire universe is said to be enfolded in its smallest parts in a holographic manner. Given the "Holo-Vision" of the Designer Himself, it is indeed possible for the smallest constituent parts of the universe to contain the information of the whole universe, for it was God's original vision of the whole universe that led Him to design these constituent parts the way He did, so they would be conducive to life. In this way of thinking, it isn't necessarily each constituent part in and of itself which contains the whole, it is the Holo-Vision of God Himself *which is reflected in the structure of this constituent part* that contains the whole.

Indeed, Bohm's notion of the implicate order seems to be a prior condition to our present degree of universal harmony, for the only way so many independent structures could possibly interact in so precise and delicate a manner to create such a complex end product (life) is if each constituent part somehow "contained" within itself the interactive design of the whole; otherwise, how could Structure A "know" the design of Structures B, C, and D in such a way as to enable it to interact with them to produce a common end product? Just as each constituent part of an architectural blueprint "contains" the structure of the whole, in the sense that its own structure is determined by its role in the overall blueprint, each constituent part of the universe also seems to contain the structure of the whole, in the sense that the structure of each constituent part seems to be determined by its role in the overall cosmos. Again, God's Holo-Vision seems to be the unifying factor to this universal implicate order, since His transcendent view of the whole seems to be the only way each of the universe's constituent parts could have been designed in the proper life-supporting way.

From this point of view, Bohm's implicate order is simply a way of saying that the structure of each constituent part of the universe was specifically designed with the interactive functionality of the whole universe in Mind. However, this isn't to say that each constituent part doesn't also *directly* contain all the information of the entire universe as well. This could very well be the case. But what we can say for sure is that our universe appears to be unified at all levels of its existence, from the very large to the very small.

5.11 Contrivance and the Second Law of Thermodynamics

One of the most frequently encountered scientific-based arguments for the existence of God in the literature has to do with the utter pervasiveness of the Second Law of Thermodynamics, which states that the overall disorder of a closed system always rises. But if this is so, how are we to explain the existence of so much order in the universe? Who wound up the "cosmic clock" to begin with?[39] While it is possible for order to spontaneously arise in a small part of the cosmos in spite of the Second Law (it is "paid for" by increased entropy or disorder elsewhere), what are the odds that an entire magnificently ordered universe like our own could have come into existence entirely by chance? As Boslough points out:

> Consider the odds of shaking the parts of a watch in a barrel and having them fall into place as a working timepiece. Is that the kind of event that led to the Big Bang? Is our universe an enormous, accidental reversal of entropy? Or is it—literally—a miracle?[40]

One of the chief characteristics of virtually all explosions is the violent generation of waste products that are in a state of relatively high entropy. This only stands to reason; explosions naturally give off soot, heat, and shrapnel in an entirely random manner. But what if an explosion were to happen before our eyes in such a way that the waste products spontaneously came together to form an exquisitely formed sculpture? Wouldn't we then be convinced that we had witnessed a bona fide miracle?

In the same way, the extreme amount of order that emerged from the Big Bang explosion is *itself* powerful evidence for the existence of a Divine Creator, as Paul Davies points out:

> If the universe is simply an accident, the odds against it containing any appreciable order are ludicrously small. If the big bang was just a random event, then the probability seems *overwhelming* (a colossal understatement) that the emerging cosmic material would be in thermodynamic equilibrium at maximum entropy with zero order. As this was clearly not the case, it appears hard to escape the conclusion that the actual state of the universe has been "chosen" or selected somehow from the huge number of available states, all but an infinitesimal fraction of which are totally disordered. And if such an exceedingly improbable initial state was selected, there surely had to be a *selector* or *designer* to "choose" it?
>
> A useful image here is that of a creator equipped with a pin. Before him is a vast "shopping list" of universes, each characterized by their initial state. If the creator picks a universe by sticking in a pin at random, there is an overwhelming probability that the choice will be a highly disordered cosmos with no appreciable structure or organization. Indeed, to find an ordered universe, the creator would have to scour a selection of "models" that is so vast its number could not be written down on a sheet of paper as big as the entire observable universe![41]

Davies clearly seems to be conceding that some form of Divine Influence had to have been operative at the Big Bang to account for the instantaneous creation of a low entropy universe. Stephen Hawking agrees that the tremendous improbability of our universe spontaneously appearing naturally entails a number of religious implications:

> The odds against a universe like ours emerging out of something like the Big Bang are enormous. I think there are clearly religious implications whenever you start to discuss the origins of the universe. There must be religious overtones. But I think that most scientists prefer to shy away from the religious side of it.[42]

Not all scientists are so wary of this type of theistic reasoning, however. Physicist Tony Rothman, for example, openly acknowledges the natural progression from science to religion that tempts many of his colleagues:

When confronted with the order and beauty of the universe and the strange coincidences of nature, it's very tempting to take the leap of faith from science into religion. I am sure many physicists want to. I only wish they would admit it.[43]

In my mind, it isn't the realm of religion that requires the largest "leap of faith"; it is the non-theistic interpretation of cosmogenesis itself that requires the most faith, because it is founded on an incalcuably small probability of occurrence. It takes an awful lot of faith to believe that our incredibly complex and well-balanced world could have come into existence solely as a chance event.

5.12   Order Out of Disorder?

The pioneering work of Nobel laureate Ilya Prigogine with dissipative (i.e., far from equilibrium) structures has shown that, to a remarkable extent, order can arise out of apparent chaos. The key word here, though, is "apparent." Molecules may be able to adopt spontaneous positions of order out of apparent chaos when the circumstances are right, but this type of chaos doesn't qualify as genuine disorder, because the physical molecules themselves represent a higher degree of order than could ever be expected to be found purely "at random." Indeed, atoms and molecules, along with the subatomic particles of which they are made, seem to have been constructed in such a way as to make their spontaneous assembly into higher and higher degrees of order virtually inevitable. Eigen, for instance, has shown that self-propelled "autocatalytic" systems can spontaneously arise and lead to greater degrees of order, and that, when two or more autocatalytic systems conspire together to augment each other's production, a *hypercycle* can be produced, which greatly increases the overall amount of order that can be generated.[44]

Nevertheless, while atoms and molecules are quite capable of organizing themselves into progressively higher degrees of order "on their own," they still tend to lean in the opposite direction: namely, towards returning to the lowest energy state possible (which also qualifies as the most disordered state possible as well).

Equilibrium is the scientific term that is used to describe this disordered, low energy state. It is a physical fact that the natural inclination of all atomic particles is to reach thermodynamic equilibrium. Indeed, the only way this relentless push towards equilibrium can be forestalled is if a higher degree of order is somehow imposed upon a group of molecules. In this case, the anti-equilibrium effects of the externally contrived system act to oppose the natural tendency of matter to become thermodynamically equilibrated.

All living things are thus by definition *far from equilibrium systems*. They must constantly remain far from equilibrium in order to remain alive, because thermodynamic equilibrium means instant *death* for them. Thus, it is only because of some sort of externally imposed order that living things are able to avoid self-dissipation; without it, we'd all be dead in very short order.

Indeed, if the atoms and molecules of which we are made had *their* way, we'd *never* have a chance of staying alive, because they *always* want to reach equilibrium whenever they possibly can; they are simply held back at the present time by the equilibrium-fighting effects of biological order. This raises an interesting question: if we're all just the accidental byproducts of random atomic motions, why didn't the atoms of which we are made forever remain at equilibrium?

There appears to be only one answer to this question that is consistent with the known scientific laws: someone or something *had* to have exerted a restraining force on the various atoms in the universe at some point in the past, or else they all would have remained at equilibrium forever.

The standard answer to this problem is that far from equilibrium systems can be maintained in a thermodynamically open environment without contradiction to the Second Law of Thermodynamics; therefore, the need for an order-imposing Creator is circumvented. This response, however, begs the true question at issue here in two distinct ways: 1) it doesn't explain why any type of order is possible at all in the universe, and 2) it doesn't explain how these far from equilibrium systems could have initially evolved in the absence of an Intelligent Designer. Of course, once order-prone atoms and molecules have been created, and once they have been allowed to attain higher degrees of order, it no longer becomes a problem to see how these far from equilibrium systems can be maintained in a thermodynamically open environment without recourse to an Intelligent Designer.

5.12.1 God and the Existence of Self-Generated Order

The phenomenon of self-generated order in the cosmos has long been used as an argument against the existence of a Grand Designer. The reasoning here seems to be that if we can understand *how* a given process works and *what* it consists of, using only natural cause-and-effect processes that we can understand, a larger Explanation for this order becomes superfluous. The central flaw, however, in this type of anti-theistic argument from natural processes (of which the neo-Darwinian theory of natural selection is perhaps the most notable example) is that it is predicated on the shaky assumption that the Deity would not have used natural evolutionary pathways to accomplish His Creative Ends. But such an assumption is far from obvious, for the possibility always remains that the Deity could have used natural cause-and-effect processes in His creation for a Higher Purpose.[45] *It follows, then, that any theory which posits a naturalistic-type God Who creates solely through natural cause-and-effect processes is impervious to any and all discoveries of a self-generated order in the physical realm. In this type of naturalistic world view, the phenomenon of self-generated order is simply one of the Engineering Tools which the Deity has used to accomplish His Creative Ends.*

That is to say, it is one thing to observe that matter can spontaneously become more and more organized "all by itself," and quite another to say that such "autocatalysis" obviates (removes) any need for God in the physical sciences. After all, the unanswerable question still remains: Where did matter get the curious ability, not only to exist, but also to organize itself into progressively greater degrees of order "on its own"? Of course, to reply that mindless chance is the ultimate cause of these properties in matter is to confirm that such a question cannot possibly be answered from within the domain of experimental science alone. But does such a non-answer mean that there is in fact no answer to this question to be found anywhere in the cosmos? Probably not. To assume otherwise is simply to fall victim to the ultimate scientific arrogance of assuming that the only reality in existence is the physical one that scientists can understand and measure.

Indeed, if we assume that God has delegated as much creative responsibility onto the physical universe as He possibly could, then it stands to reason that He would have designed the capacity for "self-attained" order into the very atoms and molecules themselves, which would have subsequently enabled them to organize themselves into living tissue "all by themselves." In reality, though, it would have been God's initial Engineering Genius that would have endowed these microscopic particles with the marvelous capacity for self-generated order in the first place.

In fact, this conception of a naturalistic Creator, who delegates as much creative responsibility onto the physical universe as He possibly can, is far more impressive than the parochial conception of a God who has to continually intervene in the world to make things happen. The same thing can be said in the realm of automobile manufacturing: a car maker who can design a self-building and self-repairing car is far superior to the car maker who must build and repair his cars piecemeal all by himself!

5.13   Natural Selection and the Origin of Life

In the previous chapter we saw how the Earth employs thousands of highly complex structures and mechanisms in order to ensure that all forms of natural waste are regularly recycled back into the environment, where they can be used again to advantage by living organisms. We humans, by contrast, *excel* at producing unrecyclable waste products. Despite the many impressive technological achievements of the twentieth century, we are still generating billions of tons of unrecyclable toxic waste every year, and there doesn't appear to be any realistic solution to the problem in sight.

This brings to mind a very interesting question: why is it that the Earth has been able to successfully recycle *all* of its toxic waste products over the millennia, but *we* cannot? One would think that if the Earth's ecosystem had truly evolved by chance alone, it wouldn't possibly have been able to reach such a perfect level of environmental harmony all by itself. After all, we're talking about some of the most complex engineering pathways in existence, which chance processes alone almost certainly could never have duplicated, even over millions of years of cumulative selection. Indeed, although we humans are quite ingenious in our own right, our best engineers haven't even been able to *approach* the 100% recycling efficiency that is routinely employed by nature.

Put another way, why should a mindless evolutionary process succeed where intelligent humans have repeatedly failed? It doesn't help matters any to say that our world couldn't have survived to the present day without such a high degree of recycling efficiency. For while this may be true, it doesn't explain *why* it is true. This is the chief difficulty of all theories of natural selection, for while the selective process may explain why certain forms have been able to survive to the present day, it doesn't explain *where* this initial survival capacity itself originally came from. For this we have to look somewhere deeper and more substantial.

This is why all non-theistic evolutionary theories are ultimately unsatisfactory: because natural selection is only capable of explaining the process of differential survival amongst self-replicating species; it can't explain where the initial capacity for self-replication *itself* originally came from. Evolutionists thus beg the true question at issue here when they try to explain our current existence by means of natural selection. For while the selective process may help to explain why certain groups, and not others, have been able to survive the test of time, it doesn't tell us a thing about where the original survival capacities *themselves* originally came from. For this we have to look somewhere else—to a creative power that is entirely capable of producing self-replicating objects like living organisms.

Nevertheless, many non-theistic evolutionists insist on crediting natural selection for bringing about the phenomenon of life, despite the severe *category mistake* that is involved in this line of reasoning. They mistake the first category of explanation, that of differing rates of survival amongst self-replicating objects, for the first category of explanation, that of the original generation of self-replicating properties. These two categories of explanation are both ontologically and causally distinct, so there is very little, if any, realistic chance that the first category of explanation could ever substitute for the second. Even so, many non-theistic evolutionists still spend their entire careers trying to do this very thing.

This is an important point that can perhaps be better illustrated by means of an analogy with automobiles. It is a well-known fact that certain car models are able to survive the test of time in the marketplace from year to year, while others are not. The models that are "lucky" enough to survive do so because they fulfill a dual criterion of fitness: they are popular with the public and they are profitable for the parent company.

However, it would be ludicrous to suppose that this profitability and public popularity somehow explains the ultimate origin of the various car models themselves. For while it may be true that the corporate executives in the automobile industry are aiming for maximum profitability and public popularity when they initially choose to take certain car models to market, these dual intentions still do not explain how these models were originally made. For this we have to look beyond the dual intentions of popularity and profitability, to the tremendous *ingenuity* of the automobile designers and engineers themselves.

In the same way, the fact that certain groups of living creatures can survive better than others in the wild doesn't explain where this original capacity for survival *itself* came from. For this we have to look beyond the selective process, to the ultimate Creative Powers that rule the heavens.

Non-theistic evolutionists, however, do not believe this. They are instead convinced that the self-replicating process could have come into being by pure chance, in the form of a relatively simple primeval replicator. Over time, they believe that these simple chemical replicators could have accidentally developed into increasingly complex forms, primarily through the agency of natural selection acting upon random variations. Eventually, these successful variants are thought to have developed into plants, animals, and ultimately, human beings.

Significantly, the overall trajectory traced out by the evolutionary process has consistently been in the direction of increasingly greater levels of organic complexity. While the ascent of each major zoological group is known to have taken place through a highly contingent process of repeated fits and starts, the overall trend has nevertheless been towards increasingly greater levels of organic complexity. An analogy can be drawn here with the stock market. In the same way that the Dow Jones Industrial Average can trend upwards in spite of short-term setbacks in the individual stocks themselves, the overall trend of life on this planet, at least as far as biological complexity is concerned, has been upwards.

This trend is so pronounced that Paul Davies has actually defined a new arrow of time in terms of it.[46] As far as Davies is concerned, standard evolutionary theory is incapable of explaining the origin of this trend, because it defines success solely in terms of differential reproduction; the more offspring a species leaves behind, the more successful it is thought to be. However, this definition makes the myriad members of the microbial world the most successful species of all, since they leave behind by far the most off-spring. Nevertheless, this unprecedented rate of reproductive success in the various bacterial lines has *not* been accompanied by any significant increase in evolutionary complexity, since most microbes today remain unchanged from prehistoric times. Therefore, according to Davies, reproductive success alone cannot account for the existence of biological complexity.[47]

Evidently another mechanism, intrinsic to the organic replicators themselves, must have been at work fueling the rise towards increasingly greater levels of complexity in the biosphere. Natural selection in this case would have functioned in a *secondary* capacity to this internal drive, amplifying and refining it, but in no case substituting for it.

It isn't difficult to see that a replicator's ability to stand the test of time cannot in and of itself account for this gradual progression towards greater levels of organic complexity. For as Davies has pointed out, just because a replicator's internal degree of complexity enables it to survive the test of time without contradiction to the Second Law of Thermodynamics, doesn't mean that its complexity is *explained* by its ability to survive.[48] Freedom from the constraining influences of the Second Law cannot explain why this trend towards greater complexity occurs in the first place:

> Biosystems are not closed systems. They are characterized by their very openness, which enables them to export entropy into their environment to prevent degeneration. But the fact that they are able to evade the degenerative (pessimistic) arrow of time does not explain how they comply with the progressive (optimistic) arrow. Freeing a system from the strictures of one law does not prove that it follows another.
>
> Many biologists make this mistake. They assume because they have discovered the above loophole in the second law, the progressive nature of biological evolution is explained. This is simply incorrect. It also confuses order with organization and complexity. Preventing a decrease in order might be a necessary condition for the growth of organization and complexity, but it is not a sufficient condition. We still have to find that elusive arrow of time.[49]

Davies' identification of the arrow of time with this trend towards greater organic complexity elevates this trend to the level of a *fundamental cosmic principle*. However, it just doesn't seem possible that this trend could have ever occupied the status of a universal cosmic principle if it were merely the result of the differential process of survival. Something more direct and fundamental seems to be necessary for that.

Indeed, if natural selection alone were the sole arbiter of the trend towards greater complexity, life probably never would have evolved to begin with, because natural selection in all likelihood would have never had anything to select *from*. We mustn't forget that the phenomenon of self-replication is *itself* a fairly sophisticated property, which inherently requires a substantial level of complexity in order to be operative. But if there is no drive towards self-organization internal to matter (i.e., if individual atoms interact with one another by chance processes alone), then the property of self-replication probably would have never come into being, and we wouldn't be here.

In other words, the process of natural selection *presupposes* a significant degree of self-organization in matter. This is due to the fact that the only objects that natural selection can act upon are self-replicators, and self-replication is a sophisticated form of complexity that requires the prior existence of self-organizing atoms and molecules. Hence, natural selection in all probability could not have been responsible for generating the property of self-replication, since natural selection could not possibly have taken place before self-replication ever existed.

It follows, then, that the twin properties of self-organization and self-replication are necessarily *prior to* the property of being subject to natural selection, which in turn means that there *had* to have been a sufficient cause for matter to have originally become self-replicating in the first place; otherwise, natural selection almost certainly would have never become operative at all. This sufficient cause was in all likelihood a self-organizing drive internal to matter, because chance processes alone do not seem to be capable of producing self-replicating atoms and molecules, even over vast stretches of time.

This argument can be summarized in the following manner:

1) Matter must be self-replicating before natural selection can act upon it.
2) Self-replication is a highly sophisticated property that requires an impressive level of material complexity in order to be operative.
3) If no tendency towards greater levels of complexity is intrinsic to matter, then the property of self-replication in all likelihood would have never evolved, which in turn means that matter would have probably remained in the simplest form possible.
4) The simplest forms of matter are not self-replicating, because of (2). Furthermore, the simplest forms of matter are known to be *incapable* of self-replication.
5) Therefore, even the simplest forms of self-replication require the prior existence of an impressive level of material complexity.
6) Natural selection can only act upon matter that possesses a certain minimum level of complexity, which is the level that would enable it to be self-replicating.
7) It is next to impossible for natural selection to have initially created this level of material complexity, because prior to this point, matter *could not* have been self-replicating by definition, so there would have been nothing for natural selection to select from (barring the existence of highly creative chance processes).
8) If no tendency towards greater levels of complexity exists in matter, and if natural selection can only operate upon substantially complex self-replicators, then it follows that matter should exist in its simplest form only, which by virtue of its very simplicity, is not subject to natural selection, because it is not self-replicating.
9) Natural selection, however, is a fact.

10) Therefore, something internal to matter must have caused it to become complex enough to become self-replicating, because chance processes alone do not seem to be capable of producing self-replicating atoms and molecules.

The only way the evolutionist can escape from this bind is to assert that matter could have *accidentally* acquired the property of self-replication with no outside help. However, it is very hard to see how this could have ever been the case, especially if it is asserted that no natural tendency towards self-organization exists in matter (apart from the action of natural selection) and if it is acknowledged that natural selection is inoperative in a positive sense at this simple level of organization. Davies agrees:

> Since the work of Boltzmann, physicists have appreciated that microscopic random shuffling does not alone possess the power to generate an arrow of time, because of the underlying time symmetry of the microscopic laws of motion. On its own, random shuffling merely produces what might be called stochastic drift with no coherent directionality. (The biological significance of this has recently been recognized by the Japanese biologist Kimura who has coined the phrase 'neutral evolution' to describe such directionless drift.)[50]

Indeed, in order for matter to have accidentally acquired the property of self-replication, it had to have first discovered a means of becoming stable at the subatomic level. But as any particle physicist will immediately attest, this is a very tall order indeed, because subatomic stability is an *exceedingly* complex phenomenon that is only just beginning to be understood by theorists.

For one thing, stable atoms, as we have seen, must follow the Pauli Exclusion Principle, which explicitly forbids two subatomic particles from occupying the same quantum state at the same time. If this Exclusion Principle did not apply, all electrons would occupy the lowest quantum state, since it is the orbital with the lowest energy. This would cause the spontaneous rearrangement of the various positively and negatively charged particles in an atom, so that interactions between their nearest neighbors would predominate. This would result in the spontaneous collapse of the entire atomic structure into a single particle of enormous density, thereby destroying any further possibility for life. Our world is thus intimately dependent on the existence of the Pauli Exclusion Principle, yet we have no idea where it comes from or why it works the way it does. All we know is that it does indeed work, and that it is this very functionality that has enabled life to form.

The second stabilizing force at the subatomic level is the quantization of electronic energy levels. As Bohr originally showed in 1913, electrons can only exist at discrete levels about the nucleus, which amount to multiples of Planck's universal quantum of energy. The great benefit of this quantum nature of the atom, as we have seen, is that it allows for all atoms of a particular atomic number and weight to be both identical and stable in the face of a continual bombardment of energy from without. In a non-quantum atom, electrons could possess all possible energy states, and therefore all possible orbital distances from the nucleus. This of course would render all atoms different from one another, and would allow electrons to continually change their energy levels in response to the slightest amount of incoming energy, be it in the form of photons, cosmic rays, or whatever. This in turn would make a given atom's chemical properties subject to change at a moment's notice, thereby making any stable form of chemical interaction absolutely impossible. Fortunately, the existence of discrete quantum states greatly stabilizes each individual atom, because an entire quantum of energy is needed to alter a given electron's particular energy level.[51]

Even so, physicists still have absolutely no idea where the phenomenon of quantization comes from, or why it operates the way it does. All they know is that it is a strict prerequisite for atomic stability, and hence, for the existence of life.

In order for matter to have accidentally stumbled upon the property of self-replication, then, the atom had to have first discovered a reliable means of employing the Pauli Exclusion Principle within itself, and secondly, it had to have discovered a means of operating in a quantum fashion only. It is unlikely to the highest degree that matter could have accidentally stumbled upon these two discoveries by chance alone, again due to their overwhelmingly complicated nature. Indeed, these stabilization mechanisms are so profoundly complex that we humans haven't even *begun* to understand how they actually operate at the subatomic level.

Now, if these two properties are so complex that our best minds continue to be baffled by them, it is exceedingly unlikely that matter could have discovered a means of employing them purely by accident, which in turn means that matter in all likelihood did not acquire the twin properties of self-organization and self-replication by chance alone.

5.14   A Cosmic Blueprint?

In *The Cosmic Blueprint* Paul Davies examines the latest scientific findings regarding the universe's amazing self-ordering ability, and comes to a radical conclusion: there does indeed seem to be a "cosmic blueprint" acting "behind the scenes" which has enabled the universe to order itself so precisely from its primordial beginnings.

The very fact that the universe *is* creative, and that the laws have permitted complex structures to emerge and develop to the point of consciousness—

in other words, that the universe has organized its own self-awareness—is for me powerful evidence that there is "something going on" behind it all. The impression of design is overwhelming. Science may explain all the processes whereby the universe evolves its own destiny, but that still leaves room for there to be a meaning behind existence.[52]

It is the theistic implications of most design arguments which has made them unattractive to many scientists. Indeed, as Davies points out, the very idea of a cosmic blueprint in nature is often rejected as being too mystical, "for it implies that the universe has a purpose and is the product of a metaphysical designer. Such beliefs have been taboo for a long time among scientists."[53]

One wonders how *any* idea or concept, save the blatantly irrational, could possibly be taboo[54] amongst self-professed truth-seekers! The very notion of such a taboo in science smacks directly of a strong anti-theistic bias in the scientific community, which acts to severely distort most interpretations of the so-called objective evidence. Clearly, though, if one's overall goal is an accurate correspondance of one's ideas with the way things really are in life, *no* intrinsically rational ideas should be excluded from consideration *a priori* just because they happen to contradict one's own personal world view, or the biases of one's community.

In suggesting that a cosmic blueprint for the universe may in fact exist, Davies proposes a new set of *biotonic* laws[55] that act at the holistic level of the entire biological organism, yet without conflicting with the basic underlying laws of physics itself. Such a proposal amounts to an admission that an absolute reductionism in physics can never be fully adequate, since it cannot account for the miraculous existence of biological complexity; hence, the need is for new "biotonic" laws that function at the highest levels of biological organization, which, though they may not conflict with the more fundamental laws of physics, nevertheless could never be actually deduced from them.

In addition to these biotonic laws, Davies cites the need for a larger organizing principle that would apply to the entire universe itself, especially at the incipient stages of its evolution, since it appears to be impossible to account for the universe's present degree of order in the absence of such a unifying principle. Three separate criteria would have to be satisfied by any such meta-organizing principle:

1. It would have to be essentially acausal, or non-local in nature, since it would have to coordinate the behavior of large portions of the universe which have never been in causal contact with one another.
2. It would have to apply at the largest possible scale: that of the entire universe.

3. It would have to simultaneously account for the small-scale irregularities that produced galaxies and clusters of galaxies.

Such a universal meta-organizing principle hasn't yet been discovered, although there have been several tantalizing suggestions put forth in recent years. One of the most intriguing has come from British mathematical physicist Roger Penrose, who believes that such a principle would have to be in the form of a time asymmetric universal law, because it appears as though the time-reversible nature of the Second Law of Thermodynamics must first be broken before any type of entropy reduction and spontaneous ordering can occur. Penrose has conceived of the early universe in terms of what he has called the *Weyl curvature*, which is a measure of the distortion of the cosmic geometry away from perfect homogeneity and isotropy.[56] In Penrose's conceptualization, the Weyl curvature of the initial conditions surrounding the birth of the universe had to have been zero, otherwise we could never observe the type of homogeneous and isotropic universe we presently have. According to Penrose, then, if a meta-organizing principle does in fact exist, it would have to be capable of ensuring that the Weyl curvature of the early universe be *exactly* zero.

Needless to say, this is a very tall order indeed for any potential meta-organizing principle. But even if such a principle were to actually be discovered one day, we would still be faced with the question of how this principle came to be so efficacious to begin with, i.e., we would need a larger organizing principle to account for this meta-organizing principle, which would then need a larger organizing principle to account for *itself*, and so on, *ad infinitum*. Clearly, the only way to avoid an infinite regress here is if we posit an Ultimate Organizing Principle for the entire universe *which would contain within Itself all the necessary organizing principles for Its Own Existence*. Such a Limitless Role, it seems, can only be ascribed to a Divine Creator.

This shouldn't be surprising. What other principle could possibly satisfy Davies' and Penrose's stringent criteria for the ultimate law of the universe? What other principle could possibly work at both the largest and the smallest scales, be acausal, and still be capable of ensuring that the Weyl curvature of the early universe be exactly zero? And finally, what other principle could possibly fine-tune the many fundamental parameters of our biocentric universe, out of an infinity of possible choices? It seems as though only one Principle could possibly satisfy all of these stringent requirements simultaneously.

5.15   The Empirical Nature of the Biocentric Principle

Many scientists find the theistic explanation of cosmogenesis unconvincing on empirical grounds: since any type of religious explanation appears to be non-empirical by its very nature, the religious hypothesis doesn't seem to be as credible as the traditional scientific explanation. However, this distinction between religious and scientific explanations is fallacious, because there is no necessary connection between a given mode of explanation and its empirical content. In fact, depending on which mode of explanation is more consistent with the available evidence, the religious mode of explanation can be just as empirical as the scientific one, if not more so.[57]

Indeed, the evidence for contrivance in the universe appears to be about as "empirical" as we can reasonably expect, given the fact that we cannot directly observe the postulated Contriver in action. That is to say, a rational interpretation of the empirical evidence at hand indicates that some form of Intelligent Contrivance is the most probable explanation for the profound order and design that is observed everywhere and everywhen in the universe. Since the evidence itself is empirical, and since we are forming a direct interpretation of this evidence that is based primarily on its intrinsic characteristics, there is a legitimate sense in which our conclusion can be said to be "empirical."

Indeed, most of the "empirical" conclusions that are reached by modern scientists involve a similar type of subjective interpretation. Since experimental results don't automatically come tagged with their own correct explanation, scientists must invariably propose an interpretation of the evidence that is most consistent with the evidence's basic character. The more this interpretation appears to be self-evident (i.e., the more likely it is that any rational individual would reach the same conclusion), the more this interpretation can be said to be "empirical." On the other hand, the more ambiguous the evidence appears to be, the more subjective will be its interpretation, and hence the less "empirical" will be its conclusion.

Since the evidence for contrivance in the universe is suggestive of Intelligent Design, even to atheistic scientists (many of whom admit this in their writing), we can say with a reasonable degree of certainty that this is as "empirical" a conclusion as we could possibly expect, given the constraints that are inevitably imposed by the nature of the evidence and by our own limitations.

Unfortunately, the evidence for an "anthropic" interpretation of the cosmological evidence isn't nearly so direct. It tends to rely primarily on a subjective interpretation of the evidence, instead of on the intrinsic nature of the evidence itself. Hence, any argument for an anthropic interpretation of the evidence cannot be said to be "empirical" in the same sense that the argument for contrivance might be empirical.

Of course, this lack of absolute empiricism doesn't necessarily deter us from coming to conclusions that are logically valid or inductively sound. It only prevents us from saying that our conclusions are directly and unquestionably indicated by the evidence at hand.

Notes

1. Stephen W. Hawking, *A Brief History of Time* (New York: Bantam Books, 1988), p. 171.
2. Philip E. Johnson, *Darwin on Trial* (Washington, DC: Regnery Gateway, 1991), p. 110.
3. The Standard Model of particle physics attempts to describe all the known elementary particles and their interactions in terms of fields.
4. Larry Abbott, "The Mystery of the Cosmological Constant," *Scientific American*, Vol. 3, No. 1, 1991, p. 78.
5. Ibid., p. 72.
6. Ibid., p. 78.
7. Newton and Boyle would have wholeheartedly agreed with this idea, because they routinely allowed their theological beliefs to guide their scientific pursuits.
8. Ibid., p. 79.
9. John D. Barrow, *The World Within the World*, p. 220.
10. It is possible that some of the laws of Nature are simply a consequence of the underlying structure of the physical realm. In this case, atoms and molecules would behave the way they do largely (but not entirely) because of the way they are constructed. This seems to be Rupert Sheldrake's point in his conception of physical laws as "habits." But the perennial question still remains: why are atoms and molecules constructed the way they are? This type of question seems unintelligible in the absence of a Larger Creative Intellect, who would have designed atoms and molecules in such a way as to make a certain type of large-scale behavior possible in the universe.
11. Gerald L. Schroeder, *Genesis and the Big Bang*, pp. 93–94.
12. Ibid.
13. Ibid., p. 94.
14. Gribbin and Rees, *Cosmic Coincidences*, p. 46.
15. Hawking's attempt to get around the need for a Big Bang singularity seems to be more a consequence of his desire to avoid the singularity's religious implications than it is a consequence of any tangible scientific evidence *per se*. Furthermore, the denial of a Big Bang singularity doesn't at all eliminate the need for some sort of "cosmic egg" at the very beginning. It only eliminates the need for an infinitely dense Big Bang singularity.
16. It helps to think of the "matter" in a singularity in terms of its energy equivalent, since matter and energy are related through the famous formula $E = MC^2$. It is easier to see how an infinite amount of energy could be squeezed into a point of infinite density than it is to see how the same could be true for matter.
17. John D. Barrow, *The World Within the World*, p. 315.
18. Hugh Ross, *The Fingerprint of God*, p. 50.
19. Gerald Schroeder, *Genesis and the Big Bang*, pp. 57–58.
20. Ibid., p. 56.
21. Ibid.
22. Ibid., pp. 56–57.
23. Ibid., p. 58.
24. Ibid.
25. Ibid.
26. Ibid., p. 59.
27. Ibid.
28. Black holes, which result when massive dying stars collapse in on themselves

until a point of infinite density is reached, are hypothesized to have the same effect on light today.

29. *Babylonian Talmud,* Section Haggigah 12a.
30. Interestingly enough, the Talmud's emphasis on creative potential at the very beginning of time leaves room for a more deistic interpretation of the Divine Power, in which God would have initially created the potential for an evolving universe and then allowed it to evolve more or less on its own power. At all times, though, such a deistic universe would be metaphysically sustained by God's own Creative Power; it would simply function in a cause-and-effect manner according to its own intrinsic laws.
31. Schroeder, *Genesis and the Big Bang,* p. 92.
32. In Einstein's Twin Paradox, one twin takes off in an interstellar spacecraft bound for the stars while the second twin stays here on earth. Travelling near the speed of light, the first twin stays in space for five years before he returns home, at which time he is horrified to learn that his twin brother has been dead for several centuries. Time passed differently for the two brothers because of the profound difference in their individual velocities. A wealth of experimental evidence has subsequently confirmed Einstein's radical assertion that time does indeed slow down as one approaches the speed of light.
33. Ibid., pp. 50–54.
34. Mathematically speaking, the odds that any one thing will be chosen out of an infinity of possible choices is precisely zero.
35. C.B. Collins and S.W. Hawking, *Astrophys. J. 180,* 137 (1973).
36. Barrow and Tipler, p. 250.
37. Ibid.
38. Although it is possible that the Universal Creator is not the God of traditional theism (who is Omniscient, Omnipotent, Omnipresent, etc.), this issue is largely beyond the scope of the present work. However, because some aspects of cosmic evolution nevertheless seem to imply Omnipotent Coercion (more on this important point later), I will, in the interests of simplicity, assume that this Creator is the God of traditional theism.
39. Although the universe appears to be more organism-like than machine-like, the overall entropy of the universe had to have been constricted in some manner; otherwise, given the apparent universality of the Second Law, the present degree of order would be impossible to explain. The image of a wound-up clock is intended to represent this initial entropy constriction.
40. Boslough, *Stephen Hawking's Universe,* p. 123.
41. Paul Davies, *God and the New Physics* (New York: Simon and Schuster, 1983), pp. 167–168.
42. Boslough, p. 121.
43. Taken from John Casti's *Paradigms Lost* (New York: William Morrow and Company, 1989), pp. 482–483.
44. Ervin Laszlo, *Evolution: The Grand Synthesis* (Boston: Shambhala, 1987), pp. 31–35.
45. Please refer to my book *Back to Darwin* for a thorough discussion of the possible nature of this Higher Purpose.
46. Paul Davies, *The Cosmic Blueprint* (New York: Simon & Schuster, 1989), pp. 112–113.
47. Ibid., p. 112.
48. Ibid., p. 113.
49. Ibid.

50. Ibid.
51. Barrow and Tipler, p. 305.
52. Paul Davies, *The Cosmic Blueprint*, p. 203.
53. Ibid., p. 8.
54. Although philosophical speculation about the existence of God is supposedly beyond the methodology of the emprirical scientist, it is obviously *not* a forbidden topic amongst the many scientists who openly make the claim that modern scientific knowledge disconfirms the theistic hypothesis. These individuals can't have it both ways. If they are going to speculate about God in a negative fashion, they can't use scientific arguments in support of their position, since religion is supposed to be beyond the ken of ordinary experimental science. In the real world, however, the border between science and religion is exceedingly fuzzy, because each interpretation of a scientific phenomenon necessarily brings with it a question of meaning, and meaning is the central province of religion, not science. This is undoubtedly why science and religion were once united in the same discipline of study, called "natural philosophy."
55. The concept of a "biotonic" set of laws was originally formulated by physicist Walter Elsasser to explain the apparent emergence of new biological laws with increasing organismic complexity.
56. Ibid., p. 153.
57. Religious explanations can be more empirical than traditional scientific explanations if they go beyond the frontiers of normal scientific understanding to the very origins of science itself. This bypassing of traditional scientific barriers can bring with it a greater understanding of life's origins than ever would have been possible otherwise. Moreover, to the extent that this greater understanding yields a series of hypotheses which are more consistent with the existing evidence than the traditional scientific views, we can say that they are more empirical overall.

CHAPTER 6

Making Sense of the "Coincidences"

Whether or not it is clear to you, no doubt the universe is unfolding as it should.

MAX EHRMANN

What are we to make of the many remarkable "coincidences" discussed earlier in this book? Canadian philosopher John Leslie has suggested an appropriate analogy that we have already briefly alluded to. Imagine a condemned man about to be executed before a hundred-man firing squad. As the command to fire is given, though, each rifle spontaneously misfires, with the result that the condemned criminal is allowed to remain alive (albeit temporarily).

On one level, of course, this orchestrated misfiring represents nothing mysterious. No physical laws are actually violated; each rifle simply experiences an ordinary mechanical malfunctioning. But even though the odds for a single misfiring are finite enough, few of us would ever be satisfied with the contention that *each* of the hundred rifles had misfired purely by chance. The very fact that all the rifles misfired *simultaneously* seems to indicate beyond question that some sort of external unifying principle had to have been at work to coordinate the misfiring.

In the same way, by all "natural" accounts we should not have ever had the opportunity to evolve on this planet, because there are far too many disorganizing influences at work in the universe to ever allow such a coordinated masterpiece of engineering to occur purely by chance. However, due to the existence of a large number of cosmic "coincidences" throughout the physical realm, these potential roadblocks to our own evolution have somehow been bypassed, with the result that life did in fact have the opportunity to evolve on this planet.

The challenge, of course, is to find a suitable explanation for these "coincidences." Asserting that they were merely the result of a colossal cosmic accident does not seem to constitute a sufficient explanation because, again, their very coordination towards a common goal seems to suggest a strong degree of deliberateness, and hence contrivance.

157

6.1   The Probabilistic Significance of the Cosmic "Coincidences"

In *Reason & Religious Belief,* authors Michael Peterson, William Hasker, Bruce Reichenbach, and David Basinger reject the assertion that a naturalistic explanation for these coincidences renders the theistic hypothesis unconvincing.

On a non-teleological schema, the *a priori* probability of the particular scenario occurring that resulted in carbonous life is extremely remote. However, on a teleological schema, viewed from our *a posteriori* perspective, the features of the scenario become probable as necessary for the present state of affairs (specifically, human observers); there is a purpose to the events. Thus, though we can describe the development of the prior, causally unrelated physical events naturally, that they occurred at all and in the pattern and narrow range necessary for life that they did points to the existence of a conscious designer. Hence, it is reasonable to claim that the best explanation for the particular concatenation of the universe will appeal to more than mere natural causes and laws.

It might be objected that the fact that an event is *a priori* unlikely does not entail that it cannot be adequately explained naturally. That it has a probability at all indicates that natural explanations can be given. Hence, to evaluate its necessity from our present perspective is misleading; it is looking for an explanation after the fact. The effect, as it were, is already there in the causes, and nothing need be added to those causes to account for it.

However, the possibility that these facts about the universe have a natural explanation does not affect the argument, for the point of the argument is that what is sought is the best possible explanation not only of the conditions themselves, but also of the fact that among all the possibilities only those that make intelligent life possible exist. What requires explanation is not so much that those conditions exist, as that they are what they must be for life to be possible at all. The appeal to a conscious, purposive designer better explains the life-anticipating conjunction of these extremely narrowly ranged physical conditions and natural laws.[1]

Nevertheless, there are two possible ways to interpret the meaning of these "coincidences." The first is the method employed by the scientific agnostic: it is simply to note that since "something has to happen" in the universe, that something might just as well have been our own biocentric universe. As paleontologist Stephen Jay Gould of Harvard University has put it:

Any complex historical outcome—intelligent life on Earth, for example—

represents a summation of improbabilities and becomes thereby absurdly unlikely. But something has to happen, even if any particular "something" must stun us by its improbability. We could look at any outcome and say, "Ain't it amazing. If the laws of nature had been set up just a tad differently, we wouldn't have this kind of universe at all."

Does this kind of improbability permit us to conclude anything at all about that mystery of mysteries, the ultimate origin of things? Suppose the universe were made of little more than diprotons? Would that be bad, irrational, or unworthy of spirit that moves in many ways its wonders to perform? Could we conclude that some kind of God looked like or merely loved bounded hydrogen nuclei or that no God or mentality existed at all? Likewise, does the existence of intelligent life in our universe demand some preexisting mind just because another cosmos would have yielded a different outcome?[2]

There are two ways to respond to this serious attack. First, it is far from obvious that "something has to happen" in the universe. Indeed, if Thomistic philosophy is correct, then *nothing at all* could ever be expected to happen in a "universe" devoid of any Supernatural Power. The reason for this, of course, is that only God Himself is capable of acting as the First Cause for any contingent chain of existence. Without this First Cause, nothing else is presumably capable of existing whatsoever.

The Principle of Sufficient Reason supports this contention, as it demands that everything which occurs in the universe must possess an adequate reason for its occurrence. Traditionally, this adequate reason has been understood as being God, the very ground of all finite being. On this view, there couldn't possibly be anything at all, not even a universe, without the deliberate existence-sustaining action of the Divine Power. As a consequence, we cannot just flippantly conclude that "something has to happen" in the universe, because such an assertion is not apparent by any means.

On a deeper level, it simply isn't true that the existence of a concrete life-supporting world can even *partially* be explained by the "something has to happen" argument. Such a bare assertion commits the well-known fallacy of circular reasoning (in which one posits an argument's conclusion in its premise). For while it may be true that "something has to happen" in the world, this is only true in a world that *already* exists. But it is precisely the origin of the world that we are trying to explain here. Therefore, one simply can't observe the present-day reality of events and then argue that things are the way they are because "something has to happen." Before the birth of the universe 15 billion years ago *nothing at all* was apparently happening. What's more, scientists have no good explanation for why anything *ever* happened to begin with. To be sure, given the existence of absolute nothingness, we would *never* expect a highly organized universe to suddenly spring

into existence out of nowhere; that is, without some Larger Power intervening and orchestrating the whole affair.

Indeed, science itself is based on the conviction that nothing ever happens
in the universe without a sufficient prior cause, and this presumably includes
the birth of the universe itself.[3] But if this is true, then there is no way to
explain the sudden creation of matter out of absolute nothingness apart from
the creative activity of a "Disembodied Mind." The perfect symmetry of
absolute nothingness and perennial non-existence would thus be the cosmic
status quo in such a Mindless cosmic reality, simply because there would be
no compelling reason for anything concrete to happen in the first place.[4]

But even if, for the sake of argument, we assume the prior existence of a
coherent material realm, it still does not follow that all events are equally
impressive or meaningful, just because "something has to happen." Some
events are, by virtue of their internal degree of order, far more impressive
than other events, which possess lesser degrees of order. A straight flush,
for example, is far more impressive than a pair of twos during a poker game,
and the fact that some combination of cards had to be dealt does not diminish
this degree of impressiveness in the least.

Our present biocentric world, with its plethora of life-supporting constants and other physical parameters, represents the ultimate example of
such a complex historical outcome. Each and every one of the many variables that went into making it happen seem to have been deliberately contrived to enable life to evolve here, yet the combined improbability of all
these events is not diminished in the least by the observation that something
had to happen. The astonishment of the prisoner who survives a firing squad
of 100 riflemen because all their guns happened to misfire is not diminished
in the least because something had to happen. Similarly, our astonishment
at finding ourselves in a perfectly designed world should not be diminished
in the least by the belief that because something had to happen, our own
world is to be expected just as much as any other.

The fatal flaw in Gould's reasoning concerns the critical *perspective* from
which he is performing his overall probability evaluation. There are two
possible perspectives that can be taken in any such evaluation: an *a priori*
perspective, which is situated *before* the event in question actually occurs,
and an *a posteriori* perspective, which is situated *after* it occurs. Gould is
clearly taking the latter perspective in the above passage, since he is looking
back at the event and noting the number of "improbable" things that went
into making it happen. From this point of view, it *is* true that *all* complex
historical outcomes are exceedingly "improbable," insofar as they are all
comprised of an intricate combination of events, each of which is unique
and "improbable" in its own right. And since a precise duplication of each
particular combination will probably never occur again, due to the unique-
ness of all of its various constituents, there is a sense in which *all* complex

historical outcomes are so improbable as to never be able to happen again. Yet, these complex historical outcomes happen all the time, and since "something has to happen," it *is* in fact true that we shouldn't be unduly impressed by any particular combination of these "unlikely" events; that is, as long as we're viewing them "after the fact," from an *a posteriori* point of view.

In speaking about the probability of life's spontaneous origin, however, the natural theologian isn't taking this *a posteriori* point of view at all. He is, to the contrary, taking an *a priori* point of view, since he is convinced that life is so complex and important that it actually existed *before* the spectre of the Big Bang in the Eternal Mind of God Himself. To the extent that such a belief is true, it follows that the cosmic "blueprint" for the evolution of life actually *preceded* the birth of the universe itself, which in turn means that there is a sense in which the evolution of life was actually *predicted* before it actually occurred.

Two related factors justify our use of an *a priori* point of view in estimating the probability of our universe's evolution: 1) the intrinsic value represented by life itself (a more or less self-evident assumption), and 2) the many complex physical parameters that are necessary if life is to be capable of existing at all.

It follows, then, that when we are referring to the evolution of our present biocentric universe, we aren't talking about an *a posteriori* point of view. We are, instead, talking about an *a priori* point of view, since: 1) life itself does indeed possess a highly significant degree of intrinsic value, and 2) there is a sense in which the individual specifications for the evolution of biocentricity in the universe have existed for all eternity.

We can conduct a thought experiment to help clarify the second assertion. If we imagine ourselves as disembodied observers who are suddenly projected back in time before the the Big Bang, it would be quite clear to us that the universe had not yet come into being. Furthermore, we would know that any future universe would have to possess a certain constellation of fundamental features before it would be capable of supporting carbon-based life forms.[5] It is this timeless specification of the basic parameters for a biocentric universe *prior to* the actual occurrence of the Big Bang that constitutes an *a priori* point of view concerning the process of universal evolution.

Now if, after noting the essential requirements for a biocentric universe, we were to watch one suddenly come into being, we would justifiably be overwhelmed. Indeed, we would be convinced that we had witnessed a genuine miracle.

There are two reasons why such an event would automatically be construed as being miraculous. First and foremost, *any* complex historical outcome that is accurately predicted beforehand, when there is no possible causal connection between one's prediction and the actual occurrence, seems to be miraculous by its very nature. Secondly, the miraculous nature of life itself would automatically compel us to believe that the universal process that had brought it about was genuinely miraculous. Although it is possible that no conscious being would have been in existence prior to the Big Bang to make this momentous prediction, such a "prediction" nevertheless would have been made by the eternally existing requirements for the evolution of carbon-based life forms.

Amazingly enough, this very same sort of miracle actually occurred with the evolution of our own biocentric universe. For regardless of whether or not there was a Mind in existence at the Big Bang, it is nevertheless true that the various requirements for the evolution of a biocentric universe have existed for all eternity. It doesn't matter whether they had a concrete place in which to exist or not, since the fact remains that a certain series of requirements had to be met before life could evolve. It is these perennial requirements that have existed for all eternity. But if this is true, then it is also true that at a definite point in the past, these eternal requirements for life became fulfilled when our own biocentric universe came into being. In this sense, the "prediction" of life would have been made by the eternally-existing requirements for the evolution of carbon-based life forms. Thus, one doesn't even have to be a theist in order to affirm the claim that the evolution of life was actually "predicted" before it ever occurred. For the theist, however, this affirmation is a good deal easier, since he can simply place this *a priori* prediction in the Mind of God Himself.

From this *a priori* perspective, it is very hard to avoid the conclusion that some sort of miraculous Principle of Contrivance has been at work in the evolution of our life-supporting universe. Just as the accurate prediction of 100 straight hands of poker *before* the cards are actually dealt is infinitely more impressive than an *a posteriori* appreciation of the "improbability" of each hand *after* each is dealt, the actualization of an exceedingly complex life-supporting universe whose specifications have been in existence for all eternity is infinitely more impressive than a haphazard universe whose constitutive entities are viewed as being "improbable" after the fact.

The astronomical improbability of life's evolution of course only compounds the impressiveness of our biocentric universe. Just as being dealt a royal flush is far more impressive than being dealt two pairs, the evolution of a biocentric universe with its inherent degree of complexity (and hence improbability) is vastly more impressive than the evolution of a universe comprised exclusively of diprotons.[6]

Of course, the reason we are so impressed when we are dealt a royal flush is that we have preestablished the importance of this hand by virtue of its inherent degree of order. This is one aspect of the *a priori* sense of prediction referred to above. The evolution of life is the same way, insofar as its importance was "preestablished" by: 1) its internal degree of order, and 2) the intrinsic value of life itself. It follows, then, that when life came into being, something truly special *really did* happen: a part of the universe actually became *alive*, and this set the stage for the most monumental achievement of all: self-consciousness.

In reference to this *a priori* point of view we find that, against all the odds, the eternal specifications for life were spontaneously fulfilled when our biocentric universe exploded into being. This unprecedented event, which was heralded by a large number of stunning cosmic "coincidences," is so utterly miraculous that it would seem to have a probability of zero in the absence of some sort of larger Creative Principle.

Gould further attempts to downplay the cosmic importance of our world by arguing that any other type of cosmos would have been just as good in the end, all things considered. According to this view, our world is actually nothing special, because any other cosmos would have been just as acceptable overall (to whom?); therefore, we shouldn't be particularly impressed that it happens to exist as it does.

This type of argument is easy enough to dismiss, because it is undermined by its own propagation. The very act of attempting to form a concrete conceptualization of the universe, so that one can present a logical evaluation of it to the rest of the world, is *itself* one of the most impressive acts that can possibly be performed by an individual. To the best of our knowledge, no other being or power in the entire universe is capable of performing such a feat. But Gould would have us believe that there is really nothing special about this ability, because it would have been just as good overall if only diprotons were in existence. If there is nothing special about this ability, then there is nothing special about any of its *conclusions* either; therefore, on Gould's own terms we should ignore his conclusions completely!

However, the very fact that Gould continues to make such grand, all-encompassing statements provides strong evidence that, deep down, he really does believe that human life is special, even miraculously so. It simply would not be possible to take such an authoritative position about the meaning of life if there was nothing special about human existence.

6.2 Coincidence or Contrivance?

In its barest sense, the word "coincidence" refers to the co-incidence of two or more distinct events which may or may not be causally related. Although the simultaneous occurrence of two or more such events doesn't *necessarily* mean that the events themselves are causally related, many people like to believe in just such a causal relationship, especially when a higher degree of meaning can be attributed to the "coincidence." Indeed, the Swiss psychiatrist Carl Jung observed such a large number of meaningful coinci-

dences in his therapeutic career that he actually coined a term—
synchronicity—to refer to the underlying causal mechanism of the universe
that allows these meaningful constellations of events to occur.

It should be pointed out, however, that this larger degree of meaningfulness doesn't necessarily guarantee that the co-incident events in question
are *in fact* causally related; it only makes it more likely overall, since there
is always the remote possibility that the events themselves could be the
result of chance. The highly selective nature of human consciousness significantly increases the likelihood of this latter possibility, since we only tend
to notice those things in our lives that have some relevant degree of meaning
for us. Indeed, given the trillions upon trillions of causally unrelated events
that occur daily in the world, we would naturally expect a certain small
percentage of them to work together by chance to occasionally produce a
higher degree of meaning for us.

Not all meaningful coincidences, then, can be said to be causally related.
However, when the relationship between two or more events seems uncanny
(i.e., when the cooperation between distinct events is judged to be too elaborate to be the result of chance alone), there is a tendency to conclude that
such a co-incident occurrence *could not* have transpired without a common
cause. The strength of this tendency increases in geometric fashion as additional co-incident events are added to the "event pool."

For instance, the co-incident occurrence of five or six seemingly separate
events, which together hold some larger degree of meaning for us, is generally held to be far more indicative of a common cause than the meaningful
co-occurrence of only two or three such events. This is because the cumulative probability that any given co-incidence is due to chance vastly decreases
as more and more events are taken into consideration. This is why it is so
unreasonable to believe that the misfiring of all 100 rifles in the previously
mentioned example could have been a mere chance event—there are far too
many distinct events involved to be due to chance alone.

This conclusion is buttressed by the larger degree of meaning that is
conveyed by the cumulative rifle failure. As a consequence of this one event,
a condemned criminal is able to survive against truly overwhelming odds.
Rationally speaking, this appears to be too significant a consequence, in
light of the laws of probability, to have been due to chance alone.

It is thus the phenomenon of multi-faceted cooperation towards a single
meaningful end that compels us to posit a common cause to a series of
distinct events. In general, we can say that the larger the number of cooperat-
ing events and the greater the extent of cooperation between them, the less
likely it is that they could have been due to chance alone. The addition of a
final meaningful result makes the conclusion of a common cause virtually
irresistible.

When we speak of a common cause behind co-incident events, we usually have in mind some sense of underlying deliberateness that is aimed toward a particular result. The more relevant this result is perceived to be, the more likely we are to suspect that some type of deliberate causal mechanism must be behind it, linking the events in question together to form a single meaningful result. This tendency is greatly accentuated by the perceived degree of improbability of the co-incident events themselves: the more improbable these events are deemed to be on their own (i.e., apart from the activity of an unseen common cause), the more likely we are to conclude that they could not have been due to chance alone. It is thus the conjunction of two distinct characteristics, the personal relevance of a given constellation of events and the perceived unlikelihood of their occurrence, that compels us to conclude that they could not have been due to chance alone.

These criteria are implicit in the popular image of a "coincidence," which can be defined as the co-occurrence of two or more distinct events that is judged to be sufficiently remarkable as to warrant special attention. The question of what could be causing the coincidence is thus not directly addressed by the popular conceptualization. Such an explanation, if one is deemed to be necessary at all, is generally left to the individual's own preconceived view of the world.

While almost any such co-incident occurrence can simply be explained away as being a mere chance event (especially in scientific circles), most people tend to suspect the activity of a common causal element when the meaning and extent of a particular coincidence is judged to be sufficiently noteworthy. Nowhere is there a more noteworthy coincidence by these two criteria than in the case of the universe itself, where there are literally *dozens* of "coincidences" in existence, each of which is outrageously unlikely in and of itself, and all of which are coordinated together in an exceedingly precise fashion to allow for the evolution of biological life. This uncanniness is further supported by the apparent fact that life as we know it would be incapable of existing if even a single one of these fundamental structural parameters were minimally altered.

Going one step further, the cosmological evidence overwhelmingly seems to indicate that these cosmic "coincidences" could not have been due to chance alone. Five separate factors can be shown to work together in support of this radical conclusion:

1. The tremendous number of distinct co-incident events at work in the universe.
2. The outrageous unlikelihood that any one of these events could have occurred by chance alone.
3. The intimate degree of cooperation that is displayed by all of these co-incident events in their mutual support of biological life.

4. The intolerance to change of even a single one of these basic parameters if the biocentricity of the universe is to be maintained.
5. The unprecedented significance of life itself.

By these criteria, it is apparent that some type of underlying causal relationship does in fact exist behind these cosmic "coincidences." The big question concerns the actual identity of this causal influence. There seems to be only two possibilities. On the one hand, it is possible that some form of mindless cosmic force could have orchestrated the co-incident occurrence of these life-supporting events. This possibility, however, is strongly disconfirmed by the stupendous degree of intelligence and foresight that is repeatedly displayed by the cosmic coincidences themselves; it is hard to see how anything less than a Being of Infinite Intelligence and Power could have possibly been the creative agent behind these events.

The obvious inference, then, is that a Divine Creator Being *really did* calibrate the underlying parameters of the universe in such a way as to allow life to evolve on this planet. Indeed, it is the almost self-evident nature of this inference that explains why so many secular books on cosmology end up repeatedly mentioning God in one way or another. Even so, most of these non-theistic authors fail to take the required "leap of fact" by openly acknowledging God's Creatorship in the universe. The majority of these scientists, however, do not use the scientific evidence itself to justify their continuing non-belief (because it almost always points in the opposite direction); they instead appeal to historical and personal reasons to justify their continued resistance to theism.

Physicist George Greenstein, for example, openly mentions the idea of God several times in his book *The Symbiotic Universe*. After observing that the laws of physics seem to conform themselves to the rigorous demands for life, he wonders whether it was:

> . . . God who stepped in and so providentially crafted the cosmos for our benefit . . . Do we not see in its harmony, a harmony so perfectly fitted to our needs, evidence of what one religious writer has called "a preserving, a continuing, an intending mind; a Wisdom, Power, and Goodness far exceeding the limits of our thoughts"?[7]

Incredibly, though, after he makes the obvious inference from the scientific facts to the reality of God, Greenstein rejects the whole idea, arguing that "God is not an explanation."[8] Given the magnitude of the issues in question, such closed-minded dogmatism simply will not do. God may not be an efficient cause *within* the universal cause-and-effect scheme,[9] but He *can* be the original cause of the causal system itself (along with the internal characteristics of that system). That is to say, God may not be a physically measurable Entity Who can be directly studied in the laboratory, but this is a far cry from arguing that God cannot be a metaphysical explanation for the present character of physical reality as a whole, especially when the obvious inference is that He is. Greenstein seems to be aware of this glaring inconsistency, as he openly admits that the mere thought of a Divine Creator God makes him squirm in his seat!

Another "reason" Greenstein uses for rejecting a Supernatural explanation for these anthropic "coincidences" is that it would go directly against the historical tendency of science to oppose religion.[10] The origins of this opposition are easy enough to understand. For centuries the Church persecuted pioneering scientists out of its fear that new scientific discoveries would cast a shadow on its claim to inerrant truth; it even put some, such as Giordano Bruno, to death. Accordingly, the scientific establishment rapidly became conditioned to reject most religious matters out of hand, especially those that tried to use religious explanations to account for scientific phenomena.

But even though the scientific establishment has a legitimate gripe against the Church, it is fallacious to use this historical feud as objective evidence against Divine Creation. *Merely human activities in and of themselves have absolutely nothing at all to do with how the universe itself came into being.* Indeed, just as one would never believe that a group of lunatics who formed a religious cult around the science of biochemistry could ever destroy the validity of that science, the malicious behavior of Christians in the past can never alter the basic facts surrounding the universe's coming into being. We must therefore sharply distinguish between merely human events, on the one hand, and objective physical reality, on the other. Once we do this, however, it quickly becomes apparent that the historical clash between science and religion has absolutely nothing at all to do with whether or not God is the Author of the physical universe as a whole.

Interestingly enough, once we do away with the two incoherent objections to a scientific theism mentioned above, there no longer appears to be any reasonable way to avoid the obvious inference that some sort of Grand Designer *had* to have been at work in the genesis of our life-supporting universe.

Greenstein tries to get around this inference by invoking the Participatory Anthropic Principle (PAP): Since some form of living consciousness seems to be necessary in a quantum sense in order to collapse the cosmic wave function and give the universe a concrete reality, Greenstein argues that the universe somehow designed itself to support life so it could be "observed" into being. For Greenstein, then, a gigantic symbiosis is at work in the universe between life, on the one hand, and the physical machinery of the universe, on the other, as both seem to need each other in order to survive.

This clever method of trying to explain God away also appears to be fallacious. For even if we affirm the quantum suggestion that life is necessary to collapse the universal wave function so as to give the cosmos a concrete reality, this idea can never coherently be used to explain how the universe *itself* originally came into being, or how it first came to exhibit the unique life-supporting parameters that it now in fact possesses. The reason is simple enough: modern science knows for a fact that there was a definite time in the past before which any life at all ever existed on this planet. Moreover, this rule is known to apply to extraterrestrial life forms just as much as it does to Earth-based life, because there is a definite time before which physical life of *any* kind could have existed anywhere in the cosmos. For instance, no physical form of life could have existed 3 minutes after the Big Bang, since coherent atoms and molecules hadn't yet formed. Indeed, since any conceivable form of life must contain significant quantities of the heavier elements, life could not have evolved until after the first generation of supernovae had already exploded, since it is in these dying red giant stars that the heavy elements themselves are slowly cooked. Since the lifetime of a typical red giant star is on the order of 10 billion years, this means that approximately 70% of the history of the entire universe was probably spent in a state of lifeless cosmic evolution (assuming that by "life" we mean finite, biological life). *But if life is necessary to give the universe a concrete existence, how could the universe have ever evolved for at least 10 billion years without so much as the hint of life?*

There are two ways to get around this problem. To begin with, we can simply reject the PAP outright and assert that life is *not* necessary to give the universe a concrete existence. This alternative of course destroys Greenstein's hypothesis and puts him face to face with the need for a Cosmic Designer. On the other hand, if we accept the validity of the PAP and affirm the need for life to collapse the universal wave function, we need to find *another* kind of life in the universe that would have been in existence from the Big Bang onward, because this is the only way the entire physical universe itself could have been observed into being. Needless to say, the only conceivable form of life that could have possibly been around at the very beginning of spacetime is the "Ultimate Observer" Himself, who would have functioned to observe the primordial universe itself into being. Ironically, then, Greenstein's superficially clever ploy to use the findings of quantum physics to get around the need for a Grand Designer actually ends up supporting God's Existence in the end.[11]

6.3 Cosmic Coincidences and the Odds Surrounding the Evolution of Life

There is an interesting parallel between the cosmic "need" for "coincidences" in order to make life possible, and the actual odds against any sort of life ever evolving on earth without an external Designer, even in a perfectly hospitable world. Roger Penrose, for example, has estimated[12] that the odds of our present universe forming by chance are a whopping 1 in $10^{10^{30}}$. DeLey in like fashion has calculated the odds against the human genome forming by chance at approximately 1 in $10^{240,000}$, which is thousands of orders of magnitude above the widely-accepted level of statistical non-possibility.[13] Such observations—and there are many more like them—lead one to believe that were it not for some other "loading of the cosmic dice," life would never have evolved on this planet, in spite of the earth's possessing the ideal conditions for the sustenance of life.[14]

The unifying theme which appears to be at work here between those coincidences necessary to make the universe habitable and those necessary to enable life to actually evolve is one of *Deliberate Design by a Higher Power.*

With this in mind, the next thing we need to do is to ask ourselves the following question: What are the specific criteria by which we can judge a given object to be deliberately contrived by an intelligent power? There are several:

1. The existence of a coherent object that is comprised of a complex concatenation of interconnected parts which work together towards the achieving of a practical end.
2. A state of complex *coordination* between the various constituent structures of the object and their mutually interactive functions.
3. An overall *design* (i.e. formal cause) to the object which can be laid out in an intelligible, coherent fashion.
4. The exploitation of well-known technological and engineering principles which are utilized for a common, constructive end.

By these criteria, it is evident that the universe has been deliberately contrived by a Higher Power for a particular goal. For one thing, it is hard to question the assertion that the universe is itself a coherent mega-object which has, as one of its functions, the goal of supporting biological life.

With the advent of modern physics and cosmology it is also evident that there is a complex state of cooperation between the various structures of the universe and their resultant functions. The cosmic "coincidences" themselves which we have discussed previously are perhaps the most exquisite examples of this sort of functional cooperation. Moreover, these coincidences are known to exploit a wide variety of technological and engineering principles in their mutual cooperation to produce a viable life-supporting universe.

Lastly, it is hard to question the assertion that there exists a larger design (i.e. formal cause) to the universe itself. Indeed, it is the very intelligibility of this design which has provided scientists with a rational subject to study and to experiment with.

Of course, there are those who argue that the very "naturalness" or seemingly uncontrived nature of the world is itself somehow evidence against the existence of a Grand Designer. Such an assertion is fallacious, however, for the following reason: as long as we characteristically judge the overall contrived appearance of a given created object to be inversely related to the artist's creative skill, then we must conclude that the creative work of a *perfect* Artist must itself seem perfectly *un*contrived (in the sense of not appearing to be the deliberate handiwork of a conscious designer), and this is precisely what we observe to be true in the natural world. Thus, the seemingly uncontrived naturalness of the existing world is itself evidence *for* the existence of a Grand Designer.

But, if it is evident that the universe must have had an Intelligent Designer, then why have so many scientists found this notion so hard to believe? To begin with, not all scientists find it so unbelievable. On the contrary, our modern scientific enterprise was itself based on the efforts of those who possessed a fundamentally theistic view of the cosmos. Kepler, Boyle, Newton, and Copernicus, for example, were all ardent believers, and in fact, it was their passionate belief in a rational Creator that initially led them to look for order in the creation. Today, tens of thousands of practicing scientists believe in a theistic world view without having their faith negated by the details of scientific learning. As far as the remaining unbelievers themselves are concerned, one can only appeal to the existence of a deep, historically-conditioned anti-theistic bias in their innermost souls, which causes them to repeatedly misinterpret the existing scientific evidence in a non-theistic manner.

6.4   A Humean Objection

It is instructive to note that Scottish philosopher David Hume, whose general ideas on natural theology will be discussed at greater length in Chapter 11, would have rejected the underlying basis for Leslie's previously mentioned analogy of the misfiring rifles, for the following reason. Since the evolution of our present universe is by definition a unique occurrence, we have nothing else to compare it to. But since we need an objective frame of reference in order to judge the relative probability of any event or series of events, it would seem that there is no coherent way to assess the inherent probability of the various "coincidences" that have occurred during the history of the Hubble expansion. According to Hume, then, we are not justified in drawing *any* sort of analogy from a part within the universe to the character of the entire universe itself, because we have no objective standard to compare our judgments to.

. . . can a conclusion, with any propriety, be transferred from parts to the whole? Does not the great disproportion bar all comparison and inference? From observing the growth of a hair, can we learn anything concerning the generation of a man?

. . . But allowing that we were to take the operations of one part of nature upon another for the foundation of our judgment concerning the origin of the whole (which never can be admitted), yet why select so minute, so weak, so bounded a principle as the reason and design of animals [that are] found to be upon this planet. What peculiar privilege has this little agitation of the brain which we call "thought," that we must thus make it the model of the whole universe?[15]

This turns out to be a fallacious argument indeed, for while the universe itself may be a unique occurrence, the individual events themselves that have gone into comprising the universe are probably *not* unique in terms of their basic nature. Insofar, then, as they are similar to events in our own experience that we *are* familiar with, we *can* use them to make certain rational judgments concerning the nature of the entire universe as a whole.

That is to say, the many constitutive parts and relations that are contained within the universe are known to possess their own descriptive laws and behavior patterns that can, in principle, be generalized to the behavior of the universe as a whole, because they seem to represent basic universal principles that apply in all places and in all times. Indeed, the very nature of cosmology itself is based upon the universality of certain physical laws and processes. By coming to know and understand the underlying basis of these fundamental patterns, we can develop a theoretical series of rational expectations that *can* in principle be extrapolated out to the universe as a whole, assuming, of course, that our choice of explanatory principles is appropriate. Indeed, while it may be true that, in many cases, the whole is greater than the sum of its parts, it is also true that there are many instances where a given part of a whole *can* tell us something significant about the character of its larger environment.

In fact, with the advent of modern science, we now know that it *is* often-times appropriate to argue from certain parts to their corresponding wholes. For instance, the discovery of the DNA molecule in the nucleus of the cell—which contains the genetic information for the entire body, and not just the genetic information for the particular cell it is found in—shows that one can indeed deduce the structure of a complex whole (the genetic information of the entire body) by studying a single microscopic part (the DNA of any given cell). Thus, Hume's sarcastic accusation that the growth of a hair can never tell us about the generation of a man, has turned out to be empirically *false* in the light of our modern understanding of the DNA molecule. For it is now known that an analysis of the DNA of a single hair-generating follicle *will in point of fact* yield a complete genetic description of the entire body.

Indeed, if the views of quantum physicist David Bohm are correct, all the information in the *entire universe* is somehow "enfolded" into each of its most fundamental constituents. According to Bohm, then, each fundamental constituent of the universe contains a type of holographic "picture" of the entire cosmos. On this view, if we could somehow tap into this "implicate order," we could learn all there is to know about the entire universe, Hume's protestations notwithstanding.

If we use this holistic principle judiciously, it is quite possible to identify characteristic patterns of behavior *within* the universe that will apply equally well to the entire universe as a whole. Indeed, if this were not the case, astronomers and cosmologists would be out of a job, since they would be prevented from drawing any significant conclusions about the universe through the study of anything that is contained within it.

The fact is, Hume's dogmatic argument is fatally undermined by its *own* underlying premise. For if it is true that *no* analogies can be drawn to absolutely unique events, then this is a principle that has *itself* been learned from within the overall body of the present universal structure. But if this is so, then by Hume's own admission it cannot be applied to the universe as a whole, because this too would amount to the drawing of an analogy from a part within the universe (the assertion that one cannot draw an analogy to absolutely unique events) to the whole (that the universe itself is beyond analogy). If the universe is truly beyond analogy, then we can never prove it to be so, because in the very act of asserting such a proof we can't help but commit the same cognitive error that we are trying to legislate against. Hence, not even Hume can utilize a part contained within the universe to help explain the whole.

Another recent scientific discovery has helped to further disconfirm Hume's argument against holism. A high degree of cosmic order is now known to extend, not only to the farthest reaches of the observable universe, but also to the most distant reaches of time as well. Cosmologists are now reasonably sure that the entire universe began some 15 billion years ago in a primordial explosion whose initial conditions were so highly ordered that, against all the odds, a life-supporting biocentric universe subsequently formed. Indeed, as physicists are learning more and more every day, had even a single one of these initial conditions been even slightly different, life could never have evolved on this planet. Hence, an exceedingly high degree of cosmic order can be found to extend as far into space and time as the human mind can probe.

On this level, then, the natural theologian's argument from the part to the whole has been almost fully vindicated. While it is possible to imagine that our entire universe, dating back to the Big Bang, is *itself* a small pocket of order in a much larger abyss of disorder, there is not a shred of evidence to be found in support of this extremely remote possibility. As a consequence, doesn't it make far more sense to stick with what we know, than to resort to idle speculation about a theoretical possibility that has no supporting evidence and very little likelihood of being valid?

Hume also questions the appropriateness of thought as a model for the entire universe. He wants to know what "peculiar privilege" this "agitation of the brain" possesses to justify its use as the creative paradigm for the rest of the universe. The fact is, though, human thought is by far the most advanced and "privileged" facility of its kind that has yet been discovered in the entire known universe! For not only can it go back in time to within 10^{-43} seconds of the Big Bang to ponder the universe's origins, it can also construct intelligent space probes that can travel beyond the confines of the entire solar system, amassing important scientific data during each step of the way. On a more ominous note, the human mind has also been "privileged" with the capacity for unlocking the secrets of nuclear power, which can either be used for good or ill. Most impressive of all, however, is the fact that the mind can understand and even predict the mathematical foundations that the whole of physical reality seems to be based upon.

Now, if human thought is capable of such grandiose accomplishments, it no longer seems ludicrous to use it as a model for the origin of the entire universe. Indeed, the facility of human thought appears to be *one step ahead* of the physical universe in one important respect. For while both are capable of producing spectacular instances of intelligent creation and nuclear destruction, only humans are capable of *thinking* about the past history of the universe, as well as about the future. On this score, the "privileged" status of human thought is unrivalled by anything else in the entire known universe.

Notes

1. Michael Peterson, William Hasker, Bruce Reichenbach, and David Basinger, *Reason & Religious Belief* (New York: Oxford University Press, 1991), p. 83.
2. Stephen Jay Gould, *The Flamingo's Smile* (New York: W.W. Norton & Co., 1985), p. 395.
3. Although it has been claimed that there are events in the quantum world that have no cause, this has yet to be firmly established. All we really know for sure is that we can't identify any specific causes to the events of the quantum world, but this is a far cry from saying that no such causes actually exist. In all likelihood we are probably just ignorant of the true identity of these quantum-level causes. Moreover, while it may indeed be true that some quantum events may not have an immediate or proximate cause, there may not need to be any such cause in order for these quantum events to be able to function properly. In this case, the very existence of matter within a larger quantum field would *itself* be the cause of these "uncaused" quantum events.
4. While some thinkers attempt to get around this problem by positing an eternally existent material realm, which was simply reorganized at the Big Bang, there

isn't a shred of scientific evidence for this position. Such a belief also leaves the existence of matter itself unaccounted for, since an eternal material realm would not seem to contain within itself a sufficient reason for its own existence.

5. Although other forms of life that are not centered around carbon are conceivable, I am focusing here only on those that *are* carbon-dependent, for three reasons: 1) because *we* are carbon-based, and we are primarily concerned about a universe that caters to *our own* existence, 2) because carbon-based life forms are the only kind we know about for sure, and 3) because carbon seems to be the only element that is sufficiently versatile to support *any* physical kind of life (see Chapter 4 for more on this point).

6. Our own existence attests to this fact: we are the most impressive objects in the entire known universe, but we are only able to exist because of the exceedingly improbable universe that evolved before us.

7. George Greenstein, *The Symbiotic Universe*, p. 27.

8. Ibid., p. 28.

9. If God does act as an efficient cause within the present universal scheme, this causal influence cannot be directly detected.

10. Ibid., pp. 126–128.

11. Although this support for an "Ultimate Observer" in the universe would not exist if one simply rejected the PAP, Greenstein himself actually *accepts* it, so he *does* inadvertently end up supporting the existence of God in the end.

12. Barrow and Tipler, p. 448.

13. Ibid., p. 565.

14. In saying that God may have "loaded the cosmic dice," I mean to say that God increased the inherent probability that life would evolve to the point of being weakly necessary. This gets back to Hick's fundamental distinction between an outcome being logically necessary, and one that is merely necessary in fact. Thus, given the underlying structure of the present universal order, it was virtually inevitable that life would evolve, though it still wasn't *logically* necessary. Although each step in the evolutionary process may have been weakly contingent, the overall trend, given the fundamental structure of matter, was inexorably towards the rise of life.

15. David Hume, *Dialogues Concerning Natural Religion* (London: Penguin, 1990), p. 58.

CHAPTER 7

Alternative Viewpoints

The most incomprehensible thing about the universe is that it is comprehensible.

ALBERT EINSTEIN

7.1 The Many Worlds Interpretation of the Weak Anthropic Principle

One way in which the Weak Anthropic Principle has been used to explain the current life-supporting character of the universe is in conjunction with Everett's Many Worlds interpretation of quantum mechanics. One version of Everett's theory postulates a different branch of the universe for every possible value of an observable quantity.[1] This produces an infinite number of "worlds" or regions in existence, only a few or even just one of which has the right characteristics to support biological life.[2] And since we are alive to speculate on this issue, we must naturally be living in one of these accidentally perfect regions.

There are, however, five severe problems with this explanation:

1. It fails to consider *where* the original matter for these different worlds came from and *how* it initially came to possess the miraculous quality of self-organization.
2. There is no concrete evidence for Everett's theory whatsoever.
3. If the scope of the cosmic whole is infinite, this approach leads to the nonsensical conclusion that there are an infinite number of worlds in existence which contain an infinite number of slight and not-so-slight variations on our present world. For instance, an infinite number of Hitlers would exist in this scheme, with a widely varying array of personal characteristics, ranging from similar body structures to radically different personality qualities. Some of these Hitlers would even be kind and loving individuals, for if there are an infinite number of worlds in existence, there must also by definition be an infinite number of gradations on all possible basic themes.
4. It is difficult to see how a single coherent world could possibly be maintained in the face of each successive splitting of all possible worlds with each successive moment, not just in a single quantum location, but in *all possible* locations.

175

5. It is far too complicated and burdensome an explanation for the existence of life (in fact, infinitely so) when a much simpler and vastly more elegant explanation already exists, namely that a Divine Creator God is personally responsible for designing our fine-tuned biocentric universe.

There is a principle of theoretical economy in the world of science called Occam's Razor, which basically says that the simpler of any two competing theories is usually the one that ends up being true. If we apply Occam's Razor to the question of the origin of life, we find that we must sacrifice the infinitely complicated Many Worlds theory in favor of the much simpler notion of Intelligent Design.

Before moving on, it should be pointed out that although Everett's Many Worlds interpretation seems to make an appeal to many *distinct* universes, they must nevertheless all be a part of the *same* universe, since they all seem to be descended from the same ancestral point of origin, and since they all presumably follow the same general physical laws. Indeed, if we define the "universe" as the sum total of *everything* that exists in the physical realm, then we cannot properly call Everett's idea a many "universes" interpretation at all; it is much more appropriate to call it a "many worlds" approach, as we have done.

Most thinkers who utilize the WAP to help explain the existence of our present life-supporting world really have in mind a *single* all-encompassing universe that possesses a large number of differents realms or compartments within it, each of which is thought to possess a different underlying set of structural parameters. The notion of spontaneous symmetry breaking can help us here, because it is possible that different areas of the early universe took on different underlying structural values following the initial collapse of the universe's primordial symmetry. This could conceivably have produced a large variety of different values for the fundamental constants of Nature in different areas of the cosmos. Life would then have arisen only in those compartments which happened to contain the "right" structural values.

This attempt to explain the present universal order without appealing to an Intelligent Designer suffers many of the same problems that plague Everett's Many Worlds approach. It also takes the prior existence of self-organizing matter for granted, without making any attempt to explain where it could have originally come from. (Saying that it has always existed amounts to little more than a non-explanation, because matter does not seem to contain within itself the capacity for self-existence, as we have seen.) Moreover, no concrete evidence for this theory—which would amount to the discovery of other universal realms where true disorder reigns supreme—has ever been found. Although it is possible that the entire visible universe is simply an "oasis of order" in a much larger realm of disorder, this possibility runs counter to everything we have ever learned about the cosmos. It also seems to be terrifically improbable. In addition, if the universe is judged to be infinite in spatial extent, then this "many compartments" approach also leads to the nonsensical conclusion that there are an infinite number of other worlds in existence that are only slightly different from our own world. Finally, the postulation of a multiplicity of worlds in order to explain our own world violates the Principle of Theoretical Parsimony (i.e., Occam's Razor) that we have already alluded to, so once again we are better off sticking with the simpler of the two alternatives (i.e., Intelligent Design).

7.2 Campbell's Criticism of the WAP

As we have seen, one of the ways in which the WAP has been utilized to "explain" the existence of our life-supporting world has been in terms of a self-selection principle: out of a multiplicity of possible worlds, we inevitably find ourselves living in the one possible world that is capable of supporting our existence.

This position has been severely criticized by UCLA molecular biologist John Campbell, whose selection-based criticism is reminiscent of Alfred Russell Wallace's criticism of Darwin's hyper-selectionist explanation of the human mind. Campbell notes that if the character of the visible universe were merely dependent on the fact of our existence, we wouldn't expect the exceedingly perfect universe that we presently observe; we would instead expect to observe a barely adequate universe whose qualities are just minimally sufficient to support our own existence.

The central premise behind Campbell's argument against the WAP is that our universe is far better than it has to be in order to support human life. He bases his value judgement primarily on the anomalously long lifetime of our present universe, when presumably a much shorter universal lifetime would have easily sufficed to support human life. Campbell believes that these extra universal years will be used to greatly extend the biological and psychological evolution of the human race, and he even goes so far as to conclude that the purpose of these extra years is partially explained by the needs of our own future evolution.[3]

In order to account for our unexpectedly perfect universe, then, Campbell believes that we have to go beyond the WAP to a higher level of explanation, which is capable of taking the future evolutionary needs of the human race into account. In a similar fashion, Wallace believed that the evolution of the human brain could not be explained merely by natural selection, which would have fashioned a brain that was barely superior to that of an ape, since our survival needs in the wild wouldn't have required significantly more intelligence. Instead, Wallace noted how the brain of the most rudimentary savage is more or less identical in capacity to that possessed by more advanced European races, so he concluded that natural selection could not therefore be used to account for the brain's evolution.

Campbell's argument against the WAP is both sound and convincing. We would never expect a universe that was selected by the mere fact of our own existence out of a multiplicity of possible universes to be so overly perfected for the task, when presumably a much less adequate universe would have been sufficient to generate observers. This being the case, the ultimate reason for our universe's existence probably transcends mere selectionist explanations (though it is nevertheless possible that our overly perfected universe could have been selected for by mere chance).

7.3   The Sum Over Histories Interpretation

In *A Brief History of Time* Stephen Hawking suggests that the use of a modified version of Richard Feynman's sum over histories method of explaining subatomic particle behavior may possibly help us to understand how our present highly-ordered world could have come into existence.[4]

Briefly, Feynman's sum over histories approach states that any given subatomic particle will traverse the distance from Point A to Point B by taking all possible physical paths between the two points. These paths are then added together in terms of their individual probabilities so that a single real-world probability pattern can be determined.

Hawking maintains that if we use this sum over histories approach for the entire universe, all possible paths will be taken by all possible particles. Assuming this to be true, it would then seem to follow that a chance combination of particles could conceivably have produced our present life-supporting world, especially if we allow for the passage of huge stretches of time. This being the case, it would then no longer be a mystery why we happen to find ourselves living in the particular type of world that we do: we would simply have evolved in the only part of the universe that could have supported our existence. It this type of self-selection that constitutes the very essence of the WAP.

The problem with this "explanation" is that it does not explain why the universe does not deteriorate into total disorder with each successive instant. If all possible paths are routinely taken by all possible particles, one would expect the entire range of possibilities to repeatedly be explored. But there are many more disordered states possible than ordered states; hence, a macroscopic interpretation of Feynman's sum over histories approach should produce a wildly disordered universe, not the highly ordered one we presently observe. Even if we allow for the accidental creation of self-ordering atomic particles in the distant past, the resulting complex systems would nevertheless be comprised of subatomic particles that would constantly be exploring all possible behaviors, thereby making any lasting state of order impossible to maintain. The only way out of this dilemma is if the order that is produced is somehow able to constrain the subsequent range of possible paths taken by the constituent particles. It is very hard, however, to see how any such constraining influence could have ever come about apart from the faculty of Intelligent Design. Indeed, it may be through precisely this type of constraining influence that God has exerted His creative energies upon the world.

But let us return for a moment to the idea that our biocentric universe may be the result of a colossal cosmic accident. If this is indeed the case, we would naturally expect to see some evidence of its accidental character, as in perhaps a physical feature of the universe that could somehow be improved upon.[5] In point of fact, though, we don't observe this to be the case at all. To the contrary, apart from the problem of evil, there doesn't seem to be a single aspect of our present world and universe that could conceivably be improved upon.[6]

At least on an underlying structural level, then, we do indeed seem to be living in the best of all possible worlds, as the German philosopher and mathematician Gottfried Leibniz deduced over three centuries ago. Despite heroic attempts to the contrary, no one has been able to suggest better values for the fundamental constants than the ones we presently observe. It is very hard to see how this could possibly be the case if the universe were merely the result of blind chance. Such an accidental universe would almost certainly have left behind some trace of its random origin, which we would now identify as a theoretically correctable flaw. But no such flaw can be identified.[7] Therefore, the universe is probably not of accidental origin.

This was the argument the physician Galen made concerning the glorious structure of the human hand. Since he could not think of a single way in which the structure of the hand could possibly be improved upon, he surmised that the human body had to have been Intelligently Designed. The same argument can be applied to the universe as a whole.

Of course, we probably would have never been able to evolve if the universe originally possessed any significant flaws in its underlying structure. Therefore, the fact of our own existence testifies to the flawlessness of the present universal structure as far as our own existence is concerned. The critic, however, turns this argument around and says that we were only able to evolve because our region of the universe *just happened* to take on the "right" structural parameters for life. The natural theologian responds to this statement by asserting that the accidental formation of such a profoundly complex physical realm is unintelligible in the absence of Intelligent Design.

The work of British mathematical physicist Roger Penrose[8] is strongly supportive of this conclusion. His research indicates that a random explosion of the Big Bang would have created a universe full of black holes, instead of the thin, even dispersal of matter we now observe. Only a specially chosen initial state could have thus led to our present life-supporting universe. Building on this foundation, Penrose has estimated that the odds against our universe appearing by chance are on the order of $10^{10^{30}}$ to 1!

To thus presume, as many scientists have, that our region of the universe just happened to take on the right characteristics for supporting biological life, is to believe in miracles of the most stupendously unlikely kind. Paradoxically, then, the only way the non-theistic scientist can reject the Creatorship of God in light of the known cosmological facts is by resorting to a truly in-credible scientific faith with no known precedent.

7.4   The Genesis Paradox Resolved

As we have seen, the modern cosmological picture is beset with a whole host of theoretical difficulties, ranging from the apparent isotropy of the universe to the many cosmic "coincidences" that have made life possible on this planet. The one thing all these problems have in common is that they can all be solved by appealing to an ideal set of initial conditions.

The problem with this "explanation" is that it leaves the initial conditions themselves unaccounted for. Paul Davies has termed this "the genesis paradox." It is a paradox because nothing outside the realm of the supernatural is able to account for these very special initial conditions, or even for the very fact that there was any kind of "bang" at all.

In fact, Davies goes so far as to say that:

> . . . with gravitational attraction as the only cosmic force available, the big bang must simply be explained as god-given, an event without a cause, an assumed initial condition. Furthermore, it was an event of quite astonishing fidelity, for the present highly structured cosmos could not have arisen unless the universe was set up in just the right way at the outset. This is the genesis paradox.[9]

Davies goes on to seek a non-theistic resolution to the genesis paradox by appealing to the previously mentioned "free lunch" hypothesis of universal origins. In this conceptualization, the universe would simply pop into existence out of some form of quantum "nothingness" and then, solely in response to natural processes, undergo a period of extremely rapid inflation. This is alleged to account for the initial appearance of the universe, as well as how it could have achieved its present highly organized form without a very large reliance on special initial conditions.

The problem with this "explanation" is that it explains precisely nothing.

As we have seen, the quantum "nothingness" that the universe is supposed to have arisen out of doesn't really qualify as being true nothingness; rather, it is a highly complex quantum field that is capable of bringing matter into existence through some type of unknown process. However, the "bootstrap theory" that Davies appeals to doesn't even attempt to account for the existence of this quantum field; it simply treats it as a given. Moreover, cosmic inflation, if it is true at all, simply cannot bypass the need for very special initial conditions in cosmogenesis, as we saw in Chapter 5. Hence, the genesis paradox remains as the chief obstacle facing modern theoretical cosmology.

It is clear, however, that the genesis paradox is only a paradox in a nontheistic conceptual framework. With a supernatural Creator to deliberately give the universe its special initial conditions, any hint of paradox instantly vanishes. Davies seems to be aware of this kind of theistic solution, since he explicitly claims that in the absence of some sort of naturalistic explanation for the present universal configuration, the special initial conditions surrounding the Big Bang must simply be accepted as "god-given."

In other words, the "problems" of modern cosmology are only problems in a chance-ridden, atheistic universe, because the theoretician must find a way to explain the appearance of Intelligent Design without actually referring to a Creator. This is tantamount to trying to explain the origin of a computer without referring to humans, so any such endeavor is bound to be extremely problematic.

In an Intelligently Designed Universe, on the other hand, the Divine Creative Force would have deliberately adjusted the various initial conditions of the Big Bang in such a way as to purposively bring about a biocentric universe. To many orthodox scientific minds, this may seem like an *ad hoc* "solution" to the problems of modern cosmology, in which the rules of explanation are inappropriately revised in order to advance the cause of a particular religion.

Such is not the case, however. The use of a Creator in this context is *not* an *ad hoc* explanatory device, whose purpose is simply to fill in the gaps of our scientific understanding wherever they happen to exist. Rather, it is the logically inevitable conclusion that naturally follows the positing of a Sufficient Cause to the present universal scheme.

In other words, the apparent fact of Intelligent Design in the universe can legitimately be used to compensate for our lack of full understanding when it comes to cosmogenesis, because the very concept of Intelligent Design includes within itself its own self-sufficient "explanation." To many agnostic or atheistic scientists, of course, this may seem like an "easy way out," which inherently negates the very purpose of science, but this isn't necessarily true at all. The reality of Intelligent Design does *not* preclude the scientific pursuit of knowledge; rather, it *facilitates* it, because it assures us that a logical and coherent explanation for the universe really does exist, and can be discovered by probing human minds.

Newton, Boyle, and the other founding fathers of the modern scientific movement were well aware of this relationship between science and Intelligent Design. Indeed, it was this relationship that motivated them to search for scientific answers to begin with. Without such a belief in an Intelligent Creator, these men of faith would have had no pressing reason to believe in the existence of an underlying mathematical Plan to the universe.

This brings us to a consideration of the relationship between mathematics and the underlying structure of the universe. In the absence of an Intelligent Creator, there is no good reason to believe that our idiosyncratic mathematical constructs would ever actually correspond to the hidden structure of the cosmos, because there would be no larger Mathematician to make it so. The fact is, though, that such a correspondance does indeed exist, and has provided the theoretical basis for the recent revolution in science and technology.

Most atheistic and agnostic scientists, of course, continue to believe in the power of mathematics to describe the ultimate nature of reality, even though such a belief is very much out of place in any kind non-theistic world view. This leads us to conclude that some form of naturalistic creationism is an implicit feature of science itself, the beliefs of non-theistic scientists themselves notwithstanding.

7.5   Murphy's Law and the Anthropic Design Argument

With the preceding discussion as a backdrop, we can now use Murphy's Law, in conjunction with the Weak Anthropic Principle, to deduce the necessity of Intelligent Design in the universe.

Murphy's Law, of course, states that anything that *can* go wrong in any given state of affairs *will* go wrong eventually. The probability that this type of malfunctioning will occur in any given system is determined by two related factors: 1) the overall complexity of the system itself (which is determined by the number of independent parts involved and the complexity of their interconnections), and 2) the quality of the system's design and execution. These two factors are very intimately related to one another, insofar as an increase in a system's complexity tends to produce an increased probability for error, whereas an increase in its overall quality of design tends to hold this proclivity for malfunctioning in check. It follows, then, that as the complexity of any given system rises, its overall quality of design must also increase in commensurate fashion if a constant probability of malfunctioning is to be maintained.

The upshot of this relation is that an optimal quality of design can act as a "solution" to the problems generated by Murphy's Law, since an optimal level of design translates into a situation where as little *can* go wrong with any given system as possible. This means that the best way to inspire confidence that little or nothing will go wrong with a particular system is to make sure that as little *can* go wrong with it as is humanly feasible, and this in turn requires a level of design that is commensurate with its internal degree of complexity.

With these ideas in mind, we find that we can utilize the degree of functionality of any given system to deduce the overall quality of its original design. For instance, if the present-day performance of a particular system is found to be optimal, we can reason *backwards* from this fact and deduce that its original quality of design must have similarly been noteworthy as well. This is an anthropic style of reasoning that we can now apply to the universe as a whole.

Incredibly, though, the latest findings in fractal geometry and chaos theory indicate that the physical universe itself is *infinitely* complex in terms of its underlying structural design and degree of functionality.[10] This is a momentous conclusion indeed, because it means that the only level of design that would have initially been sufficient to ensure the evolution of our infinitely complex universe is one that was *itself* infinitely elaborate and ingenious.

This expectation is borne out by the latest findings in astrophysics and cosmology. As you will recall, a detailed examination of the conditions necessary for our own existence has revealed an exceedingly complex web of independent factors which are known to have all worked together in very precise fashion to enable the evolution of intelligent life on this planet. It would seem to be a self-evident consequence of this observation that had anything significant gone wrong on the way to intelligent life, we would not be here to discuss the fact. But Murphy's Law tells us whatever *could* have gone wrong on the way to intelligent life *would* have gone wrong eventually. Therefore, the fact that humans did in fact evolve seems to indicate that things were probably *incapable* of going significantly wrong during the entire course of biogenesis. This in turn seems to require the existence of some sort of larger organizing principle that would have been capable of ensuring the rightness of all of the important events leading to intelligent life. Without this hypothetical principle, many of these events would have undoubtedly gone wrong, and we would not be here.

Going one step further, it seems to follow that this Murphy's Law-breaking principle had to have been a power that was entirely sufficient for the infinitely complex anthropic task being proposed, otherwise no such universe could have formed and we would not exist. The stature of this universal ordering principle can be inferred from the realization that in its absence, the precursors of life should have gone wrong trillions of times before life ever formed. After all, we're talking about the most complex thing known (a life-supporting universe), and billions of years in which these potential errors could have occurred. Yet no such errors can be identified, despite the universe's profound complexity and enormous age. Therefore, we can infer that an exceedingly competent organizing principle must have acted to keep life's precursors from malfunctioning during all the stages that initially led to our own evolution. While some have conceived of chance acting in this capacity, it is very difficult to see how chance processes could have repeatedly compensated for the universe's great tendency to go wrong over the thousands of millions of years of its formative evolution. The odds[11] against the accidental formation of our present universe support us in this conclusion, as they have been calculated to be approximately 1 in $10^{10^{30}}$! This being the case, we are compelled to conclude that some sort of larger organizing power probably acted throughout cosmic history to keep the universe "on track" in its extremely straight and narrow anthropic trajectory.

This Argument from Murphy's Law reduces to the following:

1. Murphy's Law is applicable to all physical systems and to all stages of cosmic history.
2. Any system of infinite complexity requires an infinite amount of ingenuity in order to function properly.
3. Our present universe is infinitely complex in terms of its underlying structure and design.
4. Therefore, an infinite number of things had to have gone right for thousands of millions of years before intelligent life could have ever evolved on this planet.
5. Barring the activity of some sort of larger ordering influence, things *should* have gone wrong many times on the way to life, given the infinite complexity of our biocentric universe and the enormous amount of time in which it took to form.
6. Had things been capable of going significantly wrong in the distant past with respect to biogenesis and the evolution intelligent life, they *would* have gone wrong at one time or another (especially given the tremendous age of the universe), and we would probably not be here.
7. But we *are* here.
8. Therefore, things must *not* have been capable of going significantly wrong in the early universe as far as the evolution of intelligent life is concerned.[12]
9. Chance processes in the early universe were probably incapable of maintaining such a high degree of order in the universe over so many thousands of millions of years.
10. Therefore, some sort of larger organizing principle, entirely sufficient to the task, must have been at work throughout cosmic history to

ensure that the universe did not descend into life-negating chaos at all stages of its evolution.

11. This universal organizing principle for all practical intents and purposes can be called God.

7.6 The SAP to the Rescue

The "strong" version of the Anthropic Principle takes into account the immense unlikelihood of our present life-supporting world by asserting that the universe *must* possess those characteristics which enable it to support biological life. Exactly *why* it must possess these life-supporting qualities, though, is not directly addressed.

However, two corollaries to the Strong Anthropic Principle *do* attempt to explain how and why the universe came to have its present biocentric character. The first asserts that:

> There exists one possible universe "designed" with the goal of generating and sustaining observers.[13]

This version of the SAP is obviously a return to Paley's Designer God, Who deliberately fine-tuned the characteristics of our present universe so as to enable it to evolve intelligent life. As far as we are concerned in this book, this theistic corollary to the SAP offers by far the most plausible accounting of the existing cosmological evidence.

A second corollary to the Strong Anthropic Principle is the Participatory Anthropic Principle (PAP), which we have already examined. Although it asserts that life is necessary in a quantum sense to bring the universe into being, it doesn't attempt to explain the *source* of this reality-breeding consciousness before the evolution of life on this planet. Since God Himself is the only Being who could have observed the universe into existence from the very beginning, the PAP turns out to be yet another anthropic argument for the existence of God. Barrow and Tipler are aware of this possibility, insofar as they refer to God as the:

> . . . Ultimate Observer who is in the end responsible for coordinating the separate observations of the lesser observers and is thus responsible for bringing the entire universe into existence.[14]

Barrow and Tipler state a third version of the SAP known as the Final Anthropic Principle (FAP), which asserts that some form of intelligent life *had* to have come into existence, and having done so, will *never* die out. It further states that intelligent life will become infinitely knowledgeable in the future and will end up molding the universe to its own will.

These are remarkably religious words to come from the mouths of scientists, for they are virtually identical to the assertions that theologians have been making for centuries! Indeed, the Bible tells us that we are destined to become the literal "children" of God one day, which of course means that we will be like little "gods" ourselves. While we may never become *infinitely* knowledgeable, as the FAP asserts, we *will* presumably have access to an Infinite Database of Knowledge, so we will undoubtedly become far more knowledgeable in the future than we are now. The Bible also tells us that one day in the distant future we will judge angels. This is usually taken to mean that we will serve an important function in the upcoming Universal Economy, much as the FAP predicts.

There is, however, one important difference. The only reason the traditional theist would say that intelligent life *had* to form was because God Himself deliberately chose this alternative; had He not chosen to do so, it would never have formed at all. Similarly, the theist would argue that the only reason intelligent life will continue living forevermore is because God has deliberately willed it to be so. Hence, a theistic restatement of the FAP might be as follows:

Once God freely elected to create intelligent life, the universe automatically became such that it *had* to bring intelligent life into being, and having arrived, this intelligent life will continue living for the rest of eternity, during which time it will attain near infinite knowledge and perform many important universal functions.

In stark contrast to the unbounded optimism of the FAP, scientists tell us that one day in the distant future our Sun will run out of fuel and die, thus extinguishing all life on Earth. This dysteleological "Heat Death" seems to run directly counter to the FAP's assertion that intelligent life will go on living forever (as does the brute fact of our own impending death).

Barrow and Tipler attempt to get around this pitfall by suggesting several far-fetched technological "solutions" to the coming Heat Death of the universe and to the problem of bodily death in general.[15] For one thing, they suggest that intergalactic space travel will one day become so sophisticated that it will enable humankind to escape the coming Heat Death of our own solar system. This would allegedly allow them to buy more time in which to discover novel ways for escaping the proposed recollapse of the universe into a final cosmic singularity, which, strangely enough, is deemed to be the only possible cosmic fate which is compatible with their version of the FAP.[16] The reason for this has to do with the "compressive" effect of a finite, collapsing universe, which supposedly will act to push humanity upward towards the eventual attainment of the final Omega Point.

In reference to the problem of bodily death, Barrow and Tipler suggest that in the distant future it may very well be possible to embody human consciousness within such large scale structures as interstellar plasmas and fields, thereby overcoming the extremely limited lifetime of the physical body.[17] How this could conceivably be accomplished isn't mentioned, undoubtedly due to the fact that it is so fantastic that it borders on the very edge of absolute non-possibility.

However, assuming that such a grandiose "solution" to the problem of physical death is eventually attained, the secondary problem arises as to how these disembodied personalities will be able to maintain themselves against a total loss of internal energy. Not to be outdone by any sort of opposing conceptual problem, Barrow and Tipler suggest that some exotic form of asymmetrical gravitational energy, such as that seen in the phenomenon of gravitational shear, will be able to be harnessed as the universe recollapses back towards the final "Big Crunch," which the authors clearly believe in.[18]

Such a conclusion appears to be profoundly counterintuitive, because the very idea of a "Big Crunch" would seem to spell certain doom for anyone who happens to be alive at the time, even those disembodied beings who are somehow contained in some form of physical substance. However, Barrow and Tipler aren't to be outdone here, either. They propose that as the recollapsing universe approaches its final singularity, these disembodied "diaphanous" beings will have more and more gravitational shear energy to work with. This will supposedly enable them to process information at a progressively faster rate. And since subjectively experienced time is said to be dependent on the rate at which information is processed, the vastly increased rate of information processing that will supposedly occur during the final stages of the Big Crunch will cause the subjectively experienced time of these diaphanous beings to pass more and more slowly. At the limit, time will supposedly pass *infinitely* slowly for these beings, so for all practical purposes they will have attained personal immortality. It is in this fashion that Barrow and Tipler believe the ultimate purpose of the creation might finally be realized.[19]

There are three obvious problems with this precarious bit of reasoning:

1. It assumes that we will be able to undertake successfully the mammoth task of relocating our entire species to another corner of the universe. Such a goal seems exceedingly unlikely, both in terms of the number of technical problems that would have to be overcome, and in terms of the remaining amount of time we have on this planet for realizing such grandiose ambitions. Given the haunting proclivity of our species for self-destruction, we will be lucky to survive one tenth as long as it will take to develop a suitable interstellar technology.
2. It fails to take the ever-present problem of physical death seriously. It

seems immensely unlikely that the problem of physical death will ever be abolished on this planet, interstellar plasmas and fields notwithstanding.

3. It fails to take the future Heat Death of the entire universe seriously. The Second Law of Thermodynamics assures us that one day in the distant future the entire universe will run out of usable energy, even if the universe does happen to collapse back in on itself someday.[20] It seems unlikely to the highest degree that any purely physical process will ever enable humanity to escape this coming universal Heat Death.

Clearly the only realistic way around these tremendous pitfalls to the validity of the FAP is to appeal to another realm of existence that is totally impervious to the events of the purely physical realm. Teilhard's notion of "radial energy" is just such an attempt to proclaim the ultimate independence of spiritual man from the physical forces of disintegration in the universe. Postulating the existence of an everlasting spiritual realm also has the advantage of offering humanity a plausible means for defeating the ever-present problem of bodily death as well.

It follows, then, that both the coming Heat Death of the universe and the present reality of bodily death are only dysteleological to those who choose to deny the existence of a transcendent spiritual realm. As Jesus Himself states in the Book of Revelation:

"I am the Alpha and the Omega, the Beginning and the End, the First and the Last" (Rev. 22:13).

The direct implication of this famous passage is that, though the End of the physical universe is undoubtedly coming, we can nevertheless count on the Power of God to eventually provide us with a spiritual realm that is unaffected by the approaching demise of the physical universe as a whole.

In order for the FAP to be valid, then, we must return to a traditional religious perspective and affirm both God's Absolute Sovereignty in the universe and the existence of an incorruptible spiritual realm.

7.7   The Equivalence of the SAP with the Traditional Concept of Intelligent Design

Stephen Hawking is one of the many physicists who has become aware of the religious implications of the Anthropic Principle. Speaking of the remarkable degree of fine-tuning found in nature's physical constants, he has written the following:

It seems clear that there are relatively few ranges of values for the numbers that would allow the development of any form of intelligent life. Most sets of values would give rise to universes that, although they might be very beautiful, would contain no one able to wonder at that beauty. One can take this either as evidence of a divine purpose in Creation and the choice of the laws of science or as support for the strong anthropic principle.[21]

It will immediately be recognized that Hawking's final statement in the passage quoted above is not entirely accurate. He speaks of the SAP and the possibility of Intelligent Design as if they were mutually exclusive alternatives, but they are not, as we have just seen. Indeed, as the earlier quote from Barrow and Tipler well illustrates, the notion of Deliberate Design in the universe is perhaps the most sensible interpretation of the SAP. After all, how else are we to explain why the universe *must* be life-supporting if there isn't a larger Designer in existence to make it so?

But if it is true that the most sensible version of the SAP is theistic by its very nature, what are we to then make of Hawking's two above-mentioned choices for explaining the existence of our fine-tuned anthropic universe? Since the only two choices he mentions are Deliberate Design and the SAP, and since all versions of the SAP directly imply the existence of Intelligent Design, it appears as though the choice has already been made for us.

7.8   A Theistic Interpretation of Quantum Mechanics

Quantum mechanics is by far the most accurate and successful scientific theory ever devised. Virtually all of our modern technological society, from the transistor to the microprocessor, is based on it in one way or another. Yet, the philosophical view of "reality" engendered by quantum mechanics is utterly enigmatic, to say the least.

In the quantum mechanical view of the atom, each electron orbiting about the nucleus is described by a probability distribution, termed the "psi function," which describes the probability of the electron being found in any one spot. In this sense, it is possible to think of the electron as being "smeared out" over a wide range of possible locations. It isn't until the electron is actually observed by some sort of measuring instrument, though, that the quantum wave function—which determines the probability of finding the electron in any one place—"collapses," thereby giving the electron a definite location in space.

Several radical interpretations of this phenomenon have been proposed over the years, none of which have made much sense to the common mind. In the Copenhagen Intepretation, devised largely by quantum pioneer Neils Bohr, there is no "reality" at all to a given electron until it is actually measured, since it isn't until this crucial point of measurement that the electron's wave function actually collapses.[22]

The problem with the Copenhagen Interpretation is that it seems profoundly counterintuitive to state that quantum events have no reality at all until they are measured. Einstein in particular found this conclusion completely unacceptable, and he spent much of his career trying to prove it false. This absolute dependence of "reality" upon some form of measurement is thought by many physicists to extend out to the very origin of the universe itself, as it is hard to see how the early universe could have existed at all until it was actually observed into being by some sort of measuring instrument.

In an alternative view proposed by Hugh Everett III, known as the Many Worlds Interpretation, the wave function *never* collapses. In order for such a view to make sense, however, one must conclude that *all* possibilities for the electron actually occur. The only coherent way to do this is to assume that either the "real world" or the measuring instrument itself is constantly splitting into an untold number of fragments in order to realize all possible quantum states for the electron.

It is difficult to the highest degree to see how this could ever be the case. We clearly live in a coherent world that seems to realize only one possibility for each given electron and atom.

One way to solve the metaphysical problems caused by this quantum view of reality is to assume that Nature herself somehow causes the wave function to collapse. This is tantamount, however, to an admission of an unseen Deity who is the Ultimate Legislator of quantum reality. As Indiana physicist F. J. Belinfante has put it:

> If I get the impression that Nature itself makes the decisive choice about what possibility to realize, where quantum theory says that more than one outcome is possible, then I am ascribing personality to Nature, that is to something that is always everywhere. Omnipresent eternal personality which is omnipotent in taking the decisions that are left undetermined by physical law is exactly what in the language of religion is called God.[23]

Another way of saying this is that whenever decisions are left undetermined by physical law, an External Observer is the one who causes the wave function to collapse in the most appropriate manner possible. On this view, while humans and other observers might be able to cause the wave function to collapse in their own local part of the universe, God as the Ultimate Observer would cause the wave function to collapse whenever other observers aren't around to do the job. This would solve the problem of how wave functions could possibly collapse in those spatial and temporal regions of the universe where no non-Divine observers are present; God as the Ultimate Observer would simply act as the "Default Observer" who would collapse these wave functions into being.

It is even possible that God could be the ultimate cause of *all* wave function determinations, even those "caused" by non-Divine observers. This would be the case if God served as the ultimate metaphysical Mediator between non-Divine observership and subsequent quantum reality. On this view, humans and other non-Divine observers would initiate the collapse of a given wave function, but God would actually make the resulting physical reality come into being.

The Stoic philosophers of ancient Greece would have been very sympathetic to this point of view, as they were convinced that if God existed at all, He *had* to be the Logos, or Logical Mediator, between cause and effect. For the Stoics, then, it wasn't enough for humans to simply initiate physical causes in the world; they believed that there had to be a Larger Metaphysical Force in the universe to couple each cause with its corresponding logical effect. This they understood to be God.

This view has the added benefit of being consistent with the Biblical view that God is the "cause" of everything that happens in the world. If God is the Logical Mediator between cause and effect, then in a very real sense He *is* the ultimate cause of everything that happens in the world. At the same time, though, this view of God does *not* violate human free will, because God as Logos would primarily be responding to those causes that are *freely* initiated in the world.

7.9 God and Stephen Hawking's Proposed No Boundary Condition to the Universe

In *A Brief History of Time,* Stephen Hawking suggests that spacetime may be finite in spatial extent but without boundary or edge.[24] Just as one can sail completely around the world without falling off because of the no boundary condition of our spherical planet, Hawking suggests that the universe itself may be without boundary as well. This means that it may *not* have had an absolute beginning at the Big Bang, which in turn means that:

> . . . there would be no need to specify the behavior at the boundary. There would be no singularities at which the laws of science broke down and no edge of space-time at which one would have to appeal to God or some new law to set the boundary conditions for space-time. One could say: "The boundary condition of the universe is that it has no boundary." The universe would be completely self-contained and not affected by anything outside itself. It would neither be created nor destroyed. It would just BE.[25]

This is an important development, for Hawking (along with Roger Penrose) was one of the principal theoreticians who originally showed that the universe must have had a concrete beginning. Hawking has since changed his mind, as he now believes that the no boundary condition for the universe may obviate any need for a primordial singularity, or even for a beginning to space-time as such.

As Hawking explains, a proposed universe without boundary has definite religious implications:

> With the success of scientific theories in describing events, most people have come to believe that God allows the universe to evolve according to a set of laws and does not intervene in the universe to break these laws. However, the laws do not tell us what the universe should have looked like when it started—it would still be up to God to wind up the clockwork and choose how to start it off. So long as the universe had a beginning, we could suppose it had a creator. But if the universe is really self-contained, having no boundary or edge, it would have neither beginning nor end: it would simply be. What place, then, for a creator?[26]

Fortunately for the theist, Hawking's no boundary proposal is plagued by a number of severe problems. To begin with, it has absolutely no basis in experimental fact. It can't even be deduced from any existing scientific principle.[27] As such, it is only a proposal. Yet, it is a potentially powerful proposal, because it seeks to render the role of God in universal affairs superfluous.

Secondly, it seems to contradict the enormous body of modern scientific evidence indicating a formal beginning to the universe at the Big Bang. While Hawking may have intended his no boundary proposal to be a different interpretation of the existing evidence, it nevertheless directly contradicts the prevailing scientific wisdom which indicates a concrete beginning to the universe some 15 billion years ago.

Thirdly, Hawking's no-boundary proposal—based as it is upon a quantum interpretation of the universe as a whole—turns out to be plagued by the same problems that affect quantum cosmology. For as long as we accept the standard Copenhagen Interpretation of quantum physics, the entire universe necessarily remains indeterminate until an Ultimate Observer—who is God by definition—can render it determinate by collapsing its cumulative wave functions into being. The only way out of this dilemma is by assuming the simultaneous existence of all possible spacetimes in a kind of superspace, in which we would only exist in that small subset that would be capable of supporting our existence. But this highly questionable theoretical maneuver *infinitely* multiplies causes beyond necessity, and so should therefore be eliminated as being needlessly complex.

The extreme tenuousness of Hawking's no boundary proposal is well illustrated by the fact that it is only valid[28] in "imaginary time," which is a mathematical concept in which a number multiplied by itself yields a negative number. In the real world this can never happen (because the squares of both positive and negative numbers are always positive), but in the hypothetical world of modern mathematics, almost anything can be made to happen. It doesn't necessarily follow, though, that these imaginary formulations will ever apply to anything in the real world. In fact, many writers have argued that the notion of imaginary time is physically unintelligible, since it causes time to turn into space, and this clearly seems to be bad metaphysics. Hawking nevertheless assumes the validity of imaginary time with his no boundary proposal and even suggests that it may be more real than our own real time![29]

In addition, it is hard to see how the proposed no boundary condition of the universe—if it turns out to be true at all—could ever render the Creatorship of God unnecessary. Hawking reasons that if there is no boundary to space-time, there is no need to specify the behavior at the boundary.[30] This clearly isn't an explanation for the universe's beginning, however; it is simply an attempt to justify a *non*-explanation for the beginning, basically because it postulates that there *was* no beginning. It thus begs the true question at hand, which is this: where did the proposed no boundary universe *itself* come from? To argue that the no boundary condition renders an explanation unnecessary is to argue for an *eternal* space-time, which seems to be just another version of the old Steady State theory of the universe that has largely been discredited in the scientific community.

However, arguing that the proposed no boundary condition of the universe renders a larger explanation unnecessary *itself* appears to be fallacious, because there is no necessary connection between Hawking's no boundary condition and the lack of a need for a larger explanation. In other words, *even if we assume the no boundary condition to be valid, it doesn't follow that the universe would suddenly be beyond the need for a larger explanation.* To assume that it does logically follow is to confuse two separate categories of explanation which inherently have nothing to do with one another. Hawking's proposed no boundary condition is itself a description of one possible geometric configuration of the finite realm of cosmic space-time; this is one category of physical explanation. However, to say that this no boundary condition *itself* is without need of explanation by virtue of its no boundary condition alone is to appeal to a larger realm of metaphysical explanation that is entirely independent of the specific nature of the physical realm *per se*. This realm of metaphysical explanation thus constitutes a completely distinct explanatory category that cannot properly be confused with the category of physical descriptions alone.

Hawking thus commits a category mistake in his postulation that the proposed no boundary condition of the universe renders a larger metaphysical explanation unnecessary. Just as it is impossible to formally prove the existence of an Infinite Deity from the realm of finite objects alone,[31] it is also impossible to generalize from this finite realm of material objects to the much larger realm of metaphysical explanation. *As St. Thomas would have agreed, there is no possible configuration of the universe that would render it beyond the need of a larger metaphysical explanation. This would include Hawking's proposed no boundary description of space-time.*

In order to help visualize this no boundary condition, Hawking draws an analogy with the surface of the Earth. Just as the Earth curves back on itself forever, and so is without a formal boundary *per se*, the universe as a whole may also curve back on itself forever as well, and so may exist in a similar type of no boundary condition. Hawking's analogy breaks down, however, because the Earth's no boundary condition only applies to the Earth *itself*, and not to the larger universe that surrounds it. Thus, while the Earth's surface may not possess an edge or boundary in and of itself, there *is* a boundary between the Earth and outer space. Similarly, while there may not be a geometric edge to the universe in and of itself, there *must* be a boundary between the proposed no boundary universe and its immediate surroundings, that is, if the universe is finite. Even if one imagines that no form of space-time exists beyond the limits of our physical universe, this ending of space-time itself would seem to constitute a legitimate boundary. The only way such an external boundary can be avoided is if the universe itself is infinite in both duration and spatial extent, but this would contradict Hawking's proposal of a *finite* universe without boundary. Thus, the very concept of finitude seems to necessitate some sort of external boundary *by definition*. Accordingly, Hawking's claim of a self-contained universe without boundary turns out to be self-contradictory, as the very concept of self-containment implies an external realm to be contained *within*. It is this external boundary which leaves room for God as Creator.

7.10   What Is There for God to Do in the Universe?

In his Introduction to *A Brief History of Time,* astronomer Carl Sagan writes that Hawking's book:

> . . . is also a book about God . . . or perhaps about the absence of God. The word God fills these pages. Hawking embarks on a quest to answer Einstein's famous question about whether God had any choice in creating the universe. Hawking is attempting, as he explicitly states, to understand the mind of God. And this makes all the more unexpected the conclusion of the effort, at least so far: a universe with no edge in space, no beginning or end in time, and nothing for a Creator to do.[32]

It is very difficult to see what this statement could possibly mean. It cannot be considered to be a serious statement about God's larger Function in the Grand Universal Economy, because the very definition of the word "God" denotes that Spiritual Reality through which the entire cosmos derives its metaphysical being. In this sense, the "only" thing there would be for a Creator to do would be to provide the proper metaphysical conditions for the universe as a whole to come into being. Indeed, if the Copenhagen Interpretation of quantum mechanics is true, God is absolutely *essential* to the continued existence of the entire cosmos, since He alone would be capable of observing the universe into existence as the Ultimate Quantum Observer.

On this score the ancient Stoic philosophers were far more accurate in their conception of God, as we have seen. The Stoics reasoned that if God existed at all, He *had* to be the Logos, or Logical Mediator, between cause and effect. And since we now understand the law of cause-and-effect to be ubiquitous throughout the universe, God as Logos can be considered to be the larger "Ground of Being" that has enabled the entire universe to function in a logical manner.

Perhaps Sagan means in the above quotation that the most recent evidence indicating a self-sufficient universe seems to make the existence of a traditional Creator God almost superfluous. Such a conclusion, however, is mistaken on three separate grounds. First, as we just saw, a universe that operates entirely according to the natural law of cause-and-effect still needs a Creator God to bring the whole causal scheme into existence and to enable it to function in a logical and consistent manner. Secondly, a universe that is entirely self-sufficient in terms of the generation of its own natural causes is more worthy of a Divine Creator than one in which He continually has to adjust things like planetary orbits or the various stellar luminosities. Indeed, it seems as though the *only* type of being that is worthy of the name "God" is the One whose creation is so self-sufficient that it can function as a totally self-contained system (assuming, of course, the existence of a larger Ground of Being which God Himself must still provide). Thirdly, it is fallacious to argue that God's absence as a secondary cause within the physical universe itself automatically renders Him superfluous in a larger metaphysical sense, because He will always be needed as a Primary Cause for the whole spectrum of reality.

Sagan doesn't seem to be aware of the fact that the idea of God has always been an important part of the scientific pursuit of knowledge. Indeed, it was their belief in a Rational Creator that led the founding fathers of the modern scientific movement to look for—and find—a larger degree of order in the cosmos. Even Hawking himself admits that his ultimate goal is nothing less than to know the mind of God.[33]

At the same time, though, one of the hidden agendas of the scientific profession in recent years has been to render the need for God in the physical sciences unnecessary, partly in response to the Church's ruthless attack on the scientific establishment in times past. Sagan's naïve comments about God seem to be a part of this routine anti-theistic sentiment.

7.11   Ours as One of the Best of All Possible Worlds

In the seventeenth century, German mathematician and philosopher Gottfried Leibniz, whose ideas on teleology were briefly discussed in Chapter 2, made the bold claim that this is "the best of all possible worlds." In the years following this powerful assertion, Leibniz has been ridiculed for making a religiously-motivated claim that seems to fly in the face of all the known facts, most notably the problem of evil. "How," it is asked, "can this be the best of all possible worlds when one less murder, for instance, would obviously render it a better world?"

This is a disingenuous[34] argument on several scores, the most prominent one being that it is far from obvious that such an evil-free world would *in fact* be better than our own. Indeed, as I have explained[35] elsewhere, there is good reason to believe that such an innocuous world would be far more hideous than our own, insofar as each person's thoughts and behaviors would have to be controlled either from within or without in order to guarantee that no evils would be committed. This in turn would automatically transform humans into robot-like beings who would be incapable of performing destructive (i.e., evil) actions. The cost of this transformation, however, would be the complete loss of human freedom, character, creativity, and spontaneity, which are priceless qualities that are virtually synonymous with what is generally considered to be "human."

Interestingly enough, the maker of the old "Star Trek" series, Gene Roddenberry, seems to have been aware of this important metaphysical relationship between human character and moral evil, since one of his old episodes, called "The Return of the Archons," deals with this very issue. In this marvelous episode, a master computer named Landru decides to eliminate evil once and for all on his planet by externally controlling the minds and wills of all the planet's inhabitants. While this outrageous act of control succeeds in getting rid of all evils on the planet, it also has the effect of turning the "people" into lifeless sheep. Heroically, though, Captain Kirk convinces the computer—which has been programmed to bring about only good for the people—that it is *not* acting in the best interests of the people by controlling their wills. The computer responds by claiming its actions to be "good," since it has apparently eliminated all moral evil on the planet. Kirk, however, convinces the computer that it has committed a far greater evil by destroying the character and creativity of all the citizens on the planet with its relentless control of their wills. This undeniable assertion causes the computer to self-destruct, which in turn allows the people on the planet to instantly return to normal.

The crew of the Enterprise, of course, are delighted to see moral "evils," like marital arguments and bar room brawls, return to the planet, because it is a sign that the people are finally back in control of their own lives. Spock, however, is intrigued by Landru's "success" at getting rid of all moral evil on the planet, so he asks the Captain why the clever people of Earth, who have suffered an untold amount of pain and misery in their history, have never tried to implement Landru's "solution" to the problem of evil. Kirk replies that they were probably just lucky.

This penetrating statement at once reveals our world to be a far better place than is superficially apparent, precisely because the *only* logically possible alternative to moral evil (besides complete non-existence for humanity) is *far* worse overall: the death of free-willed human character. Hence, as long as we humans wish to remain in control of our lives, this world does indeed seem to be one of the best of all possible worlds, not in terms of the number of evils that occur daily here, but in terms of the underlying metaphysical conditions that allow us to be fully human, and therefore fully in control of our own lives. Leibniz apparently was aware of this important distinction, as he seems to have based his Principle of Radical Optimism on the underlying metaphysical conditions that are necessary for human existence, and *not* on the number of evils that occur in the world *per se*.

Although a complete metaphysical defense of Leibniz's claim is beyond the scope of this book, we *can* say with a large degree of certainty that *as far as the values of the fundamental constants themselves are concerned (vis-à-vis of course our own existence), this is at the very least one of the best of all possible worlds (or perhaps even the only logically possible world), because had any of these fundamental values been different with respect to all the others, life would have been unable to evolve.*[36] Of course, there is always the chance that *all* of the fundamental constants could have been different, with the possible result that an *equally* functional world could have otherwise been created. Although there is no scientific evidence for this contention, it is nevertheless possible. It is also possible that there are other worlds in existence that benefit as much as we do from an optimal arrangement of the fundamental constants. Hence, we are only justified in claiming that this is *one* of the best of all possible worlds, not *the* best of all possible worlds. *This is nevertheless a radical conclusion that follows as a direct corollary to the Anthropic Principle, insofar as the various parameters of the physical universe clearly work together to make our life-supporting environment possible.*

It is hard to see how any hypothetical manipulation of the fundamental constants would produce a *better* world ("better" in terms of an increased capacity to produce life). To the contrary, every attempted mathematical manipulation of the various constants has invariably produced a far *worse* world, or no world at all. It would appear, then, that as far as the values of the physical constants themselves are concerned, our world does in fact appear to be one of the best possible.

Indeed, in terms of the enormous amount of success our world has experienced in bringing about life (especially in comparison to what could have otherwise been the case), the assertion that this is one of the best of all possible worlds must stand as the default (e.g. standing) observation until someone can demonstrate how the world could have been improved upon through a manipulation of one or more of the fundamental constants. Given the many life-supporting "coincidences" discussed in this book, however, it is unlikely that any such hypothetical improvement will *ever* be demonstrated, precisely because our world appears to represent the optimal amalgamation of the various possible values for the physical constants.

It is important to understand, though, that once it is admitted that this may in fact be one of the best of all physically possible worlds, a cosmic precedent will have then been set. For if this is in fact one of the best of all physically possible worlds, it follows that this Leibnizian Principle of Radical Optimism must apply on at least one level of universal reality. But if it applies on one level, it becomes that much more likely to apply on *more* than one level, or even on *all possible* levels, because of the demonstrated unity of the entire universe. It is in this manner that the "anthropic" evidence discussed in this book provides indirect support for a possible affirmation of Leibniz's claim that when *all* things are duly considered, this is in fact the best of all possible worlds.[37]

Indeed, in my forthcoming book on the problem of evil, I will be arguing that nature's physical constants have their metaphysical counterparts in the various aspects of the Human Definition. Since these "metaphysical constants" could not be otherwise and still comprise the Human Essence, it follows that as far as human existence is concerned, these metaphysical constants are the best possible. Going one step further, if we extrapolate from these essential human properties to the nature of a full-scale world, the resulting world will *also* be the best possible, not in terms of itself, but in terms of being a direct and inevitable function of these anthropically-oriented metaphysical constants.

It is reported that Einstein once asked the question, "How much choice did God have in constructing the universe?" It would seem that if this is indeed the best of all physically possible worlds (or at least one of the best), then God may not have had *any* choice at all in its actual structural details, since all of the physical parameters we have discussed in this book apparently need to occupy their present values if life is to be able to exist on this planet. While God may have had the original choice of whether or not to create a world for humans, it appears fairly certain that, having made the initial decision to create humanity, the remaining creative details were themselves fixed by the necessary nature of the Human Definition.[38] Interestingly enough, Stephen Hawking has made a similar conjecture regarding God's lack of freedom in choosing the initial conditions of the universe (though he bases his ideas on his proposed "no boundary" condition of space-time, which we discussed earlier).[39]

To be sure, if it is correct to say that, given at least one of the physical constants, there is only one logically possible world capable of supporting intelligent life (which seems to be the case), then the actual details surrounding the creation event may have been beyond Divine Decision altogether (except for God's original decision to create a world in the first place). We shouldn't, however, be offended by this idea that God might have been subject to the intrinsic laws of necessity, for as Leibniz has pointed out, it is a "happy necessity" indeed, without which our wonderful world could never have come into being.

7.12 Summary

In summary, although the WAP is obviously valid (since it is apparent that we would not exist if the universe had been significantly otherwise), it does not make an attempt to explain the apparent connection between the present universal character and the existence of intelligent observers. For this reason, the SAP is much more satisfying, as one version of it explicitly states that there is only one possible universe capable of generating intelligent life, and that this one possible universe was deliberately designed with the end of producing intelligent life forms "in mind." Another version of the SAP further tells us that if some form of consciousness did not exist, neither would the universe. This of course is the position I have adopted in this book (with the proviso that God Himself was the Conscious Designer), and in my own opinion, it provides by far the most sensible accounting of the existing scientific evidence.

Notes

1. Casti, *Paradigms Lost*, p. 485.
2. In trying to make sense of the alternate possibilities seen at the quantum level, Everett himself actually felt it more appropriate to consider the measuring apparatus *itself*, instead of the universe as a whole, as splitting in two (see Barrow and Tipler's *Anthropic Cosmological Principle*, p. 476). If this is done, one no longer has an infinity of worlds to work with.
3. These ideas were communicated during a personal meeting between Professor Campbell and myself.
4. Stephen Hawking, *A Brief History of Time*, p. 137.
5. While it is possible that an entire range of random particle configurations exist

in the universe, and that we were only able to evolve in a chance configuration that happened to be perfect for our own existence (which would seem to explain why we can't find any imperfections in our immediate cosmic environment), this is immensely unlikely. Not only is it very difficult to see how such a perfect section of the universe could have formed by accident, it is even more difficult to believe that not a single trace of this accidental origin would have been left behind.

6. Indeed, as I plan to show in detail in my next work, not even the problem of evil could conceivably be improved upon without simultaneously transforming man into a subhuman creature.

7. I am only talking about credible flaws here, i.e., those which detract from the life-supporting capacity of the universe as a whole. Things like the upcoming Heat Death of the universe don't really qualify as flaws because they can be shown to be a part of a beneficial Cosmic Plan.

8. Davies, *God and the New Physics*, pp. 178–179.

9. Davies, *Superforce* (New York: Simon and Schuster, 1984) p. 186.

10. See F. David Peat's *The Philosopher's Stone* (Bantam Books, 1991), pp. 160–203.

11. Barrow and Tipler, p. 448.

12. This argument clearly minimizes the role of large-scale contingency in the evolutionary rise of life, because any such contingency seems to be strictly incompatible with the outrageous complexity and difficulty of life's evolution. While the evolution of our life-supporting universe may well have contained many small-scale contingencies, the overall thrust does not appear to have been contingent at all. It is hard to see how it ever could have been, given the enormous complexity and stringent requirements for life's evolution.

13. Barrow and Tipler, p. 22.

14. Ibid., p. 470.

15. It is not my intention to cast a shadow on Barrow and Tipler's work in any way. Their *Anthropic Cosmological Principle* stands as the most impressive treatment of this intriguing subject to date. Their conclusions regarding the future plight of the human race only begin to get far-fetched when they leave God out of their anthropic theorizing; it just doesn't seem to be possible to compensate for the shortcomings of our physical world without appealing to some form of transcendent spiritual realm.

16. Ibid., p. 670.

17. Ibid., pp. 659–660.

18. Ibid., pp. 625, 631, 646, 665.

19. Ibid., pp. 674–677.

20. Hugh Ross, *The Fingerprint of God*, pp. 104–105.

21. Stephen Hawking, *A Brief History of Time*, p. 125.

22. It is this aspect of quantum mechanics that the Participatory Anthropic Principle relies on.

23. Taken from John Barrow's *The World Within the World*, p. 157.

24. Stephen Hawking, *A Brief History of Time*, p. 136.

25. Ibid., p. 136.

26. Ibid., pp. 140–141.

27. Ibid.

28. Ibid., pp. 134–139.

29. Ibid., p. 139.

30. Ibid.

31. See John Hick's *The Existence of God* (New York: Macmillan Publishing Company, 1964), p. 7.
32. Carl Sagan in Stephen Hawking's *A Brief History of Time*, p. x.
33. Ibid., p. 175.
34. Lest the reader think that a brief consideration of the problem of evil is out of place in a book on cosmology and religion, it should be pointed out that no less a scientific personage as Albert Einstein was prevented from believing in the existence of a personal Creator by the all-important reality of evil. Einstein simply could not bring himself to believe in a personal Deity who would deliberately allow such a tremendous amount of pain and suffering to take place on this planet. Moreover, millions of people share Einstein's feelings on the matter. It follows, then, that a sensitive treatment of the problem of evil can go a long way towards making belief in such a personal Deity more forthcoming.
35. Please refer to my book *Back to Darwin* for a detailed explanation of this position.
36. Davies, *The Accidental Universe*, p. vii.
37. Once again, this Leibnizian Principle of Radical Optimism refers only to the optimal arrangement of the basic structural features of our world, not to its minute details. It must be continually borne in mind that the spectre of human freedom allows for the existence of moral evil in a world whose underlying structural format is nevertheless the best possible.
38. This isn't as much a statement about the limited power of God as it is a statement about the necessary nature of the creative process itself. In order for any coherent thing to be created, *all* of its essential defining properties must simultaneously be brought about, or else the thing itself cannot be properly said to exist.
39. Stephen Hawking, *A Brief History of Time*, p. 174.

CHAPTER 8

A Proof for God?

> I do not believe that any scientist who examined the evidence would fail to draw the inference that the laws of nuclear physics have been deliberately designed with regard to the consequences they produce inside the stars. If this is so, then my apparently random quirks have become part of a deep-laid scheme. If not then we are back again at a monstrous sequence of accidents.[1]
>
> SIR FRED HOYLE

8.1 Varieties of Proofs

The central point of the present work is that when the many ramifications of the Anthropic Cosmological Principle are duly considered, with no preconceived bias against any type of religious conclusion, the scientific evidence itself is strongly indicative of Intelligent Design in the cosmos. Indeed, many would claim that the evidence is so strong as to constitute a teleologically-based *proof* of the existence of God. Is the use of the word "proof" appropriate here? Does the Anthropic Cosmological Principle provide proof of the existence of a Grand Designer?

In order to provide a suitable answer to this question, we must first distinguish between several senses of the word "proof." As John Hick has pointed out in *The Existence of God*, God's existence can be considered to be "proven" if it is the noncontroversial conclusion of a formally valid argument.[2]

Unfortunately, it is next to impossible to "prove" the existence of God in this formal manner because the truth of the premises themselves can never be guaranteed. Although the conclusion of such an argument may very well directly follow from the stated premises, the validity of the conclusion itself is only as good as the premises which are supplied, and there are no premises concerning the existence of God that are acceptable to everyone.[3]

John Barrow agrees:

> The logical arguments [for the existence of God] are all of a piece. They begin with some assumptions ("axioms" as the logicians like to call them), and then proceed to deduce the existence of God by a series of inexorable logical steps. But in the last analysis we are left not with a conclusion, but a choice. Only if we believe the assumptions at the outset must we believe

the conclusions. There cannot be an ineluctable logical proof of God's existence or non-existence. There will always be a choice about the credibility of assumptions. Furthermore, one suspects that even the great propounders of logical arguments for the existence of God, like Thomas Aquinas, had a personal faith that would not have been perturbed one iota by the undermining of their logical or scientific demonstrations, because it was grounded elsewhere. By the same token, they could not honestly have expected their arguments to sway anyone else to accept their conclusion.

It is for reasons of this sort that the Strong Anthropic coincidences cannot be the basis of a cogent argument for God's existence from apparent anthropocentric design in the universe, although they are quite consistent with such a conclusion. The wide range of remarkable coincidences between values of constants of Nature which have allowed complex living things to evolve are only conditions *necessary* for the existence of life. They are not sufficient to guarantee it.[4]

It seems unlikely, then, that a formally valid argument *per se* will ever be able to prove the existence of God beyond possible doubt, because the premises themselves will always be dubitable. For instance, consider the Design Argument being constructed in this book, which proceeds as follows:

1. Life-facilitating coincidences between distant and causally unrelated branches of physics could not come about by chance, but only by Intelligent Design.
2. Our universe has a large number of these coincidences.
3. Therefore, our universe was Intelligently Designed.

The first premise is clearly dubitable. Therefore, the Argument from Design based on the Anthropic Cosmological Principle will always be open to doubt.

Nevertheless, it does not follow that the Strong Anthropic coincidences do not allow for *any* cogent arguments at all to be proposed in favor of the existence of God. The fact is, only sound proofs with indubitable premises are actually precluded. *Other* types of proofs—some of which are every bit as persuasive as the fundamentally sound arguments mentioned above, if not more so—can serve perfectly well in this capacity.

In fact, if an absolutely coercive logical proof for the existence of God were to actually be devised one day, there would *still* be those who would demand a more direct, *experiential* type of proof before they would be fully convinced. This would undoubtedly constitute the *ultimate* sort of proof, wherein God's Being would be amenable to *direct perception*. But even this type of proof is not beyond doubt, because there is always the possibility that one's consciousness is being externally manipulated by a sinister power, who is bent on deceiving one about the existence of God.[5] In lieu of this admittedly remote possibility, it is extremely doubtful whether any of us will ever attain a direct experiential proof of God's existence in this lifetime. This is because of the tremendous epistemic (i.e., knowledge-based) distance between God and man which, by reasonable hypothesis, must necessarily exist at this stage of our development.[6] Consequently, if we are to ever hope to prove God's existence beyond reasonable doubt, we must rely on less extreme *probabilistic* types of proofs.

Surprisingly enough, the presumed goal of absolute certainty with respect to proving the existence of God turns out to be a Red Herring, because it is a well-known fact that there is no such thing as *absolute* certainty to be had anywhere in the world (apart from the certainty that there can be no certainty). As mathematician Kurt Gödel has amply demonstrated, we can't even gain absolute certainty in such a relatively "simple" field of endeavor as arithmetic, since any such proof must contain statements that are neither provable nor disprovable within the logical system of the language itself.[7] Earlier, Kant had related this epistemological uncertainty to the nebulous realm of sensory perception, as he conclusively demonstrated that the intrinsic categories of human thought forever separate us from an absolute knowledge of *anything* in our environment.[8] The vaporous realm of quantum indeterminancy, discovered in the twentieth century by Werner Heisenberg, had the effect of further eliminating the goal of absolute certainty from the "concrete" physical world, as it suggested that there is a fundamental uncertainty which seems to be built into the underlying nature of physical reality itself: Not only can we not know both the position and momentum of a subatomic particle simultaneously, we can't even tell for sure whether or not the particle actually exists at all as a concrete piece of physical matter!

This fundamental uncertainty about the real world is so deep that we can't even prove in an absolute sense that solipsism[9] is false, because our lack of absolute knowledge about the world inevitably renders it a perpetual (though admittedly remote) possibility. This being the case, how can we ever expect to be absolutely certain about *anything* in our lives, especially something as inherently nebulous as the existence of God?

This is an exceedingly important point, for if we grant from the outset that absolute certainty can never be had in virtually any field of human inquiry, then the natural theologian's lack of absolute certainty about the existence of God cannot be used to count against the validity of his argument. While logically valid proofs may come closer to the goal of absolute certainty than other types of proofs, not even they can claim to deliver *absolute* certainty. This counts *against* Hick's fundamental criticism of natural theology, for if absolute certainty in philosophy can never be had, then in a very real sense *all* logical and philosophical proofs are probabilistic in nature. This is a momentous realization indeed, for it puts *all* proofs in the same general probabilistic category. This in turn greatly strengthens the natural theologian's probabilistic argument, because there are undoubtedly situations in which the circumstantial evidence for a given conclusion is far more convincing than a logically valid proof for the same conclusion could ever be.

This being the case, proving the existence of God is more or less on the same footing as proving that the color purple actually exists, insofar as absolute certainty cannot be had with either of them. In this sense *all* arguments and proofs in human experience are probabilistic in nature.[10] It follows, then, that the natural theologian can no longer be criticized for the lack of absolute certitude in his argument, because in reality such certitude cannot possibly exist in *any* facet of human knowledge.

Going one step further, if absolute certainty can never be had anywhere in human experience, then it follows that there will *always* be more than one possibility in *any* type of scientific or philosophical theorem. Indeed, quantum physicists have long been aware of this metaphysical enigma, since it has been a well-acknowledged fact since the early part of this century that there are many possibilities for any and all quantum events. This being the case, Hick can no longer criticize the cogency of the natural theologian's claims because two interpretations of the cosmological evidence are *possible*, since there is no such thing as a situation where only one interpretation of *anything* can possibly exist. This would require the existence of absolute certainty in epistemology, which, as we have seen, appears to be utterly unattainable.

Thus, Hick's and Barrow's claim that the Anthropic Principle can never be used to provide a cogent argument for the existence of God turns out to be a Red Herring after all, because the very basis of their argument (the desire for absolute certainty) turns out to be a fiction. It follows from this realization that *all* rational conclusions in life are probabilistic in nature. Accordingly, the cogency of *all* rational conclusions can be seen to rest on the intrinsic persuasiveness of the evidence under consideration, not on the *absolute* exclusivity of any particular conclusion in relation to other logical possibilities.

8.2   Data Coherence and Causality

One of the inevitable consequences of this lack of absolute certainty in human life is that we can never hope to establish indubitably the existence of a direct causal relationship between two or more distinct events in the real world. The very best that we can do is find some reliable means for assessing the relative probability that certain events in our experience will in fact be causally related. As it turns out, this is something that we intuitively do—and do well—every single day of our lives.

The chief criterion that we subconsciously use to determine whether or not a causal connection exists between different physical phenomena is the notion of *data coherence around a central focal point.* If most or all of the events in question are observed to cohere together in a recognizable pattern, we naturally assume that a common causal element has elicited the pattern, and is therefore responsible for eliciting the events themselves.

A good example of this process can be found in the various global weather patterns that are routinely detected by meteorological satellites. While a single photograph can show the existence of a well-developed weather pattern (through the systematic orientation of the clouds themselves), a sequence of photographs over an extended period of time is much more effective in this regard, since each repetition of the observed pattern through a variety of successive states tends to further reinforce the impression that a single causal agent has been at work in the genesis of the pattern itself.

Once such a consistent pattern has been identified, we automatically assume that a common causal agent has been responsible for eliciting the whole phenomenon. For instance, if a dense region of clouds is repeatedly observed to be swirling in counterclockwise fashion around a central focal point, we automatically assume that the entire pattern itself has been elicited by a single causal agent (and therefore that the behavior of each of the individual members of the pattern has been elicited by the same causal agent).

A similar situation can be found to exist in the area of "anthropic" cosmology, where the stucture of the entire universe can repeatedly be seen to cohere around the central focal point of living tissue. Two conclusions can be drawn from this clearly recognizable pattern: 1) that a common causal element is probably at work behind the various structural parameters of the physical universe, and 2) that the existence of biological life seems to be the explicit aim of this causal force. While these conclusions are not beyond doubt (since it possible that life could have evolved to fit the existing cosmic circumstances), they nevertheless seem to lead directly to a theistic view of cosmogenesis (though again not necessarily so, since it is conceivable that a non-divine physical force could have accidentally generated this cosmological pattern). The point is simply that given the evidence at hand, the theistic interpretation appears to be more probable overall than the non-theistic interpretation.

The statistician Bartholomew is in full agreement with this radical point of view.

Let us set up the hypothesis that there is no directing purpose behind the universe so that all change and development is the product of "blind chance." We then proceed to calculate the probability that the world (or that aspect of it under consideration) would turn out as we find it. If that probability turns out to be extremely small we argue that the occurrence of something so rare is totally implausible and hence that the hypothesis on which it is calculated is almost certainly false. The only reasonable alternative open to us is to postulate a grand intelligence to account for what has occurred. This procedure is based on the logical disjunction *either* an extremely rare event has occurred *or* the hypothesis on which the probability is calculated is false. Faced with this choice the rational thing to do is to prefer the latter alternative.[11]

8.3 A Probabilistic Proof for the Existence of God

Probabilistic proofs take the general form that, given this or that structure or feature of the world, it is more likely that there is a God than that there is not.[12] Such arguments make no claim of absolute certitude; they simply state that, given the considerations under evaluation, it is more rational to believe in God than not to.[13]

"Proving" the existence of God via the Anthropic Cosmological Principle constitutes just such a probabilistic type of argument. This type of "proof" simply says that, given the most recent findings supplied by physicists and cosmologists, it is more reasonable to believe in God than not to do so.

Actually, next to the direct experiential sort of proof mentioned earlier in this chapter, this probabilistic type of argument based on firm scientific evidence constitutes the next strongest proof of the Divine Being. This is because probabilistic proofs themselves are also based on the direct perception of a certain body of real world facts. While they may not involve a direct perception of God's Own Being *per se*, they do purport to offer a direct perception of the *effects* of God's Creative Activity in the world, from which it is possible to infer the existence of Intelligent Design. Indeed, judging from the real-world accessibility of probabilistic proofs and the relative inaccessibility of both experiential and logically valid proofs respectively, probabilistic proofs offer the strongest *practical* proof of the Divine Being.

Probabilistic proofs of God's existence in the realm of cosmology are based on *circumstantial evidence* whose existence is alleged to be hard to refute. It is the *conclusion* that is *inferred* from this circumstantial evidence that is open to doubt, because of the dubitable premise that the data in question could not have come about without Intelligent Design. In this case, the more evidence one amasses in support of one's position the better, because the entire issue under consideration here is one of probability, so a greater number of examples typically translates into the perception of a greater overall probability for Intelligent Design. This being the case, we now need to ask ourselves whether there is enough circumstantial evidence in the cosmological realm to "prove" beyond reasonable doubt the existence of a Grand Designer.

Before we can hope to provide an accurate answer to this question, one assertion must be conceded: a large number of cosmic "coincidences" have in fact occurred in our universe, and it is precisely these "coincidences" that have enabled life to evolve on this planet. In other words, it isn't the reality of these "coincidences" that is at issue here; it is how we are to *interpret* their underlying meaning that constitutes the true issue. The question thus boils down to the following: are these "coincidences" *so* numerous and *so* compelling that we are virtually forced into acknowledging a Divine Origin to them?

Interestingly enough, it is the non-theistic scientists themselves who can provide the most help in this arena. Stephen Hawking, for instance, has openly admitted that the evidence surrounding the Anthropic Principle is so compelling that there *must* be religious overtones associated with it.[14]

Theoretical physicist Paul Davies is even more emphatic in this regard, as he has openly acknowledged the need for a "selector" or "designer" to choose our exceedingly improbable universe out of the infinity of possible choices.[15]

Hawking agrees that, given the infinite number of universes which *could* have been born at the Big Bang, "there ought to be some principle that picks one initial state, and hence one model, to represent our universe."[16] Hawking admits that God could very well have been the primordial "principle" which chose the initial state of our present universe.[17]

Indeed, given the remarkable large-scale smoothness and homogeneity of the universe, along with the fact that there hasn't been time for any causal communication between areas of the universe that are separated by more than 30 degrees in the sky,[18] it seems as though our universe *had* to have begun from an exceedingly well-chosen set of initial conditions. Yet, if we assume that randomness alone was the dominant factor at the Big Bang, the universe itself:

> . . . would be unlikely to contain *any* region in which life would appear. In the hot big bang model . . . there was not enough time in the early universe for heat to have flowed from one region to another. This means that the initial state of the universe would have to have had exactly the same temperature everywhere in order to account for the fact that the microwave background has the same temperature in every direction we look. The initial rate of expansion also would have had to be chosen very precisely for the rate of expansion still to be so close to the critical rate needed to avoid recollapse. This means that the initial state of the universe must have been very carefully chosen indeed if the hot big bang model was correct right back to the beginning of time. *It would be very difficult*

to explain why the universe should have begun in just this way, except as the act of a God who intended to create beings like us (emphasis mine).[19]

George Greenstein is yet another physicist who seems to acknowledge God's apparent role in orchestrating the Big Bang (although as we have seen, he ends up rejecting the theistic hypothesis for philosophical reasons):

As we survey all the evidence, the thought insistently arises that some supernatural agency—or rather, Agency—must be involved. Is it possible that suddenly, without intending to, we have stumbled upon scientific proof of the existence of a Supreme Being? Was it God who stepped in and so providentially crafted the cosmos for our benefit? Do we not see in its harmony, a harmony so perfectly fitted to our needs, evidence of what one religious writer has called "a preserving, a continuing, an intending mind; a Wisdom, Power, and Goodness far exceeding the limits of our thoughts"?[20]

The epigraph to this chapter, taken from the work of Sir Fred Hoyle, provides yet another instance in which a non-theistic scientist has been seduced by the scientific evidence into believing in the existence of a "Super-calculating Intellect." Hoyle openly believes that the existing evidence is so overwhelming that no scientist who carefully examines it can fail to come to the same conclusion.[21]

Now, one would never expect non-theistic scientists—who have been trained from the very beginning to reject as "unscientific" all religious considerations—to openly mention God as a possible explanation for the cosmological evidence unless the data were so compelling that they almost had no choice in the matter. Indeed, judging from the many incredible things that these scientists have said about God's possible relationship to the cosmos, it is likely that deep down many of them actually believe in—and are fascinated by—the idea that God Himself may be behind the marvel of physical reality.

8.4 Scientific Proof for a Creator?

Given the many stunning "coincidences" that we have examined throughout this book, along with the pro-theistic statements of many of the world's foremost scientists, we must now ask whether or not we have discovered in these coincidences a valid "proof" of God's existence. Although one might initially object to the use of the word "proof" in this context (since, as we have seen, no absolute proof of God's existence is possible or promised), there surely must come a point where the circumstantial evidence surrounding the possibility of Intelligent Design becomes so persuasive that it can accurately be said to constitute a probabilistic proof of the Divine Being. The question is simply whether or not enough convincing evidence exists in the realm of physics and cosmology for such a probabilistic proof to be considered valid.

With this in mind, how are we to be able to ascertain whether or not a sufficient amount of convincing evidence actually exists to justify a transition from circumstantial evidence to circumstantial proof as far as the origin of the universe itself is concerned? Given the fact that God isn't going to directly make Himself known to us, at least not in this lifetime, it would seem that the only way we're going to make a realistic judgement on this issue is by appealing to some sort of *functional* criterion. For just as we tend to judge the "goodness" of a given thing in terms of how efficiently it serves its intended purpose, we can also judge the adequacy of the evidence surrounding Intelligent Design in terms of its overall *functional competence*, i.e., how well does the cosmological evidence work to attain its supposed purpose?

As long as this criterion of functional efficiency is used to determine the adequacy of the circumstantial evidence, we are compelled to conclude that the evidence is almost *perfectly* adequate for its apparent functional intention, which is the supporting of biological life. Indeed, this is where the Biocentric Principle derives its very meaning: the coincidences themselves are so well-coordinated with one another that life has been able to evolve on this planet against all the odds. It would seem, then, that as long as we posit the evolution of life as the long-range "intention" of these coincidences, we are justified in concluding that they have indeed been enormously successful in reaching their "intended" goal. It is this perfect degree of functional success in the face of overwhelming odds to the contrary that compels us to conclude that there is more than enough circumstantial evidence in cosmology to prove the "behind the scenes" activity of an Intelligent Designer. The outrageous unlikelihood that our biocentric universe could have evolved by chance alone only strengthens the validity of this conclusion.

An analogy may help to clarify this important point. Imagine coming home late one evening to find one's front door ajar, one's clothes strewn all over the floor, and one's drawers obviously mingled with. Upon further inspection, imagine finding one's diamond watch missing, one's VCR gone, and tracks of mud scattered throughout the house. One's first impression, of course, would be to conclude that one has been robbed, because *all* of the circumstantial evidence is consistent with this conclusion. Still, one cannot yet be certain about this impromptu conclusion, because there are other possible explanations that are also consistent with the available evidence. Before one can conclude beyond doubt that one has indeed been robbed, one must first consider all these other possibilities.

Upon deeper reflection, one finds that the only other conceivable explanation for one's torn-up house is that one's normally immaculate and conscientious daughter may have inadvertently flown home from the other side of the country and torn the house up in an uncharacteristic fit of anger. This explanation also fits the circumstantial evidence, because it is possible that she could have flown home, taken the watch and VCR, and left the house in a complete state of disarray. The tremendous improbability of this explanation, however, immediately causes it to be dismissed in favor of the robbery hypothesis, which is clearly the more probable explanation overall.

In other words, one typically uses the relative probability of the competing explanations to determine which one is best. The lack of absolute proof in this instance thus does not significantly detract from one's certainty about the robbery, because the enormous dissimilarity in probabilities almost completely compensates for the lack of absolute proof. It is for this reason that just about everyone would agree that the circumstantial evidence in this instance proves beyond reasonable doubt that a robbery did in fact take place.

Indeed, given the strength of the circumstantial evidence in this particular example, an absolute proof of the robbery (which would amount to a videotape or a reliable eyewitness) is almost unnecessary. While it is possible that there is another explanation for one's torn-up house that one cannot yet conceive of (such as a disorganizing local disturbance in the quantum field surrounding one's house), such an "explanation" can quickly be seen to be improbable enough to be dismissed entirely in favor of the far more convincing robbery hypothesis.

Although the notion of circumstantial evidence tends to be highly suspect, especially in legal circles, due to its intrinsically questionable nature, it is actually the only evidence we are ever presented with in our lives. Absolute experiential proof, as we have seen, is an extremely nebulous concept that may not even exist at all for beings of finite intelligence. Although a given cause and effect relation may transpire before our very eyes, this still does not amount to an absolute proof that the two are in fact causally related to one another. All we know for sure is that there is a temporal conjunction between the observed cause and the observed effect (and perhaps a physical conjunction as well); we simply use this temporal (and possibly physical) conjunction to conclude that the observed cause has in fact elicited the observed effect. In reality, though, another causative agent entirely could have actually elicited the observed effect, perhaps from another dimension. Indeed, as far as we can tell, an extraterrestrial being could be externally implanting in our minds all the cause and effect processes that we will ever experience in our lives, and we would never know the difference.[22]

From this point of view, all the evidence we ever experience in this world is *necessarily* circumstantial in nature, because we can never know all the possible forces in the universe that could causally impinge upon our lives. Because of this crucial epistemic limitation, we can only see a relatively tiny proportion of the many causal influences that happen to exist in the universe.

This being the case, we simply *assume* that the events in our world are elicited exclusively by locally visible causal influences, but we have no absolute proof of this. It is for this reason we can say that the temporal conjunction between cause and effect that we regularly observe in our world is simply circumstantial evidence of a direct causal relationship that happens to have an extremely high probability of being true (in light of all the other known explanations). Thus, when we accidentally step on a dog's tail and find that it lets out a loud scream, we can be fairly sure that *we* have directly elicited this response, even though a number of other alternative explanations are also possible. Our relative certainty in this case is justified because the temporal and physical conjunctions involved make it overwhelmingly probable that we are in fact responsible for eliciting the dog's response, instead of some unseen causative agent.[23]

Absolute proof, then, can only come about when one surveys *all* possible explanations for any given state of affairs. This is clearly impossible, though, because no mere mortal can examine all possible explanations for *anything*. Indeed, given our almost complete ignorance about the role of unseen causal influences in our world, we would have to possess *omniscient* knowledge before we could ever arrive at absolute proof for *anything*. Absolute proof is thus the exclusive province of the omniscient, but since we can never even approach the goal of omniscience in this lifetime, we must rely on less certain probabilistic proofs to explain why things happen in our world.

So it is the notion of probability that enables us to establish the relative degree of certainty of our causal explanations in life. Whenever we are in doubt about the cause of any given state of affairs, we typically weigh the relative probabilities of all the relevant alternatives in order to determine which is the most probable explanation in light of the existing evidence at hand. If the relative probabilities of the competing explanations are deemed to be similar to one another, one's decision becomes difficult and ambiguous, because it then becomes hard to tell which alternative is the most likely overall. However, when one alternative is clearly recognized as being far more probable than all the others, this is the one that is generally regarded as being "true."

All this has direct application to our goal of finding a suitable explanation for the many life-supporting "coincidences" that we have discussed in this book. These "coincidences" are so complex, so numerous, so intrinsically improbable, and yet so perfectly attuned to the goal of life that they seem to push the circumstantial evidence for Intelligent Design far beyond the critical threshold needed for a reasonable theistic proof. For just as the conclusion of robbery in the above example was based on the "success" of the evidence in indicating that a robbery had indeed taken place, the "success" of the evidence for Intelligent Design—the actual existence of the biosphere despite truly monumental odds to the contrary—compels us to conclude that the critical threshold separating circumstantial evidence from circumstantial proof has in fact been greatly exceeded as far as the origin of the universe itself is concerned.

For Hick and Barrow, however, the fact that there are two *possible* interpretations of the cosmological data (naturalistic and theistic) *automatically* renders *both* explanations ambiguous. The question of the inherent probability of either alternative does not significantly enter into the discussion, because as long as more than one explanation is *possible*, the issue is deemed to remain inherently ambiguous. But surely the existence of two *possible* alternatives does not in itself preclude the possibility that one of the alternatives may in fact be far more probable, and therefore far more likely, than the other.

In other words, just because one can conceive of two *possible* explanations for a given phenomenon doesn't *necessarily* make the choice between them ambiguous. The only way this would be true is if the two alternatives in question could be shown to be similarly probable. Clearly, however, this isn't always the case, because one can easily conceive of a situation where *one* of the alternatives is overwhelmingly more probable than the other. In this case, the fact that there might be two *possible* alternatives doesn't seriously detract from the ascertation that *one* of the alternatives is clearly to be preferred on probabilistic grounds.

For instance, while it may be *possible* that Smith is a being from another world, this possibility in and of itself does not necessarily make the ascertation of Smith's true identity ambiguous. Rather, the immense unlikelihood of Smith's possible extraterrestrial status makes our determination of his earthbound humanity almost certain. Or, in terms of the earlier example concerning the robbed apartment, the fact that it is *possible* that one's daughter *could* have disrupted the apartment does *not* significantly detract from one's conviction that a robber did in fact do so. Similarly, the fact that our universe *could* conceivably have been a great cosmic fluke should *not* significantly detract from the much more likely possibility that it was deliberately designed by a Higher Power for the purpose of sustaining biological life. As a consequence, we must reject Hick's and Barrow's surmisal that the Strong Anthropic data are unable to provide a cogent argument for the existence of God.

Of course, people differ in their overall readiness to accept a given amount of circumstantial evidence as "proof." There are undoubtedly those, for instance, who would resist the conclusion that the simultaneous misfiring of 100 separate rifles during an execution was indicative of some sort of deliberate "behind the scenes" coordinating activity. Such individuals are few in number, and of these, most would probably be resisting the above-stated conclusion for reasons other than the weight of the evidence itself. Similarly, there are those who heroically resist the conclusion that our incredible life-supporting universe is the result of Intelligent Design, in spite of the mountain of scientific evidence to the contrary. Of these "theistically resistant" individuals, it seems likely that many of them are rejecting the conclusion of Intelligent Design for reasons other than the weight of the evidence itself.

8.5   The Acceptability of Indirect Scientific Evidence

Scientists, philosophers of science, and theologians alike all tend to believe that the search for the existence of God is unscientific by its very nature, due to the indirect nature of the evidence itself: since God can never be discovered or measured directly, He is deemed to be beyond the reach of scientific investigation altogether.

Although this may superficially seem like a legitimate reason for excluding God from the realm of scientific inquiry, it is actually inconsistent with the highly abstract, indirect nature of modern science itself. As physician Larry Dossey has aptly pointed out, finding evidence for the existence of God is in principle no more unscientific than finding evidence for the existence of subatomic particles, since both are invisible and can therefore be discovered only indirectly:

It's not scientific heresy or blasphemy to settle on indirect evidence. No one has ever held a quark in his hands. The same reasoning can be applied to God. But if we start out saying we have no God meter, whatever evidence we get will be indirect and we'll be in a better position to handle whatever phenomenon we observe.[24]

From this point of view, the search for God is at least as scientifically sound as the search for quarks or antiprotons, because: 1) both types of objects stand on the same indirect epistemological footing, and 2) the phenomenon of Intelligent Design is much more accessible and comprehensible to us on the whole, since we know what it is we are talking about from personal experience and can postulate necessary conditions for its existence.

The existence of subatomic particles, on the other hand, is far more dubitable, since we only have indirect access to these hypothetical entities through our scientific models of reality, which are themselves always open to change. Indeed, many ground-breaking particle physicists have *already* disposed of the existence of discrete subatomic particles in favor of vibrating cosmic strings.

Clearly very little in the realm of theoretical physics is sacrosanct. Better scientific models invariably lead to different interpretations of the physical evidence, so *all* interpretations must remain perpetually open to doubt. This seems to put our probabilistic proof for the existence of God on a similar epistemological footing as many of science's most cherished ideas regarding the physical nature of reality.

Indeed, for most scientists the domain of scientific proof can be extended to any form of physical evidence that can plausibly be used to support a rational belief.[25] Within such a broad conceptualization of the necessary conditions for scientific proof,[26] it isn't surprising that many respected scientists now believe that science can actually provide quantifiable evidence for the existence of God within a traditional scientific framework.

As far as Tulane University's Frank Tipler (co-author of *The Anthropic Cosmological Principle*) is concerned, the existence of God is well within the domain of traditional scientific research, since science "concerns itself with the totality of existence. [Accordingly, if] science can't reach God, then God doesn't exist."[27] This is an audacious statement, to be sure, but it nonetheless appears to be valid in principle, since science *does* theoretically extend to the whole of reality.

Fortunately, we won't have to wait until the fifty-first century before science is advanced enough to be able to discover the existence of the Creator, for if the underlying structure of the universe has in fact been Intelligently Contrived, then this characteristic should be abundantly evident to the scientific researchers of *today*. And so it is. As Caltech engineer Thomas McDonough has pointed out, several of today's top scientific researchers have picked up on this pattern of Intelligent Design in the universe, insofar as they believe that the concatenation of so many "anthropic" coincidences throughout the cosmos "seems to make the universe fine-tuned to our existence." This in turn can be taken to be "a signpost that God does [in fact] exist."[28]

It would seem, then, that science's exclusion of God from the realm of legitimate scientific inquiry, on the sole basis of the indirect nature of the evidence itself, is little more than a celebrated Red Herring, whose purpose has been to keep threatening theological ideas outside of the scientific establishment altogether. While it may be true that God's spiritual nature automatically renders Him undiscoverable in a direct physical sense, His Creative Actions in the world *can* nevertheless be directly analyzed to our heart's content, since they *are* in fact physical in nature.[29]

This is the sense in which the physical evidence for the existence of God can be said to be similar to the physical evidence for quarks or positrons: since both types of objects can never be directly seen, we have no choice but to rely on the indirect process of interpretation before we can reach any definitive conclusions regarding either of them. This simple fact provides a new level of credibility to the natural theologian's quest for a scientific proof of God's existence, and explains how a popular science magazine *(Omni)* was able to devote an entire issue to the scientific search for God.[30]

Indeed, Frank Tipler goes so far as to claim that the scientific search for God will actually herald the dawn of the twenty-first century. The reason for this remarkable statement isn't far to seek: The idea of God represents the very pinnacle of human thought regarding the evolution of the universe, since such a Divine Creative Energy, if it exists at all, must constitute the metaphysical source of all being. In this sense God is the unacknowledged Goal that all scientists are striving for, since He is by definition the Author of all forms of natural science. It is only natural, then, to suppose that as science progresses, the Ultimate Goal of science will become increasingly clear to its practitioners, as it was to the founders of the modern scientific movement during the Renaissance period.

8.6   Scientific Truth via the Process of Elimination

One of the best ways to asertain which of several competing scientific theories is true is to work backwards by eliminating the more inadequate theories one by one. What one is generally left with is the *least* inadequate explanation, and this often turn out to be the one that is true in the end.

In *Paradigms Lost,* John Casti discusses four possible theories to account for the extraordinary degree of life-facilitating order in the universe: dissipation, inflation, God, and Everett's Many Worlds theory.[31] As we have seen, the concept of cosmic dissipation contains numerous internal difficulties that don't seem to square with observation, while the concept of inflation cannot legitimately be used to supplant the need for a Divine Creator. Moreover, few individuals seem to take the many worlds approach seriously enough to posit it as a realistic explanation for our biocentric universe. This leaves us with only one remaining Alternative to choose from, whose only inadequacies are that it contradicts recent scientific dogma and that it is not directly testable in the laboratory. Certainly one cannot claim that the theistic hypothesis is counterintuitive, because all major civilizations throughout history have believed in some sort of Divine Power, and all have possessed some sort of creation myth.

Moreover, just because we can conceive of several logically possible scenarios (based on premises of our own choosing) that happen to be able to "explain" the existence of our universe as a chance event, this doesn't at all mean that any of them could have ever *really* happened. It is logically possible, for instance, that a trillion repetitions of a legitimate coin toss will produce a trillion "heads" in a row, but no one in their right mind believes such a thing to be possible *in fact*.

The evolution of our biocentric universe appears to be much the same way. Although it doesn't seem to be logically impossible for it to have evolved by chance, such an accidental evolution *does* seem to be impossible *in fact*, because the odds against such a stupendous feat are far too vast to have *ever* been overcome in the relatively small amount of time that the universe has been in existence. This being the case, we shouldn't delude ourselves too much by the fact that we can dream up all sorts of self-consistent "explanations" for how our life-supporting universe could have come into being by chance alone. For in every such hypothetical instance, we must inevitably posit the self-existence of certain basic initial conditions (such as self-organizing atoms and molecules) that don't seem to be able to contain within themselves a sufficient explanation for *their own* existence. A simple examination of these non-theistic assumptions should therefore be more than enough to disconfirm all of these "accidental evolution" paradigms.

On the plus side, the theistic hypothesis is the only one that squares consistently with the observed facts, as we have seen. It thus boils down to whether one's anti-theistic inclinations are sufficiently intense to counter the striking evidence of Design at all levels of cosmic reality.

8.7 Deducing the Existence of God from the Intelligence of the Creation

It is also possible to deduce the existence of a Divine Creator from the intelligence that is exemplified in the underlying structure of the universe itself. *For it would seem to be a truism that any system that requires a certain amount of intelligence and insight to understand originally required at least as much intelligence and insight to create.* This much only stands to reason.

However, to the extent that we accept this relation as true, we find that we must attribute the creation of the universe to an intelligence that is superior to our own, since the intelligence that is displayed in even the "simplest" atom vastly exceeds our ability to understand it. And since God appears to be the only intelligence superior to our own who could have actually created the present universal order, we find that such a Divine Creator Being must indeed exist after all.

The ancient Stoic philosopher Chrysippus used a similar type of argument to prove the existence of God:

> If there is something in the world which human reason, strength and power are incapable of producing, that which produces it must be better than man. But the heavens and everything which displays unceasing regularity cannot be produced by man. Therefore that by which those things are produced is better than man. And what name rather than God would you give to this?[32]

Paul Davies reaches a similar conclusion in *Superforce:*

> If nature is so "clever" it can exploit mechanisms that amaze us with their ingenuity, is that not persuasive evidence for the existence of intelligent design behind the physical universe? If the world's finest minds can unravel only with difficulty the deeper workings of nature, how could it be sup-

posed that those workings are merely a mindless accident, a product of blind chance?

Should we conclude that the universe is the product of design? The new physics and the new cosmology hold out a tantalizing promise: that we might be able to explain how all the physical structures in the universe have come to exist, automatically, as a result of natural processes. We should then no longer have need for a Creator in the traditional sense. Nevertheless, though science may be able to explain the world, we still have to explain science. The laws which enable the universe to come into being spontaneously seem themselves to be the product of exceedingly ingenious design. If physics is the product of design, the universe must have a purpose, and the evidence of modern physics suggests strongly to me that the purpose includes us.[33]

In reality, belief in a Divine Creator appears to be much more widespread amongst physicists, biologists, and cosmologists than has heretofore been admitted. Such a belief is almost inevitable, given the theological background of modern science and the inherently mystical nature of physical reality itself. Speaking of his theistically minded colleagues, Paul Davies says that he is surprised by how many of them hold conventional religious beliefs. "In some cases," he says, "their scientific work bolsters their conventional religious positions. The majority, however, probably stand in awe of nature and aren't sure whether its subtlety and ingenuity relate to a personal God or simply an underlying order. Yet even they feel the world is more than a random accident. There has to be more to it than just fact."[34]

This gut-level feeling appears to be very firmly entrenched in American society, where 95% of the population say they believe in the existence of God, 75% say they are certain about life after death, 90% say they pray every week, and 50% say they pray every day.[35] Contrary to popular belief, the prevalence of religious belief in this country has *not* declined in recent years; it has remained more or less the same for over half a century. According to Father Andrew Greeley, professor of sociology at the University of Arizona, fluctuations in religious belief are more a function of psychological variances in the life cycle than they are an indication of any long-term societal trends: religious devotion tends to bottom out during one's late teens and early twenties, only to pick up again during one's late twenties and thirties, and finally reaches a plateau in one's mid-forties.[36]

But if this is indeed the case, why have so many jounalists and academicians, who have ready access to the sociological data and should know better, nevertheless led us to believe that there has been a serious decline in religious devotion in this country over the last several decades? According to Father Greeley, the answer is that these writers themselves have for one reason or another drifted away from their religious origins and have simply projected their own lack of belief onto the remainder of society.[37]

8.8   Holistic Proof for the Existence of God

In *Cosmos and Anthropos* Errol Harris develops an interesting line of argument in which he attempts to prove the existence of God using the philosophical principles of holism. Speaking of God as the consummation of the cosmic scale of forms, Harris writes the following:

> As totally explicit in transparent self-consciousness, this consummation of the cosmic scale is an omniscient mind. Being the actualization in full of a universal principle of order, which is immanent in every phase and every detail of the scale, it is the Alpha and the Omega of all being. Because the universal principle is immanent in every part, it is what generates and determines the nature of every entity, and its activity is nothing more nor less than its own self-differentiation in and as the spatio-temporal world. But its ultimate realization is a transcendent comprehension and self-conscious realization of the whole. It is thus all-creative and all-powerful, as well as all-knowing and absolutely self-complete. All this is necessarily entailed by the very concept of design.

> If God is conceived as the absolute universal principle of order manifesting itself in and as the universe, and transcending all finite phases, the argument from design, as a proof of his existence, can be justified in this, its modern form, without requiring any inference from a contrived plan to a Supreme Architect (unless these phrases are used metaphorically).

> . . . This conclusion has the rare advantage that it is not a resort to God as a cloak to cover our knowledge, but is the logical consequence of the very nature of our knowledge and of the structure of the universe as discovered by empirical science. Here, then, is the argument from design in modern dress, and the epithet Physico-theological describes it nicely. It is the argument for the existence of God that follows most readily from the discoveries of the empirical sciences, and I have discussed it here because it has been publicly and deliberately resurrected by the physicists themselves.[38]

One could conceivably counter Harris' holistic proof of the existence of God by asserting the possibility that the universe is *not* an undivided whole, appearances notwithstanding. However, just about all of the scientific and philosophical evidence discovered to date seems to indicate rather forcefully that the universe is in point of fact a unified, seamless whole. To the extent that this is true, Harris' conclusions seem to follow directly from the very concept of holism.

Indeed, Harris even goes so far as to claim that if the traditional proofs for the existence of God are understood in terms of a holistic and dialectical conception of the universe, *all* of them can be "resurrected, restated, and vindicated as valid."[39] These are powerful, far-reaching conclusions, to be sure, but, as Harris indicates, they seem to follow inevitably from the very concepts of design and holism.

8.9   The Overall Case for Intelligent Design

As we have seen, a grand conspiracy between a large number of seemingly unrelated events has been at work in the universe since its very inception. The purpose of this conspiracy has been, among other things, to make it possible for life to evolve on this planet.

While it is possible to "explain" the co-operation of these distinct elements in terms of chance alone, the more intuitive and probable explanation is to use the immense complexity and difficulty of life's evolution, along with the utterly remarkable nature of life itself, to conclude that these "coincidences" were deliberately planned and implemented by a Higher Power so as to enable life to come into being.

Most scientists, even the most hardened atheistic ones, will readily admit that this is the most natural and intuitive explanation for these remarkable "cosmic events." However, the notion of probability also greatly favors this intuitive explanation, since it is far more probable that these "coincidences" were the result of Intelligent Design than that they were the product of blind chance. But science operates primarily on the basis of recognized probabilities, since virtually nothing in science can be proved absolutely. Therefore, the most "scientific" conclusion with regard to these "coincidences" is undoubtedly the theistic one, since it is clearly the most probable explanation overall. The radically more improbable alternative—that life is merely the result of a stupendous cosmic accident—must therefore be dismissed as being a relatively unscientific form of self-deception, since it is sufficiently unlikely as to be virtually impossible.

Indeed, according to University of Montreal psychiatrist Karl Stern, the belief that our wondrous universe could have evolved by blind chance is ". . . crazy. And I do not at all mean crazy in the sense of a slangy invective but rather in the technical meaning of psychotic. Indeed such a view has much in common with certain aspects of schizophrenic thinking."[40]

It takes a lot of faith to believe that our enormously complex universe could have arisen by chance alone—certainly a lot more faith than it takes to believe that it is the product of Intelligent Design. Since science, as we have seen, allies itself with probabilities and recognized analogies, and not heroic unsubstantiated faith, it follows that the notion of Intelligent Design is by far the most "scientific" explanation for the origin of our biocentric universe. The founding fathers of the modern scientific movement—Newton, Boyle, and a whole host of other brilliant thinkers—would have wholeheartedly agreed with this conclusion, as they were convinced beyond doubt that our universe was in fact Intelligently Designed. Given the strength of the Anthropic Design Argument, perhaps we should return to their timeless fount of insight and wisdom.

Notes

1. Sir Fred Hoyle, *Religion and the Scientists* (London: SCM, 1959.
2. John Hick, *The Existence of God* (New York: The Macmillan Publishing Company, 1964), pp. 4–7.
3. Ibid., p. 5.
4. John D. Barrow, *The World Within the World*, p. 365.
5. A similar sort of mind deception takes place in the Arnold Schwarzenegger film "Total Recall." An artificially contrived identity, complete with its own self-consistent set of memories, is mechanically implanted into Schwarzegger's brain without "his" knowledge, and needless to say, once this mental reprogramming has already taken place, there is no way for Schwarzenegger to tell the difference between his real self and his artificially implanted personality.
6. This notion of epistemic distance, due in recent years to John Hick, will be discussed at greater length in the next chapter. The interested reader is also referred to Hick's *Evil and the God of Love* (New York: Harper and Row, 1977), pp. 280–282.
7. John Barrow, *The World Within the World*, p. 25.
8. Ibid., p. 78.
9. Solipsism is the belief that nothing in the external world is real.
10. While some extremely probable conclusions can be shown to approximate absolute certitude, there is still a vast gulf separating the highly probable from the absolutely certain.
11. Reprinted from John Polkinghorne's *Science and Creation* (Boston: Shambhala, 1989), p. 28.
12. John Hick, *The Existence of God*, p. 7.
13. Ibid., pp. 7–9.
14. Boslough, *Stephen Hawking's Universe*, p. 121.
15. Paul Davies, *God and the New Physics* (New York: Simon and Schuster, 1983), pp. 167–168.
16. Stephen W. Hawking, *A Brief History of Time*, p. 123.
17. Ibid., p. 122.
18. Barrow and Tipler, p. 420.
19. Hawking, *A Brief History of Time*, pp. 126–127.
20. George Greenstein, *The Symbiotic Universe*, p. 27.
21. Sir Fred Hoyle, *Religion and the Scientists* (London: SCM, 1959).
22. For a great demonstration of this possibility, the reader is once again referred to Arnold Schwarzenegger's movie "Total Recall." In the film's plot, sinister agents implant a brand new personality inside of Schwarzenegger's brain, in the form of a constellation of artificially contrived memories that never really happened. Since these memories never really happened, the cause and effect relationships within them never really happened either, but Schwarzenegger was unable to become objective enough to realize that he had been duped.

23. The Stoic idea of God as the Logos, or Logical Mediator, between cause and effect does not contradict this notion of circumstantial probability. For while God may actually be externally pairing all worldly causes with their corresponding logical effects, the worldly causes themselves are still ultimately responsible for eliciting the effects in question. God simply enables these causes and effects to be paired up in the most logical and sensible fashion possible.

24. Quoted in A.J.S Rayl and K.T. McKinney's "The Mind of God," *OMNI*, Vol. 13, No. 11, August, 1991, p. 46.

25. Ibid.

26. This is a much looser definition of the word "proof" than is regularly used in philosophical circles. It is more or less synonymous with the probabilistic type of proof discussed in this chapter.

27. Ibid., p. 44.

28. Ibid.

29. It is this disjunction between God's Spiritual Essence and His physical Actions in the world that necessarily renders all scientific evidence for His existence indirect by its very nature.

30. See the August, 1991 edition of *OMNI*, Vol. 13, No. 11, pp. 43–48.

31. John Casti, *Paradigms Lost* (New York: William Morrow and Company, 1989), pp. 485–488.

32. Taken from A.A. Long's *Hellenistic Philosophy* (Berkeley: University of California Press, 1974), p. 149.

33. P.C.W. Davies, *Superforce*, p. 243.

34. Quoted in A.J.S Rayl and K.T. McKinney's "The Mind of God," *Omni*, Vol. 13, No. 11, August, 1991, p. 46.

35. Andrew Greeley, "Keeping the Faith: Americans Hold Fast to the Rock of Ages," in *Omni*, Vol. 13, No. 11, August, 1991, p. 6.

36. Ibid.

37. Ibid.

38. Errol E. Harris, *Cosmos and Anthropos*, pp. 171–172.

39. Ibid., p. 28.

40. Taken from Jeremy Rifkin's *Algeny* (New York: The Viking Press, 1983), p. 114.

CHAPTER 9

An Anthropic or Biocentric Universe?

What is a man, that the electron is mindful of him?

CARL BECKER

Thus far, we have only sought to establish a principle of deliberate contrivance in the universe aimed at the emergence of biological life. Now it is time to move on to consider whether or not we can justifiably claim that this contrivance was intended to produce *human* life.

9.1 Argument for an Anthropic Interpretation of the Cosmological Evidence

As we have seen, when the physical evidence is examined *entirely* on its own terms, it can only properly be said to support the notion of a *biocentric* universe. That is to say, the various life-supporting physical parameters that have been discovered in the cosmos cannot be said to be "aimed" at the evolution of uniquely human life; at most, they can only be said to be aimed at the evolution of biological life in general. Thus, as far as the scientific evidence itself is concerned, we are only justified in arguing for a Biocentric Principle, not an anthropic one *per se*.

Yet, insofar as human beings are commonly acknowledged as being the most intelligent and highly evolved species on this planet, they appear to be the very pinnacle of creation. Generations of philosophers dating back to ancient Egypt and Mesopotamia have supported this anthropocentric dogma, which subsequently found its way into many of the creation myths of the ancient world, including the book of Genesis. Plato built upon this anthropocentric foundation with his concept of the Great Chain of Being, which states that all types of organic beings are necessary so that the highest possible good can be attained in the world. Within this organic hierarchy, human beings are generally seen as occupying the highest possible echelon of psychophysiological development.

From this anthropocentric point of view, a universe that is biocentric is also anthropic, since the Cosmic Power that would have been responsible for creating the Great Chain of Being would have been aiming primarily at *human* existence. The Scholastics in the twelfth century seized upon the obvious theistic implications in Plato's Great Chain of Being by uniting it with the abstract formulations of orthodox Christian theology. The result of this theoretical wedding was the anthropocentric enthronement of humanity as the most important of all of God's creations.

Today we have become a good deal more objective in our theorizing about man's possible role in the heavens. Thanks to the efforts of Nicholas Copernicus, we now know that the Earth is *not* located at the center of the cosmos, and modern science has extended this Copernican perspective by showing that there appears to be nothing special about our position in the heavens. In 1974, however, Brandon Carter put a strict limitation on this Copernican dogma by showing that it is *necessarily the case* that the universe cater to the physical needs of man, insofar as the structural configuration of the universe *must* be consistent with our own existence as observers. This is the essence of the Anthropic Principle, and it is significant because it seems to restore man to his former position at the very pinnacle of creation.

With this in mind, the chief question now centers around whether humans *in particular* were deliberately intended from the very beginning. This is a difficult question that strikes at the very heart of the human dilemma, for no one seems to know who we really are or what our position actually is in the cosmos.

While there is a vague sense in which the universe *must* be "anthropic" since we obviously exist, this is a far cry from saying that we were directly intended from the very beginning. It is also possible that only generic biological life was originally intended, and that we only evolved by a happy accident, not by Omnipotent Intention.[1]

Although this is admittedly a subtle distinction, it is nevertheless exceedingly important, because our interpretation of the character of both the Deity and the universe itself rests directly upon it. In the first possibility, God would have only had generic life in Mind when He first set out to create the universe; later, when He found things to be moving in the right direction, He would have "lured" the evolutionary process towards the subsequent development of humanity. On this view (which is held to varying degrees by process theists), the rise of humanity was clearly a *contingent* phenomenon, since there is a very real sense in which it might not have ever occurred.

In contrast, the Omnipotent God of traditional theism would have deliberately intended the rise of uniquely human life *from the very beginning*. In support of this Primordial Intention, He would have unilaterally determined all of the initial conditions that would have been necessary for the eventual rise of human life.[2]

It is clear from this distinction that process theism, which affirms the existence of a limited Deity, is more comfortable with a biocentric world view than it is with an anthropic one, because the biocentric viewpoint claims that humans evolved merely contingently; it is therefore directly compatible with the process theist's conception of a struggling, limited Creator.

An anthropic world view, on the other hand, directly contradicts the process position, because it claims that humans evolved *necessarily* in response to a unilateral (i.e., Omnipotent) contrivance by the Divine Power.

At first glance, the evidence of evolution seems to support an exclusively biocentric world view, since true contingency seems to have permeated virtually every step of the evolutionary process. As Harvard paleontologist Stephen Jay Gould has pointed out, there appear to have been a large number of bifurcation points in the distant past in which evolution could have gone either way. This seems to indicate a pattern of true contingency in the evolutionary process, which in turn seems to count against traditional theism's concept of an Omnipotent Creator.

There is evidence, however, that the appearance of contingency in the evolutionary past may turn out to be an illusion. For in the midst of all of these apparent bifurcation points, a single path was taken each time. This would not have been so remarkable, of course, had this single path led to a non-significant end product. But it did not. Instead, it led to the unspeakable grandeur of our present world and universe. *This is all the more remarkable when we note that this evolutionary path appears to have been the ONLY one that would have been able to lead to this conclusion.* While other sorts of worlds with different evolutionary trajectories are conceivable, the sort of world *we* inhabit only seems to have been possible given the single evolutionary trajectory that led up to it.

As philosopher Keith Ward of Oxford University has pointed out, the universe's consistent choice of the "right" (i.e., life-facilitating) evolutionary path, in the face of a near infinite range of other possibilities, gives the strong impression of Intelligent Contrivance in the universe. Indeed, one could even go so far as to say that the appearance of strong contingency throughout the evolutionary past is an appearance only. For while definite bifurcation points may truly have existed throughout the past, the "right" outcomes could have been more or less guaranteed by either: 1) the creative influence of God acting at each moment of bifurcation, or 2) the creative influence of God acting at the very beginning of spacetime, in which He could have predisposed the primordial constituents to behave in a certain intended fashion at all of the subsequent bifurcation points.

If we take this latter, deistic,[3] alternative to be true, it would seem to eradicate any form of absolute contingency in the evolutionary process. On this view, while apparent bifurcation points may have existed throughout the evolutionary past, no genuine form of contingency would have ever *really* existed in the universe, because all outcomes would have been both foreseen and predetermined by God beforehand.

However, if we take a weaker view of cosmic necessity and say that the evolutionary trajectory intended by God was only necessary *in fact* (given the preexisting nature of the evolving entities), and *not* logically necessary *per se*, we can then preserve a weak form of contingency (i.e., freedom) in the universe while simultaneously avoiding the spectre of absolute determinism.[4] On this view, the underlying freedom of the creation is consistently employed to enable the repeated choice of the one evolutionary path that leads to humanity.

It is thus possible for an anthropic universe to exist in spite of the apparent contingency of the evolutionary past. For this to have been true, though, the unsearchable ingenuity of the Creator would have had to have been employed at least once to enable the repeated choice of a single evolutionary trajectory out of a near infinity of possible choices.

Unfortunately, while we can show that an anthropic universe is consistent with the existing scientific evidence, it is impossible to prove in a strict formal manner whether or not humanity was the direct "object" of the evolutionary process. For many people, this lack of empirical support for an anthropic universe is immaterial, because they already believe in one *anyway*. Others, however, will feel compelled to believe only in a general doctrine of contrivance in the universe, because this is the most that the scientific evidence itself can be said to support.

Yet, if one accepts the notion that the universe has in fact been intelligently contrived, one must then naturally ask what the universe has been contrived *for*. Presumably any Cosmic Power that is powerful enough to have contrived the present universal system is also capable of contriving it for a specific purpose.[5] Moreover, judging from the utter immensity of this creative task, one would think that any such purpose would have had to have been important enough to justify its overall creation, all things considered.

This in turn leads us to a possible means of evaluating whether or not we live in an anthropic, or merely biocentric, universe: we can simply ask ourselves whether or not a merely biocentric universe—one in which humans evolved, not by Unilateral Design or necessity, but by contingent struggle—would possess enough *intrinsic* value to justify its own creation in an otherwise Intelligently Contrived universe. Presumably such a merely biocentric world would have had to have been worth creating entirely in its own right, because there would always have been the chance that the evolutionary process in such a world would never have reached the level of *Homo sapiens*.

But what would have been the creative justification for such an exclusively biocentric world, especially when it would have been occurring within the overall context of an Intelligently Contrived universe? The various plants and animals of the Earth (and possibly of other planets as well) may indeed possess a certain amount of intrinsic value, but do they possess *enough* intrinsic value to justify the creation of the entire physical universe just for their sake? The answer would appear to be no, especially in light of the much greater degree of intrinsic value possessed by humans. Indeed, many people find it hard enough to see how the entire universe could have been deliberately created just for the sake of human and human-like beings. This being the case, it is that much *harder* to see how the entire universe could have been created just for the sake of producing plants and non-human animals.

Of course, it is possible that a biocentric universe was first needed in order to give the cosmos a valid chance at producing humans. On this view, our biocentric universe wouldn't have been created entirely for its own sake, but for the sake of obtaining the inherently risky chance of producing intelligent life (one form of which would be human). While there would have been no *a priori* guarantee that humans would have resulted from such a contingent evolutionary process, it is nevertheless possible that their tremendous degree of intrinsic value would have made the creation of a biocentric universe worth the risk.

Such a view of the creation is consistent with the dictates of process theism, which posits the existence of a radically limited deity who simply does the best he can with metaphysical circumstances he did not create and which he does not have absolute coercive control over. Such a deity would have been incapable of contriving an exclusively anthropic universe from the very beginning, even though he may very well have wanted to.

Indeed, we can safely assume that just about any type of creative deity would have wanted to bring about the most advanced life forms that he possibly could in his creation. Everything hinges, however, on how we choose to define the word "advanced" here. The overwhelming tendency, of course, is to understand the word "advanced" in this particular context as having something to do with the faculty of intelligence.

With this in mind, we can now view our own existence in a new light, since we are in fact the most intelligent beings we know of in the entire universe. This one property alone would seem to make us one of the chief creative objects of any transcendent deity worthy of the name, including the process deity.

Such a proposition assumes, however, that humans are important enough to have been intended by the divine power all along, but such an assumption is far from obvious. Indeed, many people find such an inflated view of humanity's cosmic importance downright nauseating. Even so, it is still possible to construct a persuasive argument for humanity's central role in the present universal order.

It is easy to see how humans could be construed as being the chief creative goal of the natural world.[6] After all, they are capable of art, compassion, intelligent discourse, and a great many other highly evolved activities, each of which seems to possess a tremendous amount of intrinsic self-worth in its own right. All the other living creatures on this planet, on the other hand, seem to possess such a vastly smaller amount of intrinsic value that the value they do possess is generally evaluated, at least in the Western world, in terms of its instrumental role in the overall ecological order. Human beings, in contrast, seem to possess their greatest intrinsic value in terms of their own species, i.e., in terms of the goods they produce for themselves, and not in terms of the goods they produce for other species. As a result of this greater capacity for intrinsic self-worth, it follows that human beings could well have been worth creating for their own sake, in contrast to the lower plants and animals, who don't seem to be capable of generating nearly enough intrinsic value to justify such an independent creation. By hypothesis, then, it is the greater degree of intrinsic value that humans are capable of attaining that seems to justify the jump from the Biocentric Principle to the Anthropic Principle in many people's minds.[7]

As we have seen, it is the human capacity for intelligent thought and discourse that sets us apart from the rest of the animal kingdom. Indeed, this capacity is typically judged to be so momentous that many consider it to be the only thing in the world worth creating in its own right. This is why the majority of "believers" in the Anthropic Principle feel that it is a reasonable extension from the Biocentric Principle: because intelligence in and of itself is so intrinsically valuable that it alone seems to be worth creating for its own sake. On this view, the Biocentric Principle is overshadowed to the extent that sub-human forms of life are deemed to be an evolutionary prerequisite for the rise of uniquely human life.

In any attempt to distinguish between the Biocentric and Anthropic Principles, it is important to remember that there is no real need for the physical universe to display an explicitly anthropic character in terms of its underlying structure. Human beings don't require any special ingredient in the underlying physical structure of their world and universe to support their existence, above and beyond that required by the rest of the biosphere. Therefore, a world whose physical structure can support the existence of sub-human plants and animals is capable of supporting human beings just as easily. In view of this fact, we should never *expect* to find explicit evidence of an anthropic universe in the underlying structure of the cosmos, *because none is needed.* Since none is needed, we would expect the underlying structure of a biocentric universe to be more or less identical to an anthropic one. As a result, we should never expect to find direct evidence for an anthropic universe in the nature of the fundamental constants themselves. We can only appeal to other, more intuitive sorts of judgements when attempting to make this ascertation.

When this critical insight is coupled with the uniquely human capacity for intelligent thought and action, the extension from the Biocentric to the Anthropic Principle seems to be eminently justifiable, at least to those who are sympathetic to a moderate anthropocentric world view.

Moderate anthropocentrism refers to the belief that human beings constitute *one* of the most important reasons why the universe was originally created. It ranges in scope from the view that humans are the single *most* important creatures in the universe (amidst a plurality of other creatures who also possess a significant degree of importance themselves), to the view that humans are *one* of the most important creatures in the universe (amidst a plurality of other creatures whose importance may be equal to, or even greater than, the intrinsic importance of humans).

Strong anthropocentrism, on the other hand, is the belief that human beings *alone* constitute the *sole reason* for the creation of the universe. This outlandish point of view is to be rejected for two important reasons: 1) there is no way to know for sure the intrinsic value of the other creatures on this planet, and 2) there is no way to be certain that we are the only intelligent creatures in existence. In all likelihood we are probably *not* the sole beings of value to be found throughout the heavens.

Moderate anthropocentrism thus appears to be by far the more appealing (and plausible) of the two views, since it affirms the importance of humanity in the overall scheme of things, while still leaving open the possibility that other beings of equal or greater value may exist somewhere else in the universe (or even here on our own planet, as in the case of whales and dolphins). It is for this reason that I will be adopting a moderate anthropocentric world view throughout the remainder of this book.[8]

This brings us to consider yet another intuitive reason why many people feel justified in making the jump from the Biocentric Principle to the Anthropic Principle. If the universe's Primordial Creative Force was so powerful that it was able to contrive the Big Bang in such a way as to make the evolution of life a virtual inevitability (as seems to have been the case), then it was also probably powerful enough to have directly (i.e., coercively) brought about the evolution of humans as well.

Moreover, if creaturely intelligence is so important in its own right, and if the Creative Power of the universe is clever enough to have initially brought about the existence of life, then it is probable that human intelligence itself would have been one of the chief goals of the creation. Indeed, it doesn't seem too outrageous to suppose that an Intelligent Creator would have wanted to infuse part of His physical creation with the same mental faculty that originally enabled Him to create our biocentric universe in the first place.

It is also important to remember that the evolution of non-human biological life is an essential precondition for the evolution of uniquely human life, as we have seen. Accordingly, a biocentric universe appears to be a necessary precondition for the evolution of an ultimately anthropic one. Therefore, we would naturally expect to find a biocentric universe "embedded" within a larger anthropic scheme if humans indeed represent the ultimate cosmic "intent." And since we would never expect to find a significant difference between these two types of cosmic "intentions" in the underlying values of the constants themselves, we find that we cannot differentiate between biocentricity or anthropocentricity at this level of analysis. Accordingly, we find that the ascription of the term "anthropic" to the existing evidence is entirely consistent with the physical nature of the evidence; it is also consistent with what we would expect to find in a genuinely anthropic universe.

To the extent, then, that we intuitively accept the centrality of humanity in the overall world order, we seem justified in making the theoretical jump from the Biocentric Principle to the Anthropic Principle. For insofar as our fellow creatures are understood to be here only because we are here, then a universe that "intended" to bring them about also "intended" to bring us about as well.

Thus, the inference of an Anthropic Principle from the biocentric evidence is itself based on the assumption that some form of humanoid life was the ultimate point of this mode of the creation. Although I will be making this assumption throughout the remainder of this book, one needn't make such an assumption in order to be able to appreciate the incredible degree of intelligent contrivance displayed by the universe. One can become awestruck and mystified simply by noting the remarkable correspondence between the fundamental constants of nature, on the one hand, and the existence of complex terrestrial life forms, on the other.

9.2   The Legitimacy of the Moderate Anthropocentric Perspective

As Barrow and Tipler[9] have shown, the unique type of postdictive reasoning employed by the Anthropic Principle has been able to establish one ineluctable fact: against all the odds, the entire universe has mysteriously been able to assume precisely the right structural configuration to encourage the evolution of life on this planet. This biocentric quality extends down to the smallest subatomic particles and dates all the way back to the Big Bang itself, because the fundamental constants of nature have apparently occupied their present life-facilitating values from the very beginning, some 15 billion years ago. Moreover, since the entire universe had a single unified beginning at the Big Bang, this means that the *entire* cosmos, and not just our small localized region, is permeated with the *same* biocentric qualities that have enabled life to evolve on this planet.

From this biocentric point of view, then, life is *in point of fact* the structural "center" of the universe, insofar as: 1) the entire universe began from the same set of initial conditions that have enabled humans (and other life forms) to evolve on this planet (and possibly elsewhere), 2) the entire universe possesses the same physical constants that have been so conducive to life, and 3) all of the microscopic and macroscopic properties of the universe seem to emanate directly from the requirement that life should be able to exist.

This assertion is supported by the fact that the smallest known common denominator for the observed values of the fundamental constants is the requirement that they should be able to support biological life. In other words, the most basic thing all of the constants seem to have in common with one another is their mutual contribution to life. A strong interpretation of this phenomenon claims that these fundamental values have actually been *determined*, at least partially, by our own[10] existence as observers.

At least on an underlying structural level, then, we are perfectly justified in proclaiming the phenomenon of life to be the organizational "center" of the entire visible universe, since the universe does indeed seem to be organized around the requirement that life should be able to exist.[11] After all, if life is so important to the universe that the physical requirements for its existence have somehow influenced both: a) the initial conditions displayed by the Big Bang, and b) the specific values of the fundamental constants themselves, then there would seem to be something very special indeed about living matter (so special, in fact, that the structure of the entire visible universe has apparently conformed itself to life's strict requirements).

This strong interpretation of life's central role in the cosmos has heretofore been missed by most scientific theorists because of the long-standing assumption that the evolution of life on Earth had nothing at all to do with the structure of the universe as a whole; it was simply assumed that the evolution of life here was a merely local event. However, with the advent of our modern cosmological understanding about the intimate relationship between life and the structure of the universe as a whole, this narrow-minded view has quickly become obsolete. The Anthropic Principle has led the way in this brilliant conceptual revolution, because it is what has enabled us to see the vital connection between the existence of life, on the one hand, and the structure of the universe as a single dynamic entity, on the other.

The Anthropic Principle in its various manifestations, then, is basically an attempt by some members of the scientific community to account for the fact that many different aspects of the physical universe, down to the actual values of the physical constants themselves, seem to have been deliberately predesigned for supporting biological life. From this biocentric point of view, it is no longer appropriate to think of the universe as being indifferent to the needs of life, as we have repeatedly been told in the past, for we now know that the universe has actually *catered* to the specific needs of life from the very beginning, which explains why living cells were able to evolve in the first place. As it turns out, each and every one of nature's fundamental constants—which conspire together to determine the overall character of the macro universe—has been exceedingly fine-tuned to a *single* precise value *out of an infinity of possible choices*. For some mysterious reason, it just so happens that *each* of these seemingly "arbitrary" choices is an essential prerequisite for the development of carbon-based life forms, including humans.

This fundamental connection between biological life on Earth and the underlying structure of the universe is so intriguing that many theoreticians within the traditional scientific community have felt justified in making an anthropocentric generalization from the biocentric evidence by granting humanity a special place in the overall cosmic order. For instance, John A. Wheeler, one of the modern pioneers of quantum mechanics, has wondered whether or not the actual subatomic particles *themselves* are somehow tied into making human life possible, since "the physical world is in some deep sense tied to the human being . . . We are beginning to suspect that man is not a tiny cog that doesn't make much difference to the running of the huge machine but rather that there is a much more intimate tie between man and the universe than we heretofore suspected."[12]

An even more surprising testimony of the centrality of (human) life to the universe has been proposed by modern quantum physicists. In place of the completely objective universe that we were raised to believe would exist even in the absence of man, we are now being told that there may be no objective reality at all apart from the observership of some sort of living consciousness.[13] The strong form of this statement, dubbed "The Participatory Anthropic Principle" (PAP) by John[14] Wheeler, asserts that intelligent observership[15] is somehow necessary to give the universe its very *existence*! This is certainly a far cry from the utterly pessimistic notion that we are unimportant in the overall scheme of things.[16]

Given the persuasiveness of the evidence[17] for a moderate anthropocentric view of reality, one wonders how the opposing position, known as the Principle of Mediocrity, could have ever drawn such a huge following in the first place. The original criterion used for rejecting anthropocentrism was largely astronomical and "geographical" in nature: a cleric in the Church named Nicholas Copernicus (who, ironically enough, was an anthropocentricist himself) discovered that the Earth revolves around the Sun, and not vice versa, and this had the effect of removing humanity from the "center" of the cosmos. The cumulative effect of this discovery was the eventual end of anthropocentrism in the modern age.

In a limited sense, of course, Copernicus was absolutely correct; the Earth is *not* the literal center of the universe, but this observation turns out to be utterly irrelevant to the question of humanity's importance in the overall scheme of things. It is a childish notion indeed to assume that we need to literally be at the physical center of the cosmos in order to be important to it, and the most recent cosmological models of the universe support us in this regard, as they indicate that no such astronomical center probably exists at all. Interestingly enough, Copernicus himself seemed to be aware of this fact, as he wrote that in comparison to the vast size of the cosmos, the displacement of the Earth from the center of the universe is actually very slight.[18]

The criterion of our relative smallness in the universe has also been used to count against the spectre of anthropocentrism in the modern world. Carl Sagan, for instance, has repeatedly reminded us about how small and insignificant we are in the face of the vast sizes and distances in the universe, as well as how unprivileged the Earth's position seems to be in the overall scheme of things.[19] But when did physical size ever equal overall significance in any larger metaphysical sense? Is an elephant more significant than a man merely by virtue of its size alone? Similarly, while a rhinoceros may be much bigger than a man, no rhino could possibly create a musical masterpiece the way Jeff Lorber or Chick Corea can.

The equation of physical size with overall cosmic significance thus turns out to be yet another childish notion that is inexcusable in the realm of intellectual adulthood. While we may be infinitesimally small in terms of physical size, we're the biggest things we know of in terms of structural complexity or creative capacity.

Interestingly enough, there is a sense in which humankind (and the rest of the biosphere) *is* the "center" of the universe: when the various observable objects in the universe are plotted on a size-mass diagram, we find that the human body is located midway between the size and mass of the universe, on the one hand, and the size and mass of subatomic particles, on the other (see Figure 9.1). Although there is no proof that this curiosity bears any direct relationship to the true place of humankind in the cosmic order, it nevertheless remains as an intriguing testimony to the mystery that surrounds the meaning of our existence.

In actuality, there are several other criteria besides size and astronomical location that are far more relevant in determining humankind's relative degree of importance to the cosmos. These criteria include an object's internal degree of complexity and its capacity for self-consciousness. When these more relevant criteria are taken into account, man occupies a far more central position in the cosmos, since his body is by far the most complicated mechanism in the entire known universe and his mind is the only known object that is capable of the miraculous quality of self-consciousness.[20]

In recent years, however, a much more important argument has gradually surfaced against all forms of anthropocentrism. It is concerned with the tremendous amount of time it took after the Big Bang for humans to appear and to rise to any degree of significance on this planet. As Bertrand Russell once put it:

If the purpose of the Cosmos is to evolve mind, we must regard it as rather incompetent in having produced so little in such a long time.[21]

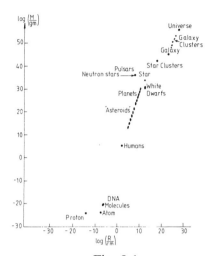

Fig. 9.1
A Size-Mass Diagram of the Observed Objects in the
Universe

However, with the tremendous increase in our cosmological understanding of the universe in recent years, a devastating anthropocentric rebuttal to this objection has suddenly made itself known: carbon-based life forms intrinsically *require* a sufficient supply of carbon and other heavy elements in order to evolve, but these heavier elements weren't in existence immediately following the birth of the universe; they had to be "cooked" in stellar interiors for billions of years and then subsequently released into the cosmos through colossal supernova explosions. When this fact is taken into consideration (along with the other temporal stipulations on planetary and biologic evolution), it turns out that ours is among the *youngest* possible universes that could have evolved carbon-based life forms through natural evolutionary pathways.[22] Furthermore, given the fact that the universe is continuously expanding, ours is also among the *smallest* possible universes that could have evolved life through these same pathways.[23] Thus, it would take a universe as big and old as our own just to evolve *a single race* of intelligent beings. Accordingly, as long as one accepts the stipulation that life must evolve through natural evolutionary pathways, the vast size and age of our universe is perfectly compatible with an anthropocentric world view.

Indeed, given the intrinsic Power of an Omnipotent Creator, it is no longer outrageous to presume that God might have created such a large universe just for the sake of human-like beings alone. To be sure, if He were anything *other* than the Infinite Creator of the universe, this possibility *really would* be outrageously unacceptable. But since He *is* presumably such an infinitely powerful Being, the present size of our universe is no more intimidating than if it were one-tenth its size. As a consequence, since the immense size of our universe wouldn't have been any more "trouble" for an Omnipotent God to create than a vastly smaller universe, it follows that such a God could indeed have created the entire cosmos primarily for the sake of human beings.[24]

What we are learning, then, as far as our overall position in the cosmos is concerned is that the ancients seem to have had it right all along. Plato and Aristotle, for instance, both taught that a certain parallelism seems to exist between the mind of man, on the one hand, and the structure of the physical universe, on the other. This they took to be evidence for the existence of some sort of Mind or Intelligence in the universe.

This parallelism first became evident in the fact that the mind of man is for some strange reason capable of understanding the same mathematics that happen to describe the activities of the natural world. Today, scientists are even going so far as to conclude that the structure of the physical universe *itself* has been deliberately "monkeyed with" so as to make human life possible, and may even depend on living consciousness for its very existence.[25]

While many of the individuals who originally argued against anthropocentrism did not have access to this important scientific data, there are nevertheless a great many scientifically trained professionals *today* who still hold on to the irrelevant criteria of size and physical centrality as evidence against an anthropocentric view of the cosmos. These individuals seem to be responding more to a deeply felt intuition regarding man's *existential* plight in the universe than to any type of raw physical data *per se*.

Indeed, it is man's existential dilemma in the universe—his extreme loneliness and helplessness in the face of an entire plethora of destructive forces— that offers the most potentially damaging evidence against an anthropocentric world view. Religious beliefs aside, all of the immediate scientific and existential evidence seems to indicate that we are utterly alone in the cosmos. If a Supreme Being really exists who is overseeing the entire universe, He clearly isn't communicating directly with us, at least not in a way that is immediately obvious. Even when horrific evils such as Hiroshima and Auschwitz have threatened entire population centers with utter doom, the Powers that be, if they exist at all, have remained curiously silent. As a consequence, sensitive thinkers on the subject have concluded that we must *not* be very important in the overall scheme of things, for if we were, we wouldn't be forced to feel so alone on this troubled planet.

The problem with this sort of reasoning is that, while it may be more compelling than the overly simplistic criteria of size and physical centrality, it still fails to consider an equally plausible alternative: namely, that a Supreme Being *does* in fact exist, but for reasons having to do with the ultimate welfare of man, He may be choosing to remain silent with respect to the human race. John Hick makes this very point in *Evil and The God of Love,* arguing that a certain amount of "epistemic distance" between God and man is a logically necessary precondition for the existence of genuine behavioral freedom in man. The idea here is that if God immediately made Himself known to us in all of His incomprehensible Glory, we would be so enamored and overwhelmed that we would *inevitably* lose all freedom to do as we pleased. Of course, God doesn't want to *force* us to come to Him by overwhelming us with His Great Glory; He wants us to come to Him *freely* on our own, when we are fully ready to do so, because this is the only way that our love for Him will be genuine. However, the only logically possible way that God can achieve this laudable goal is by temporarily making Himself *unavailable* to the human race in any direct fashion.

Humanity's freedom benefits from this "epistemic distance" between God and man in other related ways as well. For one thing, it allows us to do as we truly please in those aspects of our lives that don't directly involve the Creator. To be sure, if God were "right on top of us," as it were, we wouldn't be nearly as free to do what we *really* want in our own lives. Unfortunately, this means the possibility for such unspeakable evils as Auschwitz and Dachau, which obviously would not have been possible if an All-Good and All-Powerful God were directly involved in human affairs. Surprisingly enough, though, the alternative is even worse, for if God were to become directly involved in the world, at least at this early stage in our development, our freedom would be curtailed so severely that our larger cosmic "definition" would probably suffer irrevocable damage, since freedom of will is presumably an essential part of our intrinsic makeup.

The tragic consequence of such a curtailing of our freedom would be that we would no longer be genuinely human; having lost one of our own essential properties, we would automatically and inevitably be transformed into a completely different type of creature. Evidently such a possibility was not very appealing to the Creator, so He chose to preserve our freedom—and hence our humanity—by doing the only thing He possibly could to preserve it: removing Himself from the immediate realm of human affairs. Although such an action would temporarily serve to increase our sense of despair by exacerbating our feeling of isolation in the cosmos, it would nevertheless be well worth this tremendous "cost" in the long run, for two important reasons: 1) because our humanity will have been preserved in the process, and 2) because we will eventually attain a sense of epistemic oneness with our Creator when we are finally ready for it.

Again, we see that what seems to be evidence against an anthropocentric world view actually turns out to be evidence *for* such a view when all the relevant options are duly considered.[26] God only "neglects" man so that his freedom—and hence his humanness—can be maximized to the greatest possible extent.

A related reason that has been used to argue against anthropocentrism is the simple fact that we cannot see the Creator: since we cannot see Him, it is concluded that He mustn't exist, and that we cannot therefore be important to Him. Surely, though, our present inability to directly perceive the Creator cannot legitimately be used to count against the possibility that humans have been deliberately created by a Higher Power for a specific purpose. For just as there is an intelligible reason why a certain degree of epistemic distance should initially exist between God and humanity, there may also be an intelligible reason why humans cannot yet perceive their Creator in an unambiguous form.

To illustrate, we can regard this capacity to directly perceive the Creator as being a function of each person's individual level of psychospiritual development (which it clearly seems to be). This being the case, it would seem to follow that the immaturity which is necessarily entailed during the beginning and intermediate stages of the developmental process will automatically act to thwart the mind's capacity to accurately perceive the existence of God.

In other words, since God is by definition the most sublime of all realities, we need to be equally sublime in order to accurately perceive Him, but only the most developed forms of humanity seem to be capable of attaining such an advanced perceptual capacity. Therefore, we shouldn't be surprised that most of us are still incapable of directly perceiving the Creator at the present time: since almost all of us are relatively immature from a psychospiritual point of view, we haven't yet had the opportunity to develop our perceptual capacities to such an elaborate degree.

A useful analogy can be drawn to the process of radio broadcasting. Just as a radio receiver that is tuned to a frequency of 98.1 kHz cannot pick up a radio station broadcasting on a frequency of 105.1 kHz, even though the station may be broadcasting 24 hours a day, a psychospiritually immature individual also presumably cannot "pick up" the highly advanced "spiritual transmissions" of the Creator, even though these "transmissions" are presumably coursing throughout the cosmos all the time.

Thus, to the extent that our level of psychospiritual development determines how successful we are in perceiving God's Reality, we shouldn't *expect* to be able to directly perceive our Creator at this relatively early stage in our development, *no matter how important we are to Him*, because an initial state of psychospiritual immaturity seems to be an intrinsic property of genuine humanness.[27]

What this means, of course, is that God's apparent absence from the world cannot be used as unequivocal evidence against a limited degree of anthropocentrism in the cosmos. For if God's purpose for mankind can be conceived in such a way as to render inevitable His temporary absence from the world, then this absence can be properly accounted for from within the confines of the theist's anthropocentric view of reality.

9.3 Anthropocentrism in Light of the Weak and Strong Anthropic Principles

According to Keith Ward, there is a sense in which the Weak Anthropic Principle may be more anthropocentric than its Strong counterpart. Traditionally, the Strong Anthropic Principle has been understood as being the more anthropocentric of the two principles, since it makes the evolution of some form of life inevitable. However, it doesn't specify the precise *form* of life that must come about; in most formulations, it doesn't even specify that this life must be intelligent. Hence, there is no outstanding reason to suppose that the life specified by the SAP *must* be human, or even intelligent at all. To the extent that the SAP does refer to intelligent life, there is no outstanding reason to suppose that it refers to uniquely human life, apart from the fact that, in addition to the other forms of intelligence on this planet, we are the only intelligent beings we know of in the entire universe.[28]

The WAP, on the other hand, requires the existence of some form of intelligent observership in order to be valid, since it says that *we* can't help but observe the present universal configuration, since this configuration is necessary for our own existence as observers. This reference to human observership gives the WAP a definite anthropocentric flavor, though it doesn't do so absolutely or necessarily. The possibility remains that *other forms* of intelligent life could also be capable of experiencing the biocentric character of the present universe, though in this respect they would be virtually identical to ourselves.

In addition, although the WAP requires some form of intelligent observership in order to be valid, it doesn't require the human component of this observership to have been deliberately *intended* by any sort of Universal Creative Power; it merely says that *however* intelligent observers are able to come into existence, they can't help but note the existence of a universe that caters to their own survival. In this sense, the WAP only requires an "anthropocentric" universe that is centered around intelligent humanoid observership.

The SAP in its original biocentric formulation is thus primarily an argument for contrivance in the universe, while the WAP is a much more anthropocentric type of argument, since it requires the existence of intelligent observers in order to be valid.

In order for the SAP to support a *strong* anthropocentric view—which sees humans as the *only* source of importance in the universe—a new corollary to the SAP must be devised that takes this species exclusivity into account. We can call it the *Human-Centered Principle*. It reads as follows:

> There is one possible universe that has been deliberately designed by a Higher Power so as to allow intelligent life—represented by humans only—to come into existence, and it is for the sake of humans only that the universe was originally created.

Needless to say, the Human-Centered Principle must immediately be rejected as being both unverifiable and even preposterous in light of what we currently know about the universe. For one thing, we know that there are other forms of intelligent life on this planet besides human intelligence. Whales and dolphins, for example, are known to be remarkably intelligent by objective human standards. While they may not be able to communicate directly and extensively with humans, this limitation does not at all prevent them from being truly intelligent in their own sphere of influence.[29] The point is simply that humans are not the only intelligent species on this planet, so we can't possibly argue for an exclusively "Anthropic" (i.e., Human-Centered) Principle.

Secondly, there is no proof that intelligent beings don't reside elsewhere in the universe. Until such proof actually presents itself (it is hard to see how it ever could), we cannot ever accept the validity of the Human-Centered Principle, since there is always the possibility that intelligent life could exist on other planets.

9.4 The WAP and the Existence of Extraterrestrial Intelligences

Many scientists who believe in the existence of extraterrestrial intelligences (ETIs) use the Principle of Mediocrity—which says that there is nothing special about human beings—to support their claims.[30] The basic idea is the following: if there is nothing special about earth-based life forms, then, given the vast reaches of outer space, ETIs probably exist on thousands of different planets. This is a very tempting mode of reasoning to adhere to, and many famous scientists (such as Carl Sagan) are convinced by it.

Not all scientists, however, are so convinced. Brandon Carter, for instance, has invoked the WAP to argue very persuasively *against* the existence of ETIs, for the following reason: while the size and age of the universe may both be enormous, ours is still among the *smallest* and *youngest* universes that could possibly produce life through natural evolutionary pathways. This is a devastating "anthropic" rebuttal to the traditional argument in favor of ETIs, *for if this is one of the smallest and youngest possible universes that could have evolved carbon-based life forms, then the cosmos had to have been this big and this old just to produce a single lonely outpost of life.* Thus, if it turns out that carbon-based ETIs do in fact exist elsewhere, they will have only had approximately the same amount of time to evolve as we have. This makes it highly unlikely indeed that they will have advanced to the point of being capable of intergalactic space travel,[31] which in turn is consistent with the fact that we haven't yet been directly contacted, at least not unequivocally, by any form of extraterrestrial intelligence.

Another argument that is commonly used in favor of the existence of ETIs says that other forms of intelligence need not be limited to any of the laws governing the evolution of carbon-based life forms, since they need not be carbon-based at all. However, it is possible to show that ETIs occupying *any* physical format *must* satisfy certain basic requirements. For one thing, they must be capable of some form of reproduction, which in turn requires a chemical structure that is capable of accurately conveying millions of bits of information. The only known type of chemical structure that is capable of transmitting this amount of information is some form of polymer chain, but there are only two elements that are capable of forming long polymers: carbon and silicon.[32] Significantly, silicon is only capable of forming long polymer chains at temperatures *below* -200 degrees Celsius. While such ghastly temperatures are common in outer space, they cause ordinary chemical reactions to proceed much too slowly to support the complex metabolic reactions that are required in any physical form of intelligent life. This leaves carbon as the sole remaining choice for the complex demands of intelligent life.

Moreover, Carter has shown that there is a definite upper limit to the length of time life can evolve on *any* given planet, regardless of the composition of the particular life forms involved: the lifetime of the planet's sun. Furthermore, it is also known that the evolution of *any* intelligent life form probably entails a vast number of individually unlikely steps whose cumulative probability is correspondingly astronomical (in the absence, of course, of a larger Divine Influence). When this vanishingly small probability is coupled with the absolute time limit imposed by any given stellar lifetime, it follows that the evolution of life on *any* planet must be *exceedingly* rare, so rare in fact that we may be the only race of intelligent beings in the entire universe.

Interestingly enough, there is a general consensus in the orthodox evolutionary community which agrees that "the evolution of intelligent life . . . is so improbable that it is unlikely to have occurred on any other planet in the entire visible universe."[33] Mayr, Dobzhansky, Simpson, Francois, and Ayala, for example, all agree that given the immense improbability of the evolution of intelligence, it is unlikely to the highest degree that ETIs exist elsewhere.[34]

9.5 Solar Eclipses and the Size of the Moon

There is one additional cosmological phenomenon that is intriguing enough to be mentioned in support of moderate anthropocentrism: the solar eclipse.

The complete solar eclipse—which occurs when the Moon passes directly between the Earth and the Sun—has been an important phenomenon in human affairs throughout recorded history. It has been used both as a cosmic reference point for human time-keeping purposes, as well as a type of archetypal Universal Event for the enrichment of humanity's collective unconscious.

Interestingly enough, a complete solar eclipse is only possible because of the intimate cooperation between two independent cosmic factors: 1) the size of the Moon, which is 400 times smaller than the Sun, and 2) the Moon's orbital radius about the Earth, which is 400 times smaller than the Earth's orbital radius about the Sun (i.e. the Moon is 400 times closer to the Earth than the Sun is). As a consequence of these two independent factors, the Moon is able to completely block out the Sun from an earthbound point of view from time to time.

Computer studies have shown that our solar eclipse is a unique phenomenon amongst all the known satellites in the solar system.[35] With this in mind, how are we to explain this remarkable coincidence? How are we to explain the fact that the Moon is both 400 times smaller than the Sun, and yet 400 times closer to the Earth than the Sun is? Out of the millions of possible values that these two independent variables could have possessed, both happen to possess exactly the same value: 400, and it is precisely this equality that makes total solar eclipses possible from an earthbound point of view.

While one could simply attempt to dodge this vexing issue by attributing this coincidence to blind chance, it is hard to resist the feeling that something more is going on here. Could it be merely a coincidence that the one planet in the entire solar system that possesses intelligent life—and hence the capacity to perceive the significance of the total solar eclipse—*also* happens to possess a moon of just the right size and proximity to Earth to make total solar eclipses possible?

In order to visualize the implicit implausibility of this scenario, imagine that the Moon happens to possess rock formations on its surface that are, for some strange reason, arranged in the form of clearly discerible words and sentences. Imagine further that it is the only satellite in the solar system that possesses this curious feature. Now, if this were in fact the case, would anyone in their right mind suppose that these "rock formations with a message" were merely the result of blind chance? Probably not, since in this hypothetical case the Moon would belong to the only planet in the solar system that would be inhabited by beings who are capable of reading these messages.

In the same way, we can use the meaningfulness of the total solar eclipse in human life to justify the positing of a *transcendant causal connection* between the intelligibility of eclipses, on the one hand, and the precise size and orbital location of our Moon, on the other. While there is no way to prove the literal truthfulness of this hypothesis, the fact that it seems to possess the same intriguing coincidental quality possessed by all the other cosmic coincidences discussed previously, seems to afford it an additional degree of plausibility overall.[36]

Notes

1. Thus far, I have only argued for an element of Intelligent Design in the universe, and not for any particular type of Creator *per se*. However, the evidence for Contrivance is also evidence for the Omnipotence of the Contriver, as we shall discuss at length in Chapter 10.

2. This possibility raises the question of why an Omnipotent God would have deliberately chosen to create through the long and drawn-out processes of cosmic and biological evolution to begin with. One would think that if He were powerful enough to have unilaterally determined the initial conditions at the Big Bang, He should also have been powerful enough to unilaterally create the universe *in its final form*. The fact that He did not do so either says that God is *not* Omnipotent, or else that He deliberately chose to create the universe through normal evolutionary pathways for a Higher Reason. Although this issue gets to the very heart of the matter regarding the relationship of God to His creation, it is beyond the scope of the present discussion. The interested reader should consult my forthcoming book *Back to Darwin* for a detailed analysis of this important topic.

3. Deism refers to the belief that God set up a self-driven universal order from the very beginning, and then left it alone to function in accordance with its own laws and behavioral tendencies.

4. As John Hick has pointed out, a similar principle seems to apply in the area of Universal Salvation, where it is claimed that all will be saved in spite of the existence of true behavioral freedom. According to Hick, if the salvation of all is not *logically* necessary, but is only necessary *in fact*, human freedom *can* be preserved. On this view, all will be saved because of the nature of their underlying psychospiritual makeup *in concert with* their inner freedom. Thus, true human freedom can still exist, because humans aren't logically (i.e., inevitably) bound to be saved; they are only *predisposed* to be saved because of their underlying psychospiritual makeup. When this principle is applied to the realm of cosmic evolution, we find that it is possible for humans to have been intended all along by the Divine Power, and yet for there to simultaneously exist some form of contingency in the evolutionary process—that is, provided it is not *logically* necessary that humans evolve, only necessary *in fact* (i.e., due to the underlying makeup of the primordial entities).

5. Although the existence of biological life forms in general qualifies as a specific purpose, the fact of our own existence leads one to suspect that this purpose, if one exists at all, probably has something to do with humans directly.
6. In saying that humans might be the ultimate goal of creation, I do not mean to imply that the rest of the natural world possesses *no* intrinsic value in and of itself. To the contrary, both humans and the rest of nature can be intrinsically valuable *simultaneously*. The issue thus isn't whether or not the animal world possesses *any* intrinsic value, but whether it possesses *enough* intrinsic value to justify an independent creation in the absence of man. One can therefore have an appreciation for a limited anthropocentric perspective *without* undervaluing the rest of the ecological order, and *without* condoning any type of species-based imperialism on the part of humankind.
7. It is important to note that this jump to a limited form of anthropcentricity does *not* necessarily negate the reality of the evolutionary process in nature. Although the fact of organic evolution *does* seem to impart a certain sense of equality to the various species (since they all presumably arose together in response to the same creative forces), this does *not* necessarily mean that humanity cannot be the chief creative goal of the evolutionary process. The reality of evolution thus says nothing one way or the other about the place of humanity in the global species hierarchy.
8. Weak anthropocentrism, by contrast, is the view that God aimed only at creating beings with the greatest possible degree of intrinsic value. In some possible worlds these maximally evolved creatures might have been chimpanzees, but in our own actual world they turned out to be humans. Weak anthropocentrism is thus consistent with process theism, wherein God is believed to have aimed only at the creation of the most valuable creatures possible, given the local creative circumstances that would have been operative at the time.
9. Barrow and Tipler, *The Anthropic Cosmological Principle*, pp. 288–289.
10. From here on out I will be assuming the centrality of humanity in the overall world scheme, not because all the other creatures on this planet are unimportant, or because no other forms of intelligent life may exist in the universe, but because humans appear to be the most highly evolved creatures in our own biosphere. As always, the Biocentric Principle can be understood as being implied whenever any of the Anthropic Principles are mentioned in the text.
11. If it turns out that life exists only on our own planet, then the Earth will indeed be the "center" of the universe as far as the existence of life is concerned. However, if other life forms exist elsewhere, then the phenomenon of *life in general* will constitute a much more dispersed "center" to the universe.
12. John A. Wheeler, interviewed in Florence Helitzer's "The Princeton Galaxy," *Intellectual Digest*, no. 10 (June 1973), p. 32.
13. Barrow and Tipler, *The Anthropic Cosmological Principle*, pp. 468–471.
14. Ibid., p. 22.
15. As we have seen, the PAP contains an implicit argument for the existence of an "Ultimate Observer." For if some form of life (especially intelligent life) is necessary to give the universe its very being, then the entire universe itself could only have been brought into being by a Life Form whose existence would have *preceded* the Big Bang. Only one Being seems capable of fulfilling this lofty requirement.
16. I am not necessarily endorsing the PAP. I am simply using it to document the recent change in sensibility that has taken place in the scientific community.
17. As we have seen, the scientific data in no way suggests that we are the *most*

important beings in the entire universe. For all we know, thousands of other intelligent civilizations could very well exist which could be every bit as important as we are, if not more so. As a consequence, the discovery that we are important to the cosmos should cause us to be *more* humble, not less, *vis-à-vis* our relationship to the rest of creation.

18. Nicholas Copernicus, *On the Revolution of the Heavenly Spheres,* transl. C.G. Wallis, ed. R.M. Hutchins (Encyclopedia Britannica, London, 1952), Book 1, Ch. 6.

19. Carl Sagan, *Discovery 4* (No. 3, March), 30 (1983).

20. Although it could be argued that I am arbitrarily taking our own features to be important criteria in the overall scheme of things, I would counter that these criteria are not arbitrary at all. To the contrary, intelligence and the ability to act decisively in the world are obviously important in an objective sense, since they alone are capable of producing the awesome levels of creativity that humans routinely enjoy in the world. They are also important insofar as they allow the making of deliberate large-scale changes to the overall structure of the cosmos. For instance, humans can, by virtue of these objectively important criteria, act to completely destroy this planet, whereas nothing else in the entire known universe is capable of deliberately doing so. On a more positive side, this same capacity can also be used for equally *good* ends if it is properly used.

21. Bertrand Russell, *Religion and Science* (New York: Oxford University Press, 1968), p. 216.

22. Barrow and Tipler, *The Anthropic Cosmological Principle,* p. 385.

23. Ibid.

24. It must be continually borne in mind that human beings don't have to be the *only* intelligent life forms in the universe in order to be important in the overall scheme of things. The cosmos could in fact be *teeming* with intelligent life, without the overall importance of man being diminished one iota.

25. Quantum physicists who believe in this "Participatory Anthropic Principle" are often unclear as to what level of consciousness is necessary to "collapse the universal wave function," thereby allowing the physical universe to come into being. But even if microbial "consciousness" turns out to be sufficient for this quantum effect, what about the critical period *before* any life at all evolved on this planet? How could the physical universe have evolved to such an advanced point in the absence of *any* reality-producing consciousness? Proponents of the PAP, such as physicist George Greenstein, are unclear about this, but if we assume that consciousness is indeed necessary to produce physical reality, there is only one possible way to account for this anomaly: by positing a consciousness that would have been in existence from the Big Bang onward. Of course, there is only one conceivable Entity that could possibly fulfill this lofty requirement: a Divine Creator Being, whose Eternal Consciousness would have automatically been capable of collapsing all pre-biotic wave functions into being. A God of this magnitude would therefore act as the "Ultimate Observer" that seems to be a necessary part of the PAP.

26. Interestingly enough, the early Church Fathers anticipated the discovery of scientific evidence that would support their God-based anthropocentric notions. For more information on this intriguing subject, see David C. Lindberg's article "Science and the Early Church," in David C. Lindberg and Ronald Numbers, eds., *God & Nature* (Berkeley: University of California Press, 1986), pp. 19–48.

27. This initial inability to perceive the Creator in turn provides the further benefit

of maximizing human freedom over against God by temporarily creating a certain degree of epistemic distance between God and man.

28. For all we know, another form of intelligent life residing on a distant planet could have been the chief intention of the Creator, and we are merely a by-product of a universe that was set up for *their* evolution.

29. The argument could easily be made that humans comprise the *least* intelligent species on our planet, since they are the only creatures who actively seek their own self-destruction, when in fact they should know better.

30. John Casti, *Paradigms Lost,* p. 483.

31. Although it is possible that a world a few hundred years more advanced than our own could have developed the technology for intergalactic space travel by now, the odds appear to be strongly against it. If nothing else, the odds against the evolution of life anywhere else in the universe appear to be so astronomical that virtually all modern evolutionists are agreed that we are probably alone in the cosmos.

32. Casti, *Paradigms Lost,* p. 363.

33. Barrow and Tipler, p. 133.

34. Ibid.

35. M. Mendillo and R. Hart, "Resonances," *Physics Today,* 27:2 (Feb., 1974), p. 73.

36. There are a large number of other lunar "coincidences" which, at least in terms of their instrumental value to earth-based humans, seem to possess a remarkably contrived appearance as well. For instance, the Moon's stable orbit, capacity to evoke tides, anomalously large size relative to the Earth, and great reflective capacity, all are precisely suited for an optimal degree of functionality on this planet. If the Moon's composition, size, and location were all matters of chance only, we would never expect *all* of its properties relative to the Earth to be so beneficial to human life.

CHAPTER 10

The Prospect of Divine Omnipotence

As we look out into the universe and identify the many accidents of physics and astronomy that have worked together to our benefit, it almost seems as if the universe must in some sense have known that we were coming.

FREEMAN DYSON

Thus far I have argued for an Intelligent Creator, presupposing this Creator to be Omnipotent. In this chapter the issue of Omnipotence will be dealt with directly.

10.1 Creation *Ex Nihilo*

Theologians have long theorized that God created the universe *ex nihilo*, or out of nothing. Indeed, creation *ex nihilo* is a fundamental tenet of orthodox Christian theology. Incredibly enough, modern theoretical physicists have also speculated that the universe may have been produced through a sudden quantum appearance "out of nothing."

Speculation surrounding this notion of a quantum universal leap out of nothing began with scientific attempts to calculate the total energy content of a star. Surprisingly, calculations seem to indicate that the total energy content of a given star may be zero, in spite of its obvious energy content in the form of matter. This is because the energy that is tied up in the star's gravitational field seems to be negative. If this is so, then it would not violate the law of the conservation of energy if a star made a sudden quantum appearance out of nothing, because its positive energy content in the form of matter would exactly be counterbalanced by its negative gravitational energy content. Using this intriguing possibility as a theoretical base, Ed Tryon of Hunter College in New York has suggested that the total energy content of the entire universe may also be zero. If this is true, this would mean that the entire universe itself could have conceivably made a sudden quantum appearance out of nothing.

Physicist Paul Davies, however, has gone one step further and claimed that the particular physics involved in the Big Bang *necessitates* creation *ex nihilo*. To illustrate, Davies draws an analogy to a balloon that is being inflated:

This pictorial model enables ready visualization of the big bang. When the balloon is deflated back to time zero, its area shrinks to nothing and it disappears. The creation event thus amounts to the sudden appearance of space, as well as matter. It is *not* the explosion of a lump of matter in a pre-existing void.[1]

If Davies' account is correct, *no* form of space or matter could have pre-existed the Big Bang. This of course is the image of the creation held by traditional theologians, who believe that God created the entire universe *ex nihilo*.

Even so, a sizable contingent of non-theistic scientists continue to believe that matter in some form has always existed, even prior to the Big Bang.[2] Such a belief differs from the position of the process theologians in that it rejects the eternal existence of any type of Supreme Being; it simply posits matter and matter alone as being eternal.

The very notion of an infinitely dense singularity bringing into existence the entire universe of physical matter seems to imply a type of creation out of "nothing," as we have seen. But once we posit a Big Bang singularity, though, we still have to ask where the singularity *itself* originally came from. This type of question cannot be avoided by simply denying the existence of a Big Bang singularity, because one must then ask where the primordial "cosmic egg" that led to the Big Bang *itself* originally came from. Predictably, scientists are at an almost complete loss to answer this type of question; they simply acknowledge that whatever gave rise to the Big Bang could conceivably have made a sudden quantum appearance out of nothing.

If it does turn out to be true that the universe made its initial appearance in a quantum leap out of nothing,[3] it wouldn't amount to a cosmic "free lunch," as Alan Guth has suggested, nor would it dispose of the need for a universal Creator. Rather, such a quantum leap would only be capable of taking place in a larger quantum field that would itself be responsible for making such wild quantum fluctuations possible to begin with. It is this larger quantum field which is the "price" that must be paid for the supposed "free lunch" of an "uncaused" universal existence.

But where would the initial quantum field *itself* have come from? No one really knows for sure. The scientific theist, however, would argue that God Himself constructed this primordial quantum field *ex nihilo* as the initial background from which He could carry out the rest of His creation. Indeed, it is conceivable that this primordial quantum field could be the unsearchable interface between the physical universe, on the one hand, and God's Own Spiritual Substance, on the other.

10.1.1 The Self-Existence of God vs. the Self-Existence of Matter

Traditionally, one of the main arguments against the existence of an eternal God has been that it is hard to see how any Being can be self-existent by Its very nature.[4] Some have even argued that if God can be self-existent, then so can matter. But if the concept of self-existence makes it so difficult to believe that God had no beginning, why should it be any easier to believe that matter had no beginning, as many scientists and philosophers openly believe? Presumably the answer to this question is that we know for a certainty that matter exists, while the question of God's existence is not yet determined; therefore, if anything needs to be eternal, why can't it just be matter?

The problem with this sort of reasoning is that matter in and of itself does not seem to have any internal characteristics that make it likely to be self-existent. Certainly self-existence is not a necessary part of the traditional *definition* of matter, nor can it be deduced by examining any of the internal characteristics of matter. Indeed, virtually all scientists agree that matter is *not* self-existent, at least not in its present form, since it is thought to have originated in the Big Bang some 15 billion years ago. While it is conceivable that matter in some form did precede the Big Bang, there is no way to verify this claim or to falsify it. The best that science can do is to simply show that matter in its present form did indeed have a beginning long ago.

God, on the other hand, is *defined* as being the Self-Existent Truth who created the worlds. To be sure, it is *much* easier to see how Universal Truth could have always existed than to see how lifeless matter could have done the same. Indeed, the *only* concrete piece of evidence that favors the idea of an eternally-existing material realm (as opposed to an eternally-existing God) is that we know for a fact that matter exists, whereas we have no absolute proof that any type of God exists. Process thinkers, of course, have it *both* ways, as they believe in both an eternally existing God *and* an eternally existing material realm.[5]

10.2 Supernatural Naturalism

Traditionally, the God of theism has been understood to be a Supernatural Being whose power utterly transcends the realm of natural cause-and-effect processes. In response to this traditional view, process theologians have advanced a more natural view of the Godhead, in which God's Power to create is limited by those causal laws that are deemed to be an intrinsic feature of the natural realm of finite actualities.

It has heretofore been been assumed that these two characterizations of the Divine Power are mutually exclusive, i.e., either God is supernatural in power, in which case He is not limited to acting in accordance with natural cause-and-effect laws, or else He is natural in power, in which case He has no choice but to act in accordance with those causal laws that are an intrinsic feature of the natural realm.

I would like to suggest a third possibility that seeks to blend the best features of supernaturalism and naturalism, which we can call *Supernatural Naturalism*. In this conceptualization of the Divine Power, God is entirely supernatural, insofar as: 1) He utterly transcends all naturalistic causal laws, 2) He originally possessed all the power in the universe, and 3) He created the universe *ex nihilo*.

In accordance with this supernaturalistic conception of the Divine Power, the doctrine of Supernatural Naturalism asserts that our supernatural Creator deliberately chose to create a naturalistic cause-and-effect universe in order to be consistent with the Higher Purpose that He set out to achieve when He initially began His Creative Effort (that of creating a world that would function as a "vale of soul-making" for developing human beings).[6] On this view, although God *could* possibly act in ways that completely transcend the limits of traditional naturalism, He has deliberately chosen not to do so, so that His larger Purpose in creating humankind can be fulfilled as efficaciously as possible.

In short, the doctrine of Supernatural Naturalism hybridizes the two opposing views of God as being either supernaturalistic or naturalistic, by asserting that a supernatural God has deliberately chosen to limit the power of His creation by instituting a naturalistic cosmic order that is totally subservient to the law of cause-and-effect.[7] In this way, the supernatural God of traditional theism can be fully reconciled with the entirely naturalistic findings of modern science, without jeopardizing the coherence or validity of either ingredient.

10.3 Modern Cosmology and the Adequacy of the Process God

The process theologian envisions a God who does not have absolute coercive power over his creatures.[8] Since the creatures themselves, as well as the atomic and subatomic constituents of which they are made, all necessarily possess a certain degree of creative self-determination, God *cannot* unilaterally bring about events in the world. He can only *persuade*, and while this persuasion can sometimes take on the appearance of coercion, in the final analysis God can only provide a creative *lure* for the creatures, which they can either opt to follow or reject. As Rolston has stated, the process God:

> . . . presents possibilities in excess of actualities, together with a heading, but then draws back to suffer the entity its own increments of freedom. The routings taken are not all inlaid into the anthropic constants of the big bang, not all thrust up from superposed quantum states below, but they are actualized in part owing to elections that the organic entity superposes on the quantum states. There is provision for cocreation and continuous

creation. God is the ground of creativity "from below," and yet aloft, aboveground, creativity is removed from God enough to be assigned locally to the creatures, who actualize themselves. They do their own thing, always in God but not always of God. There is the kind of parenting that puts local integrities on their own and yet educates them as they go. This influence is not mandatory or deterministic, but enticing, prompting.[9]

Although process philosophy was originally conceived by mathematical physicist-turned-philosopher Alfred North Whitehead as a metaphysical system that was supposed to be consistent with both quantum physics and relativity theory, the findings of modern cosmology have cast a serious shadow on the process deity. If the process theist is correct, God would have been unable to unilaterally determine (coerce) the initial conditions exhibited by the Big Bang in an absolute fashion. He would only have been able to present certain creative lures to the finite actualities themselves, which is to say that He would have only been able to *persuade* them to occupy certain productive configurations. But since they necessarily would have possessed a certain degree of self-determination, it would have been partially up to them whether or not to comply with God's creative lure.

Thus, if the process theist is correct, we would never expect to find the Big Bang to have been so remarkably fine-tuned in *all* of its many initial conditions, *each* of which was essential to the later evolution of life. Rather, we would expect some of these actualities to have complied, perhaps even a majority, but we would also expect some of them to have resisted. Indeed, it is this type of resistance to the Divine Will which the process theist blames for the reality of evil in the world. He even goes so far as to assert that the possibility for this type of resistance can never be eliminated, because such a possibility is alleged to be an inevitable consequence of universal creativity, which itself is understood as being a metaphysically necessary ingredient in *all* possible worlds.

Yet, the many biocentric qualities exhibited by the Big Bang show absolutely no signs of resistance to the Divine Will at all. Indeed, given the fact that each physical constant originally assumed precisely the correct value, out of an *infinite* range of possible choices, to ensure the later evolution of biological life, we must conclude that God's determination of these initial conditions was essentially *perfect*. This initial perfection, in the face of: a) an infinite range of possibilities and b) the many precise requirements of carbon-based life forms, yields a view of the Big Bang that is more coercive than persuasive. In short, the biocentric quality of the Big Bang provides powerful evidence that it was *unilaterally determined* by a Higher Power to occur just as it did.

The evolution of the universe *following* the Big Bang also seems to have followed a similar process of coercive Design. Up until the rise of the first life forms, the universe seems to have followed a very specific biocentric course, with little or no resistance on the part of the "creatures." This provides further evidence of coercive Design. While the evolution of life itself seems to have had a certain contingent, "groping" quality to it, in which life only advanced opportunistically against the process of natural selection by a repeated process of fits and starts, this does not have to count against the Power and Sovereignty of an Omnipotent Creator. Rather, the Creator could have *deliberately* chosen to impart this opportunistic quality directly onto the natural realm for a Higher Reason, namely that of being consistent with the intrinsic necessities that were dictated by the presumed goal of His creation (namely humanity).

According to the process theist, the reason the universe must evolve is because God is *incapable* of creating it ready-made. That is, since God cannot unilaterally determine the nature of the finite actualities themselves in their final desired form, He must resort to gradually persuading them to do His creative bidding. This process of Divine persuasion correlates with the process of natural selection, because only those entities that are persuaded to evolve to a certain minimum level of complexity are able to continue surviving in the intended direction. But if the process theist is going to take the process of Divine persuasion, along with the concomitant process of natural selection, as the central paradigm for God's creative relation to the world, it follows that this relation must apply *thoughout* the process of cosmic evolution, not just in the limited area of biological evolution. Yet, as Barrow and Tipler have pointed out, there appears to have been *no* evolution by natural selection whatsoever in the values of the physical constants themselves, since they have apparently occupied their present values from the very beginning.

What's more, a strong element of determinism is also to be found in the relation of these fundamental constants to the size and structure of the entire physical universe, since the particular values occupied by these constants "render inevitable the gross size and structure of almost all its composite objects. The size of bodies like stars, planets and even people are neither random nor the result of any progressive selection process, but simply manifestations of the different strengths of the various forces of Nature."[10]

One would never expect such a strong element of determinism in the underlying structure of the cosmos, operative from the very beginning, if the process view of the Creator were in fact correct. Rather, we would expect to find the same type of gradual persuasion and evolution by natural selection that we find in the biosphere even at the level of the fundamental constants themselves. For while the subatomic realities that comprise the fundamental constants may not have been able to depart from the Divine Will as fully as more advanced individuals can, we would still expect to find *some* resistance to the Divine Will even at the level of the Big Bang itself, since it apparently contained a huge number of profoundly complex parameters that needed to be precisely determined from the very beginning. The fact that we do not find any such resistance whatsoever strongly disconfirms the plausibility of process theism, at least with respect to its view of God's creative relation to the rest of the cosmos. Although it is conceivable that God could have tried a trillion times to create a universe such as ours, and that we were only able to evolve in his most successful creation, the marvelous degree of power and ingenuity that is displayed at all levels of cosmic reality tends to strongly disconfirm this notion. A God who is competent enough to produce our own breathtaking universe would seem to be more than competent enough to get it right the first time around.

In rebuttal, the process theists would say that even their limited God could have unilaterally determined which set of mathematical formulas to present to the actualities that resulted from the Big Bang. Moreover, they would add that since there were supposedly no other competing principles in existence at this time, and since these low-grade entities would have only been capable of a very small degree of self-determination, it is indeed possible for God's "persuasion" of these primordial entities to have been more or less identical in effect to genuine omnipotent coercion. Accordingly, God could have orchestrated the Big Bang in a manner similar to that proposed by more traditional theologians.

In order to understand how mere persuasion can take on the appearance of full coercion, we must look briefly at process theism's interpretation of causality. In the process metaphysical system, all actual occasions (or entities) are necessarily bipolar in nature, in that they all possess a "physical pole," through which they take in influences from the past and repeat them, and a "mental pole," through which they respond creatively to the various possibilities that are open to them. Moreover, the relative degree of influence of each entity's physical and mental poles varies directly with the degree of complexity and organization that is intrinsically possessed by the entity: the less complex the entity, the more dominant its physical pole tends to be, and the more amenable it supposedly is to "coercive persuasion" from without. On the other hand, the more complex the entity, the more dominant its mental pole—and hence its capacity for self-determination—tends to be, and this in turn corresponds to a greater capacity for resistance to the Divine Will. Thus, less resistance to the Divine Will may be expected of such relatively low-grade individuals as atoms and molecules, as compared to more sophisticated "compound individuals" such as human beings (which is why humans are able to cause more evil than mere aggregates, such as rocks or mountains).

There are several problems with this rebuttal. First, there is no compelling reason to believe that atomic and subatomic particles are truly "low-grade" entities in themselves. While they may be "low-grade" with respect to other "higher-grade" entities (such as cells and people), they certainly aren't "low-grade" in and of themselves, since they possess a tremendous level of complexity that we are only beginning to understand. But if they are so inherently complex, shouldn't they possess a correspondingly bigger mental pole, and hence more power for self-determination? If so, then the process God couldn't have coercively persuaded all of the primordial entities of the universe so effectively from the very beginning. He could only have *gradually* coaxed them to eventually do His creative bidding.

The second problem with the process theist's rebuttal is that it does not seem to appreciate the tremendous amount of absolute creative coercion that seems to have occurred during the birth of the universe. The evidence seems to suggest that the Big Bang was perfectly designed *from the very beginning*, both in terms of its structural composition and its overall explosive intensity. The evidence does *not* suggest that these basic parameters were in any way altered or otherwise influenced after the first microsecond of the Big Bang. This primordial explosion was apparently so huge and energetic that anything less than absolute creative perfection (i.e. total coercion) *from the very beginning* would have not been sufficient to produce a biocentric universe.

That is to say, the momentum of this primordial blast at even the Planck time of 10^{-43} seconds would have probably been far too great to subsequently allow any significant alterations in the universe's constituent members via the process of Divine persuasion. The very size and intensity of the Big Bang thus seems to require a near perfect determination (i.e. coercion) of its initial conditions *from the very beginning* if the desired product (in this case a biocentric universe) is to be possible. The overall picture thus seems to be that of a deistic-type God who designed and created the Big Bang perfectly from the very beginning, and not a process God who had to resort to persuading these initial actualities to do his creative bidding at various intervals along the way.[11]

Of course, it is possible that God's initial coercive persuasion of the relatively low-grade individuals comprising the Big Bang could have set up a fundamental cosmic pattern or "habit" amongst them (through the process of "conformal prehension") that would have persisted throughout all future epochs.[12] This would have eliminated the Divine "burden" of having to continually persuade these entities in a very precise, coercive fashion throughout the steady increase in their capacity for self-determination. This possibility, however, is only a step away from the Deistic Creator who designed and created the Big Bang perfectly from the very beginning. It simply utilizes a different means to arrive at a similar end.

At the same time, though, this alternative would seem to de-emphasize the role of Divine Persuasion in the overall cosmic scheme. For if God could have coercively persuaded the fundamental entities of the Big Bang in such a way as to precisely direct them into eventually forming our present biocentric universe, in spite of their constantly growing capacity for self-determination, then what need is there to posit an ongoing process of Divine Persuasion at all? The almost perfect degree of creative coercion that is evident during all later cosmic epochs prior to the evolution of life (and even, in some respects, during the evolution of life as well) would *not* seem to be possible for a merely persuasive Divine Power, in light of the significant degree of cosmic self-determination that would almost certainly have been obtained by this point in time. However, to revert back to the *opposite* extreme by claiming that the process God could have established the current universal order *from the very beginning* in a deistic-type fashion, would seem to negate the extent of Divine Persuasion during these later epochs.

The third reason why God's persuasion of the Big Bang's primordial entities couldn't have been as complete (and therefore as "coercive") as the process theist would like to believe is statistical in nature. For even if we were to assume that the degree of self-determination that was originally possessed by these "low-grade" entities was minimal, and therefore that God's creative lure could have more or less unilaterally determined their basic configuration, there still would have had to have been some small degree of *possible* resistance to the Divine Will that would have been operative at that time, even if the extent of "conformal prehension" in the early universe was overwhelming (but still not absolute). In small samples this resistance would probably have been minimal, to the point of even being undetectable. However, in the tremendously large sample that comprised the Big Bang, there were literally trillions and trillions of "low-grade" occasions happening every microsecond, each of which could have possibly resisted the conformal prehension of all that had transpired before. This possibility for resistance would only have grown throughout cosmic history, and this in turn would have necessitated a Divine Power that was strong enough to overcome this resistance during each pre-biotic step of the cosmic evolutionary process. Statistically speaking, then, we would expect to see *some* evidence of resistance to the Divine Will during the early to middle stages of cosmogenesis, especially in such a huge population of "low-grade" occasions, but no such evidence can be found in what is presently known about cosmic evolution.

The only way out of this bind is if the process God were able to set up a state of near-perfect conformal prehension at the very beginning, thereby eliminating any significant degree of resistance to the Divine Will. But this brings us back to the notion of deism, which seems to contradict the very identity of the process Deity.

The final problem for process theism in this area has to do with the increasingly complex nature of cosmic evolution. As this evolutionary process proceeds, the "occasions of experience" that comprise it steadily move up the scale in complexity from "low-grade" occasions to "middle-grade" and then "high-grade" occasions. Concomitant with this fundamental increase in complexity is a corresponding increase in the power of self-determination, since most increases in complexity are thought to increase the mental pole's relative degree of influence over the physical pole. Thus, if the process theist is right, we would expect the amount of resistance to the Divine Will to steadily *increase* in frequency and magnitude as the process of cosmic evolution proceeds, since the overall complexity of the universe is known to have steadily increased during its expansion.

Prior to the evolution of life, though, no evidence for this type of resistance can be found.[13] Process theists, however, believe that the utilization of some 10 to 20 billion years to bring life about *itself* constitutes a significant degree of resistance to the Divine Will. Such an allegation, though, rests upon the assumption that it is logically possible for a biocentric universe to have been created in much less time, or even instantaneously. But even the process theists themselves reject this notion. Going one step further, if it isn't logically possible for a biocentric universe to be created instantaneously, then the use of several billion years in its creation cannot be construed as representing a fundamental resistance to the Divine Will, especially considering the relativistic nature of time itself.

The only way the present universal age could be construed as representing resistance to the Divine Will is if God repeatedly had to *compensate* for individual acts of resistance on the part of the finite actualities themselves. These compensatory actions on the part of the Creator would intrinsically take a certain amount of time, as God would have to start certain creative processes over and over again in order to get things right. This in turn would translate into a universal age that was directly proportional, both to the degree to which His Will was actually resisted by the creatures, and to the number of times God had to actually start a given creative process over again.

There is, however, absolutely no evidence in the cosmological literature that this was ever the case. To the best of our knowledge, the universe has evolved more or less *perfectly* from the very beginning (up until the point when life actually formed). This strongly suggests that the age of the cosmos results from logical limitations surrounding the present universal identity, and *not* from creaturely resistance *per se*.[14]

Since the requirements for biocentricity are known to be extremely narrow and specific, it is hard to see how any resistance at all could ever have been tolerated at any pre-biotic point if a genuine biocentric universe was in fact the intended result. Moreover, the very nature of the process God's mode of action requires that He be constantly involved in the luring of His creation. In order for this principle of constant persuasion to be valid, God would have had to have persuaded the universe *at all points* during its evolution. But this would have brought Him face-to-face with the "middle-grade" and "higher-grade" occasions that undoubtedly existed towards the latter part of the evolutionary process. And since these higher-grade occasions would have possessed a significant degree of self-determination *by definition*, we would naturally expect to see a significant degree of resistance to the Divine Will during the middle and later stages of cosmic evolution. *Yet, no such evidence for this type of resistance can be identified at any stage of the Hubble expansion until the process of biological evolution actually begins, and by this time the universe had already become complex enough to be capable of supporting biological life.*

Apparently, then, the only way the process position can possibly be consistent with the cosmological evidence is if the process God acted in a *deistic-type* manner by first determining the initial parameters of the universe and then allowing it to evolve more or less entirely on its own. In this way, God wouldn't have had to continually persuade the universe's constituent entities throughout the steady increase in their self-determining power. This in turn would have enabled Him to avoid any type of creature-inspired sabotage to His ultimate creative aims. However, the process theist's metaphysical system does not allow for a deistic-type God, since it requires the deity to be intimately involved in the persuasion of *all* aspects and stages of cosmic evolution. Therefore, we must conclude that the evidence from modern physics strongly disconfirms the process position with respect to cosmogenesis.

10.4 Is the Present Universe Worthy of a Divine Creator?

Throughout this book I have suggested that a theistic interpretation of the Anthropic Principle is the most sensible way to account for the existing scientific evidence. One way to ascertain the potential validity of this proposition is to ask ourselves the following question: Is the view of cosmogenesis proposed by modern science worthy of an all-knowing and all-powerful Supreme Being? That is to say, does the nature of the scientific evidence itself seem consistent with an Infinitely Intelligent Universal Power?

I believe the answer is yes, for the following three reasons:

1. The very notion of a primordial Big Bang explosion, in which all the matter in the universe emanated from a point of infinite density, only seems to make sense when it is viewed as the product of Divine Creative Activity. Who else could "squeeze" all the matter and energy in the universe into a point of infinite density except God Himself?
2. The seemingly endless expanse of outer space certainly seems "big enough" to have been created by an Omnipotent Power. Had the uni-

verse been perceptibly smaller, it would have been less consistent with God's presumed Infinitude.

3. The truly unfathomable degree of complexity found at all levels of universal reality also seems to be explicable only in terms of an all-knowing Intelligence. It just doesn't seem to be possible for a mindless product of chance to consistently produce instances of complexity that completely overwhelm our ability to understand them. It would thus seem that the origin of any complex process requires at least as much intelligence as it takes for that process to be understood by other intelligent beings. As long as we assume this to be true, it follows that the universe had to have been created by a universal power that is *infinitely* more advanced than we are at the present time, since the underlying details of the physical universe appear to be infinitely complex. The only being who is capable of such infinitely advanced creative tasks is God *by definition*.

10.5 God's True Nature

If we assume that the conclusions presented in this chapter are accurate, then a truly amazing realization suddenly presents itself. If God *really is* in fact the Creator of the Big Bang, black holes, and biological life, then He is at once far more impressive than most of us have ever previously considered.

Most of us, of course, have had our conception of God seriously damaged by the overly parochial and trite images of Him that have been handed down to us by naïve humans over the centuries. The *real* God, of course, isn't a trivial Being at all; He doesn't have a finicky temper or a long white beard. He is, rather, the unsearchable Author of the strong nuclear force, the gravitational constant, and the stupendous miracle of biological evolution. God is thus *infinitely* greater in every positive capacity than we are capable of imagining, and this in turn yields a Spiritual Essence that is *infinitely* worthy of our deepest respect and admiration.

Notes

1. Davies, *The Accidental Universe*, pp. 83–84.
2. Barrow and Tipler, pp. 185, 601.
3. Although the idea that our entire universe could have made a sudden quantum appearance "out of nothing" seems strictly in-credible, we shouldn't be surprised to hear this sort of scientific rhetoric, because for centuries theologians have been telling us that the universe was initially created out of nothing, not by a blind quantum act, but by the Great Creator Himself. Theology thus directly credits God for this original Creative Act, whereas science simply sees the *end result*, and not the Perpetrator, of the Act.
4. See John Hick's *The Existence of God* (New York: Macmillan Publishing Company, 1964), pp. 23–68.

5. One of the main reasons why the process position posits the eternal existence of a finite material realm is that it produces a coherent world view which seems to be consistent with a number of real world observations, chief among them being the ever-present problem of evil. This, however, is *theoretical* evidence for an eternal material realm, not concrete scientific evidence (although as David Griffin has pointed out, the evidence for much in science is also highly theoretical).

6. For more on the various ramifications of Supernatural Naturalism, please refer to my book *Back to Darwin*.

7. In Romans 8:20–24, St. Paul states that God deliberately created a "futile" natural realm, presumably in order to be consistent with the gradual "unfolding" of His finite "children." This notion of "futility" apparently refers to those natural causal laws that the universe must temporarily possess if human beings are to develop in the proper way.

8. Actually, the use of the word "creature" in this context is not entirely appropriate, since the process theist does not posit an absolute creation of the creatures *ex nihilo*; he only posits a *creative reorganization* of an already existing material realm, which implies a substantially weaker concept of what actually constitutes a creature.

9. Holmes Rolston III, *God and Science* (Philadelphia: Temple University Press, 1987), p. 318.

10. Barrow and Tipler, *The Anthropic Cosmological Principle*, p. 288.

11. These possibilities lead us to postulate that perhaps the process theist has confused the radical degree of freedom that may have been voluntarily *conferred* to humans and the rest of creation by God for the metaphysical requirement that all finite actualities *must necessarily* be self-determining by their very nature. To be sure, it does not necessarily follow from the observation that the cosmos is self-determining that this power for self-determination must necessarily be tied into the metaphysical nature of things. An Omnipotent God could very well have had a Higher Reason for voluntarily conferring a certain degree of freedom onto His creatures.

12. See Rupert Sheldrake's *A New Science of Life* (Los Angeles: J.P. Tarcher, Inc., 1981) for more about the laws of nature as "habits."

13. Although some form of resistance can be construed to have existed during the process of biological evolution (though not necessarily so), we are only dealing here with the evolution of our biocentric universe, and not with the evolution of living organisms *per se*. Therefore, we can confine the present discussion to the evolution of a universe capable of supporting biological life.

14. Process theists consider viruses and bacteria, along with the various disease processes they cause, as being evidence of creaturely resistance to the Divine Will. Although one could argue against this notion by showing how these organisms are actually instrumental to the overall Divine Will (many forms of bacteria, for instance, are essential for the stability of the global ecological order, and the existence of various diseases can be shown to have a certain growth-building character to them), I am avoiding this issue in the present argument by confining the discussion to the *pre-biotic* stages of cosmic history.

CHAPTER 11
The Case for Natural Theology

This most elegant system of suns, planets, and comets could only arise
from the purpose and sovereignty of an intelligent and mighty being . . .
He rules them all, not as a soul but as a sovereign lord of all things, and
because of His sovereignty He is commonly called "Lord God almighty."

ISAAC NEWTON

For since the creation of the world His invisible attributes are clearly seen,
being understood by the things that are made, even His eternal power and
Godhead, so that they are without excuse.

ROMANS 1:20

Natural theology is the attempt to infer the existence and character of the
Creator from rational thought, in conjunction with a careful study of that
which He has presumably made. It has had a long and distinguished history
in the Western world, and can be shown to have been an important precursor
to the modern scientific movement. Newton, Leibniz and Boyle were all
natural theologians just as much as they were scientists, and they all openly
stated that it was their belief in a rational Creator that led them into scientific
matters to begin with.

Although the pursuit of natural theology has fallen into severe disrepute
in recent years (due to the scientific materialism of the late modern world
view), it nevertheless remains a viable means of learning important information about the Creator (provided, of course, that one actually *believes* in the
existence of such a Being). For just as one can tell a great deal about an
automaker by examining the types of cars he has made, one can also tell a
great deal about God by examining the types of things *He* has made. Indeed,
there are many learned individuals who go so far as to say that "science
offers a surer path to God than religion."[1]

To the extent that we believe in the ability of science to teach us about
God, we now have at our disposal a virtually *unlimited* amount of indirect
information about the Creator, which we can glean from the pages of our
modern scientific textbooks. This information is freely available just for the
asking—provided, of course, that one knows *what* one is looking for.

Most scientists today are fully aware of the awesome nature of the physical world, yet many of them are still unable to make the vital connection
between creation and Creator. This is where the issue of religious belief

259

becomes important: it is very difficult to do natural theology (at least in a direct fashion) without first believing in the existence of God. Without this belief, it is exceedingly difficult to bridge the gap between scientific information, on the one hand, and the nature of the Creator, on the other. This is why the conclusions of natural theologians seem so untenable to atheistic minds: because the sensibility of such theistic conclusions becomes apparent only *after* one takes the required leap of faith and begins interpreting the natural world in terms of an Intelligent Creator.

This building of faith has been one of the primary goals of the present study, for by showing how strongly suggestive the cosmological evidence is of Intelligent Design, the way can be paved for a possible flowering of the reader's belief in a Creator. Once this belief has taken root, there is a greatly increased likelihood that the remainder of the natural theologian's claims will suddenly begin to come into focus.

Once this vital connection between creation and Creator is made, one finds that a whole new world of spiritual and intellectual intrigue instantly becomes available. There is nothing quite like the realization that an All-Powerful Universal Power is actually responsible for creating the world and everything in it. As C. S. Lewis has put it:

> The objects around me, and my idea of "me," will deceive if taken at their face value. But they are momentous if taken as the end-products of divine activities. Thus and not otherwise, the creation of matter and the creation of mind meet one another and the circuit is closed. . . . [2]

Armed with this knowledge, one can approach the world of science with a fresh new attitude, viewing it not as a dry and boring litany of useless facts, but as the miraculous product of God's Creative Hand. Such an attitude can go a long way towards making the study of science (which has long been considered to be a drab and mundane affair) both pleasant and enjoyable.

11.1 The Natural Theologian's Claims

The chief argument against the validity of natural theology is that there is supposedly no degree of physical complexity that *necessarily* demands the Intelligence and Activity of a Grand Designer. On this view, it is probable that profound levels of complexity could simply exist on their own, having been formed over billions and billions of years through an entirely naturalistic process that doesn't necessarily require the input of an Intelligent Designer.

Although philosopher of religion John Hick obviously believes in the existence of a Grand Designer, he *doesn't* believe that the scientific (i.e., physical) evidence in and of itself can be used to provide a reliable proof of the Divine Being, largely because the evidence from science appears to be ambiguous. Since the existence of profound levels of complexity can, according to Hick, just as easily be explained by an entirely naturalistic, nontheistic rationale, one cannot claim with any substantial degree of force that the evidence of the natural world provides any indication of a Grand Designer. It is for this reason that Hick finds the explanatory utility of natural theology limited at best.

In support of his position, Hick has gone so far as to claim that there is *no* conceivable degree of complexity in the physical realm that would *necessarily* point to the Activity of a Grand Designer as its only rational mode of explanation. Although such a claim is consistent with his highly critical attitude towards natural theology, it doesn't hold up under scrutiny.

An analogy will help to illustrate the weakness in Hick's position. Let us suppose, for instance, that an extremely powerful telescope trained on the planet Neptune reveals a boulder formation that spells out the following statement: "Humans are dangerous creatures who need to carefully consider the effects of their actions." The existence of a such a meaningful series of "words" on the surface of Neptune clearly could not be explained by any type of human activity, because humans have not yet been able to land on Neptune. It also could not be explained by merely appealing to mindless natural processes, because the boulder formation clearly contains an intelligible message that has a higher meaning for the inhabitants of our planet. Accordingly, the only rational conclusion we could possibly come to in this situation is that some sort of intelligent life was aware of our precarious existence on this planet, and so decided to send us a message by arranging the boulders on the planet Neptune in a certain way.[3]

In order to remain consistent with his position, however, Hick must maintain that this intelligible boulder formation doesn't *necessarily* point to the activity of an intelligent being, and to a certain point, of course, Hick is right: it is certainly conceivable that such a boulder formation *could* have resulted entirely from natural processes on Neptune's surface. Even so, it is immediately apparent *beyond any reasonable doubt* that this boulder formation *had* to have been the result of an intelligent power. The meaningfulness of the message and the immense unlikelihood that chance processes could have formed it make such a conclusion almost inescapable.[4]

The skeptic, however, would disagree vehemently with this conclusion, as he would argue that natural processes *can* conceivably produce meaningful states of complexity entirely by chance. In response, the natural theologian can argue that the type of complexity found in the boulder formation is not directly analogous to the types of complexity found in the natural realm. For one thing, all the known examples of complexity in the material realm can be understood to have reached their present degree of complexity through an entirely naturalistic process of evolution from humble beginnings, with natural selection acting along the way to preserve an increasing line of material complexity. The boulder formation, on the other hand, cannot as easily be explained in such a naturalistic manner. The reason for this, of course, is the existence of an intelligible message in the boulder formation itself: naturalistic processes don't seem to be capable of forming a coherent and meaningful statement in the English language.

At the same time, though, the material line of complexity that has led to the existence of biological organisms is far and away more complex than the simple arrangement of boulders in our hypothetical example. (In fact, it is infinitely complex.) While the message conveyed by this degree of complexity may not be in a form that is directly intelligible to us, this is not to say that no intelligent message at all is being conveyed. On the contrary, the message of *high-level functionality for a variety of advanced purposes* is the intelligent message that is being conveyed by the inherent complexity of living organisms.

Indeed, it is now a matter of common scientific knowledge that the nucleotide sequences contained within the DNA molecule are *themselves* a very real type of intelligent information, insofar as they code for the assembly of complex proteins, which in turn contain within themselves the capacity to help maintain the living process. And since the living process is trillions of times more complicated than the relatively simple arrangement of boulders in the above example, it follows that the various genetic messages contained in the DNA molecule must be afforded a *correspondingly greater* degree of respect. Thus, if one concedes that the existence of such an intelligible boulder formation offers powerful evidence of an intelligent contrivance, there seems to be no reasonable way of escaping a *similar* conclusion with respect to the intelligent information contained within the genome.[5]

The fact that the genetic information in the cell can conceivably arise by natural cause-and-effect processes does *not* necessarily invalidate the natural theologian's hypothesis, because the possibility remains that these naturalistic processes were actually the creative means that were originally used by God to create this information. For just as it is possible that an intelligent power could have utilized natural processes to arrange the boulders on the surface of Neptune into an intelligible message, God could have also utilized natural processes to produce the information contained in the genetic code. While the lack of absolute certainty concerning the origin of DNA may make it impossible for the natural theologian to formally *prove* that the genetic code had an Intelligent Origin, it does not detract from the overwhelming *probability* that in all likelihood it probably *did* have one.

There is, however, one type of evidence that *can* stand on its own to argue against a non-theistic interpretation of natural complexity. This is the evidence provided by the physical complexity itself.

If we temporarily remove from our minds the evolutionary origin of the eye, for instance, and simply consider its inherent degree of complexity, it soon becomes apparent that we aren't dealing with just another type of organizational complexity here, but rather with a truly *stupendous* degree of order, which is in fact so profound that it demands an appropriate and sufficient explanation, over and above that of the complexity-building power of the evolutionary process itself.

In other words, it is the intrinsic *quality* of the eye's complexity that seems to cry out for an element of Intelligent Design. Although this qualitative aspect of biological complexity is admittedly a nebulous notion at best, it nevertheless remains a powerful indication of Intelligent Design *if it can be properly appreciated.*

This type of appreciation of natural complexity is vitally important to the cause of the natural theologian. For while it may be easy enough to dismiss this complexity as being just another product of natural selection, one can only persist in doing so if one has not deeply contemplated its profoundly complex nature. Take the eye once again for instance. Modern molecular biologists have discovered that the eye is able to function only by virtue of the cooperation of a seemingly endless number of complexity layers, each of which seems more complex than the next. This amazing "abyss of complexity" needs to be directly experienced to be believed and properly appreciated, but the only way this can be done is by poring over a neurobiology text for a number of hours. *If one makes an honest attempt to do this, and brings to the effort an open mind that is prejudiced only in its sincere desire for truth, I am convinced that there is only one plausible conclusion that one can possibly come to.*

Although accessibility to modern scientific thought is important in any attempt to fully appreciate the Argument from Design, it is by no means necessary. One need not understand how the Krebs Cycle works in order appreciate the reality of design in the universe, or how this design naturally speaks of a Designer. Paley, for instance, had no idea about the many stupendous scientific discoveries that have been made in the last century, yet he was still able to make use of what he *did* know to argue persuasively for the Teleological Argument. What is required isn't so much a certain quantity of information *per se*, but rather a certain *quality* of information, i.e., one needs to be able to look at the existing scientific evidence with a certain state of mind. No one was more aware of this than Paley, who wrote that if all he had access to was the eye, it would have been more than sufficient to convince him of the validity of the Design Argument.

Nevertheless, the quantity of evidence under consideration can also be useful as well, as it effectively drives home the point that a Grand Designer is the most reasonable way to account for the existing evidence. A few isolated pockets of evidence might not be enough to convince some individuals of the case for Intelligent Design, but a tremendous number of them might. In Chapter 4, for instance, we discussed over 25 compelling types of evidence for contrivance in the universe, each of which seems to be far more reasonable than its non-theistic counterpart. Whereas one or two of these examples might not have been sufficient to convince one of the reality of Intelligent Design, a large number of examples automatically becomes far more persuasive. The sheer quantity of this evidence would thus seem to be more than sufficient to justify the move to a scientific theism.

However, it is the intrinsic *quality* of neurobiological complexity which, when it is fully appreciated in detail, presents one of the most forceful arguments of all for an element of Intelligent Design. That this argument is "only" intuitive does not count against its validity and persuasive power, since many of the most accurate and persuasive aspects of our conscious experience are "only" intuitively based, such as the relationship between cause and effect, for instance.

There is, to be sure, a conceivable level of physical complexity that is so profound that it would, if it were ever actually discovered, seem to be explicable only in terms of a Grand Designer. According to the natural theologian, this extreme level of complexity has *already* been discovered in the details of modern molecular biology. Unfortunately, the larger implications of this complexity tend to go undetected by the vast majority of individuals who study this material.

The fact is, the natural realm is so subtle and profound that it is a rare event indeed to find that one has accurately surmised the true inner nature of a given object or a given process within it. More often than not, this inner reality seems to evade us, *for the closer we look, the further away it seems to flee.* At the most foundational level of quantum physics, for example, a shadowy type of reality is uncovered which, as far as the basic constituents of matter are concerned, only shows an underlying *tendency* to exist. Nothing truly concrete is ever found at this fundamental level of reality. Like the confusing house of mirrors at an amusement park, where everything one sees turns out to be a mere reflection of something else, the subatomic constituents of matter consistently show a level of interdependence and evasiveness that has so far eluded our best efforts to pin them down.

In fact, we now know, thanks to fractal geometry and chaos theory, that nature is *infinitely* complex in terms of its underlying structure and design. This is an outrageous assertion, to be sure, but it is one that is very well supported in the scientific literature.[6] In fractal geometry, for instance, we find that the length of any complex physical border, say that of a coastline, is ultimately infinite, because the degree of complexity that is found in the inner details of the coastline is *itself* infinite. This fact translates into an infinitely complex physical realm, because each aspect of physical reality appears to be an infinitely complex series of fractal shapes.

The point is simply that we should never become so arrogant as to assume that we have ever finally understood the true nature of *anything* in the physical realm, because this is a goal that appears to be strictly impossible in the absence of an infinite amount of knowledge. Indeed, every time someone thinks that they've almost discovered the true nature of *anything* in the physical realm, they've always been radically mistaken. In the latter stages of the nineteenth century, for example, Lord Kelvin, one of the most celebrated physicists of his time, announced that man's quest for a complete scientific understanding of the world had more or less been completed, except for two "small clouds" on the horizon. These two clouds eventually turned into the science of quantum mechanics and modern relativity theory! Kelvin's inordinate confidence in the scientific understanding of his day thus turned out to be severely mistaken.

We too must constantly be on guard to prevent ourselves from falling into a similar sort of epistemological trap. That is to say, we must cultivate within ourselves an adequate appreciation of the underlying *subtlety* and *complexity* of the entire physical realm. Conversely, we must avoid concluding that we have *ever* come to a full understanding of how *anything* in nature operates or exists within itself. As mathematician Kurt Gödel has demonstrated, we can't even gain absolute certainty in such a relatively "simple" field of endeavor as arithmetic. The findings of modern quantum physics have only added to this fundamental uncertainty, as the most basic constituents of the physical realm also seem to exhibit a similar degree of indeterminancy. Given this limitlessly subtle nature of the material realm, is it not more sensible to maintain a healthy state of *reverence* towards it, rather than the arrogant attitude that we have finally attained an accurate understanding of its true underlying nature?

But even if, for the sake of argument, we do one day succeed in learning all there is to know about the physical universe, there will still always be the larger metaphysical implications that are posed by it which will *themselves* be in need of explanation, and these are issues that are intrinsically beyond the explanatory power of the physical sciences alone. Indeed, it is precisely here in the many ramifications of physical reality that the natural theologian believes the Limitless Intelligence of God can be found.

It is hopelessly naïve to think that a superficial perusal of *anything* as complicated as a living cell could *ever* yield an accurate appraisal of its true underlying significance and meaning. For just as living systems, along with their molecular constituents, continue to exhibit new layers of structural and functional complexity as our scientific understanding grows, we can expect the overall *meaning* of these systems to grow as well, as our capacity for comprehending it grows more mature and sophisticated with the passage of time.

No scientist worth his salt would look at a given biological structure or organism and claim to understand every aspect of its internal structure or biochemistry. But if such a healthy level of respect is appropriate at the structural level, isn't it even *more* appropriate at the larger philosophical level, where even *less* is known about life's true meaning and significance? Indeed, why should we expect the underlying meaning of life to be any simpler to explain than its internal degree of physical complexity?

For the non-theistic scientist, who cannot fall back on the mystery of Divine Intelligence to explain the awesome complexity of living systems, the *why* of cosmic evolution must remain an open question, as he cannot hope to possess an accurate understanding of life's true meaning in the absence of a complete understanding of *what* life is, *where* it came from, and *how* it evolved. Such a complete understanding, however, is nowhere near being attained. Hence, the most extreme intellectual response that is justifiable by our current level of scientific understanding is agnosticism, *not* atheism.

The non-theistic scientist, on the other hand, is typically forced by his own belief in life's accidental origins into claiming that life has *no* meaning. Is it rational, though, to assert that the cell, with its seemingly limitless degree of internal complexity, has no larger meaning, apart from the meaning we give to it? With any other (man-made) object possessing an appreciable level of internal complexity, the notion of its being ultimately meaningless is unthinkable, because structural complexity and overall meaning tend to go hand in hand. That is to say, most objects are only able to reach a relatively high level of complexity when they are judged to be meaningful by an outside intelligence.

For the non-theistic evolutionist, however, biological complexity is able to exist with no larger meaning because it is thought to have resulted from the mindless process of biological evolution. As we have seen, though, the fact that life has evolved naturalistically doesn't diminish the need for a Divine Intelligence in the least bit, *since a seemingly self-sufficient evolutionary process still requires a sufficient explanation for its own self-sufficiency.* Until an adequate explanation for this self-sufficiency is provided by the non-theistic evolutionist, then, it makes sense to assume that the very complexity of life makes life meaningful, regardless of how self-sufficient the evolutionary process is deemed to be.

That is to say, we should construct our attitude towards the material realm in a manner that is consistent with its most fundamental qualities, as they have thus far been discovered to be. Since we have uncovered a physical reality that is almost *infinitely* subtle and profound, is it not incumbent upon us to maintain an attitude towards it that is *equally* open and respectful of this seemingly endless profundity? The theistic world view that is displayed by the natural theologian is, by its very openness towards transcendent explanations, consistent with this profundity, whereas the atheistic world view displayed by the non-theistic materialist is clearly not.

It is with this underlying appreciation of the miraculousness of the natural realm that the proponents of natural theology seem to be on firmer ground than the proponents of atheistic or agnostic materialism. For by repeatedly affirming the inherent miraculousness of the universe in which we live, the natural theologian shows himself to be in line with the mystical nature of the physical realm, as it has so far been empirically discovered to be. The skeptic, on the other hand, is totally out of step with this fundamental nature, as he assumes: 1) that he has, for the most part, adequately understood the underlying nature of the physical universe, and 2) that this understanding is consistent with a non-theistic view of universal origins.

Given these observations, it now becomes sensible to ask how we can possibly hope to come to an accurate appreciation of the true nature of the physical realm. It can, I think, be safely asserted that a superficial perusal of the basic scientific facts will *not* convey such an accurate appreciation, simply due to the fact that long periods of meditative consideration are generally required *by definition* before the more sublime aspects of the natural world can be identified and adequately appreciated. If these qualities were immediately discernible, it would not be appropriate to refer to them as being sublime. So, it follows from the very postulation of a sublime natural realm that a significant degree of serious consideration must first be engaged in before this subtlety can be identified and fully appreciated.

In accordance with this basic postulate, the natural theologian assumes that the universe consists of *many* different levels and degrees of reality, each of which possesses its own form of substance and meaning. On this view, the non-theistic scientist or philosopher is judged to see only the lower levels of physical reality. Yet, as F. C. Copleston has pointed out, what is required in order to obtain a full picture of nature isn't mere sight but the act of *noticing*—noticing the higher levels of reality that are not immediately apparent to the sight-oriented materialist or philosopher. It is this deeper and more substantive act of noticing which the natural theologian claims to be the essential prerequisite before the true nature of the physical realm can be fully appreciated.

Interestingly enough, this deeper level of appreciation has much in common with the mystical modes of experience described by William James in his famous volume *The Varieties of Religious Experience.* According to James, a mystical experience consists of "that deepened sense of the significance of a maxim or formula which occasionally sweeps over one. 'I've heard that said all my life,' we exclaim, 'but I never realized its full meaning until now.'"[7]

If we translate James' view of mystical experience to the domain of the natural theologian, we find that a deeper understanding or appreciation of the inherent miraculousness of the natural realm may indeed be possible to attain, but only on the condition that a type of mystical experience be the appropriate mediating factor in its attainment. On this view, some degree of mystical insight is required before a full appreciation of the inherent miraculousness of the natural realm can be attained. The cogency of the natural theologian's claims also rests upon the attainment of this level of insight. Unfortunately, since this type of mystical insight is all too rare in the modern world, the fundamental argument of the natural theologian—which states that the experienced degree of miraculousness exhibited by the natural realm can only be properly accounted for by appealing to an Intelligent Designer—must necessarily remain obscured by the esoteric (i.e., mystical) nature of his basic premise.

Trying to explain nature's deeper significance with mere words is, of course, largely futile, because the "incommunicableness of the transport is the keynote of all mysticism. Mystical truth exists for the individual who has the transport, but for no one else."[8] As a consequence, the intrinsic power of the Argument from Design must necessarily remain inaccessible to all but a few because of the mystical requirement of its underlying premise. While this may seem like an *ad hoc* way of preserving the possible validity of the Design Argument (since it cannot be refuted unless the proposed type of mystical experience has first been attained and *then* found to be inadequate), such a stipulation nevertheless follows inevitably from the natural theologian's underlying presuppositions.

In his discussion of E. L. Mascall's natural theology, process theologian John Cobb notes how Mascall is aware of the importance of one's mental state in determining how one relates to the goals and conclusions of the natural theologian:

> The argument is not that all men capable of rationality reach the same conclusions but that those who are willing to be attentive to the right data and open to the correct interpretation can be led to see that certain conclusions follow necessarily. The obstacles to the acceptance of traditional natural theology are indifference, habit, prejudice, blindness, and laziness. Our whole urban way of life with its artificiality and emphasis on distractions militates against the kind of concern, sensitivity, and patience that is required for natural theology. Hence, it is not surprising that the arguments of natural theology seem strange and irrelevant to many moderns. But it is clear also that this understandable response does not imply the falsity or inadequacy of the doctrines themselves.[9]

11.2 Natural Theology and the Threat from Naturalistic Evolution

Earlier we saw how the natural processes of cosmic and biological evolution don't necessarily count against the claims of the natural theologian, because God could have used these natural processes as His creative tools to make the universe the way He wanted.

A second reason why the evolutionary process cannot be used to count against the claims of the natural theologian is that it doesn't provide a rational accounting for those clever atoms and molecules that have made the rise of life possible. As we have seen, non-theistic evolutionists simply take the existence of self-organizing atoms and molecules for granted, when in fact they too possess a profound level of complexity that must also be accounted for in an entirely naturalistic manner before the claims of the natural theologian can be properly discounted. To simply claim that these self-organizing bits of matter have always existed from all eternity, and so are in no need of explanation, runs counter to the present scientific consensus that they have *not* existed forever. It also contradicts the findings of modern science, for we now know that our macro world is only possible because of the many ingenious qualities that are possessed by the atomic and subatomic realms, such as the Pauli Exclusion Principle and the existence of concrete quantum states for each electron in an atom.[10]

A third reason why the evolutionary process cannot be used as legitimate evidence against the claims of the natural theologian is that there doesn't seem to be any conceivable way for the eye, or any other complex organ, to have been formed in an *entirely* naturalistic manner, even if we assume the prior existence of atoms and molecules. The eye, for instance, is simply far too complex, on far too many interconnected levels, to have *ever* been an incidental product of the mere struggle for survival. Indeed, the assumptions of the neo-Darwinian evolutionary perspective actually work *against* the prospect of an accidental evolution, for as I have discussed elsewhere,[11] the only way natural selection could have mediated the formation of the eye is if each of its incipient parts were able to serve an important function in the immediate struggle for survival. However, it is hard to see how half an eye could possibly have been functional at all.

But if the eye in all its stunning complexity could never have been formed by a fortuitous process of natural selection alone, even over millions of years of gradual evolution, we are obliged to conclude that some form of teleological striving, internal to the evolving life forms themselves, had to have been responsible for forming it, especially given the fact that the eye evolved a bare minimum of 40 separate times in the animal kingdom.[12] Such a teleological view doesn't contradict the evolutionary paradigm or the action of natural selection. It only says that there must have been some sort of internally-based directionality to the evolutionary process; otherwise, the eye in all its astounding complexity could never have been formed.

The intrinsic complexity of the eye itself supports this conclusion. For once this complexity is fully appreciated in all of its many intimate details (and not before), it immediately becomes apparent that such a phenomenal degree of complexity could never have been formed by random chance alone, no matter how much time was available. Just as it is intuitively apparent that the Space Shuttle, by virtue of its profound degree of mechanical complexity, could never have been formed in the absence of an intelligent designer, it is equally apparent that the eye in all its stunning complexity also could never have been formed in the absence of an Intelligent Designer. The fact that organic beings evolve over many generations, while inanimate structures do not, is immaterial to this line of argument, at least insofar as it can be shown that the historical evolutionary process could never have produced such organs of "extreme perfection" without some form of inner directionality.

It is for this reason that I take natural theology to be an intrinsically valid means of shedding important light on the existence of a Grand Designer, but only on the condition that the intrinsic complexity of living creatures be fully appreciated in its own right, which in turn can only take place when their scientific details are rigorously studied with an open and mystically inclined frame of mind.

11.3 Response to Hume

The classical argument against the conclusions of the natural theologian were originally levied by the Scottish philosopher David Hume[13] (1711–1776), in his famous *Dialogues Concerning Natural Religion*. In this important work, Philo, the skeptic, argues against Cleanthes, the natural theologian, and Demea, the orthodox believer, concerning the cogency of the natural theologian's claims.

Philo's first point is that, given the huge analogical discrepancy between human creativity, on the one hand, and the hypothetical creativity of a Divine Being, on the other, no legitimate means of arguing from the one to the other can possibly be said to exist. Take the human act of building a house, for instance. According to Philo, this human act is so inherently dissimilar to the supposed creation of the world by God that one cannot use any apparent degree of similarity to argue from the reality of human creativity to the possibility of Divine Creativity. As Philo himself says, ". . . whenever you depart, in the least, from the similarity of cases, you diminish proportionably the evidence; and may at last bring it to a very weak analogy, which is confessedly liable to error and uncertainty."[14]

The problem with Philo's objection is that it is largely irrelevant to the natural theologian's basic argument. While it may be true that the degree of dissimilarity between cases reduces the number and power of the conclusions that can analogously be drawn between them, it doesn't reduce *all* of them. The natural theologian isn't arguing on behalf of the dissimilarities, but rather on behalf of the *similarities* between human designership and Divine Creativity. To be sure, there are undoubtedly a tremendous number of differences between a mere human contriver and a Divine Creator Being, but to the extent that a given characteristic may overlap between the two, it is possible, at least in principle, to draw an appropriate analogy between them. *It would thus be a mistake to assume that the dissimilarities between God and man must somehow negate any similarities that might also exist between them.* On this score, the natural theologian seems to be on firm ground, as he isn't denying that a large number of dissimilarities happen to exist between God and man; he is only saying that one of the *similarities*, namely the capacity for intelligent design, is so striking that a legitimate analogy can in fact be drawn between them.

What is called for here is an acute state of *discretion* in the determination of those hypothetical similarities between God and man that are appropriate, and those that are inappropriate. Just because the natural theologian can claim that *some* similarities may exist between God and man, isn't to say that there is a *complete* state of anthropomorphic concurrence between humans and their Creator. Hume, however, takes the natural theologian's claim of a basic similarity between God and man much too far, in that he indiscriminately uses it to draw all sorts of silly anthropomorphic conclusions about the nature of God. As Philo himself asks:

> . . . why not become a perfect anthropomorphite? Why not assert the deity or deities to be corporeal, and to have eyes, a nose, mouth, ears, etc.?[15]

The problem with Hume's point is that the natural theologian is professing to exercise a considerable amount of discretion in the determination of which anthropomorphic qualities are likely to be found in the Divine Essence, and which are not. To thus blindly suppose that *no* such qualities can exist in God, just because *all* of them obviously do not, is clearly fallacious. A man and a woman may not possess a completely congruent set of descriptive properties, but this fact can never be used to argue against the routine observation that *some* common properties do in fact exist between them.

This sort of Humean argument has been extensively used to discredit the traditional Argument from Design, under the assumption that an appropriate analogy between a living organism and a human artefact cannot properly be drawn. Hume believed that it was possible for the universe to have the superficial *appearance* of intelligent design, whereas in point of fact it could be entirely natural in its basic essence. Thus, the cogency of the Argument from Design rests upon the demonstration that a living organism is, in a very real and profound sense, machine-like in its fundamental construction.[16]

Paley, of course, considered this analogy between life and machines to be perfectly appropriate, so he used the evidence for design in the natural world to argue for the existence of a Divine Creator. Paley's argument was founded on the assumption that living organisms are indeed machines, insofar as they possess a wide variety of intelligently designed building blocks that are very precisely put together to create a unified, functional whole. Functional machines, of course, require an intelligent contriver to produce them, so Paley argued that a Heavenly Watchmaker *had* to exist in order to account for the marvel of life on Earth.

However, due to the extreme paucity of biological information that existed prior to the second half of the twentieth century, it was possible to argue, as Hume tried to do, that the living cell may not be an intelligently designed machine after all. Certainly there was no way to conclusively show that the analogy between living cells and machines was in fact appropriate from a scientific point of view, because the scientists who were living at that time simply didn't know enough about the inner workings of the cell to justify such grandiose claims.

Today, however, with the advent of modern molecular biology, the situation is radically different. For the first time in history, the natural theologian has at his ready disposal thousands upon thousands of volumes of scientific information which explain the inner complexity of the cell in stupefying detail. The cumulative effect of all this molecular information has been to validate Paley's analogy between life and machines beyond reasonable doubt. As Australian medical doctor and molecular biologist Michael Denton has aptly pointed out:

> It has only been over the past twenty years with the molecular biological revolution and with the advances in cybernetic and computer technology that Hume's criticism has been finally invalidated and the analogy between organisms and machines has at last become convincing. In opening up this extraordinary new world of living technology biochemists have become fellow travellers with science fiction writers, explorers in a world of ultimate technology, wondering increduously as new miracles of atomic engineering are continually brought to light in the course of their strange adventure into the microcosm of life. In every direction the biochemist gazes, as he journeys through this weird molecular labyrinth, he sees devices and appliances reminiscent of our own twentieth-century world of advanced technology. In the atomic fabric of life we have found a reflection of our own technology. We have seen a world as artificial as our own and as familiar as if we have held up a mirror to our own machines.
>
> Paley was not only right in asserting the existence of an analogy between life and machines, but was also remarkably prophetic in guessing that the technological ingenuity realized in living systems is vastly in excess of anything yet accomplished by man. . . .
>
> The almost irresistible force of the analogy has completely undermined the complacent assumption, prevalent in biological circles over most of the past century, that the design hypothesis can be excluded on the grounds that the notion is fundamentally a metaphysical *a priori* concept and therefore scientifically unsound. On the contrary, the inference to design is a purely *a posteriori* induction based on a ruthlessly consistent application

of the logic of analogy. The conclusion may have religious implications, but it does not depend on religious presuppositions.[17]

The Argument from Design thus turns out to be valid after all, because it is founded on an analogy that has become far more empirically substantiated in recent years than anyone could have guessed in Hume's time. The fact is, living organisms are the most complex machines in the entire known universe, so we are therefore compelled to find a sufficient explanation to account for them. Since the neo-Darwinian idea of random chance[18] is clearly incapable of accounting for this technological wizardry, we are left with some form of theism as the only remaining hypothesis that makes any sense.

For his second objection to the Argument from Design, Hume attempts to use the domain of the logically feasible to argue for the possibility that the present universal order could have merely been the result of a haphazard cooperation of atoms.

> . . . let us suppose it [matter] finite. A finite number of particles is only susceptible of finite transpositions: And it must happen in an eternal duration, that every possible order or position must be tried an infinite number of times . . . a chaos ensues, till finite though innumerable revolutions produce at last some forms, whose parts and organs are so adjusted as to support the forms amidst a continued succession of matter.[19]

The natural theologian would respond that it is by no means obvious that all possible configurations between particles will occur infinitely often during an infinite duration of time. It isn't even obvious that it will happen a single time! The true question at issue here is whether certain highly elaborate configurations are possible in the absence of intelligent external manipulation. No one doubts whether certain relatively simple configurations can happen over and over again in this manner. The question is whether extremely contrived instances of order, such as Michelangelo's "David" or Plato's *Republic,* could ever spontaneously organize themselves with no outside help. It is hard to see how they ever could, even given an infinite amount of time and particles.

It would therefore seem that there must exist an unbridgable gap between those particle configurations that can happen spontaneously, and those that require the external input of a deliberate creative force. Assuming this to be the case, we cannot expect the concept of infinity to make up for this unbridgable gap, because the "distance" between the intrinsically possible and the intrinsically impossible is *itself* infinite. Therefore, it does *not* appear as though an infinite amount of time and particles would be able to explore all *possible* combinations even once, because implicit in the very *definition* of intelligent contrivance is the capacity to produce levels of order that cannot *under any circumstances* be duplicated by random combinations of particles alone.

But even if we were to concede for the sake of argument that an infinite number of particles might be able to explore all possible combinations in an infinite amount of time, we would still have to ask where the *particles themselves* came from, and more importantly, where they got the clever capacity to spontaneously interact with one another in such a way as to produce highly ordered states "on their own." We can't simply deny the question and claim that these self-organizing particles have always existed, *because it is not within the definition of ordinary matter to hold within itself the reason or explanation for its own existence. If it did, then matter itself would be God, because God by definition is the only entity that contains within Himself the reason for His own existence.*

In his famous BBC debate with Bertrand Russell, Father Copleston put forth a similar argument concerning the need for a necessary being in a world populated by contingent things. On Copleston's view, not even an infinite number of contingent beings can make up the huge amount of difference between a contingent being and a necessary being.

> . . . I don't believe that the infinity of the series of events—I mean, a horizontal series, so to speak—if such an infinity could be proved, would be in the slightest degree relevant to the situation. If you add up chocolates you get chocolates after all and not a sheep. If you add up chocolates to infinity, you presumably get an infinite number of chocolates. So if you add up contingent beings to infinity, you still get contingent beings, not a necessary being. An infinite series of contingent beings will be, to my way of thinking, as unable to cause itself as one contingent being.[20]

The analogy here is between contingent beings and relatively simple degrees of order, on the one hand, and a necessary being and highly complex degrees of order, on the other. Just as an infinite series of contingent beings will only yield more contingent beings, and not a necessary being, an infinite number of particles in an infinite amount of time will *not* by hypothesis ever be able to produce our present world in all its highly contrived complexity. It will only be able to duplicate the relatively simple degrees of order that are possible to obtain by random motions alone.

Hume's third objection centers around his fallacious conclusion that all potential possibilities that are not judged to be explicitly contradictory are equally possible.

> Were a man to abstract from everything which he knows or has seen, he would be altogether incapable, merely from his own ideas, to determine what kind of scene the universe must be, or to give the preference to one state or situation of things above another. For as nothing which he clearly

conceives could be esteemed to be impossible or implying a contradiction, every chimera of his fancy would be upon an equal footing; nor could he assign any just reason why he adheres to one idea or system, and rejects the others *which are equally possible* (emphasis mine).[21]

It is clearly a mistake to assume that all possibilities which are not judged to be contradictory are equally probable, yet this is precisely what Hume erroneously concludes. An example will help to clarify this important notion. Consider a lottery-type drawing where a million tickets are sold. If all the tickets but one are purchased by a single individual, it is clearly not impossible or contradictory to suppose that the person with the single ticket *could* end up winning the prize. Yet we know that the odds are 999,999 to 1 against him. By Hume's judgment, though, such a remote possibility is just as possible as anyone else's winning is, because it is not explicitly contradictory.

Extending this train of thought to the realm of natural theology, we find that the case against Intelligent Design is *not* significantly weakened by the remote *possibility* that our highly ordered cosmos *could* be the result of a mindless fluke. For although such a possibility cannot be judged to be logically impossible, it *can* be judged to be exceedingly improbable. This is where the "circumstantial evidence" for Intelligent Design discussed in Chapter 8 comes into play. For by showing how much more likely it is that the observed order in the universe is the result of Intelligent Design, rather than random chance, the case for a Deliberate Creation becomes almost completely established. From this point of view, the fact that it is not logically impossible for the universe to be a chance event does not figure prominently into the conclusion, since the likelihood of its accidental occurrence is so vanishingly small as to place it beyond rational consideration.

Hume's fourth objection to the Design Argument stems from the possibility that matter itself could contain a sufficient degree of spontaneity to account for all the apparent order which we find in the world. In this case, the material universe itself would be the necessarily existent Being. For we "dare not affirm that we know all the qualities of matter; and for aught we can determine, it may contain some qualities, which, were they known, would make its non-existence appear as great a contradiction as that twice two is five."[22]

There are two severe problems with this contention. First, there is no hard evidence that matter contains within itself the reason for its own being. Although a certain degree of spontaneity and self-determination may possibly be acknowledged to exist in matter, it does not follow from a postulation of these properties that the entire material realm could have formed its present degree of order entirely on its own. Indeed, as we saw in Chapters 3 and 4, cosmologists have shown that our biocentric universe originally began in a highly ordered, finely balanced configuration that seems for all the world to have been the result of an Intelligent Contrivance extending beyond the realm of matter alone.

Secondly, the definition of matter as it has been traditionally conceived does *not* include the capacity for self-existence, as we have seen. The traditional definition of God, on the other hand, *does* include this capacity. Of course, we could always redefine matter to contain these transcendent qualities, but if we did, the physical universe itself would become a God, and this seems absurd. There thus seems to be no way of escaping the need for a rational explanation for our exquisitely ordered universe.

Hume's overall point in the *Dialogues* is that there is no way to infer *for a certainty* that a Supernatural Creator has in fact created the world, based solely on the evidence of apparent design in nature. Such a conclusion, of course, follows inevitably from the "epistemic distance" that has apparently been laid between humans and God. Since God cannot be directly observed in any type of creative action in the world, it follows that no type of physical evidence can, in and of itself, *prove* beyond any doubt that God exists and is responsible for creating the world.

The natural theologian, of course, does not debate this point, as he isn't trying to obtain an absolute proof of the Divine Being. He is, rather, only aiming for a weaker "proof" of God's existence, one which states that, given the observable evidence at hand, it is more reasonable overall to believe in God than not to. Although this weaker type of "proof" cannot absolutely prove the existence of God beyond any possible doubt, it *can* come sufficiently close to this conclusion as to be virtually indistinguishable from it. Just as the number 0.9999999999999999 is close enough to the number 1.0 to warrant no significant distinction between the two, the natural theologian believes that there is more than enough evidence in existence to prove the existence of God beyond any *reasonable* doubt. The lack of an absolute proof for God thus does not trouble the natural theologian one iota, because he believes that he can increase the amount and degree of evidence for Design to the point that, while it may never amount to an *absolute* proof of a Divine Creator, it can still come more than close enough to yield the *same* conclusion.

To be sure, the rational individual does not require a videotape of his house getting robbed to infer, from circumstantial evidence alone, that his house was in fact robbed. All he need experience is a broken lock and a few missing valuables to conclude beyond any reasonable doubt that his house was broken into. Similarly, it is the firm conviction of the natural theologian that we need not witness the Divine Creative Act directly in order to infer, beyond any reasonable doubt, that a Larger Intelligence is in fact behind the observed order and complexity of our world. For just as there is a finite amount of circumstantial evidence in a courtroom that will judiciously send a convicted murderer to jail, or even to his death, there is also a finite amount of circumstantial evidence in existence to judiciously warrant the conviction that a Divine Intelligence is in fact responsible for creating our world.

To be effective, then, Hume's objection to the "religious hypothesis," echoed through the mouth of Philo, would have to state that there is *no* conceivable amount or degree of circumstantial evidence that would prove *beyond any reasonable doubt* that an Intelligent Designer is in fact responsible for creating the world. Again, the key phrase here is "beyond any reasonable doubt," for while Hume may correct in asserting that no amount of circumstantial evidence can *absolutely* prove the existence of a Designer, the natural theologian's counterargument is that it isn't absolute proof which is actually required here, since *relative proof* (which consists of a certain amount of circumstantial evidence) is *more* than enough to prove the existence of God beyond any reasonable doubt.

Indeed, we use circumstantial evidence every day to help us live decisively in a world where absolute proof of *anything* is extremely hard to come by. For instance, we use circumstantial evidence to help us read, insofar as the process of reading consists of interpreting the existence of meaningful words from a variety of marks appearing on a piece of paper. In and of themselves, each of these tiny marks are meaningless, but when they are pieced together into a recognizable pattern, a coherent meaning is finally attained. Indeed, it is the convergence of these marks into a meaningful pattern which tells us that they have been deliberately contrived by an intelligent power for the purpose of conveying a meaningful message.

To better illustrate the important relationship between circumstantial evidence and the inference of meaning, let us assume, for the sake of argument, that we are presented with a formless assortment of marks on a page. The simple fact that no recognizable form can be ascertained tells us that the marks were probably not intelligently contrived, at least not in a way that is immediately apparent. However, if we are presented with a second assortment of marks which seem to occupy the crude form of recognizable letters, we would be much more inclined to think that they had been intelligently contrived. Going one step further, if we are presented with a random assortment of clearly recognizable words, we would be almost certain that they had been intelligently contrived. Finally, if we are presented with a group of recognizable words that are put together in the form of a meaningful (and gramatically correct) sentence, we would be certain, beyond any reasonable doubt, that the marks were actually contrived by an intelligent power. The fact that this evidence would only be circumstantial in nature (i.e. that we did not directly witness this contrivance in action), would not significantly diminish our level of certainty, *because there is clearly a degree of circumstantial evidence beyond which any form of reasonable doubt is exceedingly difficult to maintain.*

The scientific facts of the natural world can be understood in the same way. Although highly elaborate forms of order exist at all levels of physical reality (which correspond to the appearance of recognizable words in the above example), it is the convergence of these independent forms of order into the magnificent edifice of a living cell (which corresponds to the linking of words into a coherent sentence in the above example) which proves beyond any reasonable doubt that life is the result of a deliberate contrivance by a Higher Power.

That is to say, it is the existence of high-level information, both within the DNA molecule and in the form of the living process itself, that shows beyond any reasonable doubt that life has been deliberately contrived. The fact that we have no absolute proof of this is immaterial to the natural theologian's overall point. We didn't have absolute proof that the marks in the above example were deliberately contrived, yet we concluded, beyond any reasonable doubt, that they *were* in fact contrived, based solely on the circumstantial evidence at hand. If circumstantial evidence works so well that it can enable us to read words and to infer that these words were contrived by an intelligent power, then why shouldn't it *also* work well enough to indicate the existence of God from the intelligence that is inherent in the living process itself?

On this view, there is a level of circumstantial evidence which is, for all practical intents and purposes, just as convincing as absolute proof. This is an assumption that we all presuppose in practice, even if we happen to verbally deny it for the sake of argument.

For the natural theologian, then, Hume's insistence that nothing less than absolute proof will suffice to validate the Teleological Argument amounts to little more than an irrelevant Red Herring, designed to distract the natural theologian from the extreme power that is an inherent part of the Argument from Design. To be sure, just as the Humean skeptic need not directly witness the shooting death of a friend to know beyond any reasonable doubt, from circumstantial evidence alone, that his friend has in fact died from a gunshot wound, the natural theologian argues that we need not directly observe the Creator in action to know beyond any reasonable doubt that He has in fact contrived our world (albeit indirectly through a self-driven evolutionary process).

Indeed, there has been speculation that, given the cogency of Cleathes' Argument from Design in the *Dialogues,* Hume's sympathies secretly lay in favor of the natural theologian.[23] According to this view, propounded in England during Hume's lifetime by Samuel Johnson and Joseph Priestly, Hume was simply trying to overcome his literary obscurity by mischievously arguing, through the mouth of Philo, against the dominant position of the era, which was that nature's order and design constituted sufficient proof of a Divine Being.

Philo's final point in the *Dialogues* builds from his basic premise that absolute proof based on the Argument from Design is strictly impossible.

In a word, Cleanthes, a man who follows your hypothesis is able, perhaps, to assert or conjecture that the universe sometime arose from something like design: But beyond that position he cannot ascertain one single circumstance, and is left afterwards to fix every point of his theology by the utmost license of fancy and hypothesis. This world, for aught he knows, is very faulty and imperfect, compared to a superior standard; and was only the first rude essay of some infant deity who afterwards abandoned it, ashamed of his lame performance: It is the work only of some dependent, inferior deity, and is object of derision to his superiors . . . You justly give signs of horror, Demea, at these strange suppositions; but these, and a thousand more of the same kind, are Cleanthes' suppositions, not mine. From the moment the attributes of the Deity are supposed finite, all these have place. And I cannot, for my part, think that so wild and unsettled a system of theology is, in any respect, preferable to none at all.[24]

There are several flaws in this line of argument. To begin with, our modern scientific understanding of cosmogenesis strongly disconfirms Hume's sarcastic suggestion that ours may, for all we know, be a lame and imperfect universe created by an infant, inferior deity. As we saw in Chapter 4, cosmologists have shown that our biocentric universe consists of a large number of finely tuned physical parameters that were somehow able to work together during the early stages of cosmic evolution to produce at least one life-sustaining world. It is very hard to see how a less than perfect creator could have been responsible for performing such an impressive feat.

Hume's final objection is doubly invalidated by his faulty conclusion that the sharing of certain basic features between God and man somehow renders God as finite as human beings. To be sure, an object or Being of infinite proportions can nevertheless possess certain features which could have their counterparts in the finite realm, and this would not diminish the Being's infinitude in the least. In other words, it is possible that certain properties, which have been postulated to exist in an Infinite Deity, could be duplicated in finite form in the mind and character of human beings. Indeed, this is what the Biblical concept of man being created "in the image of God" is all about. Hence, it is distinctly possible that the creativity of God could be mirrored in finite form in human beings without God's Infinitude being diminished in the least bit. For Hume to thus conclude that *any* sharing of basic features between God and man automatically renders God finite is clearly fallacious.

All in all, if the skeptic's only recourse is to resort to the natural theologian's inevitable lack of absolute certainty regarding his conclusions, instead of more *substantive* arguments to the contrary, the natural theologian can rest assured that his conclusions are about as sound as it is possible for human conclusions to get in the absence of direct, unmitigated evidence. Hume hints that this may be true when he states that the most a person can conclude from the existing evidence is that the universe may have arisen from something like design. But if a great skeptic like Hume goes so far as to say that the universe *may* have arisen from something like design, the real truth is that it probably *did* result from design.

11.4 Kant's Objections to the Argument from Design

The German philosopher Immanuel Kant (1724–1804) also argued that it was strictly impossible to prove the absolute validity of the Argument from Design, as he believed that it was impossible to either prove or disprove propositions about the real world using "pure reason" alone. He was, however, able to appreciate the power of the Design Argument using the facility of "practical reason" only, in spite of the fundamental degree of uncertainty that it supposedly entails.

Kant saw this intrinsic uncertainty as originating in the inevitable projection of our innate categories of thought onto the actual objects of the external world. Since there is no obvious way of ascertaining whether or not these innate categories are sufficient to the task, Kant believed that we cannot trust our cognitive conclusions about the world absolutely. While the various "things in themselves" that comprise reality may have a certain concrete reality apart from human perception, there is no way to perceive them as they are "in themselves," since in the very act of perception we inevitably use our own intrinsic categories of perception to do the perceiving. Because these categories of perception cannot be directly observed and subsequently evaluated within the mind, their appropriateness for the task can only be taken on faith alone. For Kant, then, the most that could possibly be said regarding the apparent design in the world is that the categories of the perceiving mind, when they are projected out onto physical reality, find it necessary to perceive some sort of "design" in it. Hence, it is not justifiable to conclude that there is *in fact* design in the world, because there is no way to tell whether or not this apparent design is just the projected figment of our own internal categories of perception.

This objection is at once both immensely valuable, and yet largely superfluous, to the cause of the natural theologian. It is valuable insofar as it encourages us to be as accurate as possible in the state of mind that we bring to our perception of reality. A mind that is consciously or unconsciously biased to find a certain meaning in the "empirical" facts of reality will often find it, whether it actually exists or not. Thus, we must continually exercise a great deal of caution not to project a predetermined set of expectations onto the external world. We must, instead, strive to be as objective and unbiased as possible in the conclusions that we draw about the external world.

Kant believed that this "bias of the observer" naturally went far beyond the mere possession of a certain number of conceptual prejudices. He believed that even in the most objective and unbiased cognitive state possible, the mind's intrinsic categories of thought are inevitably projected onto the external world, where they subsequently act to distort the true nature of the objects being perceived.

While it is indeed possible that such a built-in flaw in the human perceiving apparatus could actually exist, there are good reasons for believing that it does *not*, in and of itself, play a significant role in falsely coloring that which the mind perceives in the real world. To begin with, there is a large body of evidence which indicates that we are in fact capable of accurately perceiving the true nature of reality, at least superficially. For instance, we are able to pilot automobiles, boats, airplanes, and even spacecraft around all sorts of real-world obstacles, *but this would only seem to be possible if our perceptions of the real world accurately corresponded with the way things really are "in themselves."* Surgeons are able to successfully conduct microsurgery on tiny parts of the human body, and this too would only seem to be possible in a world where human perception accurately mirrored the true nature of physical reality. Most ominous of all, the theoretical mind of man has been able to cooperate with human engineering to devise horrible weapons of mass destruction that are able to exterminate all life on this planet with the mere touch of a few buttons. This capacity in and of itself shows that humans are in fact capable of perceiving and manipulating the objective nature of the physical world to a very high degree of accuracy.

Of course, this isn't to say that our cognitive perceiving apparatus can't be impaired by drugs, disease, or strong psychological factors. It obviously can. On the whole, though, there seems to be no concrete evidence for assuming that our fundamental capacity for accurately perceiving the real world is intrinsically flawed in any significant way.

Indeed, it is the observed *congruence* of the human perceiving apparatus with the objective nature of physical reality that is *itself* in want of an adequate explanation. After all, how could it possibly be the case that our inner categories of perception are able to correspond so accurately to the external nature of the physical world? The phenomenon of natural selection does not seem to be entirely capable of explaining this phenomenon, for while the process of selection may have eliminated all but the most accurate forms of these cognitive categories, we must then ask where the cognitive categories *themselves* originally came from.

There seems to be no way of escaping the conclusion that these categories are an *a priori* feature of our intrinsic cognitive setup. Although this inner setup itself has apparently risen out of a long process of evolutionary unfolding, this does not do away with the need to explain how such a complicated set of categories could have originally arisen "on its own."

In other words, the very capacity of the human mind to accurately perceive the external world does not appear to be explicable in the absence of an Intelligent Designer, regardless of the particular mode of creation that has produced it. In the end, we can only fall back on our faith in the intelligibility and appropriateness of our inherited cognitive setup, otherwise even the very process of logical thought itself loses its validity. It would seem, however, that the only way we can trust such a blind cognitive inheritance is if it originates in the Mind of God Himself. Therefore, it stands to reason that our relatively accurate categories of thought and perception probably originated with an Intelligent Creator.

Far from showing us the inherent limitations of the human mind, then, Kant has given us one more reason to believe in an Intelligent Designer, since there seems to be no other plausible way to account for the existence of so many accurate perceptual categories otherwise.

11.5   Is Theistic Belief Falsifiable?

In making a concrete set of assertions about the nature of the world *vis-à-vis* the existence of a Divine Creator Being, the natural theologian is attempting to paint an accurate picture of cosmic reality. Yet, as Flew has aptly pointed out, unless an assertion is falsifiable, it cannot claim to be a genuine assertion at all, for if it is not falsifiable, there is nothing it can be said to deny, and " . . . if there is nothing which a putative assertion denies then there is nothing which it asserts either: and so it is not really an assertion."[25]

The problem as far as the natural theologian is concerned is that the theistic world view seems to many people to be unfalsifiable in principle. That is to say, nothing concrete can usually be pointed out that would falsify the belief if it were to ever occur. This insulation of most forms of religious belief against falsification stands over against the apparent requirement that a religious belief must, at least in principle, be falsifiable before it can be considered to be a genuine assertion. Flew has reduced this requirement for falsification to a single question:

> What would have to occur or to have occurred to constitute . . . a disproof of the love of, or of the existence of, God?[26]

The natural theologian is in an excellent position to defend himself against this sort of high-level attack, because his underlying assertions contain within themselves the conditions for their own potential falsification. Since the natural theologian claims that the life-supporting order of the universe is only intelligible in terms of a Divine Power, his condition for the falsifiablity of his faith is actually quite simple: it would entail the sudden collapse of the present universal order into a formless, mindless chaos. Of course, if such a thing were to ever occur, no human consciousness would be capable of surviving to observe the fact. Hence, the very continuance of the world in its present biocentric character, and of the human capacity for perceiving this order within the mind, is taken by the natural theologian to be powerful evidence *for* the existence of an Intelligent Designer, which could nevertheless be falsified in principle.

A milder version of this condition for falsification would entail a partial collapse of the present universal order, one which would be severe enough to indicate the lack of an Intelligent Creator, and yet not be severe enough to immediately eliminate the existence of human consciousness. For example, the Earth's orbit about the Sun could slowly begin to lose its stability and integrity, so that scientists would then be able to predict a day in the near future when the Earth would finally plunge directly into the Sun's thermonuclear inferno.

The prospect of a universal Heat Death in the distant future, however, does *not* constitute a similar degree of falsification for the theistic hypothesis, because the natural theologian believes that the present functionality of our planet as a suitable home for developing human beings will be finished long before the Sun, or the entire universe itself, begins to die. If nothing else, we humans will in all likelihood see to it that our world will be uninhabitable long before the Heat Death ever occurs. (At the rate we are presently going, we'll be lucky to make it into the 21st century!)

Eschatologically, the natural theologian's belief in God's goodness would also be falsified if the afterlife turned out to be either non-existent, or full of everlasting torture that is unrelated to any type of positive purpose.

In the present earthly sphere, however, the all-encompassing nature of religious faith allows the believer to accept the existence of *all* types of events without having them necessarily count against the existence of a Divine Creator. This relative freedom from falsification doesn't count against the coherence of the natural theologian's claims, however; it counts *for* the all-encompassing nature of his faith. It is one thing for one's *faith* in the ultimate goodness of all things to be free from falsification, but it is quite another to say that one's empirically based *world view* is also free from falsification. It is thus the natural theologian's faith, and *not* his empirically based world view, that is free from falsification.

However, the natural theologian's faith in God is only free from falsification at this early point in the human developmental process. If we happen to survive beyond physical death, it is possible for this faith to be falsified by an evil, torturous afterlife that is unrelated to any positive purpose. Given the presumed goodness of God and of universal existence in general, this is unlikely indeed, because if we are fortunate enough to survive into the afterlife, the afterlife itself will probably turn out to be good in the long run. In all likelihood, then, the most probable condition for the falsifiability of the natural theologian's faith is *eternal non-existence* following death, which, ironically enough, will forever escape our perception and understanding if it ever really happens, because the very basis of this condition is our *own* annihilation.

11.6   The Positive Function of the Natural Atheologian's Criticisms

Although the persuasive arguments of the natural atheologian may end up partially hindering belief in an Intelligent Designer, on a larger level they serve the positive function of helping to maintain a certain degree of "epistemic distance" between humans and their Creator. For by rendering a certain degree of ambiguity to the natural evidence for or against God, these anti-theistic arguments help to preserve a degree of human freedom over against the existence of a Supreme Being. As John Hick has pointed out, if the existence of God were clearly evident to everyone, we would be *forced* into belief:

It is argued by some religious writers that a logical demonstration of the existence of God would be a form of coercion and would as such be incompatible with God's evident intention to treat his human creatures as free and responsible persons . . . For if God were to disclose himself to us in the coercive manner in which our physical environment obtrudes itself we should be dwarfed to nothingness by the infinite power thus irresistibly breaking open the privacy of our souls . . . Such a direct, unmediated confrontation breaking in upon us and shattering the frail autonomy of our finite nature would leave no ground for a free human response of trust, self-commitment and obedience . . . The basic principle invoked here is that for the sake of creating a personal relationship of love and trust with his human creatures God does not force an awareness of himself upon them. And (according to the view which we are considering) it is only a further application of the same principle to add that a logically compelling demonstration of God's existence would likewise frustrate this purpose. For men—or at least those of them who are capable of following the proof—could then be forced to know that God is real. Thus Alasdair MacIntyre, when a Christian apologist, wrote: For if we could produce logically cogent arguments we should produce the kind of certitude that leaves no room for decision; where proof is in place, decision is not. We do not decide to accept Euclid's conclusions; we merely look to the rigour of his arguments. If the existence of God were demonstrable we should be as bereft of the possibility of making a free decision to love God as we should be if every utterance of doubt or unbelief was answered by thunderbolts from heaven.[27]

In other words, the natural world has just enough ambiguity in it to allow individuals the freedom of believing or not believing in a personal Creator. While the cards seem to be stacked heavily in favor of Intelligent Design, such an observation is typically apparent only to those who have *already* committed themselves to a prior belief in God (because they tend to be the only ones who actually give the Design Argument serious consideration). It is in this manner that the freedom of humanity is preserved in a world that is nevertheless overflowing with evidence for Intelligent Design.

Notes

1. P.C.W. Davies, *God and the New Physics* (New York: Simon & Schuster, 1983), p. ix.
2. C. S. Lewis, *Letters to Malcolm,* ch. 15.
3. The movie "2010" was based on a similar plot. In that film, an extraterrestrial intelligence used the transformation of the planet Jupiter into a blazing star to tell the human race to abandon its self-destructive ways before it was too late.
4. Of course, this intelligent power doesn't necessarily have to be God. It *does*, however, have to be a type of power that is sufficient for the proposed task. In the above case, it would be reasonable to suppose that an extraterrestrial creature not unlike ourselves was probably responsible for contriving the boulder formation. It is only when we move to the structure of universe itself, and to the enormously complex life forms it has produced, that the positing of a Supreme Being becomes necessary, because such a Being is by hypothesis the only one who could have contrived the universe in this manner.
5. Still more evidence for the Intelligent Origin of the genetic code can be found in the fascinating realm of *genetic music*. Remarkably, it has been shown that when the four basic nucleotides of the DNA molecule are assigned musical equivalents in a major scale, a musical interpretation of the nucleotide sequences of various cell types turns out to be remarkably coherent, and even appropriate to the particular cell type being analyzed. For instance, the "genetic music" displayed by a cancer cell turns out to be surprisingly analogous to a humanly-contrived funeral march! It is hard to see how this could have ever be the case in the absence of a Deliberate Intelligent Contrivance. (The name of the computer program used in this example is "DNA Music," published by Silver Software, 1922 Purchase Brook Road, Southbury, CT.)
6. See F. David Peat's *The Philosopher's Stone* (New York: Bantam Books, 1991), 160–203.
7. William James, *The Varieties of Religious Experience* (New York: Longman, Green, & Co., 1902).
8. Ibid.
9. John B. Cobb, Jr., *Living Options in Protestant Theology* (Philadelphia: The Westminster Press, 1962), pp. 34–35.
10. Barrow and Tipler, *The Anthropic Cosmological Principle*, pp. 302–305.
11. See my forthcoming book *Back to Darwin* for a complete discussion of this important issue.
12. Figure quoted in a letter from Ernst Mayr to FJT dated Dec. 23, 1982.
13. David Hume, *Dialogues Concerning Natural Religion* (London: Penguin, 1990).

14. Ibid., p. 54.
15. Ibid, p. 78.
16. See Michael Denton's *Evolution: A Theory in Crisis* (Bethesda, MD: Adler & Adler, 1986), pp. 339–340.
17. Ibid., pp. 340–341.
18. See my book *Back to Darwin* for a detailed explanation of why chance is incapable of producing the miracle of biological life, even when the phenomenon of cumulative selection is taken into account.
19. Hume, *Dialogues Concerning Natural Religion,* pp. 92–94.
20. Taken from "A Debate on the Argument from Contingency," Father F.C. Copleston and Bertrand Russell, in Louis P. Pojman's *Philosophy of Religion: An Anthology* (Belmont, CA: Wadsworth Publishing Company, 1987), p. 9.
21. Hume, *Dialogues Concerning Natural Religion,* p. 56.
22. Ibid. p. 100.
23. Barrow and Tipler, *The Anthropic Cosmological Principle,* p. 71.
24. David Hume, *Dialogues Concerning Natural Religion,* p. 79.
25. Antony Flew, R.M. Hare, and Basil Mitchell, "Theology and Falsification," *New Essays in Philosophical Theology,* Antony Flew and Alasdair MacIntyre, eds. (London: SCM Press, 1955), pp. 96–108.
26. Ibid.
27. John Hick, "Arguments for The Existence of God" (London and Basingstoke: Macmillan, 1971), in Louis P. Pojman's *Philosophy of Religion: An Anthology* (Belmont, CA: Wadsworth Publishing Company, 1987), pp. 445–446.

CHAPTER 12

Conclusion

Science and religion are very much alike. Both are imaginative and creative aspects of the human mind. The appearance of conflict is a result of ignorance. We come to exist through a divine act. That divine guidance is a theme throughout our life; at our death the brain goes, but that divine guidance and love continues. Each of us is a unique, conscious being, a divine creation. It is the religious view. *It is the only view consistent with all the evidence* (italics mine).[1]

SIR JOHN ECCLES
NOBEL LAUREATE

The fool has said in his heart, "There is no God."

PSALM 14:1

It is commonly believed that the findings of modern science have somehow discredited the objective need for a Divine Creator. The purpose of this book has been to show that, to the contrary, the theistic hypothesis has been *greatly strengthened* by these findings, to the point of being almost irresistable.

The Anthropic Cosmological Principle has been instrumental in providing this empirical support, as it shows almost beyond question that there must be something going on "behind the scenes" in our universe to make life possible. As the reader will recall, astrophysicist Brandon Carter originally devised the Anthropic Principle in order to provide a limit to the Copernican dogma, which states that there is nothing special about our position in the universe. As Carter showed, our position in the universe is *necessarily* privileged to the extent that it *must* be compatible with our existence as observers.

At first, such a statement appears painfully obvious; *of course* our position in the cosmos is privileged in this life-supporting sense, otherwise we wouldn't be here to wonder about it. On a deeper level, though, this biocentric statement turns out to be the most important and momentous observation *ever put forth* by the scientific community, for the following reason: modern cosmology has conclusively shown that this biocentrically privileged state of affairs is *not* a local, isolated phenomenon, i.e., it is not limited to our relatively small region of the universe only. To the contrary, this privileged state of affairs extends to the farthest reaches of the entire universe, since it not only began with the Big Bang itself, it also derived its unique life-supporting features from the specific initial conditions that were in existence at that time. As cosmologists are learning more and more, had any of these initial conditions been different, our present biocentric universe would probably never have formed. It therefore follows that we owe our existence to the specific nature of these initial conditions. It also follows that the entire universe must possess this same biocentric "flavor" as well, since it emanated from the same initial conditions.

In a very real sense, then, we really *are* at the "center" of the universe after all, at least insofar as the entire universe possesses the same life-supporting constants and other structural parameters that have enabled us to evolve on this planet. This, however, is where the explanatory power of the Anthropic Cosmological Principle ends. Although it is able to tell us that the entire universe is the way it is "because" life is here, it cannot tell us *why* this is so. It remains for the discerning individual to draw his or her own conclusions about this remarkable observation.

12.1 Faith and the Modern Scientist

Astrophysicist John Barrow is one scientist who is aware of the over-whelmingly mystical nature of modern science. In his *World Within the World,* he concludes that, given the utterly mysterious nature of the universe in which we live, science may very well have to ultimately give way to faith:

> The fundamental problems at the frontiers of modern cosmology and parti-cle physics are of a unique type. They are not like the problems of labora-tory physics. They are not problems which always respect the traditional dogmas about the philosophy and practice of science. They are extraordi-nary problems, and they possess extraordinary solutions which it will re-quire extraordinary methods to coax from the Universe. If our methods ultimately fail, then any boundary between fundamental science and meta-physical theology will become increasingly difficult to draw. Sight must give way to faith. Confronted with an emotionally satisfying mathematical scheme which is "simple" enough to command universal assent, but eso-teric enough to admit no means of experimental test and grandiose enough to provoke no new questions then, closeted within our world within the world, we might simply have to believe it. Whereof we cannot speak thereof we must be silent; this is the final sentence of the laws of Nature.[2]

12.2 Apologetics and the Role of Faith

It is often said by many well-meaning theistic believers that seeking after empirical evidence for the existence of God is inherently *contrary* to the goal of religious faith for each individual. In this particular instance faith is taken to mean blind adherence to a series of religious beliefs for which there may be no rational justification.

In some ways this is an admirable goal: we should all trust in the goodness of existence no matter what may happen in our lives. In other ways, however, it presents a serious impediment to the all-important process of psychospiritual growth. For if we are content to simply "believe" in God without any critical examination of our beliefs, we may quickly become complacent in our inner spiritual lives, and complacency typically leads to psychospiritual stagnation. Surely God does not want us to stagnate in our quest for sanctification (i.e., self-actualization), nor does He want us to follow Him like blind sheep. If He exists at all, He almost certainly wants us to discover the Truth of Reality on our own, through the self-initiated process of critical thinking about our lives.

In this sense God might actually *prefer* the critical-thinking agnostic, who eventually comes to Him through a hard-won battle of conflicting beliefs, to the mindlessly subservient "believer" who hasn't even bothered to examine his or her belief structure. This is because the process of thinking for oneself is intimately related to the process of psychospiritual growth, and since God clearly wants us to grow as mature and responsible as we possibly can in our lives, He naturally wants us to do whatever we can to further this goal, including learning how to think for ourselves. Thinking for oneself, however, is more often the province of the atheist or agnostic than it is for the blind believer. Hence, it might be better in God's Eyes to temporarily be an atheist or an agnostic than a blind believer, because of the tremendous importance of thinking for oneself in the genesis of the mature personality. C.S. Lewis, for instance, went through a severe atheistic stage before he converted to Christianity, and he turned out to be one of the greatest believers in all of history. As always, the goal is to become an informed, willing believer, who freely chooses to believe because it is the most sensible thing that one can possibly do in one's life.

Had blind belief alone been sufficient in God's Eyes, He might just as well have created us as perpetually loyal automata, who would have mindlessly followed Him no matter what. Fortunately for us, however, blind belief alone was apparently not one of God's creative goals when He decided to make the world. To the contrary, God wants us to come to Him by our own free choice, but this first requires that we be able to think sufficiently for ourselves. Perhaps this is one reason why the straying of the sinner is so precious to God: because it is in this very process of straying that one tends to develop the priceless capacity of thinking for oneself.

This is the central meaning behind the Parable of the Lost Sheep: the shepherd leaves his herd to search for the one sheep that has become lost, and he searches and searches for it until he finds it, and having found it, he loves it more than all the other sheep who have not gone astray. For in the process of getting lost the sheep has become more mature, and hence more valuable to the shepherd. This is undoubtedly why Jesus tells us that there is more joy in heaven over the one sinner who repents than over a hundred "good" people who never repent: because it is the repenting sinner alone who has developed the precious capacity to think for himself.

This ability to think for oneself is also a prized commodity in God's Eyes because it acts as a motivational springboard for the attainment of the most important thing in all of human life: psychospiritual maturity. Since we apparently will not be considered worthy enough to enter the kingdom of heaven until our personalities are judged to be sufficiently responsible and mature (it wouldn't *be* heaven if irresponsible and immature people were allowed in), our primary goal in life must be to become as mature and responsible as we possibly can. And since the ability to think for oneself is one of the chief personal qualities that is capable of bringing us to an eventual state of psychospiritual maturity and responsibility, it follows that God probably wants us to develop this all-important capacity in any way we can. After all, this capacity to think for oneself is what separates us from the rest of the animal kingdom, and is therefore what makes us uniquely human. Had God wanted sheep He never would have created humanity!

12.2.1 The Origin of Our Modern Concept of Faith

The modern definition of faith in the Church took hold when the Roman Catholic Church sought to extend its power and authority over the entire western world.[3] In order to facilitate the attainment of this ambitious goal, the Catholic Church had to find a way to encourage blind subservience to their clergy. They found precisely the tool they were looking for in the doctrine that "knowledge proceeds from rational conviction" and that "faith precedes knowledge."[4] Since faith precedes knowledge, and since knowledge is required for religious conviction, faith was concluded to be needed for conviction, and faith was dispensed solely by the clergy.

According to Hugh Ross, this Church-inspired definition of faith completely contradicts the Biblical definition, which states that " . . . faith is founded on fact and on what God has clearly done."[5] Ross cites a number of Biblical verses in support of this assertion, including Isa. 41:20, 43:9–10, 50:10, Heb. 11:1, Ex. 4:5, 19:9, and John 11:15, 11:42, 13:19, 14:29, 19:35, and 20:31.

This conceptualization of faith makes perfect sense, because it is the rational mind that typically decides where its faith is to be placed. Only a fool places his faith in something of which he has no reliable knowledge, and God clearly doesn't want us to be fools. No one steps into an elevator or airplane unless he or she has reasonable evidence of its safety (unless suicide is the goal). Similarly, no one should place their faith in *any* type of being or organization unless he or she has reasonable evidence of its importance and validity, and this should include God as much as it should anyone or anything else. Not that we need to know *everything* about God's existence, though, in order to make a reasonable choice. We simply need to have a sufficient reason for placing our faith in a Being we cannot see.

For many people, the urgings of society, as represented by parental indoctrination and by the Church, are more than enough reason to place one's faith in God. Others, however, realize that society has been wrong too many times in the past to ever justify a blind subservience to *any* of its teachings, including those which bear the mark of religion. These individuals require a rational depiction of the "human condition" in some comprehensible format before they will consent to placing their faith in an invisible Being. This is the role of religious apologetics: to establish a body of rational evidence for belief in God, so that truth-seeking individuals won't have to make their all-important religious decisions blindly.

Indeed, this was one of the main reasons why I decided to write this book: to let the reader in on what has been the most remarkable discovery of my life, namely, that the world is literally *overflowing* with powerful evidence for the existence of God, so much so in fact that the truth-seeking individual need never complain about the lack of empirical information concerning the existence of a Supreme Being. As St. Paul has so elegantly put it:

> The wrath of God is being revealed from heaven against all the godlessness and wickedness of men who suppress the truth by their wickedness, since what may be known about God is plain to them, because God has make it plain to them. For since the creation of the world God's invisible qualities—His eternal power and divine nature—have been clearly seen, being understood from what has been made, so that men are without excuse (Rom. 1:18–20, NIV).

Now, if God's invisible qualities are truly visible through the things He has made, there is no excuse at all for blind belief as far as the existence of God is concerned. Since God's invisible qualities are clearly seen throughout His creation, the only excuse for blind belief is laziness, not any presumed ambiguousness on the part of the physical evidence itself. Those who believe blindly simply have not taken the time, nor have they made the effort, to consider the rationality of their beliefs *vis-à-vis* the nature of the world at large.

Notes

1. Sir John Eccles, "Modern Biology and the Turn to Belief in God," *The Intellectuals Speak Out About God,* Roy Abraham Varghese, ed. (Chicago: Regnery Gateway, 1984), p. 50.

2. Barrow, *The World Within the World*, p. 373.

3. Hugh Ross, *The Fingerprint of God*, p. 14.

4. Ibid.

5. Ibid.

Epilogue

A Call for a New Type of Scientifically Minded Universal Theorist

The time is ripe for the ascent of a new kind of universal theorist: one who attempts to view the cosmos from the Creator's point of view instead of merely the creature's; that is, one who attempts to raise himself up to the level of the universe he is trying to understand instead of lowering the universe down to his own level.

Such a universal theorist must be theistically minded by his very nature, because a universe created by a Divine Creator can only be properly understood when the Creator Himself is the overall point of focus and reference. Scientists may be able to accurately deduce the physical nature of the cosmos, but as long as they insist on leaving the Author of their studies out of consideration, they will *never* be able to reach a complete and unified view of the true nature of cosmic reality.

Contrary to popular scientific belief, though, such a God-centered theorist isn't "unscientific" at all—he actually represents a return to the original foundation of modern science: an unshakable belief in a Rational Creator God. Although it may be impossible to directly study God in the laboratory (because God is inherently unmeasurable), scientists can still utilize the concept of a Divine Creator Being in their personal attempts to make sense out of the cosmos.

Indeed, it was this basic theistic orientation which originally gave rise to modern science in the first place, since it was their overwhelming belief in a logical Creator which led many of the founding fathers of the modern scientific movement to a belief in a logical creation which could thus be understood by rational-thinking men. Sadly, modern atheistic scientists have departed from the original theistic roots of their profession, with the result that their theoretical strivings have been leading them in circles to a mass of apparent contradictions. These contradictions will by hypothesis never be fully resolved until a theoretical return is made to the Author and Creator of natural science.

One thing appears certain: if a Divine Creator God does in fact exist, modern atheistic scientists are making a tremendous *faux pas* by ignoring Him. For while the reality of God cannot be experimentally measured and verified in the laboratory, one can still posit His Existence and Creatorship in one's theoretical quest for a better overall understanding of reality. And as we have seen throughout this book, there is more than enough circumstantial evidence in the natural realm to compel one to begin thinking in this theistic-type manner.

In Defense of the Big Bang: A Theistic Response to Eric J. Lerner's Infinitely Old Plasma Universe

It has been said that the highest praise of God consists in the denial of Him by the atheist, who finds creation so perfect that he can dispense with a creator.

MARCEL PROUST

Introduction

As we have seen, the Big Bang theory of universal origins has reigned supreme in the field of cosmology for the last several decades. While other attempts have been made to explain the presently observed universal configuration, such as Hoyle's Steady State theory or Eddington's Hesitation theory, none have been nearly as successful in accounting for the existing evidence as the Big Bang.

In recent years, however, a new challenge to the Big Bang has emerged from within the ranks of plasma physics. Initiated several decades ago by Nobel laureate Hannes Alfven, this new theory has recently been set forth in a book written by plasma physicist Eric J. Lerner, entitled *The Big Bang Never Happened: A Startling Refutation of the Dominant Theory of the Origin of the Universe.*

Critique of the Plasma Universe Model

Lerner's basic premise is that the modern Big Bang theory is unable to account for many of the macroscopic structures in our universe, such as galaxy clusters and superclusters. Due to their enormous size and spatial configuration (some may be as large as 7 billion light years across), these structures appear to be much older than the 15 to 20 billion year time limit set by the Big Bang. Therefore, according to the plasma physicists, the Big Bang *cannot* be an accurate explanation of how the universe actually began.[1]

In contradistinction to the Big Bang model stands the infinitely old plasma universe, which achieves its present configuration because of the unique electrodynamics of plasma physics. A plasma, of course, is any electrically charged field extending across space and time. According to the plasma theorists, plasmas extend throughout the entire universe, and through the electromagnetic forces they naturally generate, they can explain virtually every aspect of the present universal structure.

For instance, it is known that magnetic fields and currents can concentrate matter far more quickly and efficiently than gravity alone can.[2] Furthermore, it has been demonstrated in the laboratory that plasmas can generate the same general shapes possessed by galaxies and galaxy clusters.[3] Consequently, since the age of galaxy superclusters appears to be greater than the 20-billion-year time limit set by the Big Bang, and since electromagnetic plasma forces are known to be capable of creating these same basic shapes, plasma theorists believe that the present physical universe was formed by electromagnetic plasma forces over a much greater time frame than that allowed by the Big Bang.

There is a problem with the above assumption, however. Plasma theorists assume that the universe must be greater than 20 billion years of age because there doesn't appear to be any way that such unspeakably huge galaxy superclusters could have formed in a "mere" 20 billion years or so.

This assumption is predicated on two deeper assumptions: 1) that there are no natural forces capable of forming galaxy superclusters in 20 billion years or less, and 2) that the universe arose in an *entirely* naturalistic manner, i.e., with no preconceived form of Intelligent Design. Within these two extreme limitations, the plasma theorists just may be correct: it may very well be impossible for gigantic galaxy superclusters to form in such a radically short period of time.

However, it doesn't follow from this conclusion that the universe *actually did* originate in such an entirely naturalistic manner some 100 + billion years ago. The only proper conclusion is that the universe must be older than 20 billion years in the absence of physical processes that could have given it its present configuration in 20 billion years or less. And since we clearly aren't aware of all the natural processes that were operative in the formation of our universe long ago, Lerner's conclusion that the Big Bang never happened does *not* necessarily follow from the observational evidence.

Indeed, as we saw in Chapter 4, the discovery of Big Bang ripples by George Smoot's team at UC Berkeley conclusively demonstrates that natural processes are indeed capable of explaining the existence of vast galaxy superclusters *within* the realm of the known laws of physics and *within* the 20-billion-year time limit set by the Big Bang. Although the details behind this formative process have not yet been fully worked out, cosmologists are well on their way towards doing so.

For our purposes here, though, the important thing to understand is that it is quite possible to conceive of plausible mechanisms that are capable of producing the observed cosmic structure from *within* the theoretical framework of the Big Bang. This being the case, there is no good reason to abandon the Big Bang in favor of a much less well-established theory, especially when we consider the massive amount of experimental support that has been marshalled in favor the Big Bang over the years.

But even if, for the sake of argument, we assume that no natural physical processes are capable of producing the present universal structure in less than 20 billion years, it *still* doesn't necessarily follow that the Big Bang model is invalid. The only thing we can properly conclude from such a scenario is that an entirely naturalistic (i.e., non-theistic) Big Bang model is invalid. But this clearly leaves the door open for a Supernatural Designer, who could have deliberately manipulated the known laws of physics in the specified time frame of the Big Bang to externally produce all manner of large-scale structure in the universe.

In other words, the scientifically oriented theist believes that the faculty of Intelligent Design can—through entirely natural cause-and-effect processes—compensate for the apparent shortcomings of the Big Bang model without any violation of natural law. In a randomly generated atheistic universe, on the other hand, there are definite limitations as to what kind of macroscopic objects we can expect to form in such a relatively short period of time.

If, however, the universe is in fact Intelligently Designed (which the vast body of "anthropic" literature seems to indicate that it is), then the entire formula for the age of the universe automatically changes, not because a supernatural Creator would have bypassed certain natural processes through Divine Fiat, but because the Creator would have undoubtedly had at His disposal a wide range of natural processes that could have easily produced the present universal configuration in less than 20 billion years, *assuming, of course, His Intelligent Input at the very beginning.*

Indeed, an omniscient and omnipotent Creator could, utilizing only the naturalistic properties of the physical universe itself, propel it into being "from nothing" in such a way that He could have easily imparted to it any macroscopic design He wanted, even to the point of causing certain physical events such as earthquakes billions of years later. All it conceivably would have taken is a certain meticulously planned twist of God's Creative Hand, so to speak, at the very beginning to produce the desired result, in much the same way that a twist applied to a ping-pong ball (otherwise known as "english") will naturally cause it to behave in a manner that never would have been expected otherwise.

The crucial causative factor in this hypothetical scenario that has been ignored by Lerner is thus the initial creative input of God Himself. The notion of Intelligent Design can more than make up for the perceived inability of the physical universe to adopt certain highly "anomalous" structural configurations naturalistically, since it can cause the physical constitutents of the universe to be assembed in a manner that would be strictly impossible without it. *Most importantly, this kind of Divine Contribution to the structure of the heavens could have taken place without a single violation of natural law.*

A fitting analogy can be drawn to the work of a sculptor. Such an individual can, utilizing only the natural characteristics of his creative medium and his own creative input, produce a sculpted figure that would have been strictly impossible otherwise. This deliberate creative input can cause certain "natural" configurations of matter to form in far less time than would have been possible without it, and all without a single violation of natural law. The same thing can be said of the physical universe as a whole: with God's Creative Input, the universe would have been able to attain a certain highly organized filamentous structure in *far* less time than would have been possible without it, and all without a single violation of natural law.

In order to see how the creative activity of an Intelligent Designer could account for the existence of the present universe without any violation of natural law, we must carefully distinguish between two distinct stages of the intelligently directed creative process: 1) the cerebral, conceptual stage, in which a definite creative plan is opted for and duly implemented, and 2) the physical implementation stage, in which natural cause-and-effect processes are deliberately called into play to bring about the desired effect.

Clearly an *ex post facto* analysis of such an intelligently contrived object would reveal no violation of natural law *per se*, since only cause-and-effect processes would have been used during the actual creative process. It is only the *intelligent arrangement* of these natural processes that would have transcended the intrinsic limitations of natural law, but this transcendance still wouldn't amount to any genuine *violation* of the law of cause-and-effect, since no natural laws would actually be broken. At most it would only amount to an intelligent *supplanting* of natural law, insofar as the faculty of intelligent design is capable of guiding natural processes to act in a way that would have been impossible without it. And natural processes that are guided into unique creative territory by the faculty of intelligent design aren't "violated" in any sense of the word; they are simply directed in such a way that they are allowed to show their full creative potential.

Going one step further, we must also distinguish between two types of order in the universe: 1) natural (i.e., uncontrived) order, which occurs largely in response to the laws of physics and chemistry, and contrived order, which occurs in response to the direction of Intelligent Design.

Of course, there is a significant degree of overlap between these two types of order, insofar as the laws of physics and chemistry themselves have been intelligently contrived. This initial contrivance—which seems to have been laid down in toto at the Big Bang—is more than sufficient to account for many (if not most) of the complex forms of order we see in the world around us.

The faculty of Intelligent Design can, however, supplement itself, in a sense, by consciously directing the contrived laws of physics to act upon matter in a manner that would have been strictly impossible without this additional level of contrivance. It is this further level of contrivance which the scientific theist believes is responsible for creating the great galaxy superclusters in the 15 to 20 billion year time limit set by the Big Bang.

Significantly, though, this additional input of Intelligent Design in no way violates any physical or chemical laws *per se*. To the contrary, it *utilizes* these fundamental laws in a very contrived, preplanned way to accomplish its creative ends. That is to say, it uses its capacity for Intelligent Contrivance to squeeze more creativity out of atoms and molecules than would have ever been possible without it. In this sense the faculty of Intelligent Design is like a creative "turbocharger" for the law of cause-and-effect, in that it can vastly increase the level of complexity that can be produced by this causal law.

In other words, there is a definite ontological chasm that naturally separates highly contrived instances of order from their uncontrived (i.e., randomly produced) counterparts. It is this ontological chasm that is "violated" or transcended whenever the faculty of Intelligent Design is operative in the universe. In terms of the sculptor analogy mentioned previously, the natural processes of the world can only do so much when it comes to the naturalistic production of a human statue in a limited amount of time. Intelligent human contrivance, on the other hand, can accomplish a great deal more in the same time frame, and all without a single violation of natural law.

In a similar fashion, it may very well be impossible for vast galaxy superclusters to have formed in a mere 20 billion years in the absence of some form of Intelligent Design. It doesn't follow from this statement, however, that these galaxy superclusters *actually did* take longer than 20 billion years to form, since there is always the possibility that a Divine Intelligence *really was* operative in the distant cosmological past.

The prospect of Intelligent Design, then, turns out to be the crucial theoretical element upon which our entire interpretation of cosmology naturally hinges. Accordingly, we cannot expect to reach accurate scientific conclusions about the history of the universe without first coming to some sort of conclusion about whether or not the universe was in fact intelligently designed. Unfortunately, we cannot rely on the physical evidence alone to guide us to the right conclusion, because there are usually several different ways to interpret the same data, depending on which theoretical model one chooses to adopt.

It would seem, then, that the best way to interpret the existing cosmological evidence is to *first* use it to reach the best possible conclusion about whether or not the universe was intelligently designed. Once this determination has been made to the best of one's ability, one can *then* use the resulting theoretical model to help one interpret the actual history of the universe.

Alternatively, one could attempt to develop two separate interpretations of the cosmological data—one utilizing the prospect of Intelligent Design and one omitting it—so that one could then compare and contrast the two conclusions that are subsequently reached. The conclusion that would best fit the physical evidence and seems the most plausible overall would then be one's first choice.

The obvious problem with this theoretical approach is that many people simply are not willing to carry out two separate interpretations of the cosmological data. Most physical scientists tend to shy away from even the mention of a Divine Creator, while most scientific theists tend to be so convinced of the validity of their world view that they aren't usually willing to consider the plausibility of the non-theistic alternative.

However, the problem of galaxy supercluster formation almost forces us into making some type of decision regarding the prospect of Intelligent Design in the universe. If we want to retain the standard Big Bang model, for instance, we almost *have* to affirm the existence of some form of Intelligent Design in the universe, because there seems to be no other way (apart from texture theory) to account for the formation of these huge supercluster formations in the relatively short amount of time stipulated by the Big Bang.

It is important to note, however, that the Intelligent Designer spoken of here isn't the much beleaguered "God-of-the-gaps" brand of Creator who has been repeatedly appealed to in times past to explain certain natural events that were otherwise inexplicable. The rapid increase in our scientific understanding has throroughly discredited this entirely supernatural, non-naturalistic concept of the Creator, since many of the physical effects that were initially attributed to God have since been "fully explained" in an entirely naturalistic manner.

There is a subtle fallacy, however, which is at work in this kind of God-of-the-gaps reasoning. It is the assumption that either God would have created the universe instantaneously through miraculous Fiat, or else the universe would have evolved in an entirely naturalistic manner with no Divine Input whatsoever. Within such a two-dimensional world view, it is clearly inappropriate to invoke God as a supernatural explanation for certain inexplicable phenomena, because modern science is almost always able to come up with a naturalistic explanation for them eventually. Conversely speaking, however, such a naturalistic explanation does not necessarily refute the reality of God as Creator, because the possibility always remains that God could have created the universe in an entirely naturalistic manner.

There is thus a tantalizing third alternative to the question of universal origins that has been neglected by almost all cosmological theoristics up until now, even the most theistically inclined ones. It is precisely this: that a Supernatural God could have produced the present universe through a subtle mixing of natural cause-and-effect processes with the Intelligent Foresight of Deliberate Design. This third alternative—which we have called *Supernatural Naturalism*—can account for all of the problems that are generated by a world view that is either exclusively naturalistic or exclusively supernatural.[4]

The term "God-of-the-gaps," however, *cannot* be used to describe this type of naturalistic Creator, because such a naturalistically oriented Being is not using miraculous Fiat to bypass physical cause-and-effect processes. Rather, He is using His capacity for Intelligent Design to direct a series of cause-and-effect processes to the *naturalistic* attainment of a certain desired end. Some of these natural processes, of course, are bound to be beyond our scientific comprehension at the present time, but this doesn't prevent God from using them, nor does it prevent them from being entirely naturalistic in origin.

Such a naturalistic view of the creation, however, doesn't necessarily mean that we have to posit the existence of additional physical processes or forces at work in the universe other than the ones we already know, since it is very much a possibility that a naturalistic Creator could have utilized His Intelligent Direction to guide these known processes to produce the present universe in far less time than would have been possible without His Intelligent Input. Moreover, all this could have happened without a single violation of natural law, since it is the faculty of Intelligent Design that can make up the crucial time difference between how natural processes behave "on their own" and how they actually behave in the Hands of an Able Designer.

It follows, then, that the God of Supernatural Naturalism *can* be invoked to explain certain features of the universe that are presently inexplicable, but this doesn't mean that such an "explanation" will instantly become discredited whenever an adequate physical explanation is eventually found (which it no doubt will). This is because the very notion of Supernatural Naturalism is predicated upon the *exclusive use* of such natural processes in the creation. The God of Supernatural Naturalism can thus be invoked to "explain" certain inexplicable realities of today with the full expectation that He used only natural processes to produce them, and that we will one day discover what these natural processes actual consist of.

It is quite possible, then, that the faculty of Intelligent Design could turn out to be the much-sought-after "missing link" to the present Big Bang conceptualization of universal origins. With it, the Big Bang model can, with relatively few revisions, accurately describe our physical universe in most of its structural details. Without it, *all* non-theistic cosmological theories seem to come up short in the end.

Getting back to the non-theistic plasma universe model, we are told in Lerner's book that science should only seek to describe the universe as it is actually observed, not tell us how it *must* be, based only upon a series of abstruse equations that may end up bearing little or no relationship to reality. At the same time, though, he tells us that the recently discovered galaxy superclusters *must* have taken over 100 billion years to form, based on his own calculations. This is a very large step to take, considering the fact that virtually all of the experimental evidence reveals a universe between 10 and 20 billion years of age.[5] Lerner also dogmatically assumes that there is no such thing as a natural process that could have formed the supercluster formations in less than 100 billion years. How could anyone possibly *know* that? We should never assume that our knowledge of science is so complete that we finally think we know all the natural processes that have ever been operative in the cosmos. Doubtless there are many natural processes that we have yet to discover, and there is a good chance that some of these will be able to explain the evolution of galaxy superclusters in the 15-to-20-billion-year time limit set by the Big Bang.

A belief in the notion of Intelligent Design renders the existence of such grandiose natural processes a good deal more plausible, of course, since it assumes that there is such a thing as a Creator who had access to a near-infinite range of natural processes at His disposal. A belief in a randomly generated universe, on the other hand, renders the existence of such large-scale natural processes less plausible, on the whole, since it would seem that these very large-scale processes inherently require a "big enough" Designer to implement them.

As we have seen, though, the standard Big Bang model doesn't absolutely require the discovery of new natural processes in order to be salvaged. It doesn't even require any additional input from an Intelligent Designer, since cosmic textures alone could suffice in this capacity. In lieu of this possibility, however, we can fall back on the activity of an Intelligent Designer to creatively implement *known* cause-and-effect processes in His Design of the present universal structure. And since the activity of a Naturalistic Designer does not violate natural law *per se*, such a God can indeed have been responsible for creating the physical universe in an entirely naturalistic manner.

It would seem, then, that Lerner's chief mistake is his complete neglect of the serious possibility of Intelligent Design in the universe. Although he says that the existence of a Divine Creator is not necessarily precluded[6] by the tenets of the plasma universe, he nevertheless fails to give the idea serious consideration at all. Accordingly, he boldly rejects the Big Bang theory by concluding that the universe *must* be older than 20 billion years, since the various macroscopic structures within it allegedly could never have formed within the relatively small time-frame dictated by the Big Bang.

A similar mistake could also be made regarding the evolution of life on this planet. It is a well-known fact that even the "simplest" living cell is so utterly complex that it would probably have taken trillions and trillions of years to evolve on its own entirely through random natural processes (if indeed such a random evolution is possible at all), *but no one is generalizing from this perceived limitation and arguing that Earth-based life must therefore be trillions and trillions of years old.*[7] There are obviously a great many hidden variables at work both in the evolution of the universe as a whole and in the evolution of life itself, which function to greatly reduce the amount of time needed to produce the present universal configuration (including the existence of life on Earth). These hidden variables, in turn, appear to be the direct product of Intelligent Design, since their strategic use to greatly extend the apparent limitations of physical matter, utilizing only natural cause-and-effect processes, seems to speak directly of some form of Higher Intelligence.

It follows from this postulation that as long as the prospect of Intelligent Design turns out to be true, one cannot possibly expect to ignore this larger Creative Faculty and still hope to be accurate in one's cosmological theorizing. It is thus the concept of Intelligent Design which could turn out to be the all-important factor in determining the relative degree of accuracy displayed by our cosmological theories. This is due to the previously mentioned fact that any valid cosmological theory must make an accurate statement about the prospect of Intelligent Design if it is to be ultimately true in the end. Hence, if there is no such thing as Intelligent Design in the universe, then the only truly accurate theories will be those that leave Intelligent Design out of the overall creative formula. Conversely, if the universe turns out to be Intelligently Designed after all, the only truly accurate theories will be those that take the faculty of Intelligent Design sufficiently into account.

Returning to Lerner's plasma universe once again, plasma theorists also have their own unique interpretation of the microwave background radiation, which has heretofore been assumed to be an ancient relic of the original Big Bang itself. They believe that the energy of this background radiation was released during the production of helium in stars long ago, and that its extreme smoothness was caused by the random scattering of photons by small, magnetically charged plasma filaments which are said to be spread throughout the physical universe. It is alleged that this process has produced the same background radiation that was initially discovered by Bell Laboratory scientists Arno Penzias and Robert Wilson in 1965. According to Lerner, then, "the microwave background is not the echo of the Big Bang—it is the diffuse glow from a fog of plasma filaments, the hum from the cosmic power grid."[8]

It is very difficult, of course, to accurately deduce the cause of many physical effects after the fact, because there are many possible causes that could conceivably and coherently explain them. Such appears to be the case with the cosmic background radiation. While Big Bang theorists seem to have a convincing explanation of their own for this microwave background, it is possible that other causes could either contribute to it or completely explain it. Gamow's amazingly accurate prediction (to within 2 degrees Kelvin) of the temperature of the microwave background based upon a hot Big Bang model some 19 years before its actual discovery would seem to be strong evidence in the Big Bang's favor, but this could nevertheless turn out to be a wild coincidence.

But even if the plasma explanation of the microwave background turned out to be legitimate, it would still not violate the theoretical foundation of a theistic cosmology in the least. The only thing the scientifically oriented theist is unreservedly committed to is the belief that God actually created the universe in one way or another at some point in the past. So, if it turns out that the microwave background has a completely novel explanation that ends up being inconsistent with the standard Big Bang model, then this can nevertheless be perfectly acceptable to the theist, since he or she can simply assert that this new explanation was part of God's overall Creative Plan.

Finally, plasma cosmologists claim that the apparent expansion of the universe is caused by the violent interaction of matter and antimatter at various times and points in the past. This kind of interaction is known to produce tremendous amounts of energy, so they hypothesize that at some point in the distant past enough matter and antimatter came together to cause a tremendous explosion, the results of which we interpret today as the famous Hubble expansion.

There is an obvious problem with this alternative explanation of the Hubble expansion. Unless the entire physical universe (or at least the part that we can observe today) were originally involved in this primordial matter-antimatter explosion, then each individual explosion would have been an entirely local phenomenon, involving different amounts of matter and antimatter, and therefore generating different amounts of explosive force. This of course would have produced a widely varying panorama of expansion velocities; one region of the visible universe would have been expanding at a certain rate, while other regions would have been expanding at a wholly different rate.

In other words, if Alfven and Lerner's matter-antimatter explanation of the Hubble expansion is correct, we would never expect the Hubble expansion to be so isotropic. Yet, this is precisely what is observed to be the case: the entire visible universe is expanding away from us at a constant rate, which is directly proportional to the distance each galaxy exists away from us.

Now, it would appear that the only way to explain this extreme uniformity in the entire visible universe's expansion rate is to assume that it all originated in the *same* primordial explosion, which of course is what Big Bang theorists have been arguing all along. While it may eventually turn out to be the case that this Big Bang explanation is wrong, it is still the only scientific theory that can adequately account for the Hubble expansion.

A similar argument can be applied to Lerner's explanation for the amount of helium that is presently observed in the universe, which works out to be approximately 24% of all the visible matter in existence. The traditional Big Bang explanation for this amount of helium comes a complex series of calculations involving the universe's initial expansion rate *vis-à-vis* the known reaction dynamics of hydrogen and helium. As George Gamow first predicted on the basis of these calculations alone, the Big Bang should have produced around 24% helium and 75% hydrogen. Subsequent observations confirmed Gamow's prediction, and this helped to propel the Big Bang theory to the very forefront of cosmology. More recent observations regarding the existence of trace amounts of the light elements deuterium, helium-3 and lithium-7 in the universe have provided further confirmation of the hot Big Bang model, which predicts precisely the observed amounts of these light elements.[9]

Lerner, however, tries to explain the 24% proportion of helium in the universe as the natural result of a much more massive first generation of stars, which would have scattered tremendous amounts of helium into the universe following ancient supernova explosions.[10] Calculations using Lerner's plasma universe model seem to support this conclusion, in that they predict that almost any galaxy would produce approximately 24% helium, 1% oxygen, and 0.5% carbon.[11]

There are two problems with this explanation. To begin with, Lerner's supposition of a much more massive *first* generation of stars assumes that there was indeed a first generation to begin with, and hence that there was an actual beginning to the universe. But this explicitly contradicts Lerner's prior assumption, abundantly stated elsewhere, that the universe is infinite in both age and spatial extent. If this were truly the case, we would expect a much greater proportion of helium and other heavier elements in the universe, since there would have been an infinite number of stellar cycles to produce them.

Secondly, Lerner's explanation does not account for the homogeneous appearance of helium throughout the universe, no matter which direction one happens to look. If this helium were produced by previous generations of supernovae, one would naturally expect the appearance of helium to vary considerably from place to place.[12] But this is simply not the case. Therefore, Lerner's explanation does not appear to hold up under the observational evidence.

Discussion

While Lerner's method of scientific analysis may be meticulous and even brilliant at times, this is *only* in relation to the non-theistic world view that he assumes from the start. Beginning as he does *only* from that which is already scientifically known, some of his conclusions are indeed impressive. The question, however, is whether or not his non-theistic world view is the correct one.

It hardly seems to be. He fails to give any account at all of how matter came to exist in the first place, since he strongly affirms the existence of a universe which is infinite in both age and spatial extent. Thus, his "solution" to the problem of the origin of matter is that it had no origin—like God, it has supposedly *always* existed in one form or another.

There are many problems with this conclusion. Not only is it very much at odds with almost every recent scientific discovery in the field of cosmology, it is philosophically self-contradictory as well. There is absolutely nothing about matter which would lead the unbiased observer to believe that it was self-existent. Indeed, self-existence *by definition* can only be applied to one type of being: God Himself. Thus, if matter did turn out to be self-existent, then it would be God *by definition*, as we have seen. But this is clearly ridiculous. Hence, matter is probably *not* eternal, the hopes of plasma (and process) theorists notwithstanding.

Thermodynamic considerations also strongly confirm a finite age to the universe. Given the highly entropic nature of the universe as a whole, along with the physical impossibility of an oscillating universe,[13] an infinite universe seems very implausible indeed.

Astronomical observations corroborate this conclusion. In an infinite universe, one would expect redshifts of stars at our Earth-based observational limit[14] to equal infinity, due to the light-bending predictions of general relativity (which have repeatedly been confirmed over the years). One would also expect the night sky to be bright instead of dim because of the infinite number of stars[15] in the heavens, in spite of the fact that interstellar matter would absorb some of this radiation (since in time it would radiate the same amount of radiation back out into space). Yet, neither of these features of an infinite universe obtain in the real world, as we have seen.

In contrast to Lerner's atheistic plasma universe stands the theist's Intelligently Designed universe. These two world views stand in such radical opposition to one another that both inevitably color all predictions and interpretations that are made with them.

In the atheistic plasma universe, for instance, there is no such thing as an Intelligent Creator who would deliberately use natural processes to impart a high level of design to the various galaxy superclusters. Therefore, the plasma cosmologist must rely upon physical mechanisms alone to provide an adequate explanation. In the Intelligently Designed theistic universe, on the other hand, there *is* such a thing as an Intelligent Designer who can deliberately and naturalistically impart a high level of design to the cosmos.

It would thus appear that Lerner's chief mistake is his inadvertent confusion of these two world views (which is inevitable for any dedicated materialistic scientist). As we have seen throughout this book, the evidence from cosmology strongly supports the existence of a "Supercalculating Intellect" who creates using only intelligently directed natural processes. To the extent that this conclusion is accurate, this makes the theist's God-centered universe the correct overall world view.

Now, if this is indeed the case, then it follows that there are many different aspects of physical reality that can only be properly understood in relation to a Supernatural Creator (who nevertheless creates through natural processes). Atheistic physical scientists, however, are not prepared to view the universe in this manner, since their scientific credo specifically forbids the use of any supernatural being as an explanatory vehicle within the universe itself. This being the case, atheistic scientists have no choice but to interpret theistically generated phenomena from an atheistic point of view, and it is precisely here where mistakes start to multiply geometrically (assuming, of course, that theism is correct).

A good case in point which illustrates the difference between the atheistic and theistic world views is the age-old question of whether or not the universe is progressive. On the one hand stands the Second Law of Thermodynamics, which states that the overall amount of entropy or disorder in the universe is constantly rising. On the other hand stands the fact of universal and biological evolution. Most scientists view the Second Law of Thermodynamics as the chief physical paradigm of the entire cosmos; they therefore view both the evolution of the cosmos and the evolution of life as "the accidental result . . . of an enormous concatenation of improbabilities."[16] Prigogine and Lerner, on the other hand, see evolutionary progressivism as the clear universal trend; for them, the Second Law is just a statistical reality that is clearly contradicted by the fact of cosmic and biological evolution.

The missing link in both of these interpretations of universal order is the contribution made by the Creator Himself. In the theistic universe, God Himself is responsible for winding up the cosmos at the very beginning; He is also ultimately responsible for creating the evolutionary order of biological life (albeit through natural physical processes). Thus, the overall trend in this kind of universe is clearly towards greater and greater levels of disorder, but only in the absence of Intelligently Derived instances of order.

The presence of Divine Input, on the other hand, is an entirely different matter. God can design entropic matter in such a way that it can spontaneously evolve into increasingly greater levels of complexity, but only because

He has deliberately designed it to be this way. The overall trend, of course, is still downhill; God can simply utilize this downward motion to build increasingly complex objects along the way.

It is as if a downhill skier is able to use his downward momentum to draw complex messages on the side of a snow-covered mountain. Although the total amount of the skier's kinetic and potential energy is rapidly winding down as he nears the bottom of the mountain, he is nevertheless able to use the energy he temporarily possesses to draw messages in the snow. In the same way, the entire universe itself seems to be on a relentless downward course in which its total amount of useable energy is progressively becoming less and less. At the same time, though, God has been able to channel this decreasing energy flux into increasingly greater levels of evolutionary order. It thus isn't progress *per se* which is a myth; it is progress *in the absence of Intelligent Input* which is a myth.

Hence, *both* the entropic and progressive views of evolutionary development are correct in their own respective spheres of influence. It is simply the inclusion of a Divine Creator God which is able to make sense of the apparent contradiction between them.

As a consequence, Lerner's argument that the present universal order proves that progress, and not entropy, is the absolute ruler of the heavens, is itself based on a fundamental confusion, insofar as he confuses the Divine Act of Creativity, which manufactures order *in spite of the Second Law*, with the natural tendency of the universe itself *apart from any Divine Contribution.*

So, Prigogine's contention that order can spontaneously arise out of chaos in far from equilibrium systems is certainly true as far as it goes, but it would be a question-begging mistake to project this process out to the character of the universe as a whole and to then use it as a substitute for Divine Contrivance. If Prigogine were asked about *why* order is able to arise out of chaos at all in the universe, he would have to concede that it is a natural property of physical matter. If he were pushed about the origin of this miraculous property, or about how far from equilibrium systems came to be formed in the first place, he would have to admit that he simply doesn't know.

It will not suffice to claim that self-organizing matter has always existed because we know that it has *not* always existed. Moreover, self-existence is not generally acknowledged as being an essential property of physical matter, as we have seen. Furthermore, there is no compelling reason to believe that matter would be self-organizing at all if it were not given this miraculous property from Without.

The coming Heat Death of the universe, which is implied by the Second Law of Thermodynamics, is also rendered harmless by the assumptions of the theistic universe, since a Divine Creator would always be there to either wind the universe up again or to give it a completely different format whenever the time became appropriate for Him to do so.[17]

The Second Law of Thermodynamics, then, seems to represent the natural tendency of the physical universe apart from God's Organizing Input, while the phenomenon of self-organization in spite of the Second Law seems to be indicative of some form of Divine Activity, originating in either the distant past or the present. Once again we see that it is the presence or absence of a Divine Creator which makes all the difference in how we interpret the evidence of science.

As any artist or technical designer will readily attest, it is impossible to fully understand any of their intelligent creations without taking *them* into account. It is in the very nature of intelligent design that the designer will incorporate certain idiosyncratic creative measures in his creation that simply cannot be fully grasped by looking only at the thing that has been created. Indeed, we can go so far as to say that the designer of any intelligent creation is the most important feature in any attempt to understand the object that has been created.

It thus comes as no surprise that the non-theistic Big Bang theory as it currently stands is conceptually and empirically inadequate. The problem isn't so much in the overall structure of the model itself as it is in the fact that cosmologists have deliberately left out the most important feature of the Big Bang: its Creator.

It's about time that this Divine exclusion ceased. As we have seen, the idea of God as Creator is implicit in the very concept of the Big Bang, as it is in the deductive nature of science itself. In order to be fully "scientific," though, scientists have insisted on leaving God out of the cosmic equation. And up until recently, this was largely adequate, because it was assumed that the deliberate creative activity of God, if it existed at all, brought nothing new to the cosmological puzzle. This assumption, however, may wind up being a huge mistake, because the Big Bang doesn't appear to be nearly as strong a theory in the absence of its all-important Designer. With God at the helm, though, everything changes. The Big Bang suddenly becomes transformed from being a less than totally adequate theoretical model to being a bold explanation of how the universe actually came into being.

A similar point can be made about the so-called "Beauty Principle," which says that the correct description of the physical universe is the one which displays the greatest level of simplicity, elegance, harmony, and consistency overall. As Lerner correctly points out, most conventional cosmologists are surprisingly subservient to the need for beauty in cosmic theories. Lerner is also correct in his criticism that this kind of subservience to the Beauty Principle is wholly inappropriate in a materialistic, atheistic, and completely objective world view. If there is no Larger Designer behind the universe, it is absurd to even look for cosmic order and beauty in the first place, because there probably wouldn't be a sufficient reason for it to exist. Even if it did exist, it is hard to see how we would be able to understand it if we weren't deliberately given this ability from Without.

If, on the other hand, an Intelligent Designer *is* in fact behind the phenomenon of universal evolution, everything suddenly falls into place. Within this theistic world view, the Beauty Principle suddenly takes on a much greater level of significance, because there is good reason to believe that an Intelligent Designer *would* have created the universe in accordance with principles and mathematical equations that are inherently beautiful. There is also good reason to believe that such a Creator would have given us the capacity to understand this order and beauty as well.

Although they are not aware of it, those non-theistic cosmologists who stubbornly cling to the Big Bang in spite of mounting evidence against it (at least in its non-theistic version) are privately committed to a theistic-type world view. For one thing, modern proponents of the Big Bang are heavily committed to the deductive method of scientific understanding, which makes mathematics the absolute yardstick by which everything else in physical reality can be judged. Einstein echoed this profound subservience to mathematics when he wrote that,

> It is my conviction that pure mathematical construction enables us to discover the concepts and the laws connecting them, which gives us the key to the understanding of nature . . . In a certain sense, therefore, I hold it true that pure thought can grasp reality, as the ancients dreamed.[18]

However, there is no persuasive reason to believe that our purely subjective mathematical constructions actually correspond to the objective nature of physical reality apart from the existence of a Supernatural Mathematician who would have deliberately made this so. In the absence of such an Omniscient Intellect, there would probably be no connection at all between our subjective mathematical constructions and the actual structure of physical reality. (Indeed, there would probably be no physical world at all, and therefore no living beings such as ourselves to contemplate it.)

It would appear, then, that the idea of an Omniscient Universal Mathematician is implicit within the very nature of scientific deduction, which has become the dominant method of scientific reasoning today. It is also implicit within the Big Bang conceptualization itself, since the Big Bang's extreme dependence on the special initial conditions and temporal finitude of the universe directly implies the existence of a "Supercalculating Intellect" who would have deliberately brought about a life-supporting cosmos through natural processes.

Moreover, since the chief alternative to the Big Bang at the present time seems to be a "plasma universe" of infinite duration and spatial extent, any continued acceptance of the Big Bang must also include an acceptance of its underlying suppositions as well, which include its temporal finitude, its absolute dependence upon initial conditions, and, as I have just argued, its implicit acceptance of some type of larger Designer.

Surprisingly, Lerner devotes very little space to refuting the Design Argument. He briefly mentions a few of the cosmic coincidences which have conspired together to make life possible, but hastily concludes that they really aren't coincidences at all, since they "ignore . . . the natural tendency of all matter, both animate and inanimate, to evolve continuously toward higher rates of energy flow, toward the capture of greater currents of energy."[19]

This type of argument amounts to little more than an elaborate exercise in question-begging. Lerner simply assumes the existence of order-prone matter, and thus doesn't even question where this underlying tendency could have originally come from. But this is really the bottom line which separates the theistic and atheistic world views. The atheistic view doesn't even attempt to explain the origin of order-prone matter; it just assumes that this intriguing quality has always been there. The theistic view, on the other hand, offers an eminently acceptable explanation: God Himself designed this orderliness into matter when He first created the heavens and the Earth.

Lerner also fails to mention the significant fact that the very foundation of modern science was built upon the ideas and presuppositions of traditional theism. Boyle, Newton, Kepler, Galileo, Copernicus and a whole host of science's other founding fathers were all inescapably theistic in terms of their basic world view. In fact, it was their theistic convictions which motivated them to look for mathematical order in the universe to begin with. Of course, some of these theistically minded scientists—such as Ptolemy and Kepler—were sometimes misled by their God-centered expectations. On the whole, though, theistically-motivated science was enormously successful throughout the last several centuries.

My overall point is this: if the evidence did not point conclusively in the direction of Intelligent Design, or if for some other reason one is prevented from adopting a theistic view of the universe, Lerner's brand of reasoning is entirely appropriate, and even laudable, but only from a non-theistic world view. However, the evidence *does* in fact strongly point in the direction of Intelligent Design, as we have seen throughout this book. Hence, Lerner's atheistic world view is inadequate, because a much better alternative is presently at hand.

Conclusion

As we have seen, the theist is not inescapably tied to the Big Bang theory of universal origins. Indeed, many theists have openly argued against it.

What the theist *is* inescapably tied to, however, is the general doctrine of creation. It doesn't matter how God actually went about creating the universe. All that matters is that He actually *did* create it in one way or another at some point in the past.

At the same time, though, there is a tremendous amount of empirical support for the Big Bang. There is also a tremendous amount of agreement between the doctrine of the Big Bang and the first chapter of Genesis, but only when the Big Bang theory is supplemented with the addition of an Intelligent Designer.

Even so, it is possible that the Big Bang may be overturned one day as the dominant explanation of universal origins. If this ever turns out to be the case, the theist needn't worry in the least, because he isn't inevitably tied to it. It is the doctrine of Intelligent Design which is of ultimate importance to the theist, and this is good news indeed for him, because the doctrine of Intelligent Design shows no signs at all of being seriously threatened any time soon.

Notes

1. Eric J. Lerner, *The Big Bang Never Happened* (New York: Random House, 1991), pp. 23–35.
2. Ibid., p. 44.
3. Ibid., pp. 46–49.
4. This of course raises the question of why an all-powerful God would deliberately choose to create the universe out of fallible natural processes when He presumably could have created it instantly and infallibly by miraculous Fiat. The answer, which is beyond the scope of this book, is that a natural cause-and-effect universe seems to be the most appropriate home for developing human beings, who themselves *must* grow according to natural cause-and-effect processes in order to be genuinely human. Another way of saying this is that such a radical change in the structure of physical reality would necessarily entail a corresponding change in the structure of human beings, with the inevitable result that they would no longer be "human." For more on this intriguing subject, please refer to my forthcoming book *Evil and the Essence of Man,*
5. See John D. Barrow's and Frank J. Tipler's *Anthropic Cosmological Principle* (New York: Oxford University Press, 1986) for a complete explanation of the scientific literature indicating a 15 to 20 billion year old universe.
6. Lerner, *The Big Bang Never Happened,* pp. 402–403.
7. Some, however, have used the extreme complexity of life, along with the relatively short amount of time life had to evolve here, to conclude that life must have been shipped here from another planet. This of course doesn't solve the problem of life's origin at all; it just removes it to another place and another time.
8. Ibid., p. 270.
9. Hugh Ross, *The Fingerprint of God,* pp. 87–88.
10. Lerner, *The Big Bang Never Happened,* pp. 266–267.
11. Ibid.
12. Hugh Ross, *The Fingerprint of God,* p. 87.

13. See Hugh Ross' *The Fingerprint of God*, pp. 97–105, for more details concerning the untenability of an oscillating universe.
14. Ibid., p. 81.
15. Ibid., pp. 37–40.
16. Stephen Jay Gould, *Wonderful Life: The Burgess Shale and the Nature of History* (New York: W. W. Norton, 1989).
17. The same thing can be said for the possibility of a "big crunch" if the universe turns out to be "closed" and starts falling back on itself. If this ever turns out to be the case, God would clearly be capable of intervening to save humanity long before the atmosphere ever started to heat up.
18. Albert Einstein, *Essays in Science* (New York: Philosophical Library, 1934), p. 18.
19. Eric J. Lerner, *The Big Bang Never Happened,* p. 400.

Bibliography

Abbott, Larry. "The Mystery of the Cosmological Constant," *Scientific American*, Vol. 3, No. 1, 1991.

Acton, Rush K. "Bone Disease Simulating Ancient Age in 'Pre-Human' Fossils," *Decade of Creation*, Henry H. Morris & Donald H. Rohrer, eds. (San Diego: Creation Life Publishers, 1981).

Angrist, Stanley W., and Loren G. Hepler. *Order and Chaos* (New York: Basic Books, Inc., 1967).

Aquinas, Thomas. "The Summa Theologica," in *Great Books of the Western World*, volume 19, ed. R. M. Hutchins. (Chicago: Encyclopaedia Britannica, 1952).

Ayer, Alfred Jules. *Language Truth and Logic* (Oxford: Oxford University Press, 1936).

Barbour, Ian. *Religion in an Age of Science* (San Francisco: Harper & Row, 1990).

Barrow, John D., and Frank J. Tipler. *The Anthropic Cosmological Principle* (Oxford: Oxford University Press, 1986).

Barrow, John D. *The World Within the World* (Oxford: Oxford University Press, 1990).

―――. *Theories of Everything* (Oxford: Oxford University Press, 1991).

Bogart, James P. "Evolutionary Implications of Polyploidy in Amphibians and Reptiles," *Polyploidy*, Walter H. Lewis, ed. (New York: Plenum Press, 1980).

Bohm, David. "Postmodern Science and a Postmodern World," *The Reenchantment of Science*, David Ray Griffin ed. (Albany: State University of New York Press, 1988).

―――. 'Some Remarks on the Notion of Order,' in C.H. Waddington ed. *Towards a Theoretical Biology* (4 vols, Edinburgh University Press, 1969).

―――. *Wholeness and the Implicate Order* (London: Routledge & Kegan Paul, 1980).

Bondi, Herman. *Cosmology* (Cambridge: Cambridge University Press, 1960).

Boslough, John. *Stephen Hawking's Universe* (New York: William Morrow, 1985).

Bowler, Peter J. *Evolution: The History of an Idea* (Los Angeles: The University of California Press, 1989).

Brandon, Robert N. "Adaptation Explanations: Are Adaptations for the Good of Replicators or Interactors?" *Evolution at a Crossroads*, David J. Depew and Bruce H. Weber eds. (Cambridge: The MIT Press, 1985).

Brooks, Daniel R., and E.O. Wiley. *Evolution as Entropy* (Chicago: University of Chicago Press, 1986).

Brown, Michael H. *The Search for Eve* (San Francisco: Harper & Row, 1990).

Burnet, Thomas. *Sacred Theory of the Earth* (London: reprinted by Centaur Press, 1965).

Campbell, John H. "An Organizational Interpretation of Evolution," *Evolution at a Crossroads*, David J. Depew and Bruce H. Weber, eds. (Cambridge: The MIT Press, 1985).

Capra, Fritjof, and David Steindl-Rast. *Belonging to the Universe* (San Francisco: HarperSanFrancisco, 1991).

Carter, Brandon. "Large Number Coincidences and the Anthropic Principle in Cosmology," *Confrontation of Cosmological Theories With Observation*, ed. M.S. Longair (Dordrecht: Reidel, 1974).

Casti, John L. *Paradigms Lost* (New York: William Morrow and Company, 1989).

Caullery, Maurice. *Genetics and Heredity* (New York: Walker and Co., 1964).

Christian, James L. *Philosophy: An Introduction to the Art of Wondering* (New York: Holt, Rineheart, and Winston, 1977).

Cicero. *The Nature of the Gods*, translated by H.C.P. McGregor (London: Penguin, 1972).

Clark, Ronald W. *The Survival of Charles Darwin: A Biography of a Man and an Idea* (New York: Random House, 1984).

Cobb, John B. *Living Options in Protestant Theology* (Philadelphia: The Westminster Press, 1962).

Coleman, William. *Georges Cuvier: Zoologist* (Cambridge: Harvard University Press, 1964)

Collins, C.B., and S.W. Hawking. *Astrophys. J.* 180, 317 (1973).

Copernicus, Nicholas. *On the Revolution of the Heavenly Spheres*, transl. C.G. Wallis, ed. R.M. Hutchins (London: Encyclopaedia Britannica, 1952).

Corner, E. "Evolution," in *Contemporary Biological Thought*, McLeod and Colby, eds., 1961.

Crawford, Michael, and David Marsh. *The Driving Force* (London: Heinemann, 1989).

Crick, Francis. *Life Itself: Its Origin and Nature* (New York: Simon & Schuster, 1981).

Darwin, Charles. *The Origin of Species* (New York: P.F. Collier & Son Co., 1909).

Darwin, Erasmus. *Zoonomia*, 2 vols. (London, 1974).

Darwin, F. ed. *The Life and Letters of Charles Darwin*, 3 vols. (London: John Murray, 1888).

Davies, Paul. *God and the New Physics* (New York: Simon & Schuster, 1983).

———. *Other Worlds* (New York: Simon & Schuster, 1980).

———. *Superforce* (New York: Simon & Schuster, 1984).

———. *The Accidental Universe* (New York: Cambridge University Press, 1982).

———. *The Cosmic Blueprint* (New York: Simon & Schuster, 1989).

———. *The Mind of God* (New York: Simon & Schuster, 1992).

Dawkins, Richard. *The Blind Watchmaker* (New York: W.W. Norton, 1987).

De Beer, Gavin. *Charles Darwin* (Garden City, NY: Doubleday & Company, Inc., 1909).

———. *Homology: An Unresolved Problem* (London: Oxford University Press, 1971).

DeLey, J. *Evol. Biol.* 2, 103, 1968.

Denton, Michael. *Evolution: A Theory in Crisis* (Bethesda, MD: Adler & Adler, 1986).

Depew, David J., and Bruce H. Weber, eds. *Evolution at a Crossroads* (Cambridge: The MIT Press, 1985).

Dewar, D. *More Difficulties of the Evolution Theory* (London: Thynne and Co., 1938).

Dover, G.A. "Molecular Drive in Multigene Families: How Biological Novelties Arise, Spread and Are Assimilated," *Trends in Genetics*, 2, (6), 1986.

Dyke, C. "Complexity and Closure," *Evolution at a Crossroads*, David J. Depew and Bruce H. Weber, eds. (Cambridge: The MIT Press, 1985).

du Nouy, Lecomte. *Human Destiny* (New York: Longmans, Green and Co., 1947).

Dyson, Freeman. "Honoring Dirac," *Science*, Vol. 185, September 27, 1974.

Eccles, Sir John. "Modern Biology and the Turn to Belief in God," *The Intellectuals Speak Out About God*, Roy Abraham Varghese, ed. (Chicago: Regnery Gateway, 1984).

Eccles, Sir John, and Daniel N. Robinson. *The Wonder of Being Human* (Boston: Shambhala, 1985).

Eden, Murray. "Inadequacies of Neo-Darwinian Evolution as a Scientific Theory," *Mathematical Challenges to the Neo-Darwinian Interpretation of Evolution*, P. Moorhead and M. Kaplan, eds. (Philadelphia: Wistar Institute Press, 1967).

Edey, Maitland A., and Donald C. Johanson. *Blueprints: Solving the Mystery of Evolution* (Boston: Little, Brown, and Company, 1989).

Einstein, Albert. *Essays in Science* (New York: Philosophical Library, 1934).

———. *Out of My Later Years*, rev. reprint ed. (Westport, Connecticut: Greenwood Press, 1970).

Flamsteed, Sam. "Probing the Edge of the Universe," *Discover*, Vol. 12, No. 7, July 1991.

Flew, Antony, R.M. Hare, and Basil Mitchell, "Theology and Falsification," *New Essays in Philosophical Theology*, Antony Flew and Alasdair MacIntyre, eds. (London: SCM Press, 1955).

Frye, Roland Mushat, ed. *Is God a Creationist?* (New York: Charles Scribner's Sons, 1983).

Galen. *On the Usefulness of the Parts of the Body*, translated by M. T. May (New York: Cornell University Press, 1968).

Gillespie, Neil C. *Charles Darwin and the Problem of Creation* (Chicago: University of Chicago Press, 1979).

Gingerich, Owen. "Let There Be Light: Modern Cosmogony and Biblical Creation," *Is God a Creationist?* Roland Mushat Frye ed. (New York: Charles Scribner's Sons, 1983).

Gish, Duane. *The Challenge of the Fossil Record* (San Diego: Creation-Life Publishers, 1985).

Goldschmidt, Richard. *The Material Basis of Evolution* (New Haven: Yale University Press, 1940).

Gould, Stephen Jay. *Ever Since Darwin* (New York: W.W. Norton & Company, 1973).

———. *Hen's Teeth and Horse's Toes* (New York: W.W. Norton & Company, 1980).

———. "The Ediacaran Experiment," *Natural History*, V. 93, No. 2, February 1984.

———. *The Flamingo's Smile* (New York: W.W. Norton & Co., 1985).

———. *The Panda's Thumb* (New York: W.W. Norton & Company, 1980).

Grant, Peter R. "Natural Selection and Darwin's Finches," *Scientific American*, Vol. 265, No. 4, Oct. 1991.

Grassé, Pierre. *Evolution of Living Organisms: Evidence for a New Theory of Transformation* (New York: Academic Press, 1977).

Gray, Asa. *Darwiniana* (New York: Appleton, 1876).

———. "Natural Science and Religion," *Is God a Creationist?* Roland Mushat Frye, ed. (New York: Charles Scribner's Sons, 1983).

Greeley, Andrew. "Keeping the Faith: Americans Hold Fast to the Rock of Ages," in *Omni*, Vol. 13, No. 11, August, 1991.

Greene, John C. *Science, Ideology, and World View: Essays in the History of Evolutionary Ideas* (Berkeley: University of California Press, 1981).

Greenstein, George. *The Symbiotic Universe* (New York: William Morrow, 1988).

Gregory, Frederick. "The Impact of Darwinian Evolution on Protestant Theology in the Nineteenth Century," in David C. Lindberg and Ronald L. Numbers, eds., *God and Nature* (Berkeley: University of California Press, 1986).

Gribbin, John, and Martin Rees. *Cosmic Coincidences* (New York: Bantam Books, 1989).

Gribbin, John. *In Search of the Double Helix* (New York: Bantam Books, 1987).

———. *The Omega Point* (New York: Bantam Books, 1988).

Griffin, David Ray. *God, Power, and Evil* (Philadelphia: The Westminster Press, 1976).

———. *God and Religion in the Postmodern World* (Albany: SUNY Press, 1989).

——— ed. *Physics and the Ultimate Significance of Time* (Albany: SUNY Press, 1986).

Griffin, David Ray, and Huston Smith. *Primordial Truth and Postmodern Theology* (Albany: SUNY Press, 1989).

Griffin, David Ray, ed. *The Reenchantment of Science*, (Albany: SUNY Press, 1988).

———. "Time, Creativity, and the Origin of the Universe: A Response to Stephen Hawking," in an as yet unpublished manuscript.

Hadarard, J. *Lectures on Cauchy's Problem in Linear Partial Differential Equations* (New Haven: Yale University Press, 1923).

Hadd, John R. *Evolution: Reconciling the Controversy* (New Jersey: Kronos Press, 1979).

Hahn, Roger. "Laplace and the Mechanistic Universe," in David C. Lindberg and Ronald L. Numbers, eds., *God and Nature* (Berkeley: University of California Press, 1986).

Hall, Marshall and Sandra. *The Truth: God or Evolution?* (Grand Rapids: Baker Book House, 1973).

Hardy, Alister. *Darwin and the Spirit of Man* (London: Collins Press, 1984).

Harris, Errol E. *Cosmos and Anthropos* (Atlantic Highlands, New Jersey: Humanities Press International, Inc., 1991).

Harrison, E.R. "The Dark Night Sky Riddle: A 'Paradox' that Resisted Solution," *Science*, 226. (1984).

Hawking, S.W. *A Brief History of Time* (New York: Bantam, 1988).

Helitzer, Florence. "The Princeton Galaxy," *Intellectual Digest*, No. 10, (June 1973).

Henderson, L.J. *The Fitness of the Environment* (Glouster: Peter Smith, 1970).

———. *The Order of Nature* (Cambridge: Harvard University Press, 1917).

Henderson, Charles P. *God and Science* (Atlanta: John Knox Press, 1973).

Hick, John. *An Interpretation of Religion* (New York: Macmillan Press, 1989).

———. *Evil and the God of Love* (New York: Harper and Row, 1977).

———. "Rational Theistic Belief Without Proof," in *Arguments for the Existence of God* (New York: Macmillan, 1971).

———. *The Existence of God* (New York: The Macmillan Publishing Company, 1964).

Hickman. *Integrated Principles of Zoology* (St. Louis: The C. V. Mosby Co., 1978, Sixth Edition).

Hiebert, Erwin N. "Modern Physics and Christian Faith" in David C. Lindberg and Ronald L. Numbers, eds., *God & Nature* (Berkeley: University of California Press, 1986).

Himmelfarb, Gertrude. *Darwin and the Darwinian Revolution* (New York: W.W. Norton, 1959).

Hogben, L.T. *The Nature of Living Matter* (London: Routledge and Kegan Paul, 1931).

Hoyle, Fred, and Chandra Wickramasinghe. *Evolution from Space* (London: J.M. Dent and Co., 1981).

Hoyle, Fred. *Religion and the Scientists* (London: SCM, 1959).

———. "The Big Bang in Astronomy," *New Scientist*, V. 92, No. 1280, November 19, 1981.

———. "The Universe: Past and Present Reflections," *Engineering and Science* (November 1981).

Hume, David. *Dialogues Concerning Natural Religion* (London: Penguin, 1990).

Jaki, Stanley L. *Cosmos and Creator* (Edinburgh: Scottish Academic Press, 1980).

———. *The Paradox of Olbers' Paradox* (New York: Herder and Herder, 1969).

James, William. *The Varieties of Religious Experience* (New York: Longman, Green, & Co., 1902).

Janov, Arthur. *The Primal Scream* (New York: G.P. Putnam's Sons, 1970).

Jantsch, Erich. *The Self-Organizing Universe* (Oxford: Pergamon Press, 1980).

Jastrow, Robert. *God and the Astronomers* (New York: Warner Books, 1978).

———. *Until the Sun Dies* (New York: Warner Books, 1977).

Johanson, Donald C., and M.A. Edey. *Lucy: The Beginnings of Humankind* (New York: Simon and Schuster, 1981).

Johnson, Philip E. *Darwin on Trial* (Washington, DC: Regnery Gateway, 1991).

Jones, Philip D., and Tom M T., Wigley, "Global Warming Trends," *Scientific American*, Vol. 263, No. 2, Aug. 1990.

Kaku, Michio, and Jennifer Trainer. *Beyond Einstein: The Cosmic Quest for the Theory of the Universe* (New York: Bantam Books, 1987).

Kauffman, Stuart A. "Antichaos and Adaptation," *Scientific American*, Vol. 265, No. 2, Aug. 1991.

———. "Self-Organization, Selective Adaptation, and Its Limits," *Evolution at a Crossroads*, David J. Depew and Bruce H. Weber, eds. (Cambridge: The MIT Press, 1985).

Kilby, Clyde S., ed. *An Anthology of C.S. Lewis: A Mind Awake* (New York: Harvest/ HBJ Books, 1968).

Knoll, Andrew H. "End of the Proterozoic Eon," *Scientific American*, Vol. 265, No. 4, Oct. 1991.

Laszlo, Ervin. *Evolution: The Grand Synthesis* (Boston: Shambhala, 1987).

Leakey, Richard. *The Making of Mankind* (New York: E.P. Dutton, 1981).

Leibniz, G.W. *Theodicy* (La Salle, IL: Open Court Publishing Company, 1985).

Lerner, Eric J. *The Big Bang Never Happened: A Startling Refutation of the Dominant Theory of Universal Origins* (New York: Random House, 1991).

Leslie, John. "Anthropic Principle, World Ensemble, Design," in *American Philosophical Quarterly* 19 (1982).

Lewis, C.S. *Christian Reflections* (Grand Rapids: William B. Eerdmans Publishing Company, 1967).

———. "Encounter With Light." Taken from *An Anthology of C.S. Lewis: A Mind Awake*, Clyde S. Kilby ed. (New York: Harvest/HBJ Books, 1968).

———. *Mere Christianity* (New York: Macmillan Publishing Co. Inc., 1952).

———. *The Problem of Pain* (New York: Macmillan Publishing Company, 1962).

Lima-de-Faria, A. *Evolution Without Selection* (Amsterdam: Elsevier, 1988).

Lindberg, David C. "Science and the Early Church," in *God & Nature*, Lindberg, David C., and Numbers, Ronald L., eds. (Berkeley: University of California Press, 1986).

Lindberg, David C., and Ronald L. Numbers, eds. *God & Nature* (Berkeley: University of California Press, 1986).

Lindsey, Hal and C.C. Carlson. *The Terminal Generation* (New York: Bantam Books, 1977).

Lokki, Juhanim, and Anssi Sauri, "Polyploidy in Insect Evolution," *Polyploidy*, Walter H. Lewis, ed. (New York: Plenum Press, 1980).

Long, A.A. *Hellenistic Philosophy* (Berkeley: University of California Press, 1974).

Lovejoy, C.O. *Life In the Universe*, ed. J. Billingham (Cambridge: MIT Press, 1981).

Macbeth, Norman. *Darwin Retried: An Appeal to Reason* (Boston: Gambit Press, 1971).

———. "The Question: Darwinism Revisted," *Yale Review* (June 1967).

Mayr, Ernst. *Animal Species and Evolution* (Cambridge: The Belknap Press of Harvard University Press, 1963).

———. "How Biology Differs from the Physical Sciences," *Evolution at a Crossroads*, (Cambridge: The MIT Press, 1985).

———. *Populations, Species, and Evolution* (Cambridge, MA: Harvard University Press, 1970).

Mendillo, M., and R. Hart. "Resonances," *Physics Today*, 27:2 (Feb., 1974).

Midgley, Mary. *Evolution as a Religion* (New York: Methuen & Co., 1985).

Monod, Jacques. *Chance and Necessity* (New York: Alfred A. Knopf, 1971).

Moore, John N. *Should Evolution Be Taught?* (San Diego: Institute for Creation Research, 1971).

Moorehead, P.S., and M.M. Kaplan, eds. *Mathematical Challenges to the Neo-Darwinian Interpretation of Evolution* (Philadelphia: Wistar Institute Press, 1967).

Morgan, T.H. *The Scientific Basis of Evolution* (London: Faber and Faber, 1932).

Murchie, Guy. *The Seven Mysteries of Life* (Boston: The Houghton Mifflin Company, 1978).

Novikov, Igor D., and Zel'dovich, Yakob. "Physical Processes Near Cosmological Singularities," in *Annual Review of Astronomy and Astrophysics*, 11. (1973).

Ohno, Susumu. *Evolution by Gene Duplication* (New York: Springer-Verlag, 1970).

Oldroyd, D.R. *Darwinian Impacts* (Atlantic Highlands, NJ: Humanities Press, 1980).

Opadia-Kadima, G.Z. "How the Slot Machine Led Biologists Astray," *The Journal of Theoretical Biology* (1987) 124.

Paley, William. *Natural Theology* (London: Baldwyn and Company, 1819).

Peat, F. David. *Superstrings and the Search for the Theory of Everything* (Chicago: Contemporary Books, 1988).

———. *The Philosopher's Stone* (New York: Bantam Books, 1991).

Peterson, Michael, William Hasker, Bruce Reichenbach, and David Basinger. *Reason & Religious Belief* (Oxford: Oxford University Press, 1991).

Plaine, Henry L., ed. *Darwin, Marx, and Wagner: A Symposium* (Columbus: Ohio State University Press, 1962).

Plantinga, Alvin. *God, Freedom, and Evil* (Grand Rapids: William B. Eerdmanns Publishing Company, 1974).

———. "Religious Belief Without Evidence," in *Rationality and Religious Belief*, C.F. Delaney, ed. (University of Notre Dame Press, 1979).

———. *The Nature of Necessity* (New York: Oxford University Press, 1974).

Platt, Rutherford. "DNA the Mysterious Basis for Life," *Reader's Digest* (October, 1962).

Polkinghorne, John. *Science and Creation* (Boston: New Science Library, 1988).

Pojman, Louis P. *Philosophy of Religion* (Belmont, CA: Wadsworth Publishing Co., 1987).

Popper, Karl. *Unended Quest* (Glasgow: Fontana Books of Collins, Sons and Co., Ltd., 1976).

Portmann, Adolf. "Die Ontogenese des Menschen als Problem der Evolutionsforschung." *Verhhandlungen der Schweizerischen Naturforschenden Gesellschaft* (1945).

Powell, Corey S. "Greenhouse Gusher," *Scientific American*, Vol. 265, No. 4, October, 1991.

———. "The Golden Age of Cosmology," *Scientific American,* Vol. 267, No. 1, July, 1992.

Rayl, A.J.S., and K.T. McKinney. "The Mind of God," *Omni*, Vol. 13, No. 11, August, 1991.

Raup, David M. "Conflicts Between Darwinism and Paleontology," *Field Museum of Natural History Bulletin* 50, No. 1 (January 1979).

Raymonde, *Studies in the History of Natural Theology,* (Cambridge: Cambridge University Press, 1915).

Repetski, John. "A Fish from the Upper Cambrian of North America," *Science*, Vol. 200, No. 4341, 5 May, 1978.

Rifkin, Jeremy. *Algeny* (New York: The Viking Press, 1983).

Rolston, Holmes. *Science and Religion* (Philadelphia: Temple University Press, 1987).

Ross, Hugh. *Genesis One: A Scientific Perspective* (Sierra Madre, CA: Wisemen Productions, 1983).

———. *The Fingerprint of God* (Orange, CA: Promise Publishing, 1991).

Russell, Bertrand. *Religion and Science* (New York: Oxford University Press, 1968).

Sagan, Carl. *Cosmos* (New York: Random House, 1980).

————. *Discovery* 4 (No. 3, March), 30 (1983).

Schroeder, Gerald L. *Genesis and the Big Bang* (New York: Bantam, 1990).

Schultz, R. Jack. "Role of Polyploidy in the Evolution of Fishes," *Polyploidy*, Walter H. Lewis, ed. (New York: Plenum Press, 1980).

Scriven, Michael. "The Presumption of Atheism," in Louis P. Pojman's *Philosophy of Religion* (Belmont, CA: Wadsworth Publishing Co., 1987).

Shea, William R. "Galileo and the Church," in David C. Lindberg and Ronald L. Numbers, eds., *God & Nature* (Berkeley: University of California Press, 1986).

Sheldrake, Rupert. *A New Science of Life* (Los Angeles: J.P. Tarcher, Inc., 1981).

————. "Modern Bio-chemistry and the Collapse of Mechanism," *The Intellectuals Speak Out About God*, Roy Abraham Varghese, ed. (Chicago: Regnery Gateway, 1984).

Simpson, George Gaylord. *The Meaning of Evolution* (New Haven: Yale University Press, 1967).

Skinner, B.F. *Beyond Freedom and Dignity* (New York: Knopf, 1971).

Smart, Ninian. "Omnipotence, Evil, and Supermen," *Philosophy*, Vol. XXXVI, No. 137 (1961).

Spergel, David N., and Neil G. Turok. "Textures and Cosmic Structure," *Scientific American*, Vol. 266, No. 3, March, 1992.

Stahler, Steven W. "The Early Life of Stars," *Scientific American*, Vol. 265, No. 1, July, 1991.

Stanley, S. *Macroevolution* (San Francisco: Hutchinson Publishing Co., 1979).

Stansfield, William D. *The Science of Evolution* (New York: Macmillan Publishing Co., 1977).

Stoner, Peter W, and Robert C. Newman. *Science Speaks* (Chicago: Moody Press, 1968).

Sullivan, Walter. "Evolution: A New Concept," *The New York Times* (October 25, 1964).

Sutherland, Luther D. *Darwin's Enigma* (Santee: Master Book Publishers, 1988).

Swimme, Brian. "The Cosmic Creation Story," David Ray Griffin, ed., *The Reenchantment of Science* (Albany: SUNY Press, 1988).

Taylor, Gordon Rattray. *The Great Evolution Mystery* (New York: Harper & Row, Publishers, 1983).

Tennant, F.R. "Cosmic Teleology," *Philosophical Theology*, Vol. II, chapter IV (New York: Cambridge University Press, 1930).

Thompson, D'Arcy Wentworth. *On Growth and Form* (New York: MacMillan, 1942).

Thompson, John Arthur, and Patrick Geddes. *Life: Outlines of General Biology* (London: Williams & Norgate, 1931).

Trefil, James. *Reading the Mind of God: In Search of the Principle of Universality* (New York: Charles Scribner's Sons, 1989).

————. *The Dark Side of the Universe* (New York: Doubleday, 1988).

Trumpler, Robert J. "Absorption of Light in the Galactic System," in *Publications of the Astronomical Society of the Pacific*, 42. (1930).

Van Till, Howard J. *The Fourth Day* (Grand Rapids: Eerdmans Press, 1986).

Varghese, Roy Abraham, ed. *The Intellectuals Speak Out About God* (Chicago: Regnery Gateway, Inc., 1984).

Voltaire. 'Atheist Atheism,' *Philosophical Dictionary* (1769), transl. and ed. P. Gay, 2 Vols (New York: Basic Books, 1955).

Waddington, C.H. *The Strategy of the Genes* (London: Allen & Unwin, 1957).

———— (ed). *Towards a Theoretical Biology* (4 vols, Edinburgh University Press, 1969).

Wallace, Alfred Russel. *Natural Selection and Tropical Nature* (London: Macmillan, 1895).

Weinberg, Steven. *The First Three Minutes* (London: André Deutsch, 1977).

Weisskopf, Victor F. "The Frontiers and Limits of Science," *American Scientist*, Vol. 65, July-August, 1977.

Westman, Robert S. "The Copernicans and the Churches," in David C. Lindberg and Ronald L. Numbers, eds., *God & Nature* (Berkeley: University of California Press, 1986).

Wheeler, John A., in Florence Helitzer's "The Princeton Galaxy," *Intellectual Digest 3*, No. 10 (June 1973).

Wiester, John. *The Genesis Connection* (Nashville: Thomas Nelson Publishers, 1983).

Wysong, R.L. *The Creation-Evolution Controversy* (Midland, Michigan: Inquiry Press, 1976).

Youngblood, Ronald. *How It All Began* (Ventura, CA: Regal Books, 1980).

Index

About the Author

M.A. Corey is a Summa Cum Laude graduate of West Virginia State College and an alumnus of the Claremont Graduate School, where he studied theology and the philosophical relationship between science and religion. He also studied human biological science at the West Virginia University School of Medicine. An avid proponent of old-style natural theology, his goal is to help stimulate a much-needed reconciliation between the scientific and religious communities.

DATE DUE

NOV 1 2000			